Post-Roe Reformation

Kayla Suderman

Copyright © 2024 by Kayla Suderman

All rights reserved.

No portion of this book may be reproduced in any form without written permission from the publisher or author, except as permitted by U.S. copyright law.

Scripture quotations are from the ESV® Bible (The Holy Bible, English Standard Version ®), copyright © 2001 by Crossway, a publishing ministry of Good News Publishers. Used by permission. All rights reserved. The ESV text may not be quoted in any publication made available to the public by a Creative Commons license. The ESV may not be translated in whole or in part into any other language.

Contents

The Five Tenets of Biblical Abolition	2
Preface	5
1. Secularism versus Sola Scriptura	12
2. Eroding Ecumenicalism	37
3. Catechizing Politics	57
4. Recant: The Pro-Life Cancel Culture	93
5. Repeating History: Protestant Resistance and Catholic Opposition to Abolition	129
6. License to Kill: Rise of the Mother Abortionist	163
7. Equal Justice: Loving Our Preborn Neighbors as Ourselves	195
8. The Cost of Partiality	225
9. Recovering Protestant Ethics	256
10. Reforming Judicial Dogma	281
11. Unthinkable	317
12. Ecclesia Reformata, Semper Reformanda	345
Resources	362
Endnotes	365

Because the sentence against an evil deed is not executed speedily, the heart of the children of man is fully set to do evil. – Ecclesiastes 8:11

THE FIVE TENETS OF BIBLICAL ABOLITION

ABOLITION HAS OFTEN BEEN associated with the fight against slavery, yet the legal definition means the act of annulling, eliminating or destroying an ongoing legally or socially accepted practice. Renowned slavery abolitionist Thomas Clarkson defined abolition as simply the gospel coming into conflict with evil and Christians rising up to rid their culture of that wickedness. In this sense, abolition can and should occur against all sources of wickedness and immorality as Christ's sons and daughters bring the Kingdom of Light into clash with the kingdom of darkness. Abolition should be a trademark of every Christian generation.

This book will deal specifically with abortion abolition. For purposes of clarity, terms will be defined upfront; words matter very much.

In American history, antislavery and slavery abolition were at times synonyms and other times descriptive differences. While slavery abolition culminated through the Civil War in immediate emancipation (freeing current slaves) and immediate abolition (ending slavery through criminalization without exceptions), it experienced a rough and evolving road to get there. History will most likely tell a similar story of anti-abortion and abortion abolition efforts today. This time, however, abolitionists are making a clearer and better effort at defining what the abolition movement means in the 21st century, and as such, the history books will hopefully thank them someday.

It will aid the reader to understand what abortion abolition is prior to going any further in this book. Abolition is *not* pro-life. And pro-life is *not* abolition. Yet both claim to be elements of the anti-abortion movement. Much work will go into dissecting the differences between these two anti-abortion positions, but for now it is important to understand that the Protestant abortion abolition movement is being built upon five core principles. Essentially, abortion abolition is:

1. **Biblical**. It recognizes every human being is an image bearer of God. The Imago Dei doctrine is what gives unique worth and status to human beings above all other parts of creation. As God has sovereignly chosen to reveal himself, human worth, and his decrees through his written Word for all generations, the abolition movement recognizes Scripture as its highest authority on how to address the sin of preborn murder.

2. **Providential**. It trusts in God alone and cries, "Duty is ours. The results are God's." It does not trust in pragmatism, situational ethics, secular moralism or any man to abolish abortion. Abolitionists believe remaining faithful to God's revealed commands will result in God faithfully fighting the battle on their behalf. Even when victory appears improbable, abolitionists labor under the promise that with man things are impossible but with God all things are possible.

3. **Gospel-Centered**. It believes in fulfilling the Great Commission to make disciples of all nations and teach them to obey all that Christ has commanded (Matt. 28:20). This includes "thou shalt not murder." Abolitionists believe the gospel message to be primary in efforts to change the hearts and minds of society, with arguments based in science, logic, politics, philosophy and so forth to be secondary tools. Abolitionists are not ashamed to proclaim the gospel in the public square and to the civil magistrates.

4. **Church Driven**. It preaches it is the duty and obligation of the local church and the believers that comprise those churches to catechize the culture on what is moral. Christians are to "abhor that which is evil; cleave to that which is good" (Rom. 12:9), expose evil (Eph. 5:11), and destroy the ungodly thinking that defends evil (2 Cor. 10:5). Yet the

pattern for 50 years has been to leave this fight up to legislators, political action committees, secular pro-life activists, and the Roman Catholic church to define morality on the abortion issue. As Christ reforms his Church, in return the Church should reform the culture.

5. **Immediate and Uncompromising**. It calls for the abrupt legal end – not slow, plodding, gradual steps – to the wickedness of prenatal homicide. The call of the gospel to repent and relent from wickedness is one of urgency. Following this model, abolitionists reject the idea that as a nation we can slowly choke the abortion industry out of existence through laws that enshrine prejudice against some of the unborn. Abolitionism seeks to do all it can to stop abortion *without* compromising the clear doctrines and commands of Scripture which prohibit personal and legislative partiality and becoming an unnecessary and bipartisan friend of the world. When unborn oppression continues and abolitionists cry out to God saying, "Why did you call us to this? Look how the nation suffers. And you have not yet even delivered the unborn," God may then graciously answer as he replied to Moses's faithfulness: "Now watch what *I* will do..."(Exodus 6:1).

Abortion abolition is the biblical model of what it means to be anti-abortion. The antithesis of biblical abolition is humanism. This form of anti-abortion work relies on legal positivism (or moral relativism), is pragmatic-centered, science driven, gradual, biblically compromising and prejudicial. In essence, it is the pro-life approach. By time you reach the end of this book, the variances between these two movements should be loud and clear.

Preface

"Let us be warned that while we live, to keep out of the company of such as fall away from the truth, as the devil did. All apostates are like the devil; they will not be quiet until they make others fall away with them." – Nicholas Byfield, Puritan preacher (1579-1622)

THERE IS A DANGER this book will be read with a harsh tone, so I must tell you that my intent is education and prodding toward our Lord and Savior Jesus Christ. My genuine desire is for us all to have wisdom from Christ to discern when we are living in accordance with Scripture or behaving as functional atheists.

James 3:13-18 says, "Who is wise and understanding among you? By his good conduct let him show his works in the meekness of wisdom. But if you have bitter jealousy and selfish ambition in your hearts, do not boast and be false to the truth. This is not the wisdom that comes down from above but is earthly, unspiritual and demonic. For where jealousy and selfish ambition exist, there will be disorder and every vile practice. But the wisdom from above is first pure, then peaceable, gentle, open to reason, full of mercy and good fruits, impartial and sincere. And a harvest of righteousness is sown in peace by those who make peace."

James's warning is of utmost importance as we embark on discovering the skeletons of what is heralded as the "Christian" pro-life movement and grapple with living faithfully to God's decrees amidst persecution and label of extremism. His counsel spans thousands of years and is applicable today, particularly as Christians wage war against selfish ambition, self-recognition and theological discord within the anti-abortion movement.

In brotherly love, this book is meant "To put a pebble in your shoe." We do not walk off pebbles and ignore the pain. Rather, we take off the shoe and investigate what is causing the affliction. We sit down, dig for a solution to our ache, and resolve to find peace. Similarly, when our worldview is challenged, we must resolve to be aligned biblically on whatever the topic.

This book assumes the reader is a Christian already informed of the biblical view of abortion, adheres to the view that life begins at fertilization, and that selfishly taking the life of another person with malice aforethought is murder. It heralds primarily to Protestant Christians so that we may understand the scope of the Roman Catholic church and secularism within the pro-life movement so we may then be on guard against false teaching and compromised philosophies and doctrines in the way in which we oppose abortion.

This is *not* an anti-Catholic book intended to be a personal slur against those practicing Roman Catholicism, though much of it will speak against the Catholic doctrines and influence that conflict and contrast with biblical doctrine. As Os Guinness once said, "Differences make a difference, and contrast is the mother to clarity." The contrasts are what I believe is inhibiting the end of abortion. We would be wise to reject unbiblical philosophies, ideologies and doctrines regardless of where or who they come from.

The pro-life movement's opposition to biblically abolishing abortion largely inspired this book. The idea for this book was born out of a year-long fascination with trying to understand the differences between the pro-life movement and the abortion abolition movement. I discovered the Roman Catholic church and secular ideologies primarily dominate the pro-life conversation, literature, education, organizations and political action committees within our nation. As such, the doctrine of the Catholic church and nonreligious groups on anti-abortion work have influenced how Protestant Christians respond. While Protestants enthusiastically agree with the Roman Catholic church's position that abortion is wrong, and Protestants profess life begins at conception alongside irreligious pro-life groups, we have ignored the unbiblical ways in which this anti-abortion movement has influenced policies, law, and public perception, specifically in its disapproval of completely criminalizing prenatal homicide.

So why does it matter if one is Catholic or Protestant or irreligious on the issue of abortion? We will discuss how those distinctions matter very much: specifically, how conviction on abortion is applied in law and evangelism, and how we vary on the sufficiency and authority of Scripture. Theologian Dr. James White writes in *The Roman Catholic Controversy*:

> I believe the differences that separate Roman Catholics and Protestants on the matter of the gospel itself are fundamental. I know many Roman Catholics who agree with me in that evaluation, I hasten to add. We do not share a common *evangel*, a common gospel, and therefore cannot, logically, share a common evangelistic mission, a common evangelistic goal. We do not have a common message. Yes, we both say, "Jesus is Lord," but the Apostles went beyond those three words to explain *what* that means. And when Roman Catholics and Protestants go beyond the bare confession, the hoped-for unity disappears in the particulars of what the gospel is and how people are made right before God. The gulf is too wide to be bridged by good intentions. Ultimately there is an impasse on the nature of the gospel itself.

If the difference is as substantial as White asserts, then it *cannot* be ignored: It will impact and subvert every anti-abortion initiative we approach from an ecumenical relationship.

Protestants affirm that all one needs to know about the moral law, civil government, how to treat others, reconciliation to God, and remittance of sins can be found within the Bible. From the Reformation, we call this *sola Scriptura* – by Scripture alone. Protestants believe mankind answers to the authority of Christ alone – as proclaimed by the Word of God – and are accountable directly to his headship. Protestants believe the Church is made up of all regenerate believers united to one another in Christ, through Christ, and for Christ in all generations throughout history.

Catholics, on the other hand, esteem the Bible as authoritative *alongside* Tradition and the Magisterium but never in contradiction to the church's leadership or apart from it. If disputes arise between Scripture and the papacy, Catholics are taught to follow the lead of the pope even when in contradiction to God's Word. Furthermore, the Church of Rome claims individuals are not permitted to go straight to the biblical text and conclude anything that is not aligned with Rome's teachings and declarations. If someone comes across a biblical passage that seems to say something entirely different than what Rome says it means, it is not Rome that is in error but the individual who is not granted the ability to discern what Scripture means apart from the interpretation of the Catholic Magisterium.

At the starting line, Protestants and Catholics are pushed dramatically apart. Conviction on what government means, how to work with politics, write legislation, and end abortion is all wrapped up in whether someone is looking to Rome for cues or looking to God's Word for guidance (John 18:36; Philippians 3:20).

Irreligious pro-life groups can fall within a myriad of secular moralism (determining what is "right" apart from religion), situational ethics, or postmodern humanism, but all at least share the same ideology that humans are not accountable to God or any supreme being. Their views of the Bible range from hostile irreverence to believing it is a collection of good teachings and wisdom but not authoritative for all people. Secularists create subjective doctrines from life experiences, preferences and pragmatism. The goodwill they possess often comes from a humanistic desire to elevate the human race and promote the dignity of life for everyone, including the unborn. While valuing all human life is noble, it fails to address the root issue of why women want to kill their children in the first place; it also fails to explain why human life is valuable.

Pro-life secularists will argue difficult circumstances such as poverty, single parenting, and racial disparities contribute to a perceived need for abortion. As such, they seek to alleviate *those* issues without delving deeper into the soul issue, which is a heart that loves self and not God, and therefore the heart chooses to violate God's law when it suits the individual. Social ills are important issues, but they cannot be solved apart from the gospel.

Regardless of such an eclectic mix of anti-abortion doctrinal flavors, Protestants have still taken their moral cues on the issue of preborn homicide from these largely Catholic and secular-dominated groups. Bible-believing Protestants have long forgotten the art of examining all things through the lens of Scripture, and the issue of what it means to be against abortion is no exception. To be clear, while not every pro-life organization is Catholic, the Roman Catholic church has been and still is the greatest influence on the pro-life cause. And this matters greatly.

While the Roman Catholic church associates itself with a form of Christianity, it operates in the pro-life sphere as largely secular amongst other non-Christian organizations. These religiously founded pro-life societies (both Catholic and Protestant) operate as any other secular business would but ignore the gospel as the main tenet of their mission. Many self-identified secular pro-life groups have joined the movement and often work seamlessly alongside the worldly efforts of the Catholic church on this front. Some of these secular organizations that oppose abortion support other things that most conservative Christians would distance themselves from.

Progressive Anti-Abortion Uprising, which joined efforts with National Right to Life's 2022 Open Letter to lawmakers (which will be examined in upcoming chapters), states on its website, "PAAU takes a position against capitalism. While structural economic solutions outside of capitalism vary among members, we believe that dismantling capitalism, alongside the anti-abortion view, will lead to far greater outcomes. Anti-Abortion Progressives approach abortion this way because we acknowledge that it is a systemic issue largely caused by existing inequality." The short biographies of each PAAU leader reveal how they arrived at the aforementioned mission statement. Its leadership team boasts an eccentric array of self-proclaimed "anarcho-communists," "queer progressive leftists," a "Catholic, anarcho-mutualist" and run-of-the-mill atheistic feminists. This activist organization believes abortion is an element of an oppressive economic system against minorities. Judging by PAAU's resume, one would be hard-pressed to find concern for God's laws in its mission.

Secular Pro-Life, another signee of National Right to Life's Open Letter, is led by professing atheists and states on its website, "Religious debates undermine our goal of building interfaith coalitions and distract from our focus on fighting abortion." This group also publicly states it takes no position on a rape exception for abortion as its leaders have split views on this topic. Instead, it desires to "keep the debate open," which sidesteps the determination whether to fight for *all* unborn lives or just some.

Remarkably, these groups are against humans murdering humans. What is not remarkable is that their godless ideologies have crept into the philosophy of what it means to fight abortion. Abortion is a *gospel* issue. It is the result of a culture that despises its Creator and those made in his image. Women are filled with envy, malice, selfishness and self-pity which lead them to destroy their offspring instead of nurturing them. Men are filled with lust, greed, pride and foolishness, which lead them to engage in illicit sex, encourage women they impregnate to abort, and abandon their call to lead and protect the families they create. These very men and women have darkened hearts and minds that need Jesus Christ's redeeming work on the cross to wash them anew and justify them before the Great Judge of the earth.

While many religious pro-life groups will give lip service to the gospel, it is rarely lived out in the training they provide, the policies they pressure legislators to pass, or the rhetoric they use in the public square. A good dose of secularism abounds.

The concept of a secular pro-life movement does not imply there is also a biblical pro-life model. This book will seek to show there is no biblical pro-life model, but rather that Scripture decidedly sides with an uncompromising abolitionist model. Therefore, if the nature of human hearts is not acknowledged, and we refuse to address from a biblical stance the sin of murder in the form of abortion, we will forever debate the causes of preborn homicide and how to prevent it.

If pastors abdicate their authority at the pulpit to instruct against the danger of blindly following those not led by the Spirit in this fight, we will continue to lose the battle and watch the utter demise of our nation under the continued judgment of God.

This book is an urgent petition for Protestant Christians to return to the word of God and by sola Scriptura determine how to justly and righteously address the issue of prenatal homicide within our nation. This is an appeal for all Christians to abandon the pro-life movement's prescribed ways where it errs from God's holy word and to remain faithful to our King's revealed decrees even when it flies in the face of popularity. This is a plea to repent from worldly pragmatism, which is often a fancy word for spiritual faithlessness to avoid complete scriptural obedience.

Whatever the sphere: religious, political, social, professional, or familial, *faithlessness is sin*. And we must repent. We cannot fight iniquity with iniquity but must stand wholly on the Word of God and trust in his deliverance against the Goliath of abortion. Duty is ours. The results are God's.

And what is our duty? "That which is altogether just shalt thou follow (Deuteronomy 16:20 KJV)." This is the bugle call for every Christian to put on the armor of God because we are at war. As the great Puritan preacher Richard Sibbes once said, "A Christian, so soon as he is newborn, is born a soldier, and so continues until his crown is put on him."

Our armor stands ready to be used. Abortion must be abolished. And it starts with first understanding whose side we are fighting on.

1

SECULARISM VERSUS SOLA SCRIPTURA

"We shall never be clothed with the righteousness of Christ except that we first know assuredly that we have no righteousness our own." – John Calvin, reformer (1509-1564)

A Foundation of Rock or Sand

"WHY ARE WE STILL having to talk about this issue?" Kristan Hawkins, president of Students for Life of America, was taking questions at the University of Texas San Antonio after her pro-life presentation on the campus that day. Darby, a student and abortion activist, stood in proud opposition to Hawkins with a poster board sign that read "Life begins when you understand living women matter more than potential babies." After many circular arguments with Hawkins, Darby finally asked the above question.

Hawkins had answered students with pro-life apologetic ease and given this student, like all the others, her undivided and thoughtful attention. Darby was less gracious. While zealous for abortion, she relied on personal attacks and insults and stumbled over her logic of when people have value and gain the right to life. By Darby's own reasoning, clumps of cells and those dependent on others do not have worth, which Hawkins politely reminded her by that reasoning we all lose. When Darby's logical fallacies began to pile up, she attempted to end her public humiliation by demanding Hawkins explain why the debate over abortion still rages.

"The reason we're still having this conversation is some people do not want to accept the natural consequences of heterosexual sex and be inconvenienced by another human life and want to selfishly choose to end human life in order to have their whims met," Hawkins answered.[1]

It was probably not what Darby wanted to hear. Pragmatically, though, that is very much a part of why the struggle continues. However, it is a physical symptom of a worse problem. In Hawkins' nearly hour-long presentation, not once did she mention God, the gospel message, or the biblical doctrine of human worth. Interestingly, Hawkins's answer reveals something routinely found in pro-life discourse. Apologetic pro-life arguments are usually based on embryology, fetal pain, polls, legal standards, statistics, social expectations and the logical fallacies of opponents. These are persuasive tools against the culture of death, but none touches the *heart* of the issue.

In their exchange, that was the only question Darby asked with genuine emotion. In a state of exasperation, she dropped her guard and pleaded to know why this battle could not be laid to rest. Without knowing it, Darby was asking for the gospel; but she did not hear it.

Mainstream pro-life organizations are not biblically answering the questions or objections of the culture on the topic of abortion. Science has become, for both sides of the abortion debate, the leading doctrine for determining good from evil. The inclination to default to science to persuade and establish justice, personhood and morality is in error. None of those things is answered by science. From that list, theology answers all three and philosophy answers perhaps two. The only thing in which pro-life scientific arguments can prove is that a fetus is a distinct, living, human being. Why is that not enough? It is not enough because the world has never had a problem with oppressing distinct, living, human beings. The genus of species is an entirely separate issue from the sanctity of life. While humanity is scientifically verifiable, it also implies an innate, deep worth of someone that science cannot explain.

Anti-abortion advocates often use humanity and personhood interchangeably, but humanity is more significant than personhood. Personhood is used as a legal connotation to confer rights to certain beings. It is also not limited to only human beings. The Bible makes clear that Jesus was a person before taking on humanity, God the Father is a person, as well as the Holy Spirit. Likewise, Satan and all fallen angels are persons. In addition to that, animal activists are trying to argue for animal personhood. This is why the focus of the fight must remain on our humanity and the Imago Dei doctrine.

Dr. Daniel Sulmasy, Director of the Kennedy Institute of Ethics at Georgetown University, echoed this in an interview with *The Atlantic*: "The question of whether the embryo or fetus is a person ... is not answerable by science."[2] This is not necessarily what either side wants to hear, as it requires tapping into philosophy, religion and theology to answer that question; all disciplines from which postmodern culture has drifted with each passing year.

Regardless, Sulmasy resolves we must go back to those disciplines if we want to answer such crucial problems, and ominously warns, "We've become steeped in a culture in which only the data matter, and that makes us, in some ways, philosophically illiterate...We really do not have the tools anymore for thinking and arguing outside of something that can be scientifically verified."[3]

Candidly, this should only be a problem for the secularist. As it is, culture *and* the Church are both confused. The culture is confused about what makes life valuable and the Church has outsourced that answer to secularized (even though many of these bulwark organizations have Catholic origins) pro-life groups.

Many Protestant pro-life advocates are shocked to learn the pro-life movement is largely irreligious. Pro-life adherents hear Catholic and Protestant churches claim life begins at conception and humans are made in the image of God; they see the pro-life movement talk about the intrinsic value of life and how abortion is ending that human life. The average Christian assumes the anti-abortion messages heard in his or her Christian circle and from the pulpit are equally broadcasted in the public square. Sometimes it is; more frequently, anything that hints at God or the Bible is disregarded when engaging politics and secular culture. Two different messages are used to support the pro-life agenda: one for the churches and one for society. Despite the majority of the pro-life movement being Catholic-driven, it operates irreligiously.

This secularized agenda originated in part with John Willke, founder of National Right to Life (NRTL). He wrote in *Why Can't We Love Them Both*, dubbed the "pro-life bible":

> Opposition to abortion stemming from one's religious beliefs is a very important and effective motivating factor. It, however, applies directly only to those persons who share similar religious beliefs. The counter-argument is very effective. "If you oppose abortion because you think it's against God's will, I respect that and you should live by that. However, I have a different religious belief (or non-belief). I do not think that it is against God's will and therefore you should respect my approval of abortion. You should not impose your religious belief on me." They had a point. The answer to this was as follows: "Medical, biological and natural science has long since proven that this is a living human from conception."[4]

Science has indeed demonstrated from the moment people come into existence they are human beings. DNA locks in the reality that people are of the *homo sapien* kind, but is that grounds for abandoning so quickly the religious roots of conviction against abortion? Willke continues to explain the evolution of the pro-life movement from one based on religious moral conviction to that of one steeped in science:

> The pro-life response, accordingly, was very direct. "Religious belief is a powerful motivator for the individual person. But this is not merely a religious issue, it is primarily a human rights issue, a civil rights issue, and our nation and other western nations, make laws to protect civil and human rights."[5]

There is a significant problem with this conclusion. Are we willing to use science instead of religious morality to argue any other point of the law? Rape? Kidnapping? Torture? Theft? Anarchy? Science certainly has its usefulness but human rights and civil law evolve from ethics, not a laboratory.

The Greek word *ethos* is derived from a root word which means "stall," as in a place where animals are kept. This denotes a place of permanence, a place of confinement, or an area where something is safely kept. From this derivative comes the word *ethics*. Often, ethics and morals are used as synonyms, and as theologian R.C. Sproul said, this confusion "permeates the modern ethical scene." This confusion is problematic because morals, from the Greek word *mores*, describe the behavioral patterns of a person or society. Sproul explained, "Ethics define what people ought to do; morals describe what people actually do."[6] In this way, an ethic is the place where one gets his or her morals. Ethics are always based on *something*, which then leads to the outward expression of those beliefs through tangible, observable morals. Humanistic ethics is based on what is normative. This means humanistic ethics can and do change from generation to generation. If the "norm" is to molest children less than 13 years old, that becomes what is seen as moral, or, at the very least, would not be called immoral. Eventually, what is seen as ethically good is reflected in the law. One could expect to see a repeal of laws that forbid or restrict people from engaging in sexual relations with children, and indeed, today's laws are beginning to reflect these new normative morals of 21st-century America.

An ethic derived from a biblical worldview, or any religion with moral parameters, works the opposite way. For the Christian whose ethic is rooted in the belief that humans will perform wicked deeds without proper restraint because all are sinners incapable of living just and righteous lives apart from the work of Christ on the cross and the Holy Spirit in their hearts, the law becomes a guide. It is used to restrain the normal inclinations of the human heart by recognizing that what is normative is not always productive, constructive, or life-giving. It does not view the normative as right or good but as something to evaluate.

As such, all the laws within the United States that address crimes such as rape, torture, kidnapping, theft, and murder come from religious ethics, specifically Christian ethics. Even laws of restitution correlate to the Old Testament Mosaic law given by God to the Israelites. Christian ethics are based on God's law. The ethic to not murder is predicated on God's law restraining humans in how they are to treat others.

Outside of God's design for human life and the protection of it, there is *no other ethical reason* to argue for the certain treatment of others. Humanism, within its godless constraints, has no logical conclusion for why we should not murder or enslave others. It can only say, "Just do not do it." Contrary to Willke's conclusion, human rights are *only* a religious issue. We cannot segregate religious ethics from a concern for making laws that protect human rights. They are the same. Unfortunately, as Sulmasy bemoaned, science seems to be the only tool that modern-day thinkers have in their tool belt. That is a substantial problem.

Science defines categories: if something is living or dead, human or animal, aquatic or astronomical, growing or shrinking. Science answers questions: Why is the sky blue? How do fish breathe underwater? Why can we not sneeze with our eyes open? Science cannot, however, tell us what are "good" civil laws. Religion (or more precisely, one's belief or unbelief about God as the ultimate lawgiver) informs ethics, which are reflected in what we believe about human rights, reflected as morals in what civil laws we establish, and influence the overall ethics of society.

Science only plays into the abortion debate by informing our ethical bias. Do we believe humans deserve protection because they are image bearers of God? If so, we apply that to the law to protect the preborn when science shows us life begins at fertilization. Do we believe humans are unexplainable mathematical accidents that have no inherent value? If so, we apply that in laws that discriminate against them when science shows the unborn are not yet fully developed to provide acceptable value.

Civil and human rights are not separate from moral and religious beliefs. Yet we will see how this poor philosophical thought has permeated the pro-life culture to remove the biblical motivation for being against abortion.

The Students for Life of America website lists the sole way to defend the pro-life position: "As a pro-life leader, you not only have to be knowledgeable on the facts about abortion — you must also be able to communicate it to others persuasively. This is how hearts are softened and minds are changed about abortion."[7]

The effects of softening and changing hearts are applied to "persuasively" presenting arguments against pro-choice principles without considering the impact of the gospel message on a person's hardened heart. Technically, what is happening is a change of mind, not heart. Someone's worldview is challenged to a point where they realize they must either change some of their views or live with opposing viewpoints. Is this a victory? Perhaps, but we should not stop and pat ourselves on the backs just yet. To be fair, Students for Life has plentiful articles on its website aimed at educating those against abortion on the popular arguments used by the pro-abortion community: the basics of human development, the history of abortion, and the devastating effects of abortion. While there is much benefit in understanding that information and being able to articulate it well (God can use that), Students for Life's mission statement stops there despite being a Catholic-run entity. Philosophy and science have their place in Christian apologetics, but they only confirm what Scripture authoritatively proclaims.

The same lack of biblical mention or resources is found when exploring National Right to Life's website, regardless of it also being a Catholic-founded organization. Ample information is provided through printable fact sheets on abortion statistics, abortifacients, surgical abortion methods, pain of the unborn, stem cell research, Planned Parenthood politics, and cultural reasons for an abortion. No printable sheets with Bible verses, gospel training tools, or gospel-sharing tips can be located. One cannot even discern from the website that the organization is religious.

Live Action, known for its educational videos and investigative work into the abortion industry, says on its website, "We expose the violence abortion does to both mother and child and demonstrate that the preborn child is an undeniably distinct and precious human life from the point of conception. Hearts and minds change daily about abortion through investigative reporting on the abortion industry, compelling and viral social media content, national media campaigns, and programs that activate individuals on behalf of the most defenseless within their communities."[8] Again, it attributes success to investigative videos and media campaigns, not God's inspired Word. We should not deny that these tools change minds. They *are* persuasive and do change minds; lest this be misunderstood, it is worth clarifying this is not a knock against all the hard work pro-life organizations have done to combat our abortion-crazed society. As believers, though, we are in the business of catechizing hearts. These organizations willfully stop short. As we will see later in the book, accepting work apart from the gospel has resulted in us losing on the battlefield of abortion despite cutting-edge investigative videos and educational tools.

March for Life, founded by Nellie Gray, who was described as a devout Catholic, states its mission is to "promote the beauty and dignity of every human life by working to end abortion—uniting, educating, and mobilizing pro-life people in the public square."[9] This is short and vague, but its website is absent of biblical resources that promote the dignity of human life from a scriptural perspective. Its main goal is to organize rallies of pro-life gatherings.

Susan B. Anthony Pro-Life America was founded in 1992 by Marjorie Dannenfelser who converted to Catholicism as an adult. Susan B. Anthony Pro-Life America states its mission is to "combine politics with policy, investing heavily in voter education to ensure that pro-life Americans know where their lawmakers stand on protecting the unborn, and in issue advocacy, advancing pro-life laws through direct lobbying and grassroots campaigns."[10] While this is a political organization and there is no reason Christians should avoid the political sphere, we still must ask ourselves if this entity is representing biblical philosophy in its political aspirations. The answer to that is no. Susan B. Anthony Pro-Life

America signed the NRTL Open Letter, along with March for Life, committing itself to oppose any legislation that could result in women being prosecuted for murdering their unborn children. Its public stance is to oppose equal protection and equal justice for the unborn. To summarize, these pro-life organizations oppose *completely* criminalizing abortion. As shocking as that may be, this is the majority position of the pro-life movement.

Author and Pastor CR Cali explains in *The Doctrine of Balaam* that another doctrine of the pro-life movement is the view that the woman is the second victim of abortion instead of one of the perpetrators. This doctrine is displayed through the national letter pro-life organizations proudly signed.

Thou Shalt Not Murder ... Unless You're a Woman

In May 2022, National Right to Life released an Open Letter signed by 76 pro-life organizations in the United States stating how they are against completely criminalizing abortion. Among the most prominent organizations were NRTL and its state affiliates, March for Life Action, Ethics and Religious Liberty Commission Southern Baptist Convention, Pro-Life Action League, Susan B. Anthony List, U.S. Conference of Catholic Bishops, and National Association of Pro-Life Nurses. In the letter they declared:

> Women are victims of abortion and require our compassion and support as well as ready access to counseling and social services in the days, weeks, months, and years following an abortion. As national and state pro-life organizations, representing tens of millions of pro-life men, women, and children across the country, let us be clear: **We state unequivocally that we do not support any measure seeking to criminalize or punish women and we stand firmly opposed to include such penalties in legislation.**[11]

A core issue arises from this pro-life declaration: All abortive women are classified as victims in the homicide cases of their children. Legally, there is no basis to declare complete innocence for a specific populace without due process of the law. While cases do arise with women being criminally forced into an abortion and, therefore, are victims of abuse on multiple levels, most women seek the destruction of their child's life on their own. Scripture declares that from "out of the heart come evil thoughts, murder, adultery, sexual immorality, theft, false witness, slander (Matthew 15:19)" and that "these are what defile a person." External pressures to commit murder are only part of the abortion problem. The seat of the issue resides within the affections of each woman's heart. Because pro-life groups have been influenced by worldly ideologies and accept the Catholic rejection of the biblical doctrine of total depravity, they have conceded on the issue of holding mothers accountable for the murder of their unborn children. This leads to a declaration that subverts equal justice for the unborn by excusing some of the main actors involved in their murders. How does this philosophy square with Scripture?

We are to do righteousness and justice is more acceptable to the Lord than sacrifice (Proverbs 21:3); Unequal weights and unequal measures are abominations to the Lord (Proverbs 20:10); It is not good to be partial to the wicked or to deprive the righteous of justice (Proverbs 18:5); We are not to join hands with the wicked, fall in with the many to do evil, or side with the many to pervert justice (Exodus 23:1-3); We are forbidden to show partiality and "justice, only justice" are we to follow (Deuteronomy 16:19-20); Those who pervert justice for the fatherless are to be cursed (Deuteronomy 27:19); and only debased people give approval to others to continue practicing wickedness (Romans 1:28-2:2). These Bible verses make it clear that the idea of excusing some people from the consequence of their sin of murder does *not* align with Scripture. God does not excuse the wicked or those who enjoin themselves to the unjust ways of the wicked.

The NRTL Open Letter reveals that the majority of pro-life organizations are opposed to justice. This further means they are opposed to abolishing abortion in the same way in which slavery was abolished. The United States did not partially criminalize slavery. The law today does not grant impunity for some people to own slaves and avoid prosecution. Instead, slavery was abolished, giving equal protection and equal justice to *all ethnicities of people*. If several individuals sought to enslave someone now, each person involved would be liable to criminal prosecution. Not all would receive the same punishment because due process does not mean equal outcomes or equal punishment, but it does mean all involved actors would be subject to the same laws for violating the rights of another individual. Likewise, we should do the same work for the preborn. Nevertheless, a lack of concern for the biblical definition of justice, ignorance of the American judicial system, and the indoctrination of feminine victimology prod many anti-abortion individuals in the other direction. The result is a movement that professes hatred of abortion yet works to reinstate or maintain it in its various forms. A clear example of this Catch-22 ideology took place in Arizona in 2021.

Cathi Herrod, president of Center for Arizona Policy (CAP), publicly opposed a bill of equal protection and equal justice for the unborn, saying she feared it would harm women because she believes they are also victims of abortion. Herrod urged the Arizona state legislature to repeal statute 13-3604, which was a pre-*Roe* law that made it a crime for women to kill their preborn children. Statute 13-3603 still stands, which makes it a crime for anyone *else* to abort babies. Arizonan mothers, however, are now free to kill their unborn children without repercussions. Proud of this fact, Herrod stated in a webinar, "... the pre-*Roe* law that punished women for having abortions was repealed by the legislature in 2021, at our urging. We're not trying to put women in jail for having an abortion. In the pro-life movement, we love them both. We love both mother and child. And we look at both as being victims."[12]

If Herrod, a leading pro-life advocate for the state of Arizona, had not stepped in and influenced the legislature to repeal that statute, Arizona could have been on the path as the first state in the nation to fully criminalize abortion after the reversal of *Roe v. Wade*. Nevertheless, complete abolition is what Herrod and other staunch pro-life advocates oppose because it could result in legal discomfort for future law-breaking women.

The Arizona equal protection bill Herrod opposed was replaced instead with HB 1457, which amended the state abortion laws to prohibit the termination of a baby due to genetic abnormalities and to require the proper disposal of aborted baby parts. Jeff Durbin, pastor of Apologia Church and abortion abolitionist, points out the irrelevancy and irrationality of such a bill by saying a couple could admit they are simply killing their child because they hate it and not because it has Down Syndrome, and that would be perfectly acceptable under the new law. Durbin further explains, "Now imagine that in terms of sex trafficking. Would you ever do so with sex trafficking say, 'You know, I think sex trafficking is bad, but here's the deal: We'll allow it in the state of Arizona except not the kids with Down Syndrome.'"[13]

On the surface what looks like a righteous chess move is an insidiously deceptive ploy to guide justice-loving citizens away from biblical standards. When the doctrine of women being victims, and not co-conspirators in unborn murder, drives your cause, you end up with illogical bills that protect no one, devalue the life of healthy babies, and send the philosophical message that killing because of hate or selfishness or any other reason is acceptable so long as you do not kill due to "ableism." Throwing in a proper burial for the decapitated, burned, dismembered, or poisoned baby does not lessen the wickedness of the act. As Durbin remarks, if we had done that with Auschwitz, would we feel better about the Holocaust?

Scripture in Conflict with Pro-Life Values

Efforts such as HB 1457 are not a God-fearing way to educate our culture on the severity and sin of abortion, yet this type of secular compromise occurs continually within the nation. Christians have outsourced their moral compass toward abortion to the world. Not only are Christians supporting a secularized pro-life movement that intentionally leaves out the gospel message, but they also link arms with the same movement that grants impunity to an entire class of people to commit murder without legal consequence. This is biblically disobedient, logically inconsistent, and judicially reckless.

God has established the parameters of this fight. Ephesians 6 reminds Christians the battle is spiritual and our weapons are spiritually derived. The belt of truth abstractly models steadfastness in the things of God. The breastplate of righteousness guards Christians from the wicked desires of the flesh, while our feet are busy with the word and work of the gospel. We are fortified by our faith in God to plow ahead while we fight confidently with the sword of the Spirit, which are the very words of God. All of that is bathed in prayer and is the recipe for victory that Paul outlines for believers in his letter to Ephesus. This idea of taking up armor is also found in Isaiah 59 where the King of Heaven is pictured as dressing for combat. Ephesians mimics Christians wearing this armor ensemble because believers are to be imitators of the Lord: "He saw that there was no man, and wondered that there was no one to intercede; then his own arm brought him salvation, and his righteousness upheld him. He put on righteousness as a breastplate, and a helmet of salvation on his head; he put on garments of vengeance for clothing, and wrapped himself in zeal as a cloak. According to their deeds, so will he repay, wrath to his adversaries, repayment to his enemies; to the coastlands he will render repayment. So they shall fear the name of the Lord from the west, and his glory from the rising of the sun; for he will come like a rushing stream, which the wind of the Lord drives (Isaiah 59:16-19)."

The armor of God is divine and useful in advancing his kingdom by teaching, correcting and training in righteousness so that every person of God may be a completely equipped soldier in the battle (2 Timothy 3:16). As theologian Matthew Henry noted about the armor pieces, "It is observable that, among them all, there is none for the back; if we turn our back upon the enemy, we lie exposed."[14] To the shame of God's people, the abortion debate rages because we have done just that. We have turned our backs on the seriousness of the war and left out the *only* weapons we have: God's Word and faith in his deliverance through prayer.

The reason science fails to convert the hearts of people is because it is rooted in the physical, and that is not where the fight originates. Culture is at enmity with God and, in a Romans 1 fashion, it rages against its Creator to chase what is morally filthy, depraved and eternally condemning. To further exasperate people's separation from God, the Church has been an accomplice in not treating abortion as the murder that it is, and has neglected to tutor society to understand their darkened minds and hearts and need for a Savior. As the apostle Paul says in Galatians, "the [God's] law is our tutor." Likewise, this is outlined in Paul's first letter to Timothy: "Now we know that the law is good, if one uses it lawfully, understanding this, that the law is not laid down for the just but for the lawless and disobedient, for the ungodly and sinners, for the unholy and profane, for those who strike their fathers and mothers, of the murderers, the sexually immoral, men who practice homosexuality, enslavers, liars, perjurers, and whatever else is contrary to sound doctrine (1 Timothy 1:8-10)."

Scripture makes clear that one of the functions of the law is to restrain people, yet pro-life advocates do not expect to apply any law to restrain mothers who premeditate the deaths of their preborn offspring. The law also tutors people on what God requires of humankind. From this comes the implicit understanding that if we break earthly laws that carry physical consequences, then what worse punishment awaits us for breaking God's laws? Pro-life apologists often have the right scientific and logical talking points to counter abortion, but those do not teach culture how abortion violates God's law and what judgment awaits unjustified lawbreakers. Matthew 28 sums up our ordained mission on this earth:

> Now the eleven disciples went to Galilee, to the mountain to which Jesus had directed them. And when they saw him they worshiped him, but some doubted. And Jesus came and said to them, 'All authority in heaven and on earth has been given to me. Go therefore and make disciples of all nations, baptizing them in the name of the Father and of the Son and of the Holy Spirit, teaching them

to observe all that I have commanded you. And behold, I am with
you always, to the end of the age." (Matthew 28:16-20)

Jesus's command is forceful. He begins by stating that *all* authority is his as he is the supreme and eternal King; in response to that, those who belong to him are to go into the world and teach all people to obey Christ the King *now*. To understand everything Jesus commands of his followers, one needs to read the entirety of Scripture, especially since Jesus quoted extensively from the Old Testament. For the sake of brevity, we are focusing on the Bible's commands on murder as it is certainly one of the moral issues we are charged with clarifying for the culture in which we live.

As a very basic definition, a disciple means someone who believes the doctrine of Christ and imitates his teachings and example (Matthew 10:24; Luke 14:26 Luke 14:27 Luke 14:33; John 6:69). How do we make disciples? By first knowing the Scriptures ourselves and then teaching others the Word of God and training them in what it means to look like Christ. It is by this ordinary means that God has ordained to bring salvation to the nations and blessings to the people. So what exactly does our culture need to be taught about abortion?

The Bible instructs that you shall not murder (Exodus 20:13); murder comes from within the heart of men and women (Mark 7:20-23); no murderer has eternal life abiding in him (1 John 3:15); those who murder are of their father the devil (John 8:44-45); murderers are accountable for breaking the whole law of God (James 2:11); and unrepentant murderers will be in the "lake that burns with fire and sulfur" (Revelation 21:8; 22:14-16).

By these verses, much is at stake for the unrepentant post-abortive and abortion-supporting men and women. Abortion is murder; when we refuse to endorse legal punishment to dissuade all people from this type of murder, and further educate them that *all* post-abortive women are somehow victims of prenatal homicide, the path to repentance is clouded at best and concealed at worst. We have also implied to the watching, pagan world that we are okay making some exceptions on murder, and that God's Word can be taken lightly and applied conveniently. This is wholly inconsistent with Scripture and discrediting of the anti-abortion cause to skeptics. As Pastor Brett Baggett points out, "God's disputation toward child sacrifice is severe."[15] Our attitude toward child sacrifice cannot be light, for God's hand of judgment will not be light against it and all those who tolerate it.

In Leviticus 20, God commands the immediate death penalty to be levied against anyone who gave their newborns as a sacrifice to the pagan god Molech. In the first chapter of Romans, the reader is brought back to the severity of murder (in a long list of other sins). Here, Paul explains to the Roman church that their culture has been turned over to a debased mind for its incessant practice of murder, sexual immorality, maliciousness, deceit and faithlessness. Paul said, "though they know God's righteous decree that those who practice such things deserve to die, they not only do them but give approval to those who practice them (vs 32)." When the pro-life movement refuses to condemn women for their abortions, it gives them approval to murder.

Inconsistencies within the Fight for Life

An article published on *Defending Feminism's* website starts by saying, "I will preface this piece by stating that I am strongly pro-choice and do not find the pro-life moral framework plausible..." It would be easy for an anti-abortion reader to stop reading at that point and dismiss the author as ignorant and foolish, but if one kept reading they would discover the article makes a rather good point. The author explains how the pro-life mentality is illogical and inconsistent; therefore, it is an ideological framework that should be tossed out. What leads the author to conclude the pro-life position is so dismissible? It is because mainstream pro-life groups call abortion murder but then treat it like it is not. The author continues with, "...I will argue here that if you do accept the pro-life framework, the views of Jeff Durbin, James White and other 'radical' pro-life activists are the logically consistent ones..."[16]

What makes abolitionists "radical" to this author is they deviate from the essential pro-life doctrine of women victimology and instead call for equal protection and equal justice for all people, both born and preborn, without exceptions. As the author concludes, those who say abortion is murder and believe it should be treated as such are logically consistent. This consistency is sadly "radical" and a fringe philosophy in the fight for life.

Quoting Secular Pro-Life, the *Defending Feminism's* article highlights the prominent pro-life belief that women have been duped by the abortion industry into believing that a fetus is not a living person so they are tricked into abortions (hence why women are also victims). The pro-choice author expressly continues:

> But this reasoning fails when we apply it to similar cases uncontroversially believed to represent murder. Let us look at the tragic case of Tina Isa. Tina Isa was the daughter of a highly traditional Muslim father, Zein Isa...When Tina began dating a Black American boyfriend, Zein felt she had disgraced his family sufficiently to warrant deadly punishment. He murdered Tina...despite immigrating to America, Zein clearly held on to many beliefs from his traditional past, where honor killings of a daughter would not be seen as unjustified murder. Yet the fact that he held these terrible beliefs does not seem sufficient to exonerate him from his crime. At most, one might say that his background should be a mitigating factor when he was sentenced for his crime. But arguing that men who commit honor killings should be protected from murder charges because of the belief system they grew up in seems hardly compelling. Likewise, the fact that many women do not believe that abortion is truly wrong does not seem like a compelling reason to believe they should not face punishment in places where 'abortion is murder' is uncontroversial law.[17]

While a strong abortion supporter, this author recognizes the cognitive dissonance that exists within the pro-life ideology and lays out a compelling case against mainstream pro-life exceptions that allow women to murder *ad libitum*. The author acknowledges that ignorance of the law is not enough to grant innocence under the law. She points out that the Middle Eastern cultural practice of executing family members who bring shame to the Muslim faith should never be accepted in a nation that does not recognize that as a legalized type of killing. In the author's scenario, even if the Muslim man acting in sincere faith carried out such a practice in America, we should reject its legitimacy and prosecute him under existing homicide law. Logically, the author likens this to the abortion cause and implicitly asks why the pro-life culture grants exceptions to those they claim are murdering.

Similar to the skeptical feminist writer, *The Conversation* news site published an article titled "If you're pro-life, you might already be pro-choice," and points out more irregularities within the pro-life movement. M. Scarfone, an ethicist and author of the article, says that believing all humans should be protected by the same laws and then permitting exceptions to that moral claim (such as in the case of rape, incest or life of the mother) is incoherent. He goes on further to argue how this is a gateway belief for transitioning many pro-life individuals over to the pro-choice camp as both are arguing for the same thing in the end: bodily autonomy.

> ... the moderate pro-life position says that a right to life is stronger than, or outweighs, a right to bodily autonomy, except when the fetus that has the right to life is created by a violation of ... bodily autonomy... when someone allows for an exception to abortion in cases of rape, they are acknowledging that there are violations of autonomy that can justify abortion. And if some violations of autonomy are appropriate grounds, then it cannot be true that a right to life is morally weightier than a right to bodily autonomy.[18]

Scarfone succinctly identifies the contradiction clouding the pro-life movement. His assertion that most pro-life advocates are just pro-choice is not entirely wrong. Recent polls show that the majority of Americans support exceptions for abortion in circumstances of rape, incest, or if the mother's life is at risk. Supporting abortion at all is certainly not anti-abortion but *for the option of it* even if in limited cases. This, of course, is the traditional definition of what it means to be pro-choice.

From 2021 to 2022, the largest leap from pro-life to pro-choice became evident in light of the reversal of *Roe v. Wade*. Since 2015, Americans who identify as pro-life have hovered respectively around 44-47% of the population. In 2022, however, Americans who identified as pro-life plummeted to 39% down from 47% in 2021.[19] These numbers do not take into account the "pro-lifers" who, when pressed, would align more closely to the pro-choice sentimentality as Scarfone discerns.

This is the fallout from abandoning the God-ordained, spiritually divine weapons with which God determined to outfit his army. Like the rebellious Israelites in the wilderness, the pro-life movement has decided to race into battle without the prescriptive method or the presence of God.

A Different Movement; A Better Focus

Contrary to the pro-life movement, the abolition movement seeks to do all things from a gospel-driven and biblically informed position. The guiding force behind the abolition movement of today is the belief that change will only come through the use of Scripture, the persistent application of biblical morals, and the regeneration of the Holy Spirit in the hearts of our neighbors. Perusing abortion abolition websites gives an entirely different landscape of its inspiration juxtaposed to its pro-life counterpart:

> Our mission is to exalt and vindicate the image of God by promoting sound public policy that provides all preborn human beings

the equal protection of the laws. – Foundation to Abolish Abortion.[20]

We believe that God is now raising up a unified, prophetic voice to speak into our culture and governments so this evil can finally be ended. We praise God for every baby that has been saved from the efforts of the pro-life movement up to this point. However, our conviction is that the approach to end abortion must be biblically faithful, philosophically consistent, and gospel-centered. We want to use distinctly Christian language and call abortion what God calls it: murder. We are calling for an immediate end to abortion, not an eventual strategy to regulate it out of existence through incremental policies. By standing on God's Word as our foundation, we are calling sinners to repentance and faith in Jesus because we know that it is only the gospel that has the power to change hearts and minds set on murder. – End Abortion Now.[21]

Following in the footsteps of former abolitionist movements, we aim to end one of the greatest human miseries and moral evils ever to be entrenched in our world. Human beings are created in the image of Almighty God, the very Creator of the universe. The weakest and most helpless among us have been subjected by this wicked culture to accepted, legal, and systematic destruction. We are simply attempting to answer the question: What does Christianity look like in a culture that practices Child Sacrifice? And put our answer into action. – Abolish Human Abortion.[22]

As you just read this opening paragraph, three children were unjustly slaughtered in the wombs of their mothers in the United States. By the time you finish reading the educational portion of this website, which I pray to God you will, about 200 babies will have been butchered under the cover of law. By the end of this day, around 2,400 of your preborn neighbors will have been murdered through what has so politely been termed *abortion*. This has been happening every single day for almost 50 years. The question that this website seeks to ask and to answer is this: *What does Jesus command from you and me who are in Christ when it comes to the abortion holocaust happening around us?* My answer, because it is the answer God gives in scripture, is this: *as Christ has rescued us, we must rescue others.* – Rescue Those.[23]

Abortion is a moral issue. All morality ultimately stems from one's religion. Additionally, all laws assert what is right and what is wrong and are therefore moral statements. If we want justice in our society, we have to know how to determine what justice is. Science does not give us love, mercy or justice, but the God of the Bible and His good commands do. – Not A Victim.[24]

We are not ashamed of the gospel and it is our intention that the truth, justice and mercy of God be freely and powerfully proclaimed to all the nations of the earth. We strive to make ourselves, with Christ, enemies of all that is sinful. In the context of a culture that murders its children, being a consistent Christian means being an abolitionist. It means bringing the light of the gospel into conflict with the darkness of death and child sacrifice. It means loving your preborn neighbor by demanding equal justice and protection. This is our intention. – Free the States (now Abolitionists Rising).[25]

Followers of Christ are to speak plainly on the issues of Scripture and trust in the work of the Holy Spirit in the recipient's life. When professing believers speak out of both sides of the mouth – saying abortion is murder but then allowing for it in certain pregnancy circumstances, or allowing preborn murder to be committed by one group of people but not others – it works against the cause to preserve and protect all life. It makes us fools in our opponents' eyes. It also becomes a tool of confusion in society as the lines become increasingly blurred between pro-life and pro-choice positions.

Victory cannot be minced apart from God. It is no trivial matter the church engages in logical debates, secular moralism or scientific arguments against abortion but leaves out the gospel essence. While those things can be used in our gospel conversations they should never be primary. A well-laid scientific argument does not call a person to repentance from sin and into the Kingdom of Light. At best, one might just convert someone into an agnostic pro-lifer; and while that may help the pro-life cause, it will not help the agnostic's in the eternal end. Likewise, a well-laid philosophical argument for a person being a person no matter what their stage of development crumbles the moment freedom is granted to women to kill those for whom we are trying to establish basic human rights.

Matthew 28 commissions Christ's followers to make disciples of all nations through sharing the Word of God that Jesus taught in the temple, to his disciples, to the Pharisees, in front of Pilate, when refuting Satan, and to us through the now-canonized Scriptures. Jesus simply told us to teach others how to obey what he commands. Abortion should not be excluded. God's Word must be used as the first tool in the toolbox in the public square to address the issue of preborn murder. If it was, we would not be inconsistent on when a woman could and could not kill her child but would instead allow no legal exceptions for murdering another human. We would apply the law equally to all people involved in murdering an unborn human instead of granting some exemption.

Instead, most pro-life organizations refrain from telling women abortion is murder and an act that needs to be repented. Christians have been psychologized to tiptoe around the truth for its "divisiveness" in sensitive situations and to respect the emotions of women at all costs to the gospel. Should grace and tact be used when discussing this issue? Yes, but God has given discernment to the believer to know when to use what type of language. Christians have more freedom in how we communicate than the postmodern world wants us to have. To imitate our Lord and Savior, we must look to his examples of how he addressed the sinful, hardened people of his culture. Jesus routinely commanded the crowds to "repent and believe in the gospel (Mark 1:14-15; Matthew 4:17; Luke 5:31-32)" and that the least valued in society were to have access to him (Mark 10:13-14). Jesus also did not remain silent on issues of wrong. He used those moments to teach about his kingdom, what sin is, and the need for repentance. Jesus had visceral reactions to the wickedness taking place such as when he called the unrepentant "vipers" (Matthew 23:33), "hypocrites" (Matthew 15:7) "fools" (Luke 11:39), "liars" (John 8:55), and "children of the devil" (John 8:44) and hypocrites who defiled the temple (John 2:13-22). Likewise, his disciples must be willing to imitate the same countenance in some circumstances. One of the most astonishing glimpses of Jesus' rhetorical style is briefly mentioned in Luke. In these verses, Jesus asks his disciples who the people in the culture think he is and their response gives incredible insight into his reputation:

> Now it happened that as he was praying alone, the disciples were with him. And he asked them, "Who do the crowds say that I am?" And they answered, "John the Baptist. But others say, Elijah, and others, that one of the prophets of old has risen." Then he said to them, "But who do you say that I am?" And Peter answered, "The Christ of God (Luke 18-20)."

The list of men to whom the people of the cities compared Jesus were not people-pleasing personalities. These were not men known for their quiet demeanors.

Rather, they were forceful in their condemnations against evildoers, loudly crying in the streets and in public against sin, calling the unrepentant names (Luke 13:32, Matthew 23:23), and confronting religious and political leaders with their public atrocities and imploring them to repent (1 Kings 22:8, Mark 6:14-18). A righteous zeal for God's holiness is what drove the prophets and Jesus to engage in such ways. Christians today lack this convicted vigor of their Lord, and it has been costly. Christians must engage in the abortion battle with the divinely given weapons they have to use against the forces of darkness. It is a command, not a recommendation, that Christians disciple those around them on God's law. Instead of leading the charge in this spiritual war with heavy machine guns and anti-tank guided missiles, we are rushing in with flashbangs and 9mm handguns. Those defenses might help for a while, or they might subject us to demise before we even warm up to fight. Either way, those weapons will not win the war.

Despite the need for heavy artillery, gospel training is rarely employed even in religious pro-life organizations. This is because the organizations are vastly ecumenical and there are substantial differences in the application, interpretation and understanding of Scripture between Catholics and Protestants, so it is left religiously ambiguous. Due to these fundamental doctrinal differences, the gospel cannot be central to the mission of the pro-life movement in a functional and observable way. This has allowed the pro-life movement to seek success without the gospel. While *individuals* may desire to be involved with pro-life ministries to share the Good News and see people come to Christ, the organizational entities themselves have a dedicated political mission to regulate abortion, not evangelize. The most well-meaning pro-life individuals have lost their zeal for spreading the gospel in their anti-abortion efforts. Cali uses the term "secular pro-life establishment"[26] to denote the clear lack of gospel driving the anti-abortion movement, even with many of these organizations having Catholic roots.

If the cliché "trickle-down effect" holds value, then we should be concerned that so many Christians volunteer under the leadership, vision and ideologies of secular-driven organizations on what should be a solely biblical and church effort. Even more disturbing is that many Christians believe they are working for and advancing God's kingdom while they are working against it. Efforts to promote the heresy God only requires some murderers to be held accountable but not all; that image bearers conceived through rape or incest do not have the same rights to life, liberty and the pursuit of happiness as their preferentially-conceived peers; and urging legislators to adopt these unjust and heretical ideas in law all work against God's revealed will and the created function of civil government. When secular moralists become our supreme head, we become disciples of the world and not of Christ.

"Why are we still having to talk about this issue?" we might ask with Darby.

It is because no one does good and does not sin.[27] In a fallen creation, there will always be the fight against those who desire death. People are gladly in rebellion against their Creator. Their hearts are wicked above all else, and without Jesus Christ's atoning work on the cross to share his righteousness with those who follow him in faith through repentance of sin, they will continue chasing after all sin that leads to death – even death in others.

Bigger blows could be struck against the culture of death if anti-abortion apologetic arguments were not separate from Scripture. Moralism teaches we can do right apart from God. Scripture teaches we have no righteousness of our own apart from God. These are two rivers flowing in different directions that will lead to different creeds and outcomes.

What impact might have been made in that university student's life if the response had been, "We are still having this conversation because we are all sinners and in need of God to transform our hearts from dark to light, to give us the burden to repent from sin, to gift us with the ability to love righteousness and forsake wicked deeds such as ending the life of another person for our pleasure and benefit. Repent, for God's kingdom is here. He is making all things new and is coming again in judgment against the lawless."

2

Eroding Ecumenicalism

"The church law has no force when it is opposed to the word of God." – John Wycliffe, reformer (1328-1384)

Two Movements, Two Gospels

CATHOLICISM AND PROTESTANTISM HAVE a tumultuous past. While Protestant kings and queens are no longer imprisoning or exiling Roman Catholics, and the Church of Rome is no longer burning, drowning or beheading Protestant Christians, there is still some tension between these two groups. Aside from the past physical violence, there are valid reasons for tension.

While Catholics and Protestants all claim to be followers of Christ, the beliefs behind these professions are starkly different. Once the layers are peeled back, it often becomes startling to both how divergent are their faiths and belief systems. If it seems hyperbolic to claim Protestants and Catholics have different gospels, then consider more closely what leading Protestant theologian and author on Catholicism James White remarks:

> I believe the differences that separate Roman Catholics and Protestants on the matter of the gospel itself are fundamental. I know many Roman Catholics who agree with me in that evaluation, I hasten to add. We do not share a common *evangel*, a

common gospel, and therefore cannot, logically, share a common evangelistic mission, a common evangelistic goal. We do not have a common message. Yes, we both say, "Jesus is Lord," but the Apostles went beyond those three words to explain *what* that means. And when Roman Catholics and Protestants go beyond the bare confession, the hoped-for unity disappears in the particulars of what the gospel is and how people are made right before God.[1]

The structure of faith in these two groups is so dissimilar it results in people who respond differently in culture and to the nature of sin, and the issue of abortion is no oddity. If Protestants truly have a different gospel than that of their Catholic counterparts, what does that mean for the anti-abortion movement? Are the divisions serious enough to warrant a departure from anti-abortion ecumenical partnerships?

As it turns out, the first point of division happens almost immediately with the question: *What is Scripture?* Protestants proclaim it is the infallible and all-sufficient Word of God preserved for all time to instruct the world and save the elect. The 1689 Baptist Confession of Faith (modern English), while a bit lengthy, paraphrases many verses from Scripture to express the essence of the Holy Scriptures:

> The Holy Scriptures are the only sufficient, certain, and infallible standard of all saving knowledge, faith, and obedience. The light of nature and the works of creation and providence so clearly demonstrate the goodness, wisdom, and power of God that people are left without excuse; however, these demonstrations are not sufficient to give knowledge of God and His will that is necessary for salvation. Therefore, the Lord was pleased at different times and in various ways to reveal Himself and to declare His will to His church. To preserve and propagate the truth better and to establish and comfort the church with greater certainty against the

corruption of the flesh and the malice of Satan and the world, the Lord put this revelation completely in writing. Therefore, the Holy scriptures are necessary, because God's former ways of revealing His will to His people have now ceased.[2]

Every October 31st, Protestants around the world remember the official launch of the Reformation Period when Martin Luther nailed his 95 theses to the door of the Wittenberg Castle Church. Though many came before Luther in laying the foundation for the Christian life to be oriented back to the Bible, it was Luther's time period we historically saw wide-sweeping change occur within the church. When Protestants celebrate Reformation Day they remember one of the greatest treasures recovered from that period: the Bible. Willem J. Ouweneel, from his book, *The World is Christ's* states:

> The Reformation entailed the rediscovery of the sola Scriptura, "scripture alone," in all matters of Christian doctrine and Christian practice. Protestants recognize many authorities above them—parents, elders, magistrates—but each of these authorities is seen as subordinate to the scriptures. Indeed, the main discovery of the Reformation was the insight that scripture has divine authority over the entire human life, both individually and societally—not only over the domain of grace (the sacred realm) but also over that of nature (the secular realm). Total natural depravity demands a total redemption of the person, and hence also a total reformation of human life and society under the guidance of God's Word and Spirit.[3]

While this rally cry is one of the most endearing tenets of the Protestant faith, Catholics would agree only partially with the above assertion. For the Catholic, Scripture holds power and authority so long as it is in communion with and under the guidance of the Church of Rome. In Catholicism, Scripture is subordinate to

Roman Catholic officials and is the exact inverse of the Protestant belief that all authority is subordinate to Scripture. If the Bible is read, interpreted and applied apart from the Roman Catholic church's instruction, Scripture seemingly holds no influential power for individuals or the culture. Rome strongly asserts no individual has the right to go directly to biblical text to discern what God's Word instructs on a particular subject. Why? Individuals could draw conflicting conclusions from that of the Catholic church. The Council of Trent (1546) expounds on Rome's position; since it remains the relevant dogma of the Roman Catholic church today, it is worth reading carefully:

> Furthermore, to check unbridled spirits, it decrees no one relying on his own judgment shall, in matters of faith and morals pertaining to the edification of Christian doctrine, distorting the Holy scriptures in accordance with his own conceptions, resume to interpret them contrary to that sense which holy mother Church, to whom it belongs to judge of their true sense and interpretation, has held and holds, or even contrary to the unanimous teaching of the Fathers, even though such interpretations should never at any time be published. Those who act contrary to this shall be made known by the ordinaries and punished in accordance with the penalties prescribed by the law.[4]

At first glance, this dogmatic declaration appears reasonable in its attempt to squelch heretical, unorthodox teachings. We very much see twisted interpretations and distortions of Scripture occur within secular and Christian cultures. In response to error, Catholics are taught they are impotent to understand God's Word without the interpretation and explanation of Rome. If they persist in understanding God's inspired words apart from the Magisterium, they are subject to repercussions. Perhaps Trent meant well, but it simply is not how God himself revealed Scripture to be used. Much to the chagrin of Rome, the philosophy of limiting the true meaning of Scripture to only the ruling Catholic authorities is neither reasonable nor biblical. Furthermore, it has not solved the plethora of diverse understandings, doctrinal differences or conflicting interpretations within the Roman Catholic church itself. Rome hypocritically looks at Protestants' fluctuating interpretations of biblical concepts and sees this inconsistency as vindication of its stance that correct interpretation belongs to Roman authority alone. This viewpoint ignores Rome's history with conflicting and changing papal teachings and various understandings among congregants and bishops. More importantly, if the Holy Spirit is the one who supernaturally reveals the truth to Catholic authority, what biblical text shows he is restricted from doing so with individuals who belong to him?

The issue is more complicated than the assertion that Catholics have the authority to understand Scripture and Protestants do not. The Roman Catholic church believes one can only have the full picture of God's words written in Scripture when paired with the oral tradition handed down through the Magisterium: the teaching office of the pope and bishops, whose responsibilities are to determine the authoritative application of Scripture and give an authoritative explanation of the apostolic tradition. This is the belief that Christ did and said things not recorded in Scripture and those pieces are needed to accompany written Scripture to fully understand God's saving will and requirements for holy living.

Protestants agree that not everything Christ did was recorded. Christ's apostle John wrote, "Now Jesus did many other signs in the presence of the disciples, which are not written in this book; but these are written so that *you may believe that Jesus is the Christ, the Son of God*, and *that by believing you may have life in his name* (John 20:30-31)." John tells his readers again in John 21:25 that the spectrum of Jesus' brief but powerful earthly ministry was too vast to record for future generations but that the most important elements were written down so all the knowledge one needs for *salvation* would not be neglected to be passed on.

Rome asserts that even essential saving knowledge has been withheld from written Scripture and is only contained within the secret oral tradition passed along by the Magisterium of the Roman Catholic church. The implication of this belief is huge. It asserts what Jesus said as "tradition" varies from written Scripture, and may even contradict written Scripture in some instances, concluding the need for both forms of revelation for true salvation. From this "oral tradition" flows penance, earthly priestly confession, papal infallibility and Mariology, all of which are taught as dogmatically essential Catholic truths. Gregg Allison, professor of Christian theology at The Southern Baptist Theological Seminary, provides this simple breakdown:

> Think of a three-legged stool. Now imaginatively label one of those legs "scripture," label the second leg "Tradition," and label the third leg "Magisterium"...You now have a mental picture of the threefold authority structure of the Roman Catholic Church. Now think of a marble column supporting, say, a statue. Imaginatively label that column "scripture." You now have a mental picture of the authority structure of Protestant churches....The authority structures of these two branches of Christendom are very different.[5]

The main issue between Catholics and Protestants is *authority*. Catholics are taught the supreme authority in their lives is the church and Protestants believe the greatest authority in their lives is the Word of God. The Roman Catholic church views Scripture as divinely inspired and authoritative *only alongside Tradition and Magisterium*. Protestants view Scripture as divinely inspired and authoritative because it is God's living word. Dr. Jeffery Mirus, Catholic co-founder of Christendom College, writes:

> The Catholic approach to scripture is quite different from that of most serious Protestants, especially Fundamentalists. To begin with, Protestants have neither Tradition nor Authority to enlighten their interpretations of scripture. Since scripture and Tradition are two forms of Revelation from the same God, and since the

Petrine authority in the Church is established and protected by Christ, the Magisterium combines with scripture and Tradition to give a complete and certain view of the truth. As the teachings of all three come from the same Holy Spirit, a right understanding of the Faith is possible only when all three are taken properly into account.[6]

To summarize these points, Roman Catholic church doctrine teaches no one can be saved apart from the one true church and those who believe in justification by faith alone in Christ alone are to be damned (Lumen Gentium 14). To believe in faith alone and justification alone is to reject the infallible authority and relevance of the Catholic Magisterium and Tradition. It completely dismantles Rome. As Dr. Mirus explains, individuals cannot determine the meaning of Scripture and must rely on the "inspired" interpretation imparted to them by the Magisterium. While Rome professes to believe Scripture is the Word of God, it acts in contradiction to that profession when it rejects passages such as 2 Timothy 3:15, which instructs believers to understand that God's words alone can make us wise unto salvation. Rome inserts itself into such a central role of salvation in the lives of others. To further complicate things, there are "exceptions" within Roman Catholic teachings that *some* outside the formal Catholic church can still be saved. Pope John Paul II writes in his encyclical :

> Since salvation is offered to all, it must be made concretely available to all. But it is clear that today, as in the past, many people do not have an opportunity to come to know or accept the gospel revelation or to enter the Church.... For such people, salvation in Christ is accessible by virtue of a grace which, while having a mysterious relationship to the Church, does not make them formally part of the Church, but enlightens them in a way, which is accommodated to their spiritual and material situation. This grace comes from Christ; it is the result of his sacrifice and is communicated by the

Holy Spirit. It enables each person to attain salvation through his or her free cooperation (no. 10).[7]

Pope John Paul II was quoting from *Lumen Gentium* (nos. 16), which more explicitly says people through "no fault of their own" who "do not know the gospel of Christ or his Church, but who nevertheless seek God with a sincere heart, and, moved by grace, try in their actions to do his will as they know it through the dictates of their conscience" actually may achieve eternal salvation alongside the devout Catholic. If someone has never heard of Jesus Christ, the gospel, or the supposed salvific need for union with the Catholic church, he or she may still inherit salvation through the limited amount of information given to them by the natural world found "among shadows and images," and "all goodness and truth found in these religions [serve] as 'a preparation for the gospel and given by him who enlightens all men that they may at length have life'" (CCC 843).[8]

Pope Pius XII explains this idea in his Encyclical of June 29, 1943, *Mystici Corporis*, as those outside a formal relationship with the Catholic church – that is not having been baptized into the Catholic church and professing its faiths – can still be "related to the Mystical Body of the Redeemer by a certain unconscious yearning and desire" (para. 103). He clarifies this is not the ideal position because "they still remain deprived of those many heavenly gifts and helps which can only be enjoyed in the Catholic Church," and are in a "state in which they cannot be sure of their salvation."[9]

The Roman Catholic church holds to inclusive soteriology, which states that people can still be saved *apart from direct faith in Jesus* because his saving work can be applied through their knowledge of God's general revelation. According to this Catholic dogma, as long as someone is not willfully rejecting the Roman Catholic church, that person might still be saved, though they will not have a complete assurance of their salvation until death. Since the Roman Catholic church plays fast and loose with soteriology, it gives a great insight into how the Catholic-led pro-life movement plays fast and loose with the gospel and biblical requirements for justice.

Many Hills to Die On

At the beginning of the chapter, there was a quote from the 1689 Baptist Confession of Faith. It is importantly listed as the first point in the confession. It leads with the critical issue of what one believes about Scripture as all else hinges on that position. It is beneficial to mention that Catholic and Protestant written scriptures differ drastically. The Catholic bible contains extra elements to the Old Testament such as additional sections in the books of Esther and Daniel, as well as containing the Apocrypha and its seven additional books: Tobit, Judith, Wisdom of Solomon, Ecclesiasticus, Baruch and First and Second Maccabees. From these extra-biblical books, Catholics build some of their foundational beliefs of purgatory (2 Maccabees 12:38–46), and earning eternal life (Ecclesiasticus 16:14). Protestants reject that these extra books were inspired canonical works of the Holy Spirit. As Allison says, " ... though Roman Catholic and Protestant churches share scripture, we must realize they do not share the same scripture."[10]

There are a lot of hills on which to die regarding the basic question of *what is Scripture*? Even after all the Roman dogma exerted to explain the function, role and placement of Scripture in a Christian's life, it essentially boils down to being irrelevant. Catholic apologist Tim Staples bluntly puts it:

> ... the Catholic Church technically is not a Bible-based Church. The Bible is a Church-based book. And that's what has to be remembered. The Church came first, was around for a generation or two before the New Testament was even completed, and it is the book that came out of the Church, not the Church out of the Bible.[11]

A careful reading of this quote reveals several imperative matters. The first is the Roman Catholic view of their church preceding Scripture. This is blatantly false as Old Testament Scripture, the very Scripture Jesus and his apostles referenced and quoted from extensively in the New Testament, preceded even Jesus' time by thousands of years. Scripture has always pre-dated the Church and as White says, "The Church was *never* without scripture. The Church was founded in the *midst* of the giving of revelation."[12]

The New Testament *is* the apostolic tradition written down under the inspiration of the Holy Spirit. No other "extra" apostolic traditions presently practiced by the Catholic church can be traced back from their lips to Jesus or the apostles. Secondly, if Scripture came out of the Church then the Church is more supreme than Scripture itself. This is problematic as God tells us the written Scriptures are *his very own words*, and yet the Roman Catholic church sees fit to rise above this threshold. The Catechism of Rome teaches that the church "does not derive her certainty about all revealed truths from the holy scriptures alone. Both scripture and Tradition must be accepted and honored with equal sentiments of devotion and reverence."[13]

That is a monumental sacrilegious order for serious-minded Protestants to support. Protestants reject the notion of the Holy Spirit concealing biblical interpretation from his children (Romans 8:14, John 16:13, Romans 5:5, 1 Corinthians 12:3, 1 John 3:9, Galatians 4:6). Committed Protestants hold fast to scriptural authority. Protestants see canonized Scripture teach God's word as a lamp unto their feet (Psalm 119:105); that all of God's inspired words are useful for teaching, rebuking and training in righteousness (2 Timothy 3:16-17); God's words are truth (John 17:17); the Old Testament Scriptures are compatible to the New Testament teachings and validate Jesus' fulfillment of them (Acts 17:11); God's Word personally indwells each of his people (Colossians 3:16); Scripture is one of our assigned weapons in spiritual battle (Ephesians 6:17); God's words are implanted into our reborn nature so as to instruct us against wickedness (James 1:21); that if we abide in Christ and in his words it will produce in us works of righteousness; that Christ's words will never pass away (Matthew 24:35); God opens our eyes to behold his wondrous law (Psalm 119:18); his word alone guards us against unrighteousness and wayward living (Psalm 119:9); God's words produce faith in his people (Romans 10:17); and that by God's words alone we can have hope in an eternal salvation (Romans 15:4).

Scripture makes plain that each individual in Christ is expected to be deeply changed and impacted by God's written words. Tangible actions and living are evident in an individual's life from the impact of God's Word. If the omniscient God planned for oral tradition *and* written Scripture to fully instruct his people, why did he never mention that at least once in the written portion of his revelation? God in his mercy did not stage a salvation scavenger hunt that, if not executed properly, would destroy billions of souls. Because the essence of God is sufficient, his written words are sufficient. To refute the sufficiency of his words is to refute his entire being. As famous preacher Charles Spurgeon remarked, "The mind of God is greater than all the minds of men, so let all men leave the gospel just as God has delivered it unto us."

There is no room for Rome to insist on its necessity for proper Christian living and salvation. No human supplementation to God's infallible, holy divine being is needed. To be certain we understand this, God tells Isaiah, "I am the lord; that is my name; my glory I give to no other."

A Chasm Too Wide

The chasm between Protestants and Catholics explains the lack of biblically derived politics, teaching and counseling in Catholic pro-life centers, leadership and political action committees. Why would Catholic-led, pro-life work devote so much time and adoration to scriptural faithfulness when Scripture is viewed as less valuable than the structure and authority of the Roman Catholic church? Catholics have little confidence in their ability to teach and explain biblical concepts outside of Catholic authority because they are taught they possess no degree of correct biblical knowledge apart from the Magisterium. Catholics look to Rome for guidance on how to operate in politics, culture, and the world, as Scripture alone is insufficient to understand a well-lived Christian life. Scripture is not enough to inform their consciences of what constitutes sin and what is God honoring. As long as Catholics do not contradict the teachings of Rome, then their organizations continue functioning in obvious compromise to Scripture.

Has Rome said *not* to write laws of partiality? If not, then there is no conscientious objection to doing so despite Scripture's disapproval of unjust and prejudicial laws. Has Rome said the gospel *must* be front and center when engaging the culture on preborn homicide? If not, then there is no guilt for leaving out Christ's words in their pleas for culture to stop child sacrifice. Has Rome said *not* to be yoked with unbelievers in intimate working or personal relations? If not, then there is no alarm at compromising some doctrines here and there to satisfy successful secular or interfaith working relationships.

Rome has no issue linking arms with unbelievers, and either shrouding the gospel of Jesus Christ in ambiguity or hiding it altogether. Historically, Rome frowned upon ecumenical relationships. During the 18th and 19th centuries, Catholics largely opposed slavery abolition because it was led by Protestants and they balked at aligning with those who were "anathema." Today's efforts are entirely different. It was not until The Second Vatican Council from 1962 to 1965 that the Roman Catholic church changed its position to approve interreligious relationships. In 2019, Pope Francis signed the interfaith covenant Document on Human Fraternity with Islam in the United Arab Emirates. Of this historic union between Catholicism and Islam, the Vatican website records:

> The document, signed by Pope Francis and the Grand Imam of al-Azhar, Ahmed el-Tayeb, was prepared "with much reflection and prayer", the Pope said. The one great danger at this moment, he continued, is "destruction, war, hatred between us." "If we believers are not able to shake hands, embrace one another, kiss one another, and even pray, our faith will be defeated," he said. The Pope explained that the document "is born of faith in God who is the Father of all and the Father of peace; it condemns all destruction, all terrorism, from the first terrorism in history, that of Cain."[14]

This shameless profession of Muslims sharing the same God and faith as Catholics was not spontaneous. This heretical view of cohesiveness with apostate religions pre-dates 2019 by decades. Remember, Catholic soteriology is wildly unbiblical. Consider the 1964 Dogmatic Constitution on the Church *Lumen Gentium*:

> But the *plan of salvation also includes those who acknowledge the Creator. In the first place amongst these there are the Muslims*, who, professing to hold the faith of Abraham, *along with us adore the one and merciful God*, who on the last day will judge mankind. Nor is God far distant from those who in shadows and images seek the unknown God, for it is He who gives to all men life and breath and all things,(127) and as Saviour wills that all men be saved.(128) Those also can attain to salvation who through no fault of their own do not know the gospel of Christ or His Church, yet sincerely seek God and moved by grace strive by their deeds to do His will as it is known to them through the dictates of conscience.(19*) Nor does Divine Providence deny the help necessary for salvation to those who, without blame on their part, have not yet arrived at an explicit knowledge of God and with His grace strive to live a good life. Whatever good or truth is found amongst them is looked upon by the Church as a preparation for the gospel.(20*) She knows that it is given by Him who enlightens all men so that they may finally have life. But often men, deceived by the Evil One, have become vain in their reasonings and have exchanged the truth of God for a lie, serving the creature rather than the Creator.(129) Or some there are who, living and dying in this world without God, are exposed to final despair. Wherefore to promote the glory of God and procure the salvation of all of these, and mindful of the command of the Lord, "Preach the gospel to every creature",(130) the

Church fosters the missions with care and attention.[15] [Emphasis the author's.]

The above passage is what Pope Francis referenced. It set the stage for blurring doctrinal differences between varying religions. In the Vatican quote regarding the ecumenical covenant with Islam, Pope Francis first used the plural statement "if *we believers* do not shake hands," and then shifted to a singular use of faith in "*our* faith," signifying that Muslims and Christians are unified believers in the same thing. This concept is not at odds with *Lumen Gentium,* which indicates one only needs to have a genuine desire to "acknowledge the Creator" and that sharing Abraham's faith can be sufficient for salvation. Yet *Lumen Gentium* has a perilous conclusion. The Bible warns about syncretizing faith in God alone with other religions. The first and most obvious is God's command to have "no other gods before me" (Deuteronomy 5:7). Shaking hands and affirming that a heretical religion's idea of god is the same as the biblical God is treacherously breaking the first commandment. If the pope can shake hands with an apostate religion and declare them brothers, it is clear why Catholics are so welcoming of many diverse faiths, beliefs and convictions in the fight against abortion. American Catholics were largely opposed to ecumenical work until the 1900s, and now there seems to be no one they are alarmed to work with. This lack of discernment has allowed an influx of permeating pagan beliefs to further dilute the pro-life movement.

Centralizing Scripture

Protestants and Catholics disagree on what is Scripture. We disagree on the sufficiency of Scripture. We disagree on the supreme authority in the Christian's life. We disagree on the basic tenet to not be yoked to unbelievers but to be set apart and holy. We disagree on the merits of salvation and the saving work of Christ. These differences naturally result in one of two things: ecumenical work, which dilutes faithful, scriptural adherence as the driving force in the anti-abortion movement, or segregation of these ideologically opposed religious and nonreligious groups on anti-abortion efforts.

Christians have been trained by the secularized and Catholic-led pro-life movement to believe it is worse to split efforts than to suppress gospel differences. That is an easy thing to dismiss if one's belief is in mystical unions to the Roman Catholic church and inclusive unions with false religions such as Islam. The main commitment for Protestant Christians should be to the Word of God and belief in its supernatural effect in our world, not allegiance to heretical groups or ideas. God's word achieves what it goes out to accomplish (Isaiah 55:11). We know from Scripture that God uses weak people or impossible scenarios to accomplish his work so that no one may claim the victory for themselves: "The Lord said to Gideon, "The people with you are too many for me to give the Midianites into their hand, lest Israel boast over me, saying, 'My own hand has saved me' (Judges 7:2).'" Scripture also demonstrates that God shows himself mighty in battle (Isaiah 42:13), that he fights for his people (Deuteronomy 3:21-22; 1 Samuel 17:45-47), and that we are to hold our position and stand firm while we watch God destroy our enemies and bring them to ruin (2 Chronicles 20:15-17).

God has always declared victory in himself for his own glory. This is not just an Old Testament pattern. When Jesus commissioned 12, lower-class citizens to evangelize the world, he once again took the unlikely to use for his kingdom's triumph. Two thousand years later we can see his plan for advancing his kingdom once again did not fail with the minority. This is good news for the biblically-minded believer. We do not need to be linked to compromised entities to succeed against abortion. The God who turned armies against each other, crumbled fortress walls with trumpet blasts, and toppled one of the most infamous ancient warriors with a rock is the same God fighting our battles today. Similar to our Old Testament and early church comrades, God requires faithful obedience to his word for us to be blessed. As straightforward as that may seem, this is a sticky point for many modern Christians.

We have been conditioned to approach politics, and especially the abortion debate, with a pragmatism that results in biblical compromise. Indeed, it is a competing philosophy to Scripture: One relies on sight and human capabilities while the other relies on faith and God's invisible capabilities. One way God's Word is undermined is through pro-life legislation that supports unequal justice and unequal protection for preborn humans. This is known as partial justice. Those familiar with Scripture will note God has much to say about partiality and the one who participates in compromise. A familiar verse in this regard is Revelation 2:14-16:

> But I have a few things against you: you have some there who hold to the teaching of Balaam, who taught Balak to put a stumbling block before the sons of Israel, so that they might eat food sacrificed to idols and practice sexual immorality. So also you have some who hold to the teaching of the Nicolaitans. Therefore repent. If not, I will come to you soon and war against them with the sword of my mouth.

The book of Revelation is about the victorious in Christ who do not tolerate wickedness and the triumph of Christ over all his creation. When believers tolerate evil practices, Christ's only command is to repent. There is no other option. No one is allowed the privilege of remaining in faithless mediocrity because it is comfortable or is the politically rational thing to do (John 14:15, Hebrews 10:26, James 4:17, Revelation 14:12, James 4:4).

Ecumenical work compromises gospel work in several ways. First, it suppresses the use of the gospel or adulterates it. This manifests in how pro-life organizations and advocates engage conversationally with opponents, how the pro-life movement counsels abortive women, and how pro-life centers attempt to present the gospel to clients – if presented at all. People of different faiths working together will shelve theological differences to avoid distraction from the political mission. Secular Pro-Life states this very thing on its website. While this seems beneficial, it can be costly. What we believe about Scripture dictates all other spheres of our lives.

Do we truly believe if we are ashamed of Christ he will be ashamed of us (Mark 8:38) and that friendship with the world is enmity with God (James 4:4)? Do we actually believe bad company corrupts good morals (1 Corinthians 15:33) and a little yeast works its way through the whole loaf (Galatians 5:9)? Do we confess faith comes through hearing the Word of Christ (Romans 10:17) and that God will accomplish all he intends to accomplish (Isaiah 46:10)? Do we truly believe God is angry every day with the wicked (Psalm 7:11) and that he will judge and destroy the unrepentant (2 Corinthians 5:10; 1 Peter 4:17; John 3:18)? If our answer is "yes" to those questions, then the gospel must be the driving force in every area of our lives. It should be obvious in the Christian's life that Scripture is our creed; anti-abortion work is no exception. If someone is living out Scripture and sharing it faithfully with others, it will not take long for the clash of competing ideologies within the pro-life framework to occur.

Second, ecumenical work influences us to take a soft approach to abortion policy and punishment rather than an unadulterated biblical approach. When working with those who do not esteem the Scriptures, it presents a temptation to compromise. The majority of pro-life organizations oppose criminalizing preborn murder, which is one of the clearest examples of biblical compromise. This was demonstrated when more than 70 leading pro-life organizations in the United States signed the NRTL Open Letter. Roughly 75 percent of the Open Letter pro-life signees were Catholic, nine percent were secular and the remaining were evangelical of some sort. This sampling demonstrates the dominance of Catholicism over the anti-abortion movement, as well as the marginal representation of Protestants against the backdrop of the Church of Rome and secularists. The pressure for professing Christians to depart from strong biblical convictions and commands is great within this ecumenical mix.

Unequally Yoked

This co-existent relationship between Catholics, Protestants and secularists demonstrates the warning found in 2 Corinthians 6:14 to not be "unequally yoked with unbelievers" as the union is unnatural and unworkable. The verse finishes the thought by asking, "For what partnership has righteousness with lawlessness? Or what fellowship has light with darkness?" Matthew Henry's commentary examines how the Christian is not only an ambassador of Christ to the world but the actual, living temple of the Holy God. Henry states, "Now there can be no agreement between the temple of God and idols. Idols are rivals with God for his honour, and God is a jealous God, and will not give his glory to another."[16] The stakes are high for defiling God's temple when we carelessly enter into contractual agreements with those not led by the same Spirit. Pope Francis would have done well to remember this warning before shaking hands with Grand Imam Ahmed el-Tayeb.

Henry further warns of the grave danger in dealing confidentially and religiously with unbelievers as those relations entice Christians to corrupt scriptural faithfulness in their lives. We are to govern our lives with such wisdom that we are prevented from binding ourselves to the unshakable influence of unbelievers. This means abstaining from marrying an unbeliever and wisely refraining from legal or business agreements which may carry the potential to compromise our witness to the world and our obedience to Christ. It is inevitable Christians will work with unbelievers in many areas. It is one thing to work with a pagan manager, function under the guidance of a postmodern professor, serve on a committee with atheists, and so on. It is another thing to ignore the red flags of poor partnerships and voluntarily seek out and enjoin ourselves to them and their ideologies through binding covenants, legal agreements and intimate relationships. If we align ourselves closely with unbiblical counsels, we must be prepared to count the cost of compromising our faith and integrity. As Henry puts it:

> Believers are made light in the Lord, but unbelievers are in darkness; and what comfortable communion can these have together? Christ and Belial are contrary one to the other; they have opposite interests and designs, so that it is impossible there should be any concord or agreement between them. It is absurd, therefore, to

think of enlisting under both; and, if the believer has part with an infidel, he does what in him lies to bring Christ and Belial together.[17]

Protestants must recognize that the leaders in the pro-life movement are not committed to sola Scriptura. The leading organizations are not motivated by the Great Commission or devoted to biblically sound doctrine. They have explicitly stated goals in contradiction to God's Word. The departure is not passive. Apart from Scripture, these organizations quickly deteriorate into a system of works. For the many Catholics in the movement, the good works of pro-life politics weigh greatly in their favor toward meriting God's sanctifying grace. For the secularists, subjective good works bring satisfaction to their humanistic-centered efforts and bring meaning to their otherwise philosophically hollow lives. For Protestant Christians, however, we should be motivated to abolish abortion out of love for God, love for others, love for our preborn neighbors and for the glory of God. The love produced in us by the Holy Spirit should compel us to fear for the eternal state of our culture and share the Good News we have been commissioned by Christ himself to proclaim. This Good News encompasses the spiritually dead state of all people who are only made alive through faith, given by God, in Jesus' work on the cross to justify us, to give us a heart of flesh, and to restore us to unbroken fellowship with God. Those truths compel us to faithfully declare Christ's good works and warn of the judgment that awaits the unrepentant.

When other pro-life groups do not want to be associated with the biblical gospel, it becomes a circular challenge in ministering to the culture if we also need to evangelize our pro-life colleagues. It becomes even more difficult to execute faithful, biblical legislative advocacy when others look down upon non-pragmatic means. If we truly believe the sufficiency of Christ and his Scripture, then a departure from the compromised pro-life movement becomes necessary. As White points out in the relationship between Catholics and Protestants, "The gulf is too wide to be bridged by good intentions. Ultimately there is an impasse on the nature of the gospel itself." [18]

There is an impasse within the anti-abortion movement that should cause biblically-minded Protestants to take leadership roles in fighting against child sacrifice instead of passively trusting the secular movement to continue the moral fight for us. We are not free to join secularized pro-life groups at the expense of God's Word. As Anglican bishop J.C. Ryle once said, "Never make an intimate friend of anyone who is not a friend of God." Many in the pro-life movement may grimace at this as it means potentially losing thousands of closely-working allies. In reality, this is not a loss. It is not forfeiture to trade fallible human alliances for the superiority of God. Many of these "alliances" are working against the anti-abortion individuals who want to see abortion completely criminalized anyway.

This chapter is not a slam against Catholics and secularists; rather, its highest indictment is against Protestants. Non-Catholic denominations are years behind in their involvement in the fight against abortion, and Protestants have remained subservient to the secularized pro-life movement for 50 years. This acquiescent posture has occurred all while Protestants claim they are the religiously correct denominations because they believe God's Word is enough. While boasting about abiding by Scripture alone, we have overtly failed to see how the pro-life tenets do not hold up in light of Scripture alone. Can we *really* say we believe in sola Scriptura? The secularized tendencies of the pro-life movement have revealed the hypocrisy and shallow-mindedness of most Protestants. We failed to guard our churches, flocks, families and political system against the unbiblical commitments of the pro-life movement.

3

CATECHIZING POLITICS

"If heresies did not have some pretty paint to cause them to stand out they would be condemned and detested by everyone." – Thomas Hodges, Puritan (1600-1672)

Inescapable Doctrines

"THE GREAT AGNOSTIC" ROBERT Ingersoll was known for his deep hatred of Christian doctrine. That did not prevent him, however, from admitting to the reality of doctrine as a functional part of every person's life. Ingersoll once proclaimed, "Any doctrine that will not bear investigation is not a fit tenant for the mind of an honest man. Any man who is afraid to have his doctrine investigated is not only a coward but a hypocrite."

Today, the doctrines of pro-life and abolition are bearing investigation. Their creeds are being weighed against logic, legal justice and biblical alignment – and they are in contention. The final line for each movement disputes what justice looks like for the unborn, and only one judicial philosophy will win. Both cannot and will not remain in tandem existence.

While the pro-life movement has struggled culturally to demonstrate a logical consistency between its profession of abortion killing innocent life and its belief to not hold accountable all actors involved in the killing, it has still succeeded in its catechizing efforts within the conservative political realm.

Catechizing is the process of giving repeated instruction on a set of doctrinal beliefs. Everyone is being catechized. The influence from worldly sources that dictates someone's behavior is offset only by how often that person is catechized by God's Word. If meditating on Christ's teachings, attending church, listening to sermons, reading and studying the Bible, learning from theologians and scholars, or fellowshipping with other serious believers barely makes the cut each week, the scriptural catechizing will not be enough to suppress that of the world.

Contrasting biblical and worldly doctrine should be a straightforward task for those who claim to be Christ's followers, yet modern polls would disagree. The Family Research Council's Center (FRC) for Biblical Worldview evaluated in 2021 how many American Christians actually hold to a biblical worldview on differing political, social, economic, entertainment and moral issues. Out of the individuals polled, 51 percent confidently claimed to have a biblical worldview. On the contrary, the FRC discovered a mere six percent of surveyed Christians held to a consistently biblical worldview across multiple areas of life.[1] This becomes problematic when a Christian's main task, given by Christ himself, is to teach others how to think biblically – to think like Christ. Ironically, even Tony Perkins, president of the FRC, is not immune to unbiblical error as evidenced later in this chapter.

The bottom line is Christians should spend much time teaching others biblical doctrine. This is what the Great Commission commands. Making disciples and teaching them to obey all that Christ has commanded is a mission of catechizing discipleship. It is a relationship of habitually teaching another person the words of Scripture and how to exhibit those truths in their outward life.

If Christian culture believes children need more time to attend school more than two days a week to become competent students, then there should be no confidence scriptural literacy can be imparted to individuals only on Sundays and Wednesday evenings. Mature believers thirst to grow more like Christ every day of the week, and they attempt to teach those around them biblical truths even outside of formal Sunday services. This discipleship is often done through efforts such as neighborhood friendships, home Bible study groups, mentorship relationships, back-yard VBS programs, Christian community centers, homeless ministries, single-parent ministries, prison ministries and after-school Bible studies. Interestingly, one area Christians neglect to influence through personal relationships is politics. Politician ministry rarely shows up next to prison ministry or women's ministry in the church bulletin. Very few churches, if any, take a Thanksgiving meal down to City Hall as they may do for their local fire or police station.

Perhaps this negligence is due to the common belief that "politics is downstream from culture," a catchy tagline that seems to have evolved into a Christian excuse to avoid political engagement. Many well-meaning believers explain what happens in culture is reflected in politics, so efforts are more focused on laypeople (the voters). What is dismissed is the very real threat that politicians often cave to the temptations of power and money. Christians ignore the spiritual needs of their politicians, and think that discipling voters better will influence the next election to turn out "more Christian."

President James Garfield, a gospel minister and self-taught lawyer, cautioned future generations of a reckless government:

> [N]ow more than ever before, the people are responsible for the character of their Congress. If that body be ignorant, reckless, and corrupt, it is because the people tolerate ignorance, recklessness, and corruption. If it be intelligent, brave, and pure, it is because the people demand these high qualities to represent them in the national legislature…[I]f the next centennial does not find us a great nation…it will be because those who represent the enterprise, the culture, and the morality of the nation do not aid in controlling the political forces.[2]

Tolerating corruption is not only evident through voting preference but also through how engaged Christians remain with their elected officials, especially when those officials seem to be wayward or disappointing. For modern voters, remaining engaged with politics often takes the form of complaining in their social circles about the latest political news. The more "dedicated" citizens might even publish a string of Tweets or Facebook posts to display their disgust at policies. Often, that is as far as any pushback goes.

At the very least, politics exacerbates the sin nature lying within men and women. This is perhaps what is demonstrated through Garfield's warning: If the culture is already reckless, ignorant and corrupt, those ill traits will be intensified and supported by those within the government.

Everyone needs the gospel, a call to repentance, and accountability. It is spiritually negligent to leave out such a significant part of America's cultural makeup in the Christian's catechizing efforts, because, as John Calvin observed, "the human heart is a factory of idols." The idols of powerful politicians impact all citizens. There should be great concern for the Christian to focus missional efforts on influencing politicians through godly means. While modern Christians have stayed silent on catechizing politicians, pro-life political action committees have not neglected the opportunity.

PACS: The Surrogate Constituents

Political action committees (PACs) are organized groups of individuals that raise money to donate to political campaigns or advocate on special issues such as amendments or other types of legislation. PAC's representatives build relationships with politicians in an effort to persuade them to adopt ideologies and cultural interests of the PAC. In return for a politician's support, the PAC usually offers campaign money or an endorsement in upcoming elections. If the PAC has a recognizable reputation and a substantial following, endorsements can often be more lucrative than money. Many voters rely on voter guides issued by PACs to inform them on which candidates to politically support. Garnishing the attention and gifts of a PAC often determines the political success of a politician.

The concept of political action committees was first created in 1944 by the Congress of Industrial Organizations. The purpose was to raise funds to assist with the re-election of President Franklin D. Roosevelt. PACs quickly figured out how to accumulate money and swing influence in their favor within the American political sphere. In response to a rapidly growing and unregulated political force, the Federal Election Campaign Act of 1971 sought to reduce the amount of money PACs could solicit from corporations, individuals, or unions so that a PACs campaign influence would not overshadow the influence of individual constituents on their representatives.

While there is now a cap on how *much* an individual, union or corporation can donate to a PAC, there is not a limit on how *many* individuals, corporations or unions can donate. In response to this minor obstacle, PACs evolved into strategic experts that raise more money than before by mass marketing to their target demographics. Today, political action committees are some of the biggest influencers in modern-day elections. At both state and federal levels, PACs often steer politicians along the path that most benefits the PAC, and completely ignore the people's voice. To be fair, PACs would not be successful without monetary donations from businesses and citizens; in an ironic twist, citizens feed the monster that replaces them in much of the democratic process.

The United States republic was constructed so that both state and federal representatives would answer directly to their constituents; however, in the materialism and rush of American society, it has grown more convenient to outsource Christian convictions to local political action committees and trust these entities to enforce and uphold Christians' values before their representatives. Citizens propped up a PAC industry that employs tens of thousands of workers across America. The pro-life movement has been no different. Pro-life PACs emerged almost immediately after *Roe v. Wade*, with National Right to Life founded in 1968, five years before *Roe*, and its PAC launched in 1980. Today, there are hundreds of pro-life political action committees nationwide. This would not be such a conundrum if pro-life PACs were faithful ministers of God's word to elected leaders and sought to biblically instruct their consciences with Scripture in the fight against a pre-born holocaust. The pro-life platform is the perfect place to instruct culture on what it means to be image bearers of God. It flows naturally to talk of the sanctity of life connected to the One who created it, designed it, forbade any person to unjustly kill another person, and what justice must be enacted against those who murder.

Devastatingly, politicians are being discipled to uphold the tenets of pro-life doctrine even when it errs from God's Word. This is grievous given the unique position PACs have with these influential and powerful people. In reality, PACs are well positioned to serve as missionaries to political leaders. If Christians thought about politics in those ways, the country might look quite different. As it stands, pro-life standards and goals primarily deviate from Scripture. There is no higher calling than to conform to the image of God. The conformity that is happening today is to the pro-life movement's secular ideologies.

The Robust Culture of Pro-life Catechizing

In a 2016 interview with MSNBC's Chris Matthews, Donald Trump stated women should be liable under the law if abortion were criminalized. This seemed a straightforward, logical conclusion. Many conservatives consider abortion murder, after all. To Trump's surprise, pro-life leaders vociferously rejected this claim. For a while, it seemed there was not enough online capacity to support the immediacy and activity of pro-life organizations seeking to set the record straight. The following are some responses that poured out in the aftermath of Trump's apparent faux pas:

> National Right to Life has long opposed the imposition of penalties on the woman on whom an abortion is attempted or performed…Rather, penalties should be imposed against any abortionist who would take the life of an unborn child in defiance of statutes prohibiting abortions.[3] – Carol Tobias, president of National Right to Life

Trump's suggestion that he would support punishing women seeking abortions because there are 'conservative Republicans' advocating such a policy shows Mr. Trump is ill informed in this vital issue.[4] – Tony Perkins, president of the Family Research Council

We have never advocated, in any context, for the punishment of women who undergo abortion...As a convert to the pro-life movement, Mr. Trump sees the reality of the horror of abortion – the destruction of an innocent human life – which is legal in our country up until the moment of birth. But let us be clear: punishment is solely for the abortionist who profits off of the destruction of one life and the grave wounding of another.[5] – Marjorie Dannenfelser, president of the Susan B. Anthony List

As for punishing the woman, those who have had abortions are already in prison. As the pastoral director of the world's largest ministry of healing after abortion, Rachel's Vineyard, and also of the Silent No More Awareness Campaign, by which those who have had abortions speak out about their experiences, I know this very well. We don't aim to imprison them. We aim to liberate them from the shame and guilt and wounds abortion brings.[6] – Frank Pavone, national director of Priests for Life

We know how much women suffer from abortion, and how they are lied to by the abortion industry. Any penalty for illegal abortion should fall on abortion providers, not the women who turn to them in desperation.[7] – Eric Scheidler, executive director of the Pro-Life Action League

You're not going to get me to say that I want to throw mothers behind bars. That's not the view of this entity. That's not the view of this convention. It's not the view of the pro-life movement.[8] – Brent Leatherwood, president of the Ethics and Religious Liberty Commission

These influential pro-life entities sounded the alarm to signal an aberration from their acceptable business practices and vehemently defended the doctrine of immunity against their endorsed presidential candidate. The catechizing was clear: Women are victims; leave them alone. Abortionists are the only ones with guilty intent; go after them.

While committed and passionate, these pro-life organizations espouse poor teaching. Dannenfelser's belief that the abortionist is the only one who profits from an abortion is remarkably detached from reality. It should be reflected on why women seek abortions. Are they hunted down and forced by abortionists? Do women mindlessly participate as a consumer in an industry they do not understand? Do they just "experiment" like one would with drugs, not cognizant of the consequences of that decision? Are anti-abortion women the only ones intelligent enough to understand abortion is murder? Are females so weak-minded that nearly one million women every year are tricked into murdering their offspring? None of these are rational or flattering views of women – and none are true. Women pursue abortion because it benefits them, too. Profit is not only relegated to monetary value. A woman benefits from murdering her unborn child so she can evade a difficult pregnancy, avoid caring for a child with special needs, dodge shame, avoid financial stress, travel uninhibited, shun single parenthood, prevent caring for more children, choose the gender of the child she wants, finish a degree, hide an affair, save a relationship with someone who does not want a child, pursue an unhindered career, or preserve her body image. Most women freely choose what will profit them the most, and sometimes that is murdering their preborn children.

As mentioned earlier, Family Research Council president Tony Perkins misses the biblical mark by supporting an ideology segregated from biblical justice. He advocates women should remain unpunished for their part in the murder of their preborn children. This is ironic in light of the FRC's 2021 survey which revealed only six percent of professing Christians have a biblical worldview on many theological and social issues. Regardless, many pro-life advocates like Perkins ignore biblical principles on murder. Jesus said those who murder or desire to murder are of the devil (John 8:44), and Scripture warns that unrepentant murderers will inherit God's eternal wrath (Revelation 21:8). Scripture expounds that the penalty for a citizen who destroys one of God's image bearers – who does not bear the power of the sword (Romans 13:4) – is to forfeit his or her own life (Genesis 9:5-6); and that there can be no immunity or pardon offered for a murderer (Numbers 35:31).

Likewise, Pavone's belief that women who have murdered their unborn children already suffer enough – and therefore should be exempt from the hardship of judicial prosecution – is a case of situational ethics. Should this apply to women who murder their *born* children? One could argue they suffer even more from the aftermath of taking innocent life as that life was more tangible, interactive, and personal than the life of an unborn human. If regret is enough to grant protection from a felony conviction, should we also pardon serial killers and rapists for their crimes if they express enough remorse?

Most rational people would not give legal impunity to violent criminals merely because they reflect on their decisions and acknowledge the grievousness of what they did. Rather, it should be the expected norm that murdering another human causes extreme dismay, agony, mental affliction and regret. It is such a gruesome revolt against the Creator to slaughter one of his image bearers. Anguish is an ordinary consequence for committing such a crime. Christians should not seek to remove legal consequences from women who murder their children – born or unborn – but urge them to seek repentance and restoration from God even while allowing justice to play out for their innocent victims. Pavone's aim "to liberate them from the shame and guilt and wounds abortion brings" is a noble endeavor, but the attribution of such capability to heal a murderer's heart is misapplied. No person, organization or counseling program can fix the seared or broken conscience of a murderer. Legally pardoning that person from what they have done will not repair post-abortive trauma. Whether free or in prison, a post-abortive woman must turn to Christ for forgiveness and redemption for what she has done. It will be found in no other place.

The pro-life movement holds to the belief, however, that all abortive women are victims of abortion because it views the psychological, spiritual and emotional turmoil in post-abortive women as unnatural; thus, it works to protect women not only from themselves and the abortion industry but also from the justice system. The pro-life movement is a master at catechizing Christians and conservatives on these doctrinal points and how to approach the issue of abortion. Influential pro-life leaders were quick to correct then-presidential candidate Trump on his accidental criminalization slip, and shortly following the issuance of their statements, he walked back what he said about women being culpable. The effort to teach Trump proper pro-life doctrine was successful.

Three years later, another catechizing event caught the attention of abolitionists when an incriminating letter accidentally showed up in the email of the wrong Oklahoman senator.

The Gag Rule

Numerous abolition bills have been introduced to committees in many states for almost a decade. Each of those bills has been killed in those committees by the very pro-life representatives who pledged to stand against abortion. Tabling bills is nothing new. Politicians in the 1800s implemented a method that served them well to avoid abolishing slavery. These 19th-century politicians decided to not receive into committee an abolition petition or bill. If it could not be heard in committee, they would not have to debate it and wrestle with the slave issue. This movement became known as The Gag Rule, where delegates routinely voted to table petitions and bills related to slavery abolition so as not to bring awareness to the growing abolition trend. If those concerns could not even make it to committee, there would be no chance of those concerns progressing to the House or Senate floor where they could then formulate into new laws. These statesmen were quite pleased with this new practice in American politics. As Representative Hammond bemoaned, the legislators "could not sit there and see the rights of the Southern People assaulted day after day, by the ignorant fanatics from whom these [abolition] memorials proceed."[9]

Comparable to the pro-slavery politicians who tabled abolition bills before committees, such it is with today's pro-life groups who practice the Gag Rule against abortion abolition. National Right to Life Vice President Tony Lauinger, who is also president of Oklahomans for Life, sent an email in 2019 intended for Senator Julie Daniels, but by mishap it arrived in the inbox of another state senator.[10] After considering the implications of the email, the recipient forwarded the letter to Free the States, an Oklahoma abolitionist organization now known as Abolitionists Rising, to warn of a plot intended to thwart the success of any abolition bills that were picking up steam in the state legislature.

The threat against these abolition bills did not come from pro-abortion legislators or Planned Parenthood lobbyists but rather Oklahoman pro-life leaders. At the time, abolition bill SB 13 was denied a committee hearing, which stopped its progression to the House and Senate floors to be voted into law. The effort to criminalize abortion was still a possibility, though. SB 614, regarding the abortion pill reversal, was set for a committee hearing. SB 614 carried the potential to be amended to abolish abortion and was scheduled for a hearing in the Senate Health and Human Services Committee – the very committee that sat Senator Joseph Silk, the author of SB 13. It was plausible that Silk would see the opportunity with SB 614 to amend and pass it through committee as an abolition bill. It was this very scenario by which Lauinger seemed concerned as he wrote to Daniels: "[SB

614] could be moved from Health and Human Services to Judiciary, in which Sen. Silk does not sit..."[11]

Removing a bill from the committee of an abolitionist is not an isolated event. Abolitionist politicians are also forced out of committees as punishment for not playing ball with House or Senate leadership. This sends a powerful signal to other legislators who might be sympathetic to the abolition movement to stay clear lest they also incur a penalty to their careers. Abolition opponents will look for ways to assign bills to more hostile committees that are sure to either vote against the abolition bill or not give it a hearing at all. Since SB 614 was already assigned to the committee of which abolitionist Silk participated, Lauinger offered advice to pursue disqualifying an abolition amendment on technicalities to boot it from committee. Lauinger recommended to Daniels, "An amendment regarding SB 13 could be ruled out of order: as violating the single-subject rule (as it involves charges in many different titles of law); as being not germane (for the same reason – many different titles of law); [or] a motion to amend could be tabled."[12] The strategy here was to argue the bill included irrelevant or immaterial legislation in an effort to kill it and end the matter. Regardless of the method, the goal was to keep representatives from voting an abolition bill out of committee and onto the House floor where the possibility of it becoming law would grow more probable. Lauinger, a representative from one of the largest pro-life organizations in America, was instructing a pro-life senator on how to destroy efforts to criminalize abortion. Four years later, Lauinger took it a step further in his efforts to hinder abolition.

When *Roe v. Wade* was reversed in 2022, Oklahoma trigger laws took effect, criminalizing the performance of any type of abortion *by a professional* for any type of reason. Yet women are still excused from penalty under these pro-life trigger laws. The criminal penalties for preborn murder only apply to anyone other than the mother of the unborn child. Specifically, Oklahoma statute 63 § 1-731.4 allows for an abortionist to be prosecuted up to 10 years in prison with up to a $100,000 fine but exempts women from prosecution, stating it does "not authorize the charging or conviction of a woman with any criminal offense in the death of her own unborn child."[13] To counter the very trigger laws the Oklahoma pro-life community established, the same pro-life community, led by Lauinger, shockingly put forward *pro-abortion bill SB 834* in the beginning of the 2023 legislative session. This bill's intent was to reopen abortion clinics to allow for abortion in cases of rape and incest, further enshrine legal permission for self-managed abortions, protect abortifacient drugs such as Plan B, and allow for the destruction of embryos created through in vitro fertilization. The bill also sought to lessen the criminal charges against an abortionist who violates the law by reducing the maximum sentencing from 10 years to five years.

Lauinger canvassed the Capitol the day before the Senate Health and Human Services Committee vote on SB 834, delivering memos in favor of the bill and urging lawmakers to vote "yes" to expand abortion access within Oklahoma.[14] In addition to personally visiting each lawmaker within the committee, Lauinger also delivered an email to Oklahomans for Life supporters requesting they also support the bill. The email claimed SB 834 would "strengthen Oklahoma's ability to defeat" the abortion industry's attempt to "impose unlimited abortion" within Oklahoma, and would "provide sustainable, long-term protection for Oklahoma's unborn children." Critics asked how promoting a pro-abortion bill would protect more preborn humans than the current statutes that prohibit the murder of *any* preborn human by a hired abortionist. Lauinger revealed his reasoning for this political pivot:

> Our current criminal law, passed last year by courageous pro-life legislators, reflects a position which is supported by just four percent (4%) of Oklahoma voters ....We must recognize politics as the art of the possible and find enough common ground in fine-tuning the pro-life option for the voters on the constitutional amendment so that our pro-life voting coalition will prevail ....Will the pro-life option be one that is supported by 4% of Oklahoma voters, or one that is supported by 71% of Oklahoma voters? That's what's at stake. That explains why SB 834 is absolutely essential.[15]

The flip-flop on the current laws of which Lauinger's pro-life community lobbied for in the past is apparently worth undoing in light of a possible threat of an impending "right to reproductive freedom" constitutional amendment. On October 28, 2022, Oklahoma Attorney General Brian Bingman received an initiative petition for a reproductive freedom constitutional amendment. The petition's sponsors, Roger Lee Coody-Rosamond, Rachel Anne Tafoya and Maegan Louise Kandi Richison, gave notice in the fall of 2022 of their plan to put forward a constitutional amendment that would secure the right to abortion within Oklahoma. Lauinger's response was a sickening compromise to the pro-abortion crowd in an attempt to appease them. Lauinger referenced a study conducted by WPA Intelligence which reported 74 percent of pro-life Oklahomans strongly support abortion for rape, incest, life of the mother and medical reasons alongside their pro-abortion counterparts. The study suggests "while Oklahoma continues to be a pro-life state, voters recognize the need for reforms to protect children in almost 95% of cases."[16]

What is especially interesting from this report is it lists Oklahomans – notably one of the most conservative demographic in America, – as being more pro-abortion friendly than the national average in regard to rape. According to the WPA Intelligence report, 76 percent of Oklahomans support abortion in cases of rape;[17] however, a 2022 PEW research study found only *69 percent of Americans favor abortion in instances of rape*.[18] It is confusing how the national average, which includes data from progressive states such as Oregon, Washington, California, New York, New Jersey, Colorado and Vermont, would result in *fewer* people favoring abortion in rape cases than the WPA's findings of conservative Oklahomans. Even longtime pro-life Representative Jim Olsen had this to say about Oklahomans for Life's bizarre support of pro-choice legislation:

> The group working behind the scenes to make this [SB 834] happen is Oklahomans for Life. Yes, we are speaking of one of the most well-known pro-life groups in the state! Tony Lauinger is the president of this group, and he has been working very hard

lobbying legislators to vote for the pro-choice bill, Senate Bill 834. This then, is the history being made in the pro-life movement. An ostensibly pro-life organization is working to undercut, dilute and weaken the law that protects unborn babies in Oklahoma.[19]

According to Olsen, Oklahomans for Life has always been "weak, halting and defeatist" in its efforts to fully end abortion within Oklahoma. Olsen further highlights how Oklahomans for Life routinely opposes "strong bills against abortion" that "either did or would have closed the abortion clinics." Olsen ends with a warning against blindly trusting those who claim to be against abortion: "If we had followed their advice over the years, Oklahoma's abortion clinics would *still* be open today. If we follow Tony Lauinger's advice now, those abortion clinics will reopen."[20]

Even though the WPA Intelligence data findings are suspicious and in conflict with other national statistical reports, Oklahomans for Life chose to use the questionable data to influence pro-life Oklahomans away from protecting 100 percent of preborn humans. When SB 834 failed to pass, another senate bill, SB 368, was amended to include the language from SB 834. Once again, Lauinger fired off emails to Oklahomans for Life supporters to encourage them to reach out to their representatives and support this new bill. Lauinger stated that SB 368, "would prohibit 95 percent of all abortions" and if not adopted then Oklahoma would lose protection for 100 percent of the unborn "when the constitutional amendment is adopted next year bringing unlimited, unrestricted abortion on demand to our state."[21] Lauinger did not explain that 100 percent of unborn children within Oklahoma are already protected (though not equally to born people) from the hands of hired abortionists under the current trigger law. In addition, his prophetic declaration that a pro-abortion amendment *will be passed in 2024* is brazen. State amendments typically reflect the majority of the voting demographic in relation to governor races.

In 2022, California placed on the ballot an amendment to enshrine abortion as a state constitutional right. It passed with 66 percent of votes.[22] Michigan also placed on its ballot a similar amendment to constitutionally protect abortion rights. It passed with 56 percent of votes.[23] On the east coast, Vermont's 2022 ballot included an amendment to enshrine abortion rights within the state. The amendment passed with 76 percent of the votes.[24] While the favor for these amendments seem daunting, it is important to recognize the percent at which these amendments passed closely reflects the percent of which these states also voted for high-ranking progressive politicians. California re-elected Governor Gavin Newsom with 59 percent of votes, Michigan retained Governor Gretchen Whitmer with 54 percent of votes, and Vermont elected Governor Phil Scott – a liberal, pro-choice Republican – with 71 percent of votes. Compare these patterns with Oklahoma that elected conservative, pro-life Governor Kevin Stitt with 55 percent of votes. While anything can potentially happen within politics, it is still quite barefaced to declare with such confidence Oklahoma *will for certain* adopt an abortion right's amendment to the state constitution. And even if such a ballot initiative would advance, we should not endeavor to beat the pro-abortion movement at their own game. No matter the motivation for wanting SB 368 to become law, critical information was withheld from pro-life Oklahomans in order to coerce support for a pro-choice bill. Lauinger has demonstrated on multiple accounts his interests are *not* in criminalizing abortion but in promoting what appears to be popular within the culture. His fluidity between anti-abortion and pro-choice philosophies should be a concern for any anti-abortion Christian, as Lauinger and his organizations have significant influence on state and national legislators and voters.

On a national level, pro-life efforts are operating to appear like abolition work, yet the outcome of these labors are actually more aligned with pro-choice goals. U.S. House Resolution 464, issued in June 2023, was initiated by Live Action and authored by Representative Doug Lamborn. It declares, "unborn children are legal and constitutional persons who are entitled to the equal protection of the laws." The resolution reads as an abolition declaration until the second to last line item. Section 3 tragically unravels all constitutional protection within the resolution for preborn humans. This section reads, "our constitutional duty and solemn obligation ... shall not be construed to permit the prosecution of any woman for the death of her unborn child."[25]

Resolutions are not laws, but are used as guidelines to direct future lawmakers how to write legislation pertaining to a particular subject. In this case, if a federal law or amendment were to be passed to reflect this resolution's sentiment that the Constitution does not allow for women to be prosecuted for prenatal homicide, it would effectively prohibit any state from abolishing abortion. During the same 2023 legislative session as the authorization of H. Res. 464, a U.S. House bill was crafted to reflect this sentimentality. House bill H.R. 431, called the Life at Conception Act, sponsored by pro-life Representative Alexander Mooney (WV-R), was submitted to the House floor. Like its resolution counterpart, it sounds like the work of abolitionists until its closing statement:

> To implement equal protection for the right to life of each born and preborn human person ... Congress hereby declares the right to life guaranteed by the Constitution is vested in each human being. However, *nothing in this Act shall be construed to authorize the prosecution of any woman for the death of her unborn child.* [Emphasis added.][26]

Constitutional attorney Bradley Pierce responded to these initiatives by saying "it is neither an equal protection nor a personhood bill" as it boldly "declares self-managed abortions as a constitutional right."[27] Pierce made a solemn observation: "This bill pays lip service to 'impartial protection.' Yet the bill rips the blindfold from Justice to examine the identity of the parties to determine outcomes. If the defendant is the mother and her victim is not yet born, there is no justice, which also means no protection."[28]

Despite being written by pro-life leaders, H. Res. 464 and H.R. 431 are in actuality pro-abortion initiatives seeking to lawfully enshrine the right for women to murder their preborn babies without consequence. This certainly undermines equal protection if some people will be legally allowed to still harm preborn humans. No one has special privilege to harm born people. The protection, therefore, for the unborn would not be "equal."

Our country needs men and women who will fight principally for the preborn. There are a plethora of those willing to compromise when it seems convenient. William Wilberforce, the independent British politician who helped spearhead the effort to abolish the English slave trade, was often on the wrong side of everyone politically as he was a "no party man." When he committed to criminalize the slave trade, he was ostracized even more within the political world. When explaining to Parliament why his motive to abolish the slave trade was not based upon economics or popular policies, he exclaimed:

> Policy, Sir, is not my principle, and I am not ashamed to say it. There is a principle above everything that is political. And when I reflect on the command that says, 'Thou shalt do no murder,' believing the authority to be divine, how can I dare set up any of my own reasoning against it? And, Sir, when we think of eternity, and of the future consequences of all human conduct, what is here in this life which should make any man contradict the principles of his own conscience, the principles of justice, the laws of religion, and of God?[29]

Today, there are not many principled Wilberforces with whom lobbyists and partisan politics must contend. Even professing Christian, pro-life politicians resemble the PACs that support them more than the Christ they profess. There is nothing inherently wrong with these alliances if both parties are exhorting each other to reflect Christ and obey all that he has commanded, but the case so often is the opposite. It is to look like the world, deal like the world, politick like the world, and, with abortion, make concessions instead of holding the line against all preborn murder. There are more politicians willing to shift with the political winds to remain relevant than those willing to stay anchored in truth that may cost them popularity.

Something (Almost) Historic

In May 2022, Louisiana was poised to do something historic. For the first time in the United States of America, a state voted *out of committee* a bill to completely and immediately abolish abortion. The magnitude of this event should not be overlooked. It was an act that would have provided equal justice and protection under the law for preborn humans. Even prior to *Roe v. Wade*, no state had completely criminalized abortion. Much like today, abortion was treated as a crime only for the abortionist, but even then serious felony charges were rarely ever levied against these perpetrators. Women, like today, were exempt from criminal prosecution. Forty-nine years after *Roe*, the tide appeared to shift: Louisiana plotted to change the course of history and passed an abolition bill from committee onto the House floor.

Pastor Brian Gunter of First Baptist Church Livingston (LA) testified before the House committee hearing on the moral importance of HB 813, the Louisiana abolition bill. Gunter had been an important advocate for the bill and worked with Representative Danny McCormick and Pierce to ensure its success. Gunter said the support from legislators was overwhelming and enthusiastic when they learned how the bill would provide equal protection for the unborn, and because *Roe v. Wade* held no constitutional authority, they did not need to wait for *Roe's* reversal to pursue criminalization. The energy of the room signaled a change in the wind, and elated abolitionists wondered if this was the cusp of reform they had long been awaiting.

On May 4, 2022, The Committee on Administration of Criminal Justice favorably voted 7-2 to send abolition bill HB 813 to the House floor for a vote the following week. Abolitionists across America froze in disbelief. It was a miracle in itself that HB 813 had made it out of committee without pro-life organizations' tampering. Even more significant was the fact that Louisiana's House and Senate was roughly 66 percent conservative. Moreover, Louisiana's governor happened to be a pro-life democrat. The victory of this abolition bill was not impossible. It was, for the first time, very probable – and that was a problem. The victory of HB 813 was short lived as Louisiana Right to Life issued a flurry of tweets to inform the culture about its opposition to this abolition bill:

> Louisiana Right to Life (@LARighttoLife): "Don't criminalize abortion-vulnerable women, a thread: Our culture needs restoration. Women have been lied to about pregnancy by the abortion industry, coerced by abusers and even by well-intentioned people." 8:59 PM • 5/07/22

> Louisiana Right to Life (@LARighttoLife): "Criminalize abortionists, who know exactly what they're doing: tearing a baby limb from limb and destroying a mother's soul, and sometimes even her body. Restore justice for mom and baby. Love them both." 9:00 PM • 5/07/22

> Louisiana Right to Life (@LARighttoLife): "Women who choose abortion are overwhelmingly victims themselves of domestic violence, racism, economic inequalities, & over 60% are coerced into doing so. Our policy as an organization is protecting vulnerable women from the abortion industry that preys on them for their profit." 9:01 PM • 5/07/22

> Louisiana Right to Life (@LARighttoLife): "HB 813: This bill is self-defeating with no teeth & no enforceability. This is NOT what it means to be pro-life." 10:39 AM • 5/09/22

Louisiana Right to Life (@LARighttoLife): "If criminal penalties is what you're after, check out SB 342, a bill that would criminalize the dangerous and disgusting abortion industry. " 10:39 AM • 5/09/22

Louisiana Right to Life (@LARighttoLife): "The abolish abortion law will NOT abolish abortion." 10:47 AM • 5/09/22

Mere days after Louisiana Right to Life's tweets, National Right to Life published its Open Letter to publicly make known the pro-life movement's "unequivocal opposition" to completely criminalizing abortion. For lawmakers who receive funding and endorsements from pro-life organizations, this was more than just a public relation statement of pro-life values. This was a threat: If you support equal protection and justice for the unborn, we will cut you off.

The Open Letter was distributed to the desk of every anti-abortion legislator within the Louisiana Congress to ensure each lawmaker got the memo. Louisiana Right to Life went so far as to publish on its website that HB 813 would "never save a single baby from abortion and therefore it was unnecessary."[30] It also claimed those who wrote the bill were legally misguided and did not understand the law despite the bill being written by a successful and well-known constitutional lawyer and a current Louisiana lawmaker.

The intentional and misleading rhetoric was unrelenting. Despite the national attack against HB 813 by the pro-life movement and the pro-abortion industry, abolitionists remained hopeful this would gain national attention for the abolition cause and wake up many more abolitionists across America. Amid the apparent unraveling of HB 813, anti-abortion advocates still traveled to Louisiana for the House vote. Abolition organizations End Abortion Now, Free the States, Foundation to Abolish Abortion, Rescue Those, Action for Life, as well as members from several churches, and pro-life organization Operation Save America were all present for the historic moment.

Reverend Jeff Durbin and head of End Abortion Now watched the debate and legislative vote of HB 813 with Gunter from the public gallery in the Louisiana House chamber. Earlier that day, a representative informed Durbin and Gunter that House leadership and pro-life lobbyists were planning to dissuade the Republican majority from voting in favor of HB 813. True to this representative's furtive warning, recess was called in the middle of session and *only* Republican legislators ushered into a secret meeting just prior to the vote on HB 813 – something never before seen in the middle of session, according to this legislative informant.[31] When the politicians reemerged, the bill of equal protection and justice for the preborn died on the House floor.

This flip is quite extraordinary. In committee, seven of the nine committee members voted in favor of abolishing abortion through HB 813. The only two dissenting committee members were Joseph Marino (I) and Vanessa LaFleur (D). One week and one covert middle-of-session-meeting later and the remaining Republican, pro-life committee members turned against abolishing abortion – all except McCormick, who sponsored the bill and held fast to the conviction of ending abortion even if he stood alone. Pro-life Representative Alan Seabaugh, who voted in favor of HB 813 when it was in committee, came out on the House floor with a surprise attack against it. He argued it was not pro-life to criminalize women, that not a single baby would be saved by this effort, and that those who wrote the bill were legally incompetent. His rhetoric was unmistakably an echo of the very words issued by National Right to Life and Louisiana Right to Life. When wind of the success of this abolition bill made it to the ears of major pro-life organizations, they were quick to jump in to halt efforts. The catechizing efforts of the pro-life PACs were obvious.

While watching the demise of HB 813 from the gallery, Durbin remarked, "A week goes by where they get the time to get worked on and indoctrinated by an organization that has no allegiance to Christ; no concern for consistency – they certainly aren't standing on the Word of God. They had time last week to be discipled by non-Christian organizations in terms of, 'Well, this is what *we* believe justice is,' when in turn it's not justice. It's injustice."[32]

Monkey See, Monkey Do

Almost a year to date after the Louisiana incident, Missouri had a committee hearing of its own on abolition bill SB 356. The committee allowed for two witnesses to speak in favor of the bill and two witnesses to speak in opposition of it. Pierce, along with Durbin, testified in favor of the Missouri abolition bill. Pierce opened his testimony with declaring, "I'm an abolitionist, which means I hold the supposedly extreme position that murdering anyone should be illegal for everyone."[33] Durbin challenged the legislators to do their duty before God and establish justice for the preborn within their land:

> This particular bill is just a bill of equal protection. That's it. It says something that is unassailable. What's in the womb, of course we believe, is in the image of God. What's in the womb, incontrovertibly, is a unique, distinct human being...I call you to establish justice. I call you to do your duty before God. I call you to repent, turn to Christ, to establish justice, to do what's right before God. There's a day of judgment in history ahead of us. Please do what's right.[34]

The organizations that arrived in opposition to SB 356 were Missouri's largest pro-life entities. Samuel Lee, director of Campaign Life Missouri, took a very different approach from the abolitionist testimonies. While the abolition witnesses appealed to the law of God, equal justice for both born and unborn humans, and the consciences of the magistrates, Lee appealed to far less weighty measures:

> ...[I'm here] to testify in opposition to Senate Bill 356....Last year about this time, many, many national and state groups issued a statement saying that they are opposed...'to any measure seeking to criminalize or punish women because it is not pro-life and we stand firmly opposed to such efforts.'...I would also point out that since 1825 when Missouri's first law prohibiting abortion was passed, Missouri has never, ever criminalized a woman for having an abortion. And I think that policy should stay the same.[35]

Lee's argument was based on the national letter, the cynosure for pro-life catechizing, as well as Missouri's antiquated abortion policy. While not all long-standing laws are problematic, Missouri established its soft abortion laws 40 years before it abolished slavery. It would be prudent to discern what other historic laws need revision in order to establish equal justice to all people. Instead of appealing to the nostalgia of the past, Lee should be willing to revise his doctrine of justice based on the logicalness of outlawing all types of murder for all types of people, as Pierce stated. More importantly, Lee and Campaign Missouri for Life should advocate for equal justice because it is biblical.

Susan Klein, director of Missouri Right to Life, joined Lee in opposition to abolishing abortion. Klein stated she was "going on record in opposition to the prosecution of women" and succinctly testified how Missouri Right to Life opposes criminalizing women for preborn murder.[36] What happened in Louisiana, Oklahoma and Missouri should be a dire warning to all Christians who desire to criminalize preborn murder. The pro-life catechisms reveal the silent part out loud: There is a double standard.

James Silberman, journalist for Abolitionists Rising (formerly Free the States), says, "The most influential things that can be done to abolish abortion is the defunding of National Right to Life."[37]

They and their affiliates appear to be some of the biggest obstacles to the end of child sacrifice.

Fear of God or Fear of Man

While the largest pro-life organizations oppose completely criminalizing abortion, there is another element to the sabotage of abolition efforts. Some pro-life politicians profess they *do* want to criminalize abortion, but fear of man and pragmatic money strategies inhibit them from sticking out their necks for full protection of all preborn humans. The dread of judicial challenge often results in these leaders seeking safe routes with pro-life bills that have less chance of being challenged in court. The desire to avoid costly litigation further encourages these politicians to take the middle road. Unfortunately, this is a handy scapegoat for the pro-life politicians who are more progressively-minded and *not* interested in criminalizing abortion. This makes it hard to parse out which politicians are cowards and which are cunning. In either case, the politician motivated by anything other than love for his preborn neighbor and fear of God will undermine any avowed convictions in the fight against abortion by making continual concessions.

Wilberforce once said, "In the scripture, no national crime is so condemned so frequently and few so strongly as oppression and cruelty and the not using our best endeavors to deliver our fellow creatures from them."[38] Wilberforce's idea of best endeavors was the complete abolition of the slave trade, for which he spent the majority of his life fighting. Today's best efforts are to take whatever politicians can get in the present.

Indiana House Committee on Public Policy Chairman Ben Smaltz (R-Auburn) tabled abolition bill HB 1430 in 2019 in fear of the legal attention it may have incited. The bill would have expanded Indiana's criminal code to recognize life begins at conception (a statute many states already have) and prevented any interference with Indiana's obligation to protect all human life. Just two years prior, Smaltz refused to allow the same abolition bill a committee hearing. In a 2017 interview with the *Fort Wayne Journal Gazette*, Smaltz said the Protection at Conception Act would have been "catastrophic to the [pro-life movement]." An article by *Free the States* explains his reasoning: "Smaltz was referring to the sections of the bill which would have repealed pro-life regulations of abortion which would have to be repealed in order to end abortion. He contends that a hostile judge could strike down the sections of The Protection at Conception Act which end abortion while upholding the sections which repeal regulations."[39]

Essentially, Smaltz feared the judge would strike down the abolition bill and leave Indiana without any abortion regulations. For anyone who has not read the bill, that reasoning seems plausible; however, page 13, lines 10 through 17 of the Indiana abolition bill, specified it is non-severable, and according to Indiana law, "[i]f a statute contains a nonseverability provision and if any part of that statute is declared invalid, the whole statute is void." In other words, this means if a court found the application of abolition to be incompatible with current laws, the whole new statute would be ignored and current laws would remain intact. It would be impossible for a court to strike down all pro-life regulations specified in the bill and leave the state without any abortion restrictions. Tragically, this lawmaker who should be familiar with nonseverability clauses chose to mislead the unsuspecting pro-life public.

Around the same time as the 2019 Indiana abolition effort, Idaho was experiencing its own struggle to push an abolition bill into its heavily pro-life political atmosphere. Representatives Heather Scott and John Green co-sponsored the Idaho Abortion Human Rights Act, which sought to remove state statutes that allow for abortion as a homicide exemption. Idaho Code 18-4001 defines murder as "the unlawful killing of a human being including, but not limited to, a human embryo or fetus, with malice aforethought or the intentional application of torture to a human being, which results in the death of a human being." If left there, abortion would be illegal in Idaho for all people; but Idaho Code 18-4016 continues on to grant legal impunity to women, doctors and girls' guardians to kill preborn humans without prosecution. In a press release on the Idaho Abortion Human Rights Act, Scott and Green stated:

> To accomplish this historic restoration of human rights for the unborn in Idaho, the act simply repeals the prohibition of prosecution for abortion, found in Idaho Code 18-4016 and puts

the matter within existing statute for the prosecution of murder, where it clearly belongs.⁴⁰

As logical as this bill was, not all pro-life representatives were enthusiastic about it. Idaho Senator Fred Martin told a constituent in a recorded meeting that the abolition bill would destroy the pro-life movement. As the constituent pressured Martin to get behind and support the abolition bill, Martin stressed, "That bill is detrimental to the pro-life cause. I hope it never sees the light of day. Every pro-life organization is against Representative Green and Scott's bill.... We're very cautious about the pro-life bills that we do so that we can have them hold up in court, because if we do pass pro-life bills that won't hold up in court the state has to pay the pro-life bill's legal fees."⁴¹

This is fiscal pragmatism. Nothing will evoke the fury of the abortion industry more than to criminalize it. It would certainly garner the attention of national abortion groups such as the National Abortion Federation (NAF), American Civil Liberties Union (ACLU), National Abortion Rights Action League (NARAL), and the Center for Reproductive Rights. While conservatives play cautious with money, abortion activists do not. Nothing is too expensive for them to fight for their right to exert dominance over the preborn. They know they are at war and they fight like it. While conservatives dot their i's and cross their t's, abortion groups rally unrivaled support for their side of the cause.

From 2000-2019, pro-life groups collectively raised $55 billion. During the same timeframe, pro-abortion groups raised $293 billion.⁴² Looking at the numbers, one can see why pro-life players attempt to use what little money (in comparison to the abortion movement) they have in the most strategic ways. But the reluctance to apply money to the root of the abortion atrocity by criminalizing it sends a counter-message.

Pro-abortion groups preach that abortion is a constitutional right and they fight and spend their money like they truly believe that. One way in which they do this is they rarely ask for exceptions. They ask for unfettered access to abortion through all nine months of pregnancy, and today they are receiving what they have asked for in many states. Contrast this with pro-life conservatives who claim abortion is a holocaust but then approach it as if rescuing them needs to be budgeted. Fighting war is costly. Christians need to get their heads around this and be willing to pay the price to secure the right to life for all people. Instead, pro-life politics treat the murder of their preborn constituents like another accounting line item. It is appropriate to use pragmatics and fiscal conservatism when planning a business strategy, but when it comes to murder, urgency and every resource available should be used to save the lives of others from oppression and demise. This is a costly and important distinction to remember. Pro-life politicians lose instant trustworthiness when they use strong rhetoric to condemn abortion but then default from the logical position to criminalize it.

The "Bloody Kansas" Catechizing Debacle

For devout anti-abortion Kansans, 2022 brought a shock that continues to ripple through the conservative Kansas landscape. Just three years prior, the Kansas Supreme Court "discovered" the right to abortion within the Kansas Bill of Rights. In the landmark case *Hodes & Nauser v. Derek Schmidt*, the Kansas Supreme Court ruled:

> We conclude that, through the language in section 1, the state's founders acknowledged that the people had rights that pre-existed the formation of the Kansas government. There they listed several of these natural, inalienable rights—deliberately choosing language of the Declaration of Independence by a vote of 42 to 6. Included in that limited category is the right of personal autonomy, which includes the ability to control one's own body, to assert bodily integrity, and to exercise self-determination. This right allows a woman to make her own decisions regarding her body, health, family formation, and family life—decisions that can include whether to continue a pregnancy. Although not absolute,

this right is fundamental. Accordingly, the State is prohibited from restricting this right unless it is doing so to further a compelling government interest and in a way that is narrowly tailored to that interest. And we thus join many other states' supreme courts that recognize a similar right under their particular constitutions.[43]

Similar to *Roe v. Wade* and *Planned Parenthood v. Casey*, the Kansas Supreme Court ruled the state constitution secures a woman's right to abortion. The consequence was potentially devastating to the Kansas pro-life culture. The *Hodes & Nauser* decision meant any new pro-life legislation could end up in litigation, and current standing pro-life laws were at risk of repeal. Naturally, Kansas Republicans and pro-life groups, such as Kansans for Life, Kansas Family Voice and Kansas Catholic Conference, scrambled to correct the nefarious court ruling. The option presented to the public was a new Kansas constitutional amendment known as Value Them Both (VtB). This amendment sought to correct the *Hodes & Nauser* court decision by, as Kansas Representative Pat Proctor put it, restoring "those regulations...through our legislators to regulate this industry."[44]

An expressed concern of many Kansans was that the Kansas state legislature is already granted the sole right to create and pass laws per Article 2 of the state constitution. While many pointed out the unnecessary need and redundancy for an amendment to allow legislators to perform their constitutional duty, these critics were dismissed.

Though an amendment is one of several routes that can be taken to address unconstitutional court rulings, critics had concerns with the ambiguous wording of the amendment. Leading abolitionists who opposed VtB warned that the amendment was a potential Trojan horse. The wording was confusing, with people on either side of the issue perplexed as to how it would be implemented or interpreted. The amendment read as:

> **§ 22. Regulation of abortion.** Because Kansans value both women and children, the constitution of the state of Kansas does

not require government funding of abortion and does not create or secure a right to abortion. To the extent permitted by the constitution of the United States, the people, through their elected state representatives and state senators, *may pass laws regarding abortion*, including, but not limited to, laws *that account for circumstances of pregnancy resulting from rape or incest, or circumstances of necessity to save the life of the mother*.[45] [Emphasis the author's.]

The court had done some gymnastics to "find" abortion within the bill of rights which states, "all men are possessed of equal and inalienable natural rights, among which are life, liberty, and the pursuit of happiness." What would the same court do with an amendment titled "regulation of abortion"? Abolitionists were concerned the same liberal court would use the loosely-defined amendment to prevent the future criminalization of prenatal homicide and only allow for the management of the industry. The phrase "may pass laws ... that account for circumstances of pregnancy resulting from rape or incest, or circumstances of necessity to save the life of the mother" left many to wonder if this would be interpreted by the liberal court to mean abortion in those instances is a constitutional right, further preventing a complete ban of abortion. It was not a risk some anti-abortion individuals were willing to take. Pro-life leaders insisted without the amendment all pro-life laws would be null and void and no unborn human would be protected. Therefore, VtB was marketed as the only path forward, but what transpired left many anti-abortion Kansans reeling as though the rug had been ripped out from underneath their feet.

On the steps of the Kansas Capitol building during the 2022 March for Life rally, Kim Borchers, Kansas Republican National Committeewoman, declared:

> The Value Them Both goal is clear: We believe in reasonable limits placed on the abortion industry. Safeguarding protections we have enacted over twenty years...and what is the truth? The truth is Value Them Both does not abolish abortion. The amendment

preserves existing laws that were passed with bipartisan support. You've heard that. I'm gonna say that over and over again 'cause that's the message we have to give. Because the lies will be that this is trying to abolish abortion. That is a lie.[46]

It was an emphatic speech that the amendment was *not* an initiative to end abortion. It was also a strange promise to make at a March for Life rally in the presence of hundreds of anti-abortion activists, and it certainly begged the question of who was the "we?"

Borchers seemingly testified that the Kansas Grand Old Party (GOP) and pro-life platform — both of which she represented — was to regulate, not abolish, prenatal homicide. Indeed, she was not off-base. Proctor avowed the same thing multiple times during a panel discussion between abolitionists, pro-abortion advocates and pro-life representatives on the VtB amendment, reminding voters "this isn't a ban but this does allow us to make reasonable limits on the practice of abortion."[47] This revelation forced many conservatives to face the fact that Kansas pro-life institutions and politicians do not represent them on abortion.

To amplify the confusion, the VtB campaign employed radio commercials and billboards riddled with pro-choice rhetoric to coerce the abortion crowd to vote in favor of the amendment. One of the radio bites featured two women in conversation and advertised for VtB as such: "Listen, I'm pro-choice. I'm not telling another woman what to do with her body. There just *has* to be a limit. I'm voting yes on the constitutional amendment to allow *some* regulation of abortion. Here's the deal; because at some point in the pregnancy, it becomes a baby."[48] Any anti-abortion individual paying attention would have been perplexed by that advertisement in which pro-abortion reasoning was used to obscure the humanity of the preborn in an effort to coerce voters to accept arbitrary limits on the practice of murdering those image bearers.

The abortion lobby was just as active as the VtB proselytizers. To counter the pro-life VtB agenda, abortion activists erected billboards throughout the state urging the public to "Trust women. Vote No." This became the abortion lobby mantra during the fight over the Kansas amendment. Pro-choice yard signs, bumper stickers, and social media ads employed the "Trust women. Vote No" motto as the staple opposition cry. Slyly mimicking this pro-abortion slogan, a Wichita, KS pro-life billboard used the same rhetoric but twisted it to read, "Trust women. Vote Yes."[49] The manipulative advertising demonstrated the pro-life movement's willingness to confuse the issue in order to gain votes. Appealing to the abortion crowd may have garnered a few votes from the left but it only further alienated the Kansas conservatives who were paying attention and wanted all preborn murder criminalized.

Despite the warning signs, many naïve and optimistic Kansans insisted VtB was the gateway to abolishing abortion despite there being no such assurance from pro-life leaders. In a VtB discussion panel in Leavenworth, Kansas, Proctor and Representative Tim Johnson responded once again that abolition was not the goal. To drive home this point, abolitionist panel member Jared Burdick with Abortion is Murder Kansas (AIM KS) addressed the audience and said of abolitionists, "*We* are the ones trying to end abortion." Then motioning toward the pro-life representatives next to him on stage he clarified, "Not them. They are not trying to abolish abortion."[50] Johnson and Proctor never corrected Burdick but remained silent in response to this claim.

Whether by pro-life PACs or politicians, their catechism was unified: the intent of the amendment effort was not to end abortion. This left many anti-abortion Kansans to conclude only one of two things. Either these pro-life leaders were liars who intended to turn around and stab their bipartisan colleagues and pro-choice constituents in the back once it passed and pursue abolition anyway, or they were telling the truth – there is no intent to abolish abortion within Kansas. It turns out to be the latter.

Kansas GOP House Majority Leader Dan Hawkins told multiple representatives and a campaign manager that an abolition bill will never succeed under his watch because most Republicans want abortion exceptions.[51] His proclamation bolstered the suspicion of many that conservative state leadership is working *against* criminalizing abortion. The reiterating message from the pro-life movement was clear: Kansas pro-life leaders are not interested in abolishing abortion, so if you are pro-choice there is nothing to fear from Value Them Both. Just vote yes.

The Idolatry of Bipartisan Support

The Kansas amendment debacle was a concerted effort to preserve bipartisan pro-life regulations such as parental consent, informed consent, licensed abortion physicians and clinics, and prohibition of abortions past 22 weeks' gestation (though with some exceptions to that). As stated by VtB advocates, it was a bipartisan effort, which meant both Democrats and Republicans agreed on the bill. This is disturbing. When one political group insists on the privilege to murder other humans, the opposition's position should not be one of compromise but one of unrelenting zeal to protect the endangered group of people. To do otherwise is a disregard of the warning found in James 4:4: "You adulterous people! Do you not know that friendship with the world is enmity with God? Therefore whoever wishes to be a friend of the world makes himself an enemy of God." Likewise, 1 Corinthians 15:33 cautions, "Do not be deceived: 'Bad company ruins good morals.'" Christians must be careful of the idolatry of bipartisan support. It can quickly deteriorate God's decrees so the culture of death will be happy and Christians will look falsely successful. It lures the unsuspecting into timidity to uphold what is known to be right, and it allows for an ethos of excuses (such as financial concern or court challenge) to aid in unfaithfulness to God's word.

Borchers insisted anything stricter than VtB would not have made it through the state legislature, would be rejected by the public, or challenged in court.[52] Like Martin, the strategy was to play it safe and seek common ground with those who want to allow for the murder of preborn humans. Ironically, the whole reason for Kansas' Supreme Court decision in *Hodes & Nauser v. Derek Schmidt* was the result of a 2015 Kansas pro-life bill which sought to ban dismemberment abortions. The excuse to avoid pursuing criminalization because it will be challenged is weak. The abortion industry has proven it will challenge every jot and tittle. It challenged an ultrasound bill in Kentucky; a Louisiana bill that requires abortionists to have hospital admitting privileges; and a bill to prevent abortions on pain-capable babies in Arizona. It will gladly go to court over every bill when given the chance. Conversely, the pro-life movement seems unwilling to go to court over *any* bill. Even the hint of litigation insinuates loss to pro-life politicians. Thus, for five decades, the pro-life culture has been taught to accept subpar moral results from pro-life legislative efforts.

We must remember that any restriction against preborn murder will be inflammatory to the abortion industry. Christians should be willing to go to court on righteous standing. Better to spend time in court fighting to secure the right to life for all humans rather than fighting to enforce licensing for preborn killers or a documented ultrasound before a preborn human is destroyed. The quest for bipartisan favor in regard to anti-abortion legislation has led the pro-life movement away from asking for the thing it claims it wants most: the end of legalized abortion.

Both biblical and American histories have shown that Christians can ask for and expect the impossible from God. A delay to a righteous end goal is not necessarily failure but merely future victory. Wilberforce submitted 14 abolition bills in the 18 years it took to abolish the slave trade. The pro-life movement has submitted zero abolition bills in 50 years. Wilberforce brought forward an abolition bill nearly every session. Though he knew it could fail, he hoped his efforts would convict the hearts of his countrymen and believed God would change the course of history through his diligence. Through his resolve to abolish the slave trade, he catechized parliament and the culture to hate slavery like he did. Despite this template of biblical justice and success, the pro-life regulatory approach remains the preference.

In the 50 years since *Roe*, the pro-life movement has submitted zero bills of total abolition at either the state or the federal level. The pro-life movement has catechized culture and politics to aim low and expect even less. It has also taught society to fight for legal immunity for women involved in the premediated murders of their preborn children while simultaneously claiming abortion ends the life of a distinct human being and is a grievous evil. This catechizing is heretical. It teaches the law can show partiality and favor toward women, ignoring the clear scriptural truth of not favoring some people over others; it ignores the warning of Scripture which says all will give an account before the Lord of Hosts and to make no ransom for murderers (Numbers 35:31); it imparts only image bearers who meet a certain criteria (heartbeat, gestational age, pain-capable, etc.) have the right to life, ignoring the biblical doctrine that all humans are image bearers of their Creator and worthy of life; and it teaches Christians can fight a culture of death apart from the Author of life. American politicians need the Word of God, not the word of PACS, to guide their decisions and convictions.

As such, a common catechizing tagline of pro-life politics is "we cannot legislate morality." God's Word says otherwise. The Bible comforts us in the fact that the law helps to restrain the evil intentions of the heart while at the same time revealing to people how wicked their hearts are in light of God's standard. Two hundred years ago slavery was not seen as morally wrong by the majority of Americans. Today, the majority of people would say slavery is morally wrong. What changed? The law did. If politics is downstream from culture, justice and morality are downstream from the law. If Christians do not push for righteous laws there can be no expectation of biblical justice. There is no reason to assume the pro-life movement will achieve the same results as the slavery abolitionists. The pro-life movement fears the failure of something it has not yet even attempted, which is asking for the total abolition of abortion. Anti-abortion individuals should not be surprised to never get what is never asked for.

Wilberforce once wrote, "I would suggest that faith is everyone's business. The advance or decline of faith is so intimately connected to the welfare of a society that it should be of particular interest to a politician."[53]

Those with the skill of evangelism should consider using that ability for the glory of God in the realm of politics. America's magistrates require biblical teaching on justice, and have righteous duties to shun partiality, forsake the temptations and pressures of the world, and rely on God to win earthly battles. The leading pro-life organizations have shown they are not faithful stewards of this discipleship task. Where Christians stay silent, the secular world steps in to speak. And our politicians are listening.

4

RECANT: THE PRO-LIFE CANCEL CULTURE

"We believe God's commandments, and not human statutes, save or condemn." – Heinrich Voes, martyr of Rome, 1523

Heretics

SOMETHING SCANDALOUS WAS HAPPENING. Whisperings of the rebel preacher spread across England and quickly reached the ears of the pope himself. Shocked by the damnable heresies he heard of this preacher, Pope Gregory XI quickly penned a letter to the king of England, the archbishop of Canterbury, and the chancellor of Oxford University to warn them of this certain preacher's offense and the proposed punishment against him. The crime? Challenging the Church of Rome's doctrines. The criminal? John Wycliffe.

Not only did this influential minister question what the Church of Rome taught, but he actively spoke against those teachings and repudiated with Scripture many of Rome's claims of truth. Wycliffe challenged indulgences, argued against transubstantiation, rebuked private confessional, taught the biblical teaching on faith, and worked to translate the Bible into English. Translating the Bible into the people's language was among one of the highest offenses against the Church of Rome, yet Wycliffe defended his efforts by saying, "Englishmen learn Christ's laws best in English. Moses heard God's law in his own tongue; so did Christ's apostles."[1] Still, Pope Gregory XI was unconvinced and scathingly concluded, "John Wycliffe is vomiting out the filthy dungeon of his heart most wicked and damnable heresies. He hopes to deceive the faithful and lead them to the edge of destruction. He wants to overthrow the church and bring ruin to the land. Arrest Wycliffe immediately and hold him until a church court can be convened to pass final sentence."[2] Undeterred, Wycliffe said, "The pope has no more power to judge than any other minister. His word should be followed only so far as he follows the words of Christ. I am under obligation to obey the law of Christ."

The Church of Rome hated Wycliffe so much that 44 years after his death his bones were dug up, burned and dumped into a stream called the Swift. Unfortunately for Rome, Wycliffe's "heresies" did not die with him. In 1412 A.D., Rome once again had to contend with another protestor.

Prague preacher John Huss preached and taught the people in their language of Czech and not Latin as required by the pope. In response, the pope forbade any church services to commence in Prague until Huss was arrested. Ignoring the pope's ban, Huss continued to preach and teach the people the words of Scripture. "Christ commanded his disciples to go into all the world and preach," he said. "No pope can stop what Christ taught to be done."[3] As Huss continued to preach and write about biblical truths that contradicted the teachings of Rome, tensions mounted until the church council decided to bring him to trial. It was not quite a fair process as it had been decided beforehand to condemn him. Still, the council set before Huss two options: recant or be burned. As they laid before him stacks of his writings and demanded he admit to the falsehoods contained within them, Huss responded, "I'm ready to retract anything in them if I am shown from the Holy Scriptures where I am in err."[4] In vain, the council repeatedly attempted to illicit renunciation from Huss. When it was apparent they would not succeed, they condemned him to burn at the stake. Huss accepted his fate: "It would be better for me that a millstone were hung around my neck and that I should be cast into the sea before I should deny the truths of God."[5]

Time and again Rome struggled against detractors from the Catholic doctrines. The recurring theme was for heretics to recant, admit the Catholic church to be dogmatically correct, or be silenced. Time and again protestors would challenge Rome and show from Scripture where Rome had erred. As Wycliffe once declared, "The highest service to which a man may obtain on earth is to preach the law of God."[6]

The struggle was not one of power for these Reformers and pre-Reformation agitators, but one of proper allegiance. They understood Scripture to reveal their proper fidelity to the authority of Christ above all other authorities. As such, this brought Rome's worldviews which were antithetical to Scripture into sharp contrast with sola Scriptura adherents. Ultimately, Rome was disinterested to use Scripture to prove or disprove anything. When pressuring Catholic monk Martin Luther to recant from his adherence to Scripture only and not the church's conflicting dogmas, Luther uttered his famous line, "If I am a heretic then show me from God's Word. It is better that I should die a thousand times than I should retract one word of what I have written about the sacred truth of God."[7]

Others such as William Tyndale were tried and charged with teaching "heresies" like salvation by faith alone, that God alone forgives sins without the mediation of an earthly priest, and that people should read the Bible for themselves in their own language. Through all the charges brought by Rome, Tyndale defended his position with Scripture. When Catholic authority could not rebuttal his defenses with Scripture, it still demanded he renounce his opposition to the church's beliefs. Tyndale refused to recant and was sentenced to death.

This trend painfully continued with bloody fighting until Protestantism emerged from the dictates of the Roman Catholic church as a restored version of the first century church. While this is an overly simplified version of history, it remains relevant because today there is also an authority struggle. Like the Reformation preachers, abolition preachers keep cropping up to declare a different gospel than that of the established anti-abortion movement. As it threatens the conventional traditions of pro-life politicking, the response to dissenters has been similar to the historic response of the Roman Catholic church: Those who insist on fighting abortion biblically, rather than the way prescribed by pro-life dogma, are labeled heretical, slanderers, endangering pro-life accomplishments, and not to be taken seriously. These heretics are to be silenced.

New Kid on the Block

A journalist for *The New York Times* highlighted in 2022 the growing tension between mainstream pro-life groups and abolitionists. Until the reversal of *Roe v. Wade*, the pro-life industry largely ignored the push to abolish abortion and the competing philosophies that accompanied it, but as the *Times* article notes, "Privately, some leaders of mainstream groups worry about how quickly abolitionists have gained a foothold."[8] With *Roe* dismantled, the pro-life culture must for the first time contend legitimately with abolitionists. The strategy thus far is to discredit anyone unwilling to recant and accept the incremental approach of the pro-life movement and its victimology of women.

Writer and pro-life apologist Jonathan Van Maren, communications director for the Canadian Centre for Bio-Ethical Reform, joined podcast host Josh Brahm, president of Equal Rights Institute, in 2021 to discuss the abolition movement compared to the pro-life movement. The podcast primarily focused on what Van Maren considers the shortcomings of Russell Hunter, founder of the abolition group Free the States (now Abolitionists Rising). During the podcast, Brahm and Van Maren lamented the slander they perceive abolition criticism to be and, ironically, insulted Master's historian Hunter by calling him a historical "intellectual lightweight" and the "alt-right of the pro-life movement."[9] Van Maren concluded with saying of Hunter's position on abortion, "I won't call it a philosophy because that's too kind. His ideology is just really simplistic, badly researched, almost entirely cherry-picked, and based on a false understanding of world history and theology."[10]

Van Maren's complaints of slander and abolition meanness can be interpreted as hypocritical considering he told a group of interns at the pro-life organization Created Equal that abolitionists are "jackasses" and labeled Abolish Human Abortion a "hostile" group because they rebuke pro-life leaders for not adhering faithfully to Scripture.[11] Van Maren also expressed frustration about how an abolition bill would wipe out all current pro-life legislation achieved over the past 50 years: "Here's why pro-lifers oppose these [abolition] bills. It's because if these bills pass...they would wipe all the other pro-life laws off the books. Two decades of careful legislating and strangling the abortion industry with red tape will be eliminated."[12]

He is not the only one to worry over the undoing of the pro-life resume. As explored in chapter three, Martin was equally aghast at wiping the slate clean with an abolition bill. Likewise, Maryland Right to Life said in a letter to its state pro-life lawmakers that equal protection for the unborn "poses a grave threat to the pro-life movement." It is inconceivable to these pro-life adherents to suggest erasing the legislative efforts and tradition of pro-life politics even if a better standard of morality and justice would be achieved by doing so.

This distaste for abolition touches on another sensitive issue: the belief abortion abolitionists are historically ignorant. This is a common complaint from many pro-life apologists. They frequently accuse abortion abolitionists of reinventing history to make William Wilberforce, Thomas Clarkson and William Lloyd Garrison their predecessors when, according to these pro-life experts, all those men were either incrementalists like the pro-life strategists of today or loose-cannon radicals not worth imitating. But are there substantial differences between slavery abolitionists and abortion abolitionists? And if so, are modern day abolitionists attempting to cram historical abolitionists into a box of modern strategies and ideologies?

The reason for beginning this book with the Five Tenets of Abortion Abolition is because the modern-day abolition movement hinges on building foremost upon Scripture in its response to abortion, not parroting historical characters. This informs how the movement engages culture, writes law, determines biblical morality, and interposes for the weakest among society. By default, this means some facets from various historical abolitionists align with today's declared tenets of the abolition movement because the slavery abolition movement was almost entirely Protestant, too; however, no single historical figure perfectly encapsulates 21st-century abolitionists.

One of the benefits of coming on the heels of the slavery fight 200 years later is abortion abolitionists can survey history and mimic the righteous and correct things. A template has already been laid by abolition predecessors on how they fought against the prevailing evils in their day, with their victories and failures on full display. Nevertheless, one thing both 19th- and 21st-century abolitionists have in common is the belief that evil must be halted immediately and without enshrined legal exceptions. In both eras, biblical abolitionists have maintained that the biblical response to evil is immediatism. Immediatism simply means asking for the complete end of something and not bargaining with evil. As slavery abolitionist William Wilberforce taught, "...it is not regulation, it is not mere palliatives, that can cure this enormous evil. Total abolition is the only possible cure for it."[13]

According to Scripture, if one is in sin the correct response is only instant and complete repentance. Efforts to turn from evil cannot be incremental. If a man is caught in adultery, the only option before him is to immediately cease that sin and turn to run the other direction. Choosing to fornicate only on the weekends or only with women pre-approved by his pastor would not be pursuing righteousness but would instead further enshrine his habit of sexual immorality. Likewise, abolition immediatism calls for the speedy end to preborn murder without compromising other biblical commands in the process. Immediatism does not mean the expectation that things will politically and culturally occur within milliseconds, but it does mean that the call for something to end is one of urgency and completeness. This aligns with some of the leading slavery abolitionists of the past.

Conversely, incrementalists advocated for slavery to stop when southern states were ready, or it sought to regulate slavery's expansion in hopes it would someday vanish, or it attempted to limit the amount of slaves on West Indies bound English ships, and so forth. Yet immediatism demanded slavery stop altogether and at once because it was wrong. The type of demand will influence what path is pursued politically, socially and morally to achieve what has been asked for. Today, some pro-life leaders refer to abortion abolitionists as immediatists in a derogatory manner to discredit these men and women. These pro-life enthusiasts claim abolitionists unrealistically expect their demands to be met by tomorrow. In contrast, abortion immediatists define their political efforts as repeatedly asking for nothing less than what is scripturally consistent and uncompromisingly just until those demands are achieved and an evil institution is criminalized. It is helpful to consider the parable of the persistent widow found in Luke 18 to exemplify this:

> And he told them a parable to the effect that they ought always to pray and not lose heart. He said, "In a certain city there was a judge who neither feared God nor respected man. And there was a widow in that city who kept coming to him and saying, 'Give me justice against my adversary.' For a while he refused, but afterward he said to himself, 'Though I neither fear God nor respect man, yet because this widow keeps bothering me, I will give her justice, so that she will not beat me down by her continual coming.'" And the Lord said, "Hear what the unrighteous judge says. And will not God give justice to his elect, who cry to him day and night? Will he delay long over them? I tell you, he will give justice to them speedily. Nevertheless, when the Son of Man comes, will he find faith on earth?"

Abolitionists attempt to model their efforts after the widow's example. They acknowledge, along with the pro-life gradualist, that immediate results within a day, a week or even years is unlikely, but they differ from gradualists in that the time frame should not hinder or alter the call for justice. The widow repeatedly pleaded for justice and Scripture does not give any indication she changed her request to make the judge more amiable toward her begging. Instead, her tenacity for the judge to do what was right wore him down to oblige even though his consideration for justice was not born from a desire to please God but rather to be rid of the incessant supplication of the widow. This greatly contrasts the pro-life philosophy to pass whatever biblically, logically and constitutionally compromised laws it can to regulate prenatal homicide, even if those laws leave some preborn humans on the chopping block. As Van Maren says, "I will support whatever laws save more of those human beings."[14]

Within this context, Wilberforce, Clarkson and Garrison were immediate abolitionists. Clarkson helped achieve passage of the 1807 Slave Trade Act, which fully criminalized the slave trade with no exceptions. The writings of Garrison and Wilberforce clarify themselves as abolitionists and *not* as incrementalists/gradualists. They spent their lives fighting for abolition. They did not expect instantaneous results. These men declare from the chronicles of history:

> The gradual abolitionists have been, in fact, the only real stay of that system of wickedness and cruelty which we wish to abolish; though that assertion is unquestionably true; it is trying beyond expression that they should be the real maintainers of the slave trade.[15] – William Wilberforce, slavery abolitionist

> I must at once strike every reasonable person, that the regulation of the slave trade cannot be an efficient remedy for the evils complained of. Regulation implies *continuance* upon state terms: and *so long as the trade continues*, so long will there be temptations, and so long will the needy and avaricious embrace them, to obtain the persons of men....It appears then, that an *abolition* of the slave trade would have the desired end, and that abolition only would be effectual.[16] – Thomas Clarkson, slavery abolitionist

Why ought the Slave Trade to be abolished? Because it is an incurable injustice. How much stronger then is the argument for immediate, than gradual abolition! By allowing it to continue even for one hour, do not my Right Honourable Friends weaken – do they not desert their own argument of injustice? If on the ground of injustice it ought to be abolished at last, why ought it not now? Why is injustice to be suffered to remain for a single hour?[17] – William Pitt, slavery abolitionist

I am a believer in that portion of the Declaration of American Independence in which it is set forth, as among self-evident truths, 'that all men are created equal; that they are endowed by their Creator with certain inalienable rights; that among these are life, liberty, and the pursuit of happiness.' Hence, I am an abolitionist. Hence, I cannot but regard oppression in every form-and most of all that which turns a man into a thing-with indignation and abhorrence...The abolitionism which I advocate is as absolute as the law of God, and as unyielding as his throne. It admits of no compromise. Every slave is a stolen man; every slaveholder is a man stealer. By no precedent, no example, no law, no compact, no purchase, no bequest, no inheritance, no combination of circumstances, is slaveholding right or justifiable. While a slave remains in his fetters, the land must have no rest. Whatever sanctions his doom must be pronounced accursed. The law that makes him a chattel is to be trampled underfoot; the compact that is formed at his expense, and cemented with his blood, is null and void; the church that consents to his enslavement is horribly atheistical; the religion that receives to its communion the enslaver is the embodiment of all criminality.[18] – William Lloyd Garrison, slavery abolitionist

One common claim that Wilberforce and Clarkson were incrementalists is they sought to abolish the slave trade before banning the entire slave industry. Retrospectively, their strategy may have been flawed since it took another 25 years after the slave trade was criminalized to emancipate slaves. Christians should solemnly consider this lesson. The optimism of English slavery abolitionists may have been misplaced, and this is the exact scenario today's abortion abolitionists are trying to avoid. History risks repeating itself on this axis when pro-life efforts seek only to criminalize those who perform abortions but excuse the consumers of it. This echoes the 19th-century move to criminalize the slave trade but not slave ownership, dragging the fight on for many more decades.

There is also a stark difference in legislative efforts. Today's pro-life bills are built upon the premise that pain-capable restrictions, gestational age limits, dismemberment bans, ultrasound laws, and clinic licensing requirements (to name a few) will result in the eventual death of the abortion industry. Historical abolitionists rejected this type of approach. Clarkson dedicated his essay on regulation versus the abolition of slavery as a rebuttal to Sir William Dolben's regulatory bill proposals, and, if alive today, could be imagined as writing the same rebuttal to pro-life politicians. To date, *there have been no pro-life bills that have demanded a complete ban in the sense of criminalizing abortion for all people.* This is a stark contrast from the slavery abolition bills, which demanded the immediate, legal end of the trade. Aside from Dolben's slave ship bill, slavery abolitionists did not routinely pass 1) prejudicial legislation that exempted slaves of certain physical characteristics from the industry, or 2) legislation which restricted only slaves older than an arbitrary age to be captured and sold, or 3) legislation which said slaves could not be beaten to death but could be drowned, or 4) legislation that required certain licensing of slave carrying ships. Requirements such as those could be considered parallel to pro-life laws, yet those type of efforts are what Wilberforce condemned as the hold up to complete abolition. Abolitionists today concur, though they may disagree with historical abolitionists on other points.

Abortion abolitionists are not trying to fit slavery abolitionists into the 21st-century's box of what it means to be an abolitionist, despite what Van

Maren, Brahm or other pro-life influencers may believe. It appears the opposite may be true. Pro-life apologists are trying to mesh the two centuries of abolitionists together and grow frustrated and confused because they do not understand that 21st-century abolitionists are attempting to be far more legislatively organized, clear and aligned theologically than their past predecessors. Abortion abolitionists hope to reform where historical abolitionists fell short.

Even without these distinguished men of history, the Christian should look to God's Word to know how to rightly address preborn murder. They should look at history to conclude that some leading slavery abolitionists attempted to be biblically minded and consistent on ending slavery, and those efforts should be imitated *when those labors align with Scripture,* not simply based on whether those efforts were successful. The end does not justify the means in the kingdom of God. Biblically-minded abolitionists do not argue for the idolization of any historical figure as none are without flaws, but Christians can certainly learn from history and seek not to repeat its errors. The pro-life model, however, ignores the failed efforts of incremental measures to end slavery and instead catechizes culture and politics that it somehow will work this time around. It boasts that those who diverge from mainstream pro-life thinking should be ignored or canceled.

The Defense of Pro-life Dogma

In *Public Discourse*, eight prominent men within the Southern Baptist Convention (SBC) signed onto an article titled "Why We Opposed an Anti-Abortion Resolution at the Southern Baptist Convention."[19] The SBC resolution was distinctly abolitionist and used extensive Scripture for each point listed in its reasoning, similar to how the 1689 Baptist Confession of Faith is structured, the confessional the SBC adheres to. Yet the article signees Denny Burk, Alan Branch, Andrew T. Walker, Steve Lemke, Daniel Heimbach, C. Ben Mitchell, Jeffrey Riley, and Richard Land made an unusual stance against the abolition resolution without using Scripture to defend their own positions. It was a déjà vu moment of Rome demanding its doctrines were the correct ones and to be followed without scriptural proof to validate that claim. Instead, the article focused on an incorrect representation of ectopic pregnancies, a lack of understanding abolitionist politics, and a commitment to judicial supremacy. One excerpt from the article explained why the resolution goals are wrong:

> ...(1) it rejects incrementalism and (2) embraces the abolition of abortion with no exception for the life of the mother. Both of those provisions – if carried out in public policy – would lead to more destruction of innocent human life, not less.[20]

The first objection to abolition is simply that it is not incremental. For abolitionists, that is the point. It is a rejection of legislative attempts that have no grounding in Constitutional law or the Bible. An article by Silberman explains this differentiation:

> The abolitionist demands the immediate abolition of the evil; calling the evil what it is, watering nothing down, and grounding our demands in God's Word. The incrementalist asks for a compromise with the evil. The tragic consequence of this is that the incrementalist cannot ground their argument in anything substantial. For instance, the abolitionist demand for abortion to be abolished can be grounded in God's Word ("You shall not murder") and in the U.S. Constitution ("[No state shall] deny to any person within its jurisdiction the equal protection of the laws"). An incrementalist's demand for a 20-week abortion ban or a heartbeat bill cannot be defended from God's Word or the Constitution, as these laws...violate both.[21]

The second point listed as cause for concern comes down to a fundamental misunderstanding of the American justice system, duress law, and how abortion is actually defined in state statutes. This issue will be explored in depth in later chapters. For now it is worth stating there are already legal provisions for saving the lives of individuals under duress, including the life of a pregnant woman, and this law is used every day in every single state. The right to care for and save the lives of pregnant women under duress situations was not granted or invented by abortion law. Duress law existed prior to *Roe v. Wade*, and it is a red herring to argue that protection will dissipate along with *Roe*. Still, the authors of the *Public Discourse* article are not alone in their incremental sentiment. At the Southern Baptist Convention 2021, Dr. David Norman from San Antonio also argued against the abolition resolution:

> This resolution repudiates every pro-life resolution ever passed by the Southern Baptist Convention. Therefore, I move that we lay it on the table…We are a pro-life convention. We are anti-abortion. But this resolution requires that we walk back from every pro-life resolution we've passed.[22]

Norman's opposition, much like the authors of the *Public Discourse* article, focuses primarily on maintaining the legacy of what it means to be pro-life instead of evaluating whether that approach has always been biblical or is even now biblical. Christians should welcome debate. The pro-life individual has a fundamental interest in debating these political differences the same as an abolitionist should. Debate sharpens the mind, exposes error, and provides opportunity to change course when a better or more biblical approach is revealed. The pro-life appeal is largely to nostalgia, however, not biblical truths. When nostalgia fails, then pro-life apologists often move against abolitionists in a more personal manner, some of which has already been seen.

Pro-life apologist and founder of the Life Training Institute Scott Klusendorf wrote about the SBC abolition resolution in a *The Gospel Coalition* article where he singled out a pastor for pointing out the hypocrisy of two prominent pro-life legislators:

The implications for Christian fellowship are troubling. William Ascol—the pastor who sponsored the resolution—used a 2020 sermon to say SBC churches should summarily disfellowship Christian politicians who don't vote along abolitionist lines....In short, pro-life advocates are not only mistaken; they are willfully sinning. Denny Burk summarizes what follows if abolitionists are right about that: "It would obligate churches to shun pro-lifers through church discipline.... They have to remove the impenitent sinners from among them."[23]

Klusendorf left out some specific information when disparaging Ascol's sermon. In his sermon, Ascol was referencing Oklahoman Senator Jason Smalley (R-Dist. 28) and Senator Greg Treat (R-Dist.47), both Southern Baptists and both sabotagers of abolition bills.[24] These senators were among those who prevented Oklahoma abolition bill SB 13 from clearing committee while simultaneously advocating any effort to save the lives of the unborn. The overwhelmingly conservative Oklahoma house and senate have previously stated they would sign an abolition bill. It was likely abolition would have succeeded in Oklahoma had Smalley and Treat not interfered. Ascol was rebuking the deceitful and sinful behavior of two specific legislators; however, the rebuke served as a sensationalized moment to paint all abolitionists as unreasonable outliers and to cover the sins of two faithfully committed pro-life senators.

Expounding on the idea of the "unreasonableness" of abolition, Dr. Marc Newman of Speaker for Life wrote an opinion article, co-authored with Klusendorf, for *Townhall* titled "Trading Lives for Prophets." Newman and Klusendorf argue the SBC's decision to issue an abolition resolution is insulting to the pro-life movement because championing immediate abolition without compromise insinuates that "pro-life work to date has done nothing more than promote evil" and that "any incremental strategy – rather than immediate abolition – is suddenly a shameful act of which leaders must confess, lament and repent because it makes them complicit in abortion. Such a charge is scandalous and factually untrue."[25]

Is it "factually untrue" that incremental policies maintain the abortion industry and therefore make pro-life adherents "complicit in abortion?" Frances Kissling, founding president of the National Abortion Federation (NAF) and staunch abortion rights activist, would think so. In fact, Kissling supports pro-life policy that focuses on regulation and stalls from the end-goal of criminalization. In a *Washington Post* article penned in 2011, Kissling made this startling declaration:

> We need more responsible and compassionate state policies....For too long, abortion has been treated in black and white. Any discussion that deviates from legal or illegal, women or fetus, faces criticism from the twin absolutes of choice or life. If the choice movement does not change, control of policy on abortion will remain in the hands of those who want it criminalized. If we don't suggest *sensible balanced legislation and regulation of abortion,* we will be left with far more draconian policies - and, eventually, no choices at all.[26][Emphasis author's.]

She worried that the criminalization ideology would eventually win out, especially since those arguing for equality under the law for preborn humans have the Declaration of Independence, the U.S. Constitution's 5th and 14th amendments, the abolition of the slave institution, and the Bible to legally and morally bolster their positions. To thwart any chance of possibly losing all rights to abortion, Kissling suggested to her colleagues that they needed to get onboard with pro-life incremental laws and use them to their advantage. In history, something similar happened within the anti-slavery movement.

The most popular anti-slavery position was the colonization movement, an gradualist political system conjured in the slave-holding state of Virginia.[27] John

Randolph of Virginia had this to say about the proposal to begin the "anti-slavery" colonization movement:

> I thought it necessary to make these remarks, being myself a slaveholder, to show that, so far from being connected with the abolition of slavery, the measure proposed would prove one of the greatest securities to enable the master to keep in possession his own property.[27]

Thus the "anti-slavery" colonization movement was born. It recommended incremental strategies to eliminate slavery and return emancipated slaves back to Africa. It was a clever tactic to create a movement to gradually (or never) end something much of culture despised, while still preserving the very institution for those who found it profitable. Kissling recycled this idea in her proposal to get on board with abortion regulatory laws. She does not stand alone on the pro-choice side with this strategic vision. Michael Wear, a progressive Democrat, President Obama's former campaign strategist, and guest writer for *The Gospel Coalition* and the ERLC, preaches the same thing as Kissling on abortion policy:

> What would be healthier for our politics is for Congress to ask the extremes to accept something they don't like, as a change from the current task of asking the majority in the middle to choose between two extremes.[28]

Wear advocates for policies that appease Americans who fall midway between abolitionists and abortion-on-demand radicals. Instead of catechizing culture to either criminalize preborn murder or fully embrace it, he believes the middle road is the most pragmatic path forward. He continues with some ways in which to appease bipartisan abortion politics:

> *A sustainable compromise* would include the following elements: a federal ban on abortion post-viability with exceptions for the life of the mother, rape and incest (the ceiling); the legalization of abortion up to a certain early-stage in pregnancy (somewhere, perhaps, between 8-15 weeks, depending on the makeup of the coalition to support such a bill; the floor); the codification of the Hyde Amendment; the codification of robust conscience clause protections; a prohibition of federal laws overriding state restrictions on abortion as proposed by the WHPA; and a mandate that states ensure reasonable access to a safe abortion provider.[29] [Emphasis author's.]

Wear concludes Democrats need to "let go of their policy ambitions of legal abortion through viability" and likewise Republicans need to abandon "the dream of a federal abortion ban." In his pro-choice opinion, a compromise is more reasonable than the tug-of-war between those who want unlimited abortion and those who want preborn murder criminalized. He concludes everyone should work toward "a framework that makes the post-*Dobbs* and post-*Roe* landscape *sustainable,* objectionable to activists on both sides." [Emphasis author's.]

Identical language was used in the previous chapter by self-identifying conservatives such as Lauinger, Borchers and Proctor. Following this pattern, in response to the U.S. House passage of The Born-Alive Abortion Survivors Protection Act, National Right to Life wrote in a press release, "Democrats attempted to hijack this *common-sense vote* to push their agenda of abortion without limit until birth."[30] Carol Tobias, president of National Right to Life Committee testified: "The Born-Alive Abortion Survivors Protection Act is *reasonable legislation* that would protect a baby born alive following an abortion."[31] [Emphasis author's.]

The same language initiated by leading abortion activists to keep the abortion industry functioning and relevant is now the language largely used in pro-life spheres. "Compassionate policies," "sensible legislation," "sustainable protection," "reasonable legislation," and "regulation of abortion" are the primary strategies of the abortion industry to maintain itself and are now also the primary strategy of pro-life policies.

In 1857, John F. Gee, pastor of a church in Berea, KY, published *Colonization: the Present Scheme of Colonization Wrong, Delusive, and Retards Emancipation*, in which he observed, "We do not doubt that at its *organization*, some who were then engaged, were promoted by good motives, but led by erring judgments. So with some now cooperating."[32]

It appears the anti-abortion incremental approach, while filled with well-intentioned actors, has also been tainted with bad faith actors who perpetually stall equal protection and justice for the unborn, much like bad faith colonizers perpetuated against the slaves. It is unclear whether Klusendorf and other pro-life influencers are aware of their cooperation with pro-abortion activists on gradualism. Regardless, Newman and Klusendorf argue in their article, without the use of a single Bible verse, against the Scripture-infused SBC resolution and for the continued use of pro-life incrementalism. These authors warn that those who reject pro-life ideologies will be "unwitting" allies "of Planned Parenthood." They wrap up their plea to remain with pro-life politics by claiming abolitionists are nothing but "ideological purists" who will end up killing many children. According to Kissling, incremental policies that regulate the abortion industry are exactly what abortion advocates should want. Despite this glaring conundrum for the pro-life movement, instances of the pressure to uphold pro-life tenets lacking scriptural support abound.

During the Kansas campaign for the pro-life Value Them Both (VtB) amendment, a campaign volunteer lectured a wavering voter who had biblical concerns with the amendment, "If VtB fails, our state will become an abortion destination for the industry with 50-100K babies killed every year and you will have to live with the decision you made in allowing that to happen for advocating for a Vote No. While VtB does not abolish abortion, it will ensure that our state will not become a safe haven for those who want unlimited abortion."[33]

This emotionally-laden homily was not an isolated event. Another volunteer with VtB who identified herself as "Jane" also sent a message to a Kansas voter during a mass text campaign to encourage support for the amendment. When the recipient expressed concern that the amendment's wording could be interpreted by the courts to prevent a future abortion ban and that the Bible makes clear Christians cannot compromise on just laws, the volunteer responded:

> If you vote YES, we can have back regulations and limitations. Now, if you vote NO, together with Planned Parenthood, the Satan Church and the Democrat Party, we will become like California or New York. Do you really believe God wants you with the NO side? Do you really believe [it] is better not [to] have regulations just because it is not the perfect solution?[34]

In both instances, instead of addressing the concerns of the voter, the approach was to shame and emotionalize the issue. Each time the voter made clear he or she did not want to regulate abortion but wanted to abolish it, and instead of receiving clarification on how the VtB amendment would play out with a future abortion ban, there was only backlash for being anti-abortion and having the audacity to go against the pro-life narrative. The sentiment was not to educate voters and offer peace of mind to encourage a "yes" vote. Rather, amendment advocates used isolating tactics and fear that a voter's non-compliance would result in great doom upon the state.

The message continues to be if people do not accept pro-life philosophies then anything bad that happens is the nonconformist's fault. Echoing Pope Gregory XI's accusation of Wycliffe wanting "to overthrow the church and bring ruin to the land," pro-life politics proclaim this same allegation against anti-abortion detractors, charging them with wanting to destroy all the pro-life industry's hard work and bring ruin to the land by "killing many children" with their "ideological purist" fantasies.

The Religious Alt-Wrong

Religious leaders who should model biblically-led lives are not exempt from these hyperbolic tendencies when defending the pro-life model. While some mock abolitionists as the "alt-right of the pro-life movement" there is a section of religious leaders who are alternatively wrong on what abolition is and is not.

Timothy Keller, Presbyterian pastor, theologian and author, was a powerful influence in the American Christian sphere for decades. Founder of *The Gospel Coalition*, Keller's prominent power was widely formative in the evangelical world, and still is even amidst his recent death. In April 2022, Keller wrote, "I know abortion is a sin, but the Bible doesn't tell me the best political policy to decrease or end abortion in this country, nor which political or legal policies are most effective to that end. The current political parties will say that their policy most aligns morally with the Bible, but we are allowed to debate that and so our churches should not have disunity over debatable political differences."[35]

Keller's chastisement of abolitionists is more passive-aggressive than other staunch pro-life supporters, but his message remains the same: There is nothing morally wrong with writing anti-abortion policies that show partiality to some preborn image bearers over others, despite the clear biblical commands against writing and supporting such laws. Keller later wrote that some policies align closer to biblical tenets, yet refused to acknowledge how abolition political goals would fit that statement over current pro-life politicking models. The subtle but present idea Keller promoted was for abolitionists to stop insisting that their doctrines are the most biblical and instead allow varying political and moral disagreements on the abortion front.

One of the most unpleasant public antagonisms toward abolitionists occurred within the single largest Protestant denomination in America. Three months after being elected the new SBC President, Bart Barber took to Twitter to make known his commitment to pro-life doctrines by slandering a Southern Baptist abolitionist preacher.

Pastor Dusty Deevers of Elgin, OK issued a statement after Brent Leatherwood was appointed next president of the SBC Ethics & Religious Liberty Commission (ERLC). Deevers had grievance with this appointment because Leatherwood had signed the anti-criminalization of abortion letter released by National Right to Life and opposed the 2021 SBC abolition resolution. These acts are noticeably ironic for someone who now spearheads an ethics commission to promote equal rights for all humans. Deever's tweet pointed out this duplicity:

> Deevers, Dusty (@DustyDeevers): "In Louisiana this spring and at SBC annual meeting this summer, Brent Leatherwood sided against the innocent preborn; now he leads the ethics and policy arm of the SBC. We glory in our shame." 10:59 • 9/14/22

Within a day, Barber launched a Twitter attack against Deevers without discussing the context and history of Deever's criticism:

> Barber, Bart (@bartbarber): "This tweet represents the lowest point of dishonesty to which we can descend when we sell out to the crass tone of secular politics instead of following the way of Christ." 06:53 • 9/15/22

Keeping with the trend of Van Maren, Klusendorf and Newman, Barber's accusation of Deever hit at the offense of rejecting the historicity and tradition of the pro-life position. He equates Deever's rejection as being rooted in secular policies without using Scripture to explain how Deever's viewpoint is secularized and, conversely, his viewpoint biblical.

Sharing and embracing history provides identity and solidarity to people in an intimate way, but solely appealing to history to continue doing something should not be acceptable to Christians. God calls his people to discern through the lens of Scripture everything they think, say and do to determine if it aligns with his will and commandments. This includes the decision to continue with historical practices (on any issue) or reform them. The SBC's offense over its pro-life political history being disregarded or challenged is especially paradoxical coming from an organization founded on its pro-slavery sympathies and opposition to the anti-slavery attitudes of northern Baptists. Reverend Lucius Bolles, who served on the Baptist Board for Foreign Missions, declared in 1834: "There is a pleasing degree of union among the multiplying thousands of Baptists throughout the land...our southern brethren are generally, both ministers and people, slaveholders."[36]

Regardless of the multitude of Baptists who supported slavery, the chasm between northern and southern Baptists grew too wide to bridge, causing the 1845 formation of the Southern Baptist Convention. This opposition continued into the 20th-century with the SBC opposing the civil rights movement of the 1950s and '60s. Because of God's grace and sanctifying means in the lives of his people, the SBC adopted a resolution in 1995 that denounced its pro-slavery roots and resistance to equal rights for minorities. The organization reformed into one of the most diverse ethnic Protestant denominations today. Given this history, one would expect the SBC to be exceptionally cautious about appealing to its past. In particular, one would expect it not to be dismissive of cries from fellow Christians who warn that the SBC is making the same human rights mistake toward their unborn neighbors as was done toward their black brothers and sisters.

Still, Barber issued more than a dozen statements lashing out at Deevers, other abolitionists and Kansas abolition group AIM KS. In his attacks, he maligned multiple SBC pastors and members, profusely misquoted coercion and duress laws, and misrepresented abolition legislation. His errors were so widely drawn that a constitutional attorney and others knowledgeable of law and abolition legislation joined the thread in an effort to help correct the record and educate Barber. It escalated with Barber tweeting how Deever was obsessed with "sending 16-year-old girls to prison" for being coerced into abortion by their parents.[37] Deevers had never promoted any such thing. The justice system accounts for instances of people forced into criminal activity against their will and holds the instigators with guilty mens rea accountable, all of which Deevers is well aware from his years in working with legislation. In light of this, no 16 year old would go to jail for the crimes of her parents. It was an unsubstantiated insult from a high-ranking Southern Baptist leader. Calls for Barber to repent and ask forgiveness for his defaming remarks and ignorance poured out. What followed was a less than powerful apology attempt:

> Barber, Bart (@bartbarber): "A little more than a month ago, I used the word 'obsession' to describe @DustyDeevers's approach to abortion law, specifically with regard to coerced minors. I repent of that. The word 'obsession' not only assumes motivation but also implies something bordering upon mental instability. It's an inflammatory and accusatory word. What makes it worse is that I did it intentionally because I was angry—angry at Deevers's unwarranted and unprovoked attacks against @LeatherwoodERLC. In my anger, I sought to match Deevers's own hyperbolic incivility. But my actual job is not to mimic Deevers hyperbolic incivility; my actual job is to imitate Christ's gracious truth-telling. And I know...everyone moved past this weeks ago. But the Holy Spirit has not. And so, I apologize for my intemperate tweeting, I retract the word 'obsession,' I thank those of you who called me out on it back then, and covet your prayers for me to do better." 06:53 • 9/15/22

Repentance is one of the main doctrines of the Christian faith. It is an ongoing act of the sanctification process as Christians are changed by the Holy Spirit to look more like the image of their Savior. Martin Luther wrote in his 95 theses, "When our Lord and Master Jesus Christ said, 'Repent' (Matthew 4:17), he willed the entire life of believers to be one of repentance." Using repentance as a moral posture to continue grandstanding against another person is an affront against the Holy Spirit who draws believers to true repentance. Insincere repentance makes a mockery of the Holy Spirit's sanctifying work. It is also indicative of a heart that is unmoved to consider its own faults.

The Sphere of Sovereignty and the Consequence of Doctrines

Why is there such a schism between pro-life and abolition politics? Why is there pressure for all those against abortion to align with the pro-life model and recant other views of justice? Ultimately, it comes down to differing kingdom views. The idea to incrementally push back against a wicked society comes from an entirely different worldview and ideology than that of most abolitionists. As explored in chapter two, it assumes a soft touch to appear loving toward abortive women and a pagan culture. Instead of an abrupt demarcation against the pro-abortion movement, the pro-life industry draws vanishing lines in the sand based on what it gauges to work in the moment. Abolitionists believe in holding the line firmly against *all* preborn murder, as Scripture is clear on the punishment for murder and other unjust laws. As such, abolitionists are concerned with loving God (1 John 5:2-3) more than loving a culture that is hostile to their King. A morally debased culture is unable to determine what true love is as defined by the Bible, and rejects the appeal of biblical love. The culture prefers to redefine 1 Corinthians 13 to mean Christians must permit the evil that pleases others, never say anything that could be misconstrued as offensive, and "live and let live" instead of discipling others in biblical ethics as Christians have been commissioned to do (Matthew 28). Fundamentally, as all Scripture ties back to the One who breathed it, Christians know popular Bible verses on love always have in mind their imitation of their Lord. Christ was kind. Christ was patient. He certainly did not insist on his own way but submitted to the Father's will (Matthew 26:39). But Christ also never allowed evil to go unrebuked (Matthew 12:34), he never compromised loyalty to the Godhead (Matthew 4:1-11), and he spoke truth even when the culture took offense (John 10:31-39). This is what Christians are to imitate, even in politics. When the culture takes offense at a stubborn stance against compromised bills, believers can take solace in knowing their obedience to God is all that is required for victory (1 John 5:2-5).

Coincidentally, this stance puts abolition doctrine at odds with secular pro-life doctrine because of the difference between piety and pietism. Leading Protestant theologians have warned for a century the danger of growing pietism within

Christian culture that seduces individuals to pursue personal holiness at the cost of evangelizing the greater culture. Theologian R.C. Sproul Jr. describes pietism as "deeply gnostic" and "radically individualistic" and that the movement "eschews political involvement, denigrates the exercise of dominion and sometimes adds to the law of God."[38] Because of pietism's heightened focus on improving the individual soul, the biblical command to advance the gospel and kingdom of God falls by the wayside. In fact, the idea of improving oneself spiritually is often used as an excuse to recoil from the culture rather than to exert Christian change. Pietism shifts the focus from living Christian theology in all spheres of life to instead living it primarily privatized. Pietism teaches individuals that God only holds accountable their personal lives such as at church and in the family but that God understands compromises and gray areas in public policies. This results in delineating God's kingdom from politics, saying it treats government as a separate entity from God's sovereign reign and establishment. This leads to a bifurcated view of God's kingdom. Instead of taking Christ at his word that *all* visible and invisible realities are under his sovereign control, Christians excuse the use of secular tactics, pragmatism and postmodern moralism within the domain of politics, careers, or other "secularly allotted" areas. It is helpful to represent this with a picture.

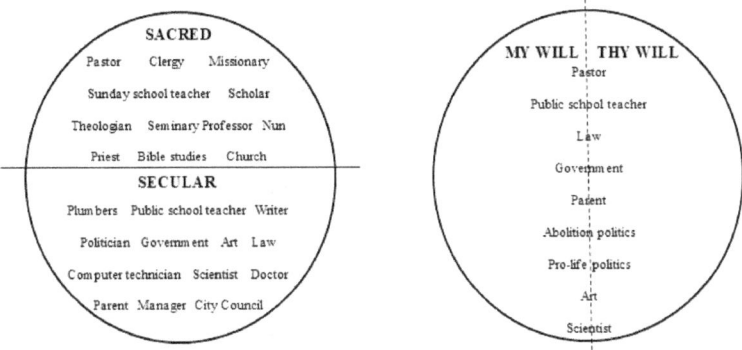

The first sphere denotes pietism's view of God's kingdom, the Christian's role in culture, and the use of ethics. It promotes spheres of life as either secular or sacred, a philosophy to which Plato ascribed. Those things that fall within the "sacred" category are ones Christians should uphold according to God's law.

Those that fall within the secular domain are not necessarily bound by God's law but are acceptable before God on a "best effort" mentality. Piety, on the other hand, is the godliness of character across *all* spheres of life. It seeks to integrate one's faith into all life dimensions. Piety views all of life as subordinate to Christ's reign and as a mission field for expanding the kingdom of God. Abraham Kuyper emphasizes, "There's not one square inch in the whole domain of human existence as to which Christ who is sovereign over all does not cry out, 'Mine!' And my opinion is, if Christ calls out, 'Mine!' over every square inch of human existence, the church has to call out, 'His!'"[39]

Piety, therefore, sees every issue as being used either to glorify the self or to glorify God. Whatever the scenario, piety teaches a response to any stimuli is either an opportunity to obey or rebel against God's commands. This is not hard to envision. Can a man sin or honor God in ministry? Certainly. A preacher can preach the whole counsel of God and live a life of consistent biblical ethics, or he can become conceited, teach a false gospel, and lead people astray. Can a woman sin or honor God with abortion? Certainly. A woman can choose to observe the biblical command to not murder and honor God through that obedience, or she can choose to end the life of her unborn child and break God's law. The list is endless; but it always comes down to an individual operating as a covenant keeper or a covenant breaker. Author Gary North says "there is a political-theological war going on throughout history" between covenant keepers of God's laws and covenant breakers. Covenant breakers seek to set up secular ethics as sovereign in place of God. The issue that results from this continual battle is never a cease-fire but constant tension, as there is no way to reconcile the differences between the kingdom of light and the kingdom of darkness. Presently, as the secularist fights the hardest to advance a culture of anti-God ethics, American Christians delve deeper into pietism, which only puffs up the individual. The result is relinquishing godly dominion over the land to those who hate their Creator, and falling in line with a culture ashamed of the gospel. North continues his thoughts on this war every Christian is engaged in, whether he or she desires to be or not:

> *This is a war for the hearts and minds of men. It is also inevitably a war for the lawful control over all of mankind's institutions.* There is not one grain of sand, not one soul, not one seat or authority, that is outside this battlefield. What is the official god of society? A *society's god is its publicly designated source of law.* Thus, a society's legal order will testify to the nature and character of its god. The legal order will support that god and its followers .... Civil law inevitably promotes one group's goals for society and suppresses other groups' goals. This is why there can be no religious neutrality in history. This is also why there can be no religious neutrality in politics and civil law.[40]

Society can only surrender to one source of absolute authority. If Christians concede ground, they are giving permission to the irreligious to construct idols in their own images in which to govern the whole of society. Every person must choose which laws will be established and followed within our land – the rules of God, or the lawlessness of man.

As cultural theologian P. Andrew Sandlin says, "Pietism inevitably leads to worldliness, because if we limit Christian concerns to the family and church, dominant anti-Christian ideas in the culture will shape our thinking. Unless we claim all areas of life for Christ the King, those areas we refuse to contest will eventually rule over us."[41]

Pietism is spiritually dangerous because it leads Christians to excuse themselves from understanding what is morally expected of them in all areas of life. This comes in quite handy for the cultural or nominal Christian who is always searching for the most comfortable and least offensive position to take in difficult circumstances. Because of this, pietism makes way for situational ethics to replace biblical ethics in the political sphere, the exact issue seen between pro-life politics and abolition politics. Pietism permits pragmatism. Piety pursues God.

R.C. Sproul wrote, "Obviously there must be a relationship between our ethical theories and our moral behavior."[42] With pietism, Christians are served an inconsistent model of professing one thing to be wrong (abortion is murder) and then writing and passing laws that teach it is not *always wrong* (abortion only on the preborn younger than twenty weeks). This ultimately reveals pro-life morals as not overly concerned with abortion as murder despite its confessed ethics of it being such. Sproul Jr. further explains:

> It is commonplace to hear the lament that some Christians, notably conservatives, are so rigidly bound by moralistic guidelines that everything becomes for them a matter of "black and white" with no room for "gray" areas. Those who persist in fleeing from the gray, seeking refuge in the sharply defined areas of white and black, suffer from the epithets "brittle" or "dogmatic." However, the Christian must seek for righteousness and never be satisfied with living in the smog of perpetual grayness. He wants to know where the right way is located, where the path of righteousness lies. There is a right and there is a wrong. The difference between them is the concern of ethics.[43]

When abolitionists voice concern with wanting to understand how to biblically address abortion through legislation and ministries, they are often met with scoff from critics. It should be the concern of every Christian to seek "where the path of righteousness lies" on every issue, especially abortion. If not, pietism marches us down the path toward statist doormats. When Christians refuse to take the hardline against a calloused culture, that same culture turns around to happily stomp all over such craven believers. Dr. Joseph Boot writes many Christians "have lost their cultural memory of God-given, *pre-political* institutions, rights and responsibilities that are to be protected, but are not *created, controlled* or *governed* by the state."[44] As such, he direly describes the reality of the average American Christian:

As a consequence, believers have floundered in their response to unprecedented and illegal lockdowns of the church, the growing collapse of civil liberties, the total control of education, expanded abortions, euthanasia, no-fault divorce law, the redefinition of marriage and the family, homosexuality and transgender issues, largely because a scriptural world and life view norming our understanding of these questions and the role of the state with respect to them has collapsed."[45]

Many well-meaning brothers and sisters in Christ dedicate themselves to the secular bipartisan politics of the pro-life movement and passionately embrace gradualism without a second thought. Leading this charge are those who intellectually and theologically should know better but denounce abolitionist biblical principles and expect their recantation from piety.

The Call to Recant is Empty

Through the modern day vitriol one can almost hear ancient Rome's accusations against Protestants being "dangerous heretics," "haters of the Christian religion," "denier of doctrines", and "infected" with poor ideas. The Waldensians, John Wycliffe, John Huss, Martin Luther, William Tyndale, John Calvin and hundreds of other Reformers had to contend with hostility from an organization that despised the threat against it. Through the allegations, both against past Reformers and today's abolitionists, Scripture is left off the table as the means for convincing and converting. Ancient Rome was not interested in persuading Protestants with Scripture because the structure of the Roman Catholic church ultimately is not to the allegiance of God's Word but to the office of the Magisterium. Karl Keating, a leading Catholic apologist puts it simply:

> But the basis for one's belief in its inspiration directly affects how one goes about interpreting the Bible. The Catholic believes in

inspiration because the Church tells him so – that is putting it bluntly – and that same Church has the authority to interpret the inspired text. Fundamentalists believe in inspiration, although on weak grounds, but they have no interpreting authority other than themselves.[46]

Keating says that Catholics' confidence in the inspiration and use of Scripture comes from the assurance of it from the Roman Catholic church leadership. By contrast, Protestants, or "fundamentalists" as Keating writes, draw their belief of inspiration and use of Scripture from God's Word itself. For the Catholic, the Magisterium is logically deduced to be in a position of higher authority than that of Scripture. White remarks in *The Roman Catholic Controversy*, "In either case the issue will not be *what the actual text of Scripture says*, but what the Roman Catholic church, claiming Christ's special empowerment, *says* it says."[47]

During the Reformation period, Rome took offense at *its* authority being challenged, not any supposed misuse of Scripture. This relationship between Protestants' desires to obey Scripture alone and Rome's claim that it alone can understand and teach what Scripture actually means provides an important lesson today. Because of the severe and obvious lack of Scripture used by pro-life advocates to convince abolitionists to recant, one can only conclude that once again Scripture is not the priority to preserve. Christians and conservatives are expected to obediently accept the official position of the pro-life movement as correct and submit. Scripture appears unnecessary in the defense of pro-life doctrines; thus, the threat against the pro-life movement is against its authority, not concerns with abolition doctrine being unbiblical.

Protestant Christians tend to dismiss the seriousness of this. Many professing Christians ignorantly think that pressure to bend on God's Word comes from the world, not from within the church. When ostracism occurs within the religious pro-life sphere on the basis of abolition politics, many believers dismiss it as the abolitionist just being off his rocker. This is because pro-life politics have been accepted as "Christian" by the majority of church-goers. When someone is viewed as dissenting from pro-life ideologies, that individual is ultimately viewed as apostating from Scripture. It is not necessary to vet through the lens of the Bible the differences of these political viewpoints because the pro-life political model is already commonly accepted as being in alignment with Scripture. Apparently, it is the thought that counts, not the evidence.

One has only to look at the Reformation period to understand the great pressure and persecution those Christians experienced came *primarily* from within the church, and the Christian slavery abolitionists were ridiculed, disciplined by their churches, or declared heretics by Presbyterian, Baptist, Methodist and Congregational ministers. As anti-slavery colonizationist minister Joel Parker said in regard to slavery abolition, "Abolitionism might be pronounced a sin as well as slavery."[48] Despite these historical lessons, many modern Christian leaders remain resistant to denounce worldly practices of the pro-life movement because they view it as "Christian" and give it unfettered approval. It is proving costly and difficult to criticize. Many seminary leaders, renowned Christian apologists and pastors strongly adhere to pro-life political tactics and are ready to vigilantly beat back any dissenters who question it. For either side, it is a dangerous game to play when custom usurps the clear truths of God. Matthew 15:1-9 provides a powerful lesson for both pro-lifers and abolitionists:

> Then Pharisees and scribes came to Jesus from Jerusalem and said, "Why do your disciples break the tradition of the elders? For they do not wash their hands when they eat." He answered them, "And why do you break the commandment of God for the sake of your tradition? For God commanded, 'Honor your father and your mother,' and, 'Whoever reviles father or mother must surely die.' But you say, 'If anyone tells his father or his mother, "What you would have gained from me is given to God," he need not honor his father.' So for the sake of your tradition you have made void the word of God. You hypocrites! Well did Isaiah prophesy of you, when he said: 'This people honors me with their lips, but

their heart is far from me; in vain do they worship me, teaching as doctrines the commandments of men.'"

The Jewish leaders were offended the disciples were not adhering to the rigorous handwashing rituals of the Pharisees. The offense was so great these leaders considered the disciples to be breaking the "tradition of the elders" which they considered authoritative and divinely handed down through the ages. To their shock, Jesus harshly rebukes and accuses them of nullifying the very commands of God to satisfy man-made tradition, which in this case was the corban rule, a Jewish law that authorized a man to leave all his belongings to the Temple instead of upholding God's command to care for his parents in their advanced age. How is this relevant? In the case of the pro-life cause, it claims a moral obligation to legally compromise on preborn murder if that is what needs to be done to have some immediate success. The compromise over which image bearers receive legal protection varies from the age of the unborn human, to how a baby is conceived, to whether the child can feel pain yet, and the list continues. In this sense, the man-made tradition to politically take whatever conservatives can get when it comes to anti-abortion legislation nullifies God's commands on establishing justice.

The Bible gives clear instructions to not murder (Exodus 20:13), to show no partiality (James 2:1-4; Leviticus 19:5; 1 Timothy 5:21; Deuteronomy 1:17), to do good and love justice (Amos 5:7), to not make ungodly alliances (Isaiah 30:1), to not withhold justice from the oppressed (Isaiah 10:1-3), to not make friends with the world (James 4:4), and to do no evil so that good may come (Romans 3:8). Instead, the pro-life philosophy teaches if one does *not* violate these commands in order to save what babies they can, then that person's position is evil and he or she will be liable for the blood of slaughtered babies.

It is an emboldened move to call evil that which God calls righteous. God's law says thou shalt murder *no one*. Pro-life law says thou shalt not murder *that* one. It is a direct contradiction to the clear message of the Bible and rings of the serpent's message in the garden: "Did God really say?"

If You Love Me You Will Keep My Commandments

Whether it is pietism versus piety, immediate versus incremental, or tradition versus Scripture, abolitionists and pro-lifers must both decide between two choices: obey God's Word regardless of the consequences, or defy God's Word for humanistic victories but at the cost of God's judgment. One route is accepted on the basis of faith and the other pursued on the basis of pragmatism. Christians should not be hesitant or fearful to faithfully follow God's commands. The limitation of what people can achieve forces Christians to rely on the sufficiency of Scripture and the promises of God. Regrettably, the pressure from the pro-life position suggests it is worse to reject situational ethics than to reject God's Word. Scripture offers a different perspective.

When Moses was first commissioned by God to stand before Pharaoh, he had only one simple demand: that Egypt should allow the Israelites to worship their God in the wilderness. Pharaoh was less than impressed with such a bold appeal and replied, "Who is the Lord, that I should obey his voice and let Israel go? I do not know the Lord, and moreover, I will not let Israel go." Moses implored Pharaoh to listen "lest God fall upon us with great pestilence or the sword" for any delayed obedience. Multiple times Moses petitioned Pharaoh with what God had commanded of him. Each time Moses returned with the same demand: Let the Israelites worship their God in the wilderness.

Pharaoh, growing noticeably annoyed, began responding with compromises. He offered for them to serve their God within Egypt (Exodus 8:21); he then proposed they could serve their God in the wilderness but not travel the required three days' journey (Exodus 8:24); later he offered for only the men to travel to the wilderness despite God's command for *all* of Israel to go including women and children (Exodus 10:11); and lastly, Pharaoh was willing to allow all the people to go but they had to leave their flocks behind, the means necessary for offering sacrifice and feasting in celebration to the God of Israel (Exodus 10:24). Moses refused to accept any of the proposed compromises. Pharaoh likewise remained steadfast in his refusal, and, in response to Moses' brazen appeal, he increased the work and sufferings of the people saying, "They are idle. Therefore they cry, 'Let us go and offer sacrifice to our God.'" Moses' lack of compromise came at great temporary expense to the people of Israel, and the Israelites made known their displeasure with Moses' faithfulness to God and ruffling of Pharaoh:

> The foremen of the people of Israel saw that they were in trouble when they said, "You shall by no means reduce your number of bricks, your daily task each day." They met Moses and Aaron, who were waiting for them, as they came out from Pharaoh; and they said to them, "The Lord look on you and judge, because you have made us stink in the sight of Pharaoh and his servants, and have put a sword in their hand to kill us" (Exodus 5:19-21).

Feeling the pull between honoring God or acquiescing Pharaoh for temporary reprieve, Moses turned to God and cried out, "O Lord, why have you done evil to this people? Why did you ever send me? For since I came to Pharaoh to speak in your name, he has done evil to this people, and you have not delivered your people at all" (Exodus 5:22-23). Only after Moses remained committed to God's way, and Pharaoh had stored up wrath for himself, did God respond with the powerful statement, "*Now* you shall see what *I* will do to Pharaoh."

Did God respond in anger that Moses had not done something on his own to alleviate the groans of the people? Did God question why Moses did not take what he could get in order to save the Israelites from *some* persecution? No. In fact, God's response shows it went exactly as planned. Likewise, Christians should be just as committed to God's way in their anti-abortion methods. Though it is uncomfortable, Christians must trust God will someday deliver the nation from its bloodguilt. When believers are tempted to meet half-way with the world on the issue of prenatal homicide, and they comfort themselves by saying, "Surely God will understand the good intentions of our hearts and bless our nation and give us victory over great evil even though we have purposely neglected to uphold his full commands," it would be prudent to heed God's disposition toward unjust laws and those who propagate them.

Scripture declares "woe to those who decree iniquitous decrees and make the fatherless prey (Isaiah 10:1-3), it forbids that we do injustice in court or show partiality (Leviticus 19:15), it commands that we cease to do evil, learn to do good, and seek justice (Isaiah 1:16-17), it warns that "he who justifies the wicked and he who condemns the righteous are both alike an abomination to the Lord (Proverbs 17:15)", it implores that we defend the rights of the needy (Proverbs 31:8), and says unequal weights and measures are an abomination to the LORD (Proverbs 11:1; 16:11; 20:10; 20:23). Most importantly, Scripture explains "We must obey God rather than men (Acts 5:29)" and that if we belong to Christ we will keep his commandments (John 14:15).

Protestant Christians should take these Scriptures seriously and scrutinize legislation through a biblical lens. A bill of compromise means merging God's standard (do not murder) with secular ethics (do not murder *those over 12 weeks*). Worldly wisdom says those who refuse to accept compromised bills are unreasonable, self-righteous and ideological purists. But the God-breathed words of Scripture praises the one who resists worldly wisdom (2 Corinthians 1:12;17; Titus 2:11-12; 1 John 2:15; James 3:17) because the foolishness of God is still yet wiser than men (Corinthians 1:25), because his ways are higher than man's ways and his thoughts higher than man's thoughts (Isaiah 55:9), and the faithful, not the cowardly, will be rewarded (Revelation 21:5-8) in their perseverance until the end. Rejecting pragmatism means rejecting what can be seen and controlled and obediently embracing through faith what only God can see and control. It makes Christ greater and man less (John 3:30) in the victory of ending abortion. More importantly, as John 14:15 teaches, if we love God we will keep his commandments on the issue of impartial lawmaking.

Siphoning politics away from God's authority as practiced by pro-life pietism reveals a fractured understanding of Christ's tri-fold position as prophet, priest and king. Jesus came as a prophet to declare what God's law requires and the judgment that awaits the disobedient and unrepentant (Matthew 5:17). As priest,

Christ intercedes for his people continually and stands to satisfy fully the commandments of God on their behalf (Hebrews 7:25-26). As king, Christ expects nothing less than full submission to his kingship in all areas of life for both the believer and the unbeliever (Matthew 28:18-20). He makes no concession for pietism. The bride of Christ would be biblically wise to apply these truths logically and literally in advocated policies. For the abolitionist, the ultimate goal is to look like Christ on the issue of abortion and to submit to his kingship, even in the face of pro-life calls to recant immediatism. God will abolish abortion for he detests wickedness and injustice, and he will work the means of ending abortion through his faithful people *for his glory alone* despite all odds. The call to be obedient sets Christians apart from the world as holy (1 Peter 1:14-15) and testifies to their love for their Lord over any love of man (John 14:15). When the calls to recant, be silent or be reviled ring loud from either culture or the church, abolitionists must say with the Reformers of old, "Show us where in Scripture we have erred and we will gladly renounce our beliefs." There can be no compromise with evil.

5

REPEATING HISTORY: PROTESTANT RESISTANCE AND CATHOLIC OPPOSITION TO ABOLITION

"Where God's image is lost, Satan's image is introduced." – William Williams, Puritan (1666-1741)

The Power of the Church

PRESBYTERIAN MINISTER ALBERT BARNES once grieved, "There is no power out of the church that could sustain slavery an hour, if it were not sustained in it."[1] This blunt criticism against his American Christian counterparts was not without merit. After all, 19th-century churches were mixed with a heavy dose of those who supported slavery or others noncommittal to ending it. A spirit of apathy and compromise flowed from church-goers who considered themselves anti-slavery but still supported each state to do what it wanted with the institution, desired to regulate slavery to prevent its expansion, or championed returning emancipated slaves back to Africa instead of giving them the same rights as whites within the Union.

Immediate abolitionists, however, demanded something entirely different. Immediatists argued for the quick, uncompromised end of the slave industry throughout the *entire* union and also demanded their black neighbors be integrated equally into society and given the same privileges and protections under the law. This rarely succeeded within the churches. Historian John McKivigan observes, "Although some northern churchmen publicly supported anti-slavery political positions and parties, before the Civil War no major denomination endorsed immediate emancipation."[2]

While the slavery abolition crusade was almost entirely Protestant driven, scholars are referencing *individual members* with evangelical roots rather than denominations at large. Even though the abolition movement was primarily comprised of Protestant Christians, it did not mean they were a representation of the majority of their faith groups "for all but a few denominations refused to condemn slaveholding as sinful or to endorse immediate emancipation."[3]

The unfortunate reality is abolition was unpopular within churches as much as it was outside of them (This is an important correlation to the abortion crisis today). A bulk of Protestant religious leaders considered themselves anti-slavery, yet argued their primary concern was the gospel and not political issues. This mantra became a comfortable and common excuse to avoid entering the slavery debate. As one Baptist minister said, "Slavery is a political institution. As a Christian minister, I have nothing to do with politics. My business is to preach the gospel, and try to save men's souls."[4]

While much of the clergy tried to avoid scuffling over the slave issue, abolitionists were not so bashful about it. As such, abolitionists were by far the minority. The movement was "a powerless and marginal handful of practitioners"[5] and drew far more powerful insults against it than it could affect politically. Church resistance to abolition swelled from pacifist excuses to outright vehement opposition. Many ministers, both anti- and pro-slavery, were not restrained in their detestation of immediate abolitionist principles:

> Abolitionism might be pronounced a sin as well as slavery.[6] – Reverend Joel Parker, anti-slavery President of the Presbyterian Theological Seminary in New York

That slavery as it exists in the South is no evil, and is consistent with the principles of revealed religion; and that all opposition to it arises from a misguided and fiendish fanaticism, which we are bound to resist in the very threshold. That all interference with this subject by fanatics is a violation of our civil and social rights – and is unchristian and inhuman, leading necessarily to anarchy and bloodshed; and that the instigators [abolitionists] are murderers and assassins.[7] – J. H. Thornwell, pro-slavery Methodist minister

Abolitionists are like infidels, wholly unaddicted to martyrdom for opinion's sake. Let them understand that they will be caught [lynched] if they come among us, and they will take good heed to keep out of our way.[8] – William S. Plummer, anti-slavery Presbyterian minister

I design to offer a preamble and string of resolutions on the subject…of the treasonable and abominably wicked interference of the Northern and Eastern fanatics with our political and civil rights, our property and our domestic concerns. You are aware that our clergy, whether with or without reason, are more suspected by the public than the clergy of other denominations. Now, *dear Christian brethren*, I humbly express it as my earnest wish, that you *quit yourselves like men*. If there be any stray goat of a minister among you, tainted with the blood-hound principles of abolitionism, let him be ferreted out, silenced, excommunicated, and left to the public to dispose of him in other respects.[9] – Robert N. Anderson, pro-slavery Presbyterian minister

> From 1838 to 1857 we were among their sturdiest opponents, and in our own sphere, we have done as much as any other man in the country to set Catholics against the abolition movement.[10] – Orestes Brownson, anti-slavery Catholic clergyman

> I subscribe myself, the friend of the Bible, and the opposer of Abolitionists.[11] – J.C. Postell, pro-slavery Methodist minister

Abolitionism was not popular, but abolitionists had high expectations of changing the moral landscape of the churches they attended. These reformers expected comradery with the clergy as most ministers from various denominations "were thought to be sympathetic to reform" and had been "involved in the movement to colonize free blacks in America."[12] Yet abolition optimism came despite historical forewarnings.

In the early post-Revolution era, most denominations expressed concern about the potential economic fall-out of immediate emancipation. Many Americans worried that freeing thousands of black men and women all at once would create job loss for free whites, create permanent class disparity between what they believed to be superior and inferior ethnic groups, induce violence against white people, and encourage intermarrying of the races. Despite those concerns, freeing slaves without exceptions remained a main tenet of abolition.

Congressman James Henry Hammond complained, "Although I am perfectly satisfied that no human process can elevate the black man to an equality with the white – admitting that it could be done – are we prepared for the consequence which then must follow?"[13] The resounding conclusion was no. The majority of Americans – even anti-slavery professing Christians – were not eager to suffer any economic or cultural hardship that accompanied the abolition of slavery. Instead, "gradually eliminating the system without destroying Southern culture" and the greater American culture became a primary objective of the anti-abolition, anti-slavery movement.[14]

A Sin or Not a Sin: That is *the* Question

While colonization and abolition both claimed to be tenets of the anti-slavery movement, they were at points starkly different from one another. Abolitionists generally believed all people, both white and black, should have equal protection and justice under the same laws. This meant the criminalization of slavery. Immediatists also believed that freed slaves should be integrated into white society without segregating them to separate church pews, schools, businesses, careers and housing districts. More importantly, they argued slavery was a sin because it violated the Great Commandment to love one's neighbor as oneself. Those who supported slavery or turned a blind eye to it needed to repent before God, abolitionists argued, so the nation could heal and judgment from God be withheld. Because sin is strictly a biblical concept of being in rebellion to God's will and law, the only appropriate response when caught in it is what God has prescribed: an abrupt departure from that sin. God's word has defined anything less than immediacy in repentance to not be true repentance but willful disobedience. Abolitionists sought to apply this immediacy to the concept of law. This set them apart from other anti-slavery sects.

The belief that human chattel slavery was sin is what fueled the abolition call for the immediate end of it in all forms. As famous slavery abolitionist William Lloyd Garrison titled a speech, there could be "no compromise with slavery."[15] Abolitionists were resolved to not cooperate with what they believed to be evil. Catholic intellectual Orestes Brownson, though himself an anti-slavery colonizer, wrote that "abolitionists demand the abolition of slavery on the ground that slavery is unjust, a sin, and no people has the right to tolerate it." He observed they "demand not only the freedom of the slave as a man, the complete and unreserved recognition of his manhood, but the full and unreserved recognition of the equality of the negro race with the white race."[16]

Abortion abolition is on par with this historic ideology. Abolitionists today argue the preborn should be legally equal to born people under homicide laws. They also argue for urgency to legally protect the lives of the preborn and to cease heralding regulatory legislative efforts. Slavery abolitionists contested the same thing in their era. They were against the idea of regulating slavery and trying to contain it within only the southern states. These forerunners rejected partially ending slavery through voluntary manumission efforts. Abolitionists adhered to the biblical view on the sanctity of every human life and the complementary view of the Declaration of Independence, which states, "all men are created equal; that they are endowed by their Creator with certain inalienable rights; that among these are life, liberty, and the pursuit of happiness."

Garrison once put this charge to abolition opponents: "Convince me that one man may rightfully make another man his slave, and I will no longer subscribe to the Declaration of Independence."[17]

On the other hand, anti-slavery colonization opposed almost all abolition beliefs. Colonizers did not desire to integrate freed blacks into white culture. Some feared the slave population was such an oppressed class of humans that they would never survive against a thriving white class. For these colonizers, they thought it best to return former slaves to their country of origin. The more sinister attitude within colonization was the belief black people were by nature inferior to whites and did not deserve, nor could they maintain, the same legal, political or social equality to white men and women. Those who held that viewpoint, while they may have disdained slavery, felt no urgent compulsion to eradicate it.

Regardless of the reason someone was drawn to colonization, one thing almost all colonizers agreed upon was an incremental strategy to end slavery. Their efforts focused on regulating slavery's expansion, managing how slave masters treated their slaves, offering money as an incentive to release slaves, and advancing their primary goal of returning emancipated slaves to Africa. Their end goal was never equality under American law.

The most important distinction between abolition and colonization is that most colonizers did not view slavery as a transgression; therefore, colonizers were not fundamental about applying the label of sin to slavery. Colonization largely garnered support from individuals who grimaced at the idea of slavery but believed blacks would remain intellectually and economically inferior to whites. These colonizers argued black men and women would suffer if they were left to compete among a "superior race."[18] This position was used to brand colonization as sympathetic to both slave owners *and* slaves. Colonization insisted it wanted what was best for the black person while simultaneously showing compassion to slave holders' needs and concerns. Once all the fancy marketing was removed, whether intentional or unintentional, the anti-slavery colonization was nothing more than a movement to continue propping up the interests of white men and women over the interests of enslaved individuals. Freed blacks, who felt forced into the colonization views and chose to emigrate, admitted, "No well-informed colonizationist is a devoted friend to . . . people of color."[19]

Another reason colonizers did not frame slavery as sinful is because many believed chattel slavery was permissible by the Bible and the Constitution. They fretted very little about the immorality or illegality of it. Much of anti-slavery America desired for slaves to be *less oppressed* rather than *unoppressed*. As such, the movement consisted of those who wanted to feel as if they were doing something to combat a distasteful institution without having to commit to offering the same benefits whites enjoyed to those whom they saw as mistreated.

To further detract from whether or not slavery was a sin issue, and to prolong its incremental response, many colonizers complained that criminalizing slavery would not change the hearts of people. This tagline gained popularity in efforts to stall or thwart abolition efforts to criminalize the "peculiar institution," as the South called it. "You can't change hearts by law,"[20] abolition opponents complained. These same individuals insisted ethnic discrimination would only end through the "slow process of education"[21] and time, not legislative efforts. McKivigan writes, "...church anti-slavery sentiment concentrated instead on ameliorative programs such as missionary work among slaves and advocacy of colonization."[22]

The quest for this enlightened education of the slave's humanity moved colonizers toward a method of emancipation which offended abolitionists and the slave population alike. One emancipation proposal was to pay slaveholders to release their slaves. By using monetary enticement to convince masters to do right by their slaves, it helped avoid the states' rights debate and avoided offending the South by calling their way of life sinful. It was also meant to cover any financial hardships associated with choosing freedom for their "property." Brownson boasted Catholics were prepared to "pay the slaveholders their pound of flesh,"[23] and Hammond argued "even the British Government did not dare to emancipate...without some compensation" and, therefore, the United States could "scarcely be expected...to free our slaves without paying for them."[24]

Immediatists abhorred this arrangement. "Slaveholders insist upon compensation if they emancipate their slaves," they cried. "...for what? For averting the wrath of God?"[25] It was unsettling to most abolitionists that the nation should pay for the wicked to flee from evil. Not only was it an unbiblical means to call someone away from transgression, but it was further insulting to the slaves who would benefit nothing while their slave masters profited further for their ill-misfortunes. The message marketed by colonization matched the slave trade's own messaging: A slave's life was only worth what one was willing to pay for it. Their lives certainly were not worth the protection of the law, according to mainstream anti-slavery doctrine.

Offering financial incentive to not harm others infuriated both abolitionists and former slaves who believed the best incentive would be the protection of the law, not the purse of the government. Out of frustration at this cowardly bargain with slaveholders, the abolition American Anti-Slavery Almanac printed this in 1841:

> A rescue from weakness, sterility, corruption of morals, bankruptcy, disunion, Lynch-law, servile wars, and universal execration is not enough – the slaveholder must have a *money* compensation

besides! If you save him from *ruin*, you must pay a round sum for the privilege![26]

Today, there is a common push from pro-life entities. Abortion ameliorative programs come in the form of covering financial burdens of women, paying adoption fees, throwing baby showers, and providing formula and diapers to convince mothers not to murder their preborn children. While caring for the needs of others is biblical, the context is reserved to aid those who would otherwise care for themselves but are prohibited from doing so in some capacity. Biblical charity should not be a bribe to turn from evil.

Regardless of a Christian's view on how to handle ministries for pregnant women who would otherwise choose to murder without some form of assistance, this has become the normative mode in response to abortion instead of a temporary solution. The greater goal should be insisting politically, morally, legally and socially for the criminalization of the act of abortion. Instead, it is common for pro-life advertisements to litter social media begging for financial assistance to help some anonymous woman "choose life." The mother is decidedly for preborn murder unless the fundraising efforts become more appealing. What is not asked for by these pro-life organizations is to raise money to lobby legislators *to fully criminalize preborn murder*. Once again, the best incentive would be the protection of the law for the preborn, not the purse of the people.

A Good Cover for Bad Actors

The problem with any movement not grounded in biblical principles is the possible infiltration of bad actors. This is what transpired in the anti-slavery colonization movement. Blatant racists and pro-slavery sympathizers joined this anti-slavery coalition. They were not interested in calling slavery a sin: They wanted to avoid a society in which their once-owned property could now roam equally with them, or even hold office over them. The lukewarm colonization lobby provided perfect cover for pro-slavery sympathizers to preserve the industry or control what happened with their slaves if the peculiar institution were ever to be erased. It was from their distaste of mixing the races that the emotionally-charged warning of "miscegenation" was invented.[27] Anti-slavery colonizers, as well as pro-slavery advocates, spread fear that emancipated black men would steal white women, force them to become their wives, and inbreed. This was one of the more horrifying realties to anti-slavery colonizers and pro-slavery Americans of what could come to fruition if the African race were to ever be in the same legal and social standing as whites. This provided a dilemma.

While some within the anti-slavery colonization movement were true racists, many more hated slavery but also loathed the idea of white society being altered. Some sort of conciliation had to be found. That fence-sitting solution came in the form of shipping away freed blacks from white society so they would not take jobs away from European immigrants, be privileged to the same benefits free whites experienced under the law, or flounder and remain an inferior ethnic group compared to white people, or inbreed and create a new, less-than-desirable mixed race. This poignant reason for sending away the black population was to protect white society from "Africanization."[28] Sending black Americans back to Africa was almost like hitting one bird with two stones: It alleviated the post-slavery concerns for the majority of Americans and, for those actually opposed to slavery, it looked as if something was being done to address the slave issue. As Pulitzer Prize winning Civil War historian James McPherson states, "All colonization plans had one thing in common: the belief that Negroes and whites in America could never live together peacefully as equals."[29]

This, however, created little peace between colonizers and abolitionists. Colonizers, influenced by anti-black sympathies, disliked abolitionists almost as much as they disliked equal protection and justice for their black neighbors. American Colonization Society (ACS) officer Andrew Judson – later a congressman and judge – ranted that the abolitionists were ignorant nuisances. Judson was not one to hide his motives for being a colonizer. He proudly proclaimed that "colored people never can rise from their menial condition" within the United States and "they ought not to be permitted to rise here." Like many other anti-slavery colonizers, Judson believed slaves were "an inferior race of beings, and never can or ought to be recognized as the equals of whites." As observed in chapter four, Randolph reassured those in favor of slavery that the "anti-slavery" colonization movement was nothing to fear. He said, "I thought it necessary to make these remarks, being myself a slaveholder, to show that, so far from being connected with the abolition of slavery, the measure proposed would prove one of the greatest securities to enable the master to keep in possession his own property."[30]

As a rebuttal to the calls of immediatists, many slavery sympathizers responded by muddying the waters of the anti-slavery movement. They buckled down on incrementalism in an effort to stall the criminalization of slavery. In the mind of most anti-slavery Americans, equal rights were not the solution for freed blacks but rather "Africa is the place for them."[31] If they were to be taken from their plantations and made free, colonizationists voted they be free elsewhere…such as the other side of the world. Because equal justice and protection were not the end goal for the colonization movement, it was easy for pro-slavery individuals to keep the movement from ever advancing.

Today, historians largely agree the main activities of the ACS "seemed more calculated to rid the nation of free blacks than of slaves."[32] Despite this back-handed ideology, colonization remained the most popular anti-slavery, incremental and unbiblical position, even among Christians. Shipping emancipated slaves back to their country of origin was a scapegoat to avoid having to hash out what equality would look like for former slaves – and what comforts or preferences would need to be relinquished by free whites to make that happen. As President Abraham Lincoln told a group of newly emancipated slaves from the District of Columbia, "I think your race suffers very greatly, many of them by living among us, while ours suffers from your presence."[33]

There is an echo of this in pro-life policy. While many in the pro-life movement profess to hate abortion, they also loathe the idea of abortive women being inconvenienced by punishment. They find it unfathomable to disrupt the legal and social comfort of mothers who choose to murder their preborn children. Today's scapegoat is maternal legal exemption that avoids hashing out what equality would look like for the preborn. The pro-life movement acknowledges how the preborn suffer while promoting the doctrine that women will suffer if justice for preborn humans is pursued. Both the viewpoints of colonizers and the pro-life movement slight the oppressed people group from true justice, and allows for actors of bad faith to join an already compromised movement to delay the end of an evil institution. Much like Kissling's call to continue regulatory practices, pro-slavery sympathizers used colonization to also manage – not abolish – the slave industry.

Disruptive and Impossible

Immediate emancipation was the prodigal position of the 1800s. It was seen as economically disruptive, politically impossible and morally reckless. It was criticized as economically disruptive because abolitionists demanded that slavery end without pay-offs or financial incentives to plantation owners, and, in some cases, demanded reparations for emancipated slaves. This was a hard-sell considering the colonization movement promoted either voluntary or paid manumission, and most slave masters frowned upon their "property" being compensated instead of them. Anti-slavery colonizers also despaired how immediately setting every slave free would work pragmatically. It seemed impossible to eliminate slavery because it infiltrated every American ecosystem, from the cotton fields to the pulpits to the presidency. William Lee Miller, Professor of Political and Social Thought at the University of Virginia, pens this reality:

> Slavery was not only an immense industry of itself, but had fundamental ties to other industries – cotton, rice, indigo, and tobacco and others directly, many others indirectly. Slavery was integral to the life and culture...of almost half the nation.[34]

The economic fear helped develop gradualism as a political response to the institution of human bondage. Abolition skeptics searched for ways to slowly acclimate an entire nation's existence without one of its main sources for industrial advancement and income. The far-reaching tentacle of slavery was another reason why defeating it politically seemed a fantasy. Abolition was seen as politically impossible because it opposed slavery to remain intact in some states but not others. States' rights defenders would be the loudest critics of this request. Despite pushback, abolition demanded the *entire nation* criminalize the slave industry, thereby disrespecting state sovereignty on the issue. Anti-slavery pragmatists warned that total abolition throughout the Union would never come to fruition because the South would never be convinced of it. The sentiment of Southern politics and culture is evidenced by an excerpt from the Southern news outlet *Augusta Chronicle*: "The cry of the whole South should be death, instant death, to the abolitionist, wherever he is caught."[35]

As if deaf to such common threats, American immediatists continued to urge political leaders to abolish slave ownership *as well as* the slave trade. English abolitionists had already demonstrated how unsuccessful it was to abolish one but not the other. After the English slave trade was criminalized in 1807, English abolitionists continued battling slavery for 20 more years as traders became crafty at operating on the black market. Once slaves made it into the hands of slave owners little could be done to mitigate the problem. Slave owners still retained legal protection and it was difficult to prove which slaves they had possessed before the end of the slave trade and which were newly acquired. Despite the template of successes and failures already laid out by English abolitionists, most of American anti-slavery society still preferred to end it slowly. As McKivigan notes, church leaders warned "that the adoption of undiluted abolitionist doctrines would destroy the church's powerful influence in behalf of amelioration and gradual emancipation."[36]

The pro-life movement and churches today take this position against abortion abolition. Pro-life leaders warn that it will destroy pro-life work. The pro-life movement fears losing its gradual victories. Even if those victories hinder criminalizing abortion, they are valued.

Substitutes for Immediate Abolition

One reason slavery abolitionists rejected gradual measures is because it often created more obstacles politically and psychologically and made it more difficult to end the slave industry. In 1833, the Anti-Slavery Convention printed one of its primary doctrines on how to fight slavery:

> We regard as delusive, cruel, and dangerous, any scheme of expatriation which pretends to aid, either directly or indirectly, in the emancipation of the slaves, or to be a substitute for the immediate and total abolition of slavery.[37]

The Anti-Slavery Convention strongly argued that gradualism only pretended to address an evil:

> That the slaves ought instantly to be set free, and brought under the protection of law...That all those laws which are now in force, admitting the right of slavery, are therefore before God utterly null and void; being an audacious usurpation of the Divine prerogative, a daring infringement on the law of Nature, a base overthrow of the very foundations of the social compact, a complete extinction of all the relations, endearments, and obligations of mankind, and a presumptuous transgression of all the holy commandments—and that therefore they ought to be instantly abrogated.[38]

Gradualists design their entire strategy around compromise and conflate their successes to justify the approach. The pro-life movement will point to ending the slave trade and then slave ownership as an incremental step to bolster its gradualism commitment. This is not a reasonable comparison. Slavery abolitionists did not seek compromises regarding enslaving children of certain ages, releasing slaves with disabilities, or freeing slaves based on gender. Instead, they aimed to emancipate all remaining slaves without conditions. Wilberforce set the tone with his first submitted bill of abolition when he said, "It will appear from everything which I have said, that it is not regulation, it is not mere palliatives, that can cure this enormous evil. Total abolition is the only possible cure for it."[39] In his extensive speech, Wilberforce finally concluded, "It is the intention after passing these resolutions, to move for leave to bring in a bill for the total abolition of the Slave Trade."[40]

Abolitionists did not seek to regulate where slaves had to work, or stipulate whether to starve or dismember unwanted slaves, or introduce legislation that only allowed women to keep slaves but criminalized slave ownership for everyone else. They put forward the same criteria to emancipate slaves. When abolitionists asked for emancipation, it was on behalf of *all slaves*, not just a random few. Abolitionists chose to criminalize the entire slave institution for everyone. Compromises within an oppressive system are tactics the pro-life movement employs, which sets it apart from historical and present-day abolition. While the pro-life lobby seeks protection for certain preborn humans, it has not sought protection for all preborn individuals.

Pro-life gradualists and slavery abolitionists have another important distinction. Slavery abolitionists never promised legal immunity for slave owners. They did not plan to defeat the slave trade and then retire. Their plan from the beginning was to criminalize every last inch of slavery. In contrast, the pro-life movement has sworn to retain the legal right for all women to pursue preborn murder without consequence.

In the end, the English slave industry continued to thrive apart from the demise of the legalized slave trade until 1833. Like ending slavery when slave owners retained legal protections, it will also prove unachievable to abolish abortion as long as women retain legal immunity to do it. The pro-life movement is fighting to end the abortion trade only. It shares almost nothing in common with slavery abolitionists.

The Tug-of-War Between States' Rights and Human Rights

Not only did abolitionists and other anti-slavery individuals disagree on how to treat freed slaves, but they also disagreed on the issue of states' rights.

Most Americans upheld state sovereignty even if states violated God's law and the sentiment of the Declaration of Independence. This was the hill upon which American Catholics were willing to die. Catholics fiercely resisted abolition. Brownson, considered the first American Catholic intellectual, wrote: "The Union, or as we prefer to say, the national question with us always took, and still takes, precedence of the slavery question....We are no advocates of slavery, but we are at the same time no abolitionists."[41]

Brownson and many other anti-slavers believed if one was forced to choose, the rights of the states were far more important than the rights of the slaves. In fact, Catholics were opposed to ending the slave trade in the South until it became opportunistic to do so. They believed immediate abolition was dangerous to the peace of the Union. Once the Civil War erupted and peace was destroyed anyway, Catholics switched gears and decided to join the abolition call for the complete end of slavery within the whole Union.

> We did not advocate emancipation of the slaves on abolition principles, nor out of consideration for the slaves themselves, but as a necessary war measure, as the only means left us of breaking power of the Confederacy, and of restoring the Union. – Orestes Brownson[42]

By this admission, the Catholic and anti-slavery colonizing push to completely criminalize slavery was not done for the benevolence of the slaves but to "restore the Union." Legal and societal equality for the slave was never at the top of their priority list. There was always another concern that took precedence. By the end of the Civil War, Catholicism was one of the only religious denominations that, as McKivigan states, "failed to condemn slavery and demand its speedy destruction."

The perception that American Catholics avoided abolition is further backed by the existing record of the American Anti-Slavery Society (AASS), the prominent 19th-century abolitionist group founded by William Lloyd Garrison alongside Lewis and Arthur Tappan. The record reveals not a single Catholic is listed in its membership from its conception in 1833 to its dissolution in 1870. This is significant because members from almost every other religious denomination *are* represented in the AASS record.

Professor of religious studies at Marymount College, Kenneth Zanca, explains that while many Catholics sympathized with the humanitarian push of the abolitionists, they were overall opposed to the abolition movement because it was Protestant-led and conflicted with core values and concerns of which Catholics held dear.[43] Brownson summed up best the situation between the anti-slavery Catholics and the Protestant abolition camp:

> Herein we have differed, differ still, and probably always shall differ from the abolitionists. They place the slavery question before all others, and prefer the division of the Union to a union with slave-holding states. We have differed, still differ, and always shall differ from them on the question of negro equality. They demand the recognition of the negro not only as a man, and as a free man, but as the political and social equal of the white man. They are hardly willing to accept of emancipation unless coupled with negro equality, and we are hardly prepared to accept it if coupled with that equality. We recognize in the negro a man, and assert for him in their plenitude all the natural rights of man, but we do not believe him the equal of the white man, and we would not give him in society with white men equality in respect to those rights derived not immediately from his manhood, but mediately from political or civil society, and in this we express, we apprehend, *the*

general sentiment of the Catholic population of this country [Emphasis added]."⁴⁴

The desire to maintain peace of the Union and to respect state sovereignty trumped any concern Catholics had for the plight of slaves. As such, they were committed to the incremental ideologies of anti-slavery colonization. Catholic priest Owen F. Campion notes the absence of Catholics on the crusade to join Protestant abolitionists:

> For Catholics, reading the history from that [slave] period is uncomfortable. Abolitionists were many — the Grimke sisters in South Carolina, William Lloyd Garrison, Frederick Douglass, from Maryland — but no Catholic is prominent among them.⁴⁵

With the overturn of *Roe*, history is repeating. Leading Catholic pro-life organizations and citizens are using the same pro-state sovereignty and anti-abolition rhetoric today. The defense of states' rights is raucously defended by both pro-life and pro-abortion supporters. Once again, opponents of ending abortion are using states' rights as an excuse, just as it was used to avoid ending slavery. It is elevated to a position higher than any biblical command and the Constitution, both of which all state laws should be subservient.

Biblically and legally, no state has the right to violate any person's Constitutional and God-given human right to life. Abolitionists 200 years ago argued the same. Immediatists argue today that no state has the right to allow for any type of murder of any person by any individual in any type of circumstance. As straightforward as this seems, it is vehemently ignored, just as it was in the 1800s.

Sadly, Catholics defended states' rights at the expense of keeping the slave population oppressed. Usurping state sovereignty was not the only reason for their distaste of abolition. The Catholic church taught from the sixth to the 20th century that slavery was a legitimately recognized social, economic and legal institution. The main concern of the Roman Catholic church was the spiritual care of the enslaved, so it therefore encouraged humane treatment of the slaves by their masters.

Catholics also upheld amelioration, like many Protestants, which promoted the idea of evangelizing the institution of slavery by converting the souls of enslaved black men and women from superstitious African beliefs. This eventually developed into the larger proselytizing goal of manumission. Both manumission and emancipation were acts to free slaves. These concepts differ, however, in that manumission was the voluntary freeing of slaves by slaveholders while emancipation was a legal act to compel them to do so. Catholics supported manumission and worked to urge slaveholders to choose freedom for their slaves. They converted slaves to Catholicism and discipled slaveholders on the humanity of the black person and how to show compassion to them.

However, Catholic and Protestant colonizers were not the only ones to thwart abolition goals. Southern pro-slavery advocates also resisted the political notion of ignoring states' rights on slavery. The *Charleston City Gazette* published in one of their editions in 1830, "We protest against the assumption – the unwarrantable assumption – that slavery is ultimately to be extirpated from the Southern States. Ultimate abolitionists are enemies of the South, the same in kind, and only less in degree, than immediate abolitionists."

At the time of this writing, the Catholic-led pro-life movement resists abortion abolition. History will record two human rights tragedies within this nation that the Catholic church refused to help fully abolish: slavery and abortion.

The Bulwarks of Slavery

The hurdles for 19th-century abolitionists were many. One such hurdle included the accusation that abolition was morally judgmental and reckless. Its staunch doctrine that slavery was a sin led abolitionists to reject segregation of the races and to call out the hypocrisy, apathy or sin of slavery in the lives of others, especially church leaders. In

1842, James G. Birney published a fiery indictment against the American churches. Birney, "a repentant slaveholder and an active, earnest abolitionist,"[46] decided to poke the consciences of professing Christians who either openly supported slavery or who held to the compromised anti-slavery colonization ideologies. Birney decided not to beat around the bush with his book's title: *The American Churches, the Bulwarks of American Slavery* seemed direct enough. Birney opened his small dossier with a startling declaration:

> The extent to which most of the churches in America are involved in the guilt of supporting the slave system is known to but few in this country. So far from being even suspected by the great mass of the religious communities here, it would not be believed but on the most indisputable evidence. Evidence of this character it is proposed now to present – applying to the Methodist Episcopal, the Baptist, the Presbyterian, and the Protestant Episcopal churches. It is done with a single view to make the British Christian public acquainted with the real state of the case – in order that it may in the most intelligent and effective manner exert the influence it possesses with the American churches to persuade them to purify themselves from a sin that has greatly debased them, and that threatens in the end wholly to destroy them.[47]

The primary audience for his book was, interestingly, British Christians, who were leaps and bounds ahead of their American counterparts in efforts to abolish slavery. Birney must have hoped their influence would pressure Christian Americans to follow suit politically and legally with abolition. Birney and other immediatists believed slavery a sin – just as British abolitionists did. McKivigan notes, "Abolitionists condemned slavery largely on moral grounds and sought the sanction of established religious institutions for their views...abolitionists branded slave owning a sin that required repentance in the form of immediate emancipation."[48]

Because churches preached repentance as a key attribute of the Christian life, abolitionists were hopeful their political and moral efforts would be supported. Yet their rebuke and persuasion often fell on deaf ears. Garrison's own minister Lyman Beecher told Garrison his zeal "was commendable, but misguided."[49] Some anti-slavery colonizers sympathized with abolition goals but did not think abolition would ever be realistic, so they clung to the workable pragmatics of the ACS. By the 1830s, most clergymen "shied away from involvement in the controversial abolition cause," marooning their abolitionist church members politically, socially, morally and spiritually, and ultimately surrendering the nation to a bloody war. McKivigan gives a dim review of what happened when the churches refused to heed the call of repentance and work to completely and immediately abolish slavery:

> ...despite the efforts of thousands of anti-slavery men and women both inside and outside the churches, all but a few small denominations balked at a commitment to uncompromised abolitionist principles and programs. As a result, civil war and government coercion, not moral suasion and church discipline, became the instrument that finally ended slavery in 1865.[50]

Instead, "American churches were satisfied to encourage gradualist programs of amelioration and voluntary manumission that held out only faint hope for eventual abolition."[51] These slow, plodding steps toward justice and repentance from the sin of man stealing and unbiblical bondage was inadmissible for the abolitionists. Garrison explained, "Urge immediate abolition as earnestly as we may, it will alas! be gradual abolition in the end. We have never said that slavery would be overthrown by a single blow; that it ought to be we shall always contend."[52] Abolitionist George Bourne agreed:

> Is not the plea, that emancipation is impracticable, the most impudent hypocrisy and the most glaring absurdity ever propounded

for contemplation? Can any supposititious expediency, any dread of political discord, or any private advantage justify the prolongation of corruption, the enormity of which is unequaled, or repel the holy claim to its extinction? The system is so entirely corrupt that it admits of no cure but by a total and immediate abolition. For a gradual emancipation is a virtual recognition of the right, and establishes the rectitude of the practice. If it be for just one moment, it is hallowed for ever; and if it be inequitable, not a day should it be tolerated.[53]

Immediatism's dispute with gradualism was it set the tone for a lack of urgency and undermined the moral seriousness of the issue. This is the same concern expressed by abortion abolitionists. As Bourne described, slowly moving to criminalize something props that thing up as legitimate whether intended for that to be the outcome or not. The hesitancy to end a professed system of wickedness is interpreted by the culture as a weak stance against that matter, inviting opposition to move in with strength against the perceived softness of gradualism. At the very least, gradualism tells others something is disliked but it is not all *that bad* because there is no demand to cease *right now*.

Professing one thing but acting contrary to one's conviction is hypocrisy. The weightiness of calling abortion murder is downplayed when it is likened to healthcare by writing pro-life legislation that requires clean clinics (for murder), licensed doctors (to murder), safe facilities for women (in which to murder), waiting periods (to murder), and ambulatory services (for when preborn murder goes "wrong" and the child survives or the woman does not). Which is it; a felony or medicine? What was a slave; a person or property? What is the preborn; a human or a woman's choice? It is a disjointed approach to evil. It allows for deceptive compromise as America's historical counterparts discovered. Despite the subpar morality of colonization, church clergy (Protestant and Catholic alike) sang the praises of the anti-slavery efforts of the ACS, which claimed to be against slavery but was an enemy of true abolition and thus the slave.

Gradualism: the Masterpiece of Satanic Policy

The main goals of the ACS were antithetical to abolition goals. Even if political increments led to slavery abolition, there was no legal equality for black citizens. In most anti-slavery Christian America, the white person had priority over the enslaved one. Minister John Gregg Lee penned a book in 1857 where he stated, "'Tis certain, then, that the Colonization Society had not that holy origin generally ascribed to it. And it is also apparent, that it originated, not so much for the good of the colored man here, or in Africa, but for the benefit of the slaveholder."[54] English abolitionist Elizabeth Coltman Heyrick also noticed the double-agent initiatives of gradualism within her nation and scathingly wrote to expose it:

> But this GRADUAL ABOLITION, has been the grand marplot of human virtue and happiness; the very master-piece of satanic policy. By converting the cry for immediate, into gradual emancipation, the prince of slave holders, " transformed himself, with astonishing dexterity, into an angel of light," and thereby " deceived the very elect." He saw very clearly, that if public justice and humanity, especially, if Christian justice and humanity, could be brought to demand only a gradual extermination of the enormities of the slave system; if they could be brought to acquiesce, but for one year, or for one month, in the slavery of our African brother, in robbing him of all the rights of humanity, and degrading him to a level with the brutes; that then, they could imperceptibly be brought to acquiesce in all this for an un- limited duration.[55]

Tragically, despite these warnings, the tenets of slavery abolition were largely rejected by the churches. Abolitionists wanted Christian America to repent of oppression and apathy and choose the slave's rights over their worn-old comforts, even in the face of political improbability. The response from the churches and culture was that political abolition was ludicrous, abolitionists were dismissible fools, and there was nothing of which to repent:

> Slavery can never be abolished.[56] – James Henry Hammond, pro-slavery congressman

> He who thinks it is a feasible act to abolish at once the system of African slavery in this country – granting that some political power existed to do it, – he who so thinks seems to us to be at best, an honest simpleton...Abolitionism is the most sterile foolishness that ever afflicted a guessing, speculative fault-finding and inquisitive community.[57] – James McMaster, anti-slavery Catholic apologist and journalist

> We have always believed, and we believe today, that liberty and humanity are more interested in maintaining the national integrity and the federal constitution unimpaired, than they are in the abolition of negro slavery.[58] – Orestes Brownson, anti-slavery Catholic clergyman

> [Abolitionists] aim at arriving the slave and his master over the head of the FEDERAL CONSTITUTION, which is, in its very nature, highly seditious if not treasonable![59] – Eleventh Annual Report of the Indiana Colonization Society

> [Abolitionists are] noxious and pestilent" and a body of "moral invalids and intellectual imbeciles.[60] – *Freeman's Journal*, an anti-slavery Catholic news outlet

> [Immediate abolition] is turbulent invective and acrimonious clamour.[61] – J.R. Tyson, anti-slavery judge and politician

Anti-abolition sentiment among the majority of pro-life Protestants and Catholics has been recycled from the 19th century. The pro-life plan is to end abortion through incremental measures; but like colonization, even if those increments bring about the end of the abortion industry, there is no equality under homicide law waiting for the preborn. It is not the pro-life goal to subject mothers, who commit preborn murder with malice aforethought, to the criminal justice system. Pro-life godfather Willke promised this when he said, "We don't know of a single pro-life or pro-abortion leader, or congressman, or member of Parliament in any nation, who would want this...women should not be punished."[62]

The main perpetrators against the preborn will have no legal deterrents from continuing to destroy them under the vision of what it means to "end" abortion by current pro-life standards. Priority is for the mother over the preborn person for most of anti-abortion America. Much like their incremental predecessors, anti-abortion gradualists see abortion immediatists as politically incompetent and dismissible fools:

> Nobody has defended the incrementalist approach better and debunked the political silliness of immediatism than Scott Klusendorf.[63] – Seth Gruber, pro-life founder of The White Rose Resistance

[abolitionists] are not good faith actors.⁶⁴ – Jonathan Van Maren, pro-life communications director for Canadian Centre for Bio-Ethical Reform

And it is THAT – this [abolition] Faustian bargain with the devil of politics, this gossipy accusing of the brethren, this focus-group-tested rabble-rousing that tramples truth in the quest for quote tweets – that represents one of the gravest threats to the work of the SBC today.⁶⁵ – Bart Barber, pro-life president of the Southern Baptist Convention

Let it be perfectly clear: I charge that abolitionists and their organizations act in a manner contrary to the gospel; that they are unreflective and misguided, blind teachers leading others astray; that their actions, if ever successful, threaten the lives of thousands of women and children; that they want to unjustly prosecute women for abortion the moment they can; and that they refuse to learn from history or rebukes to their sinful mistakes.⁶⁶ – Andrew Kaake, pro-life lead editor at Equal Rights Institute

Yesterday, the SBC passed a very foolish abolition resolution that just threw pro-lifers under the bus. The resolution essentially says that those who work incrementally to protect all unborn humans are moral compromisers.⁶⁷ – Scott Klusendorf, pro-life apologist and founder of Life Training Institute

There are two very distinct types of pro-life advocates. One type wants to end abortion, has an actual working knowledge of what that requires in our judicial and legislative systems, and uses strategic expertise to save as many lives as possible while setting the table to topple Roe v. Wade. The other type wants to lie on the floor kicking and screaming like a child throwing a tantrum, expecting the wider world to capitulate to that. Their strategy might end abortion in Fantasy Land, but not in the United States of America.[68] – Dana Hall McCain, 2021 pro-life Southern Baptist Convention Resolutions Committee member

Abolitionists sacrifice babies right now for the sake of promoting its long-range goal, which may be unobtainable in any case. For abolitionism, babies are poker chips. The endgame is to win the jackpot. The abolitionist is all-in. He's prepared to lose everything in the hopes of winning everything.[69] – Steve Hays, pro-life Christian apologist and writer

These people in the abolitionist movement have absolutely zero concept of what pro-life legislation looks like. They don't understand the repercussions. They are legislatively ignorant.[70] – Abby Johnson, pro-life activist

Despite the pro-life community's putdowns, Christian abolitionists should be encouraged. The pessimistic prophecies and unfounded insults from 19th-century skeptics did not come to fruition: Slavery *was* abolished – and abolitionists were not crazy. There is little reason to listen to 21st- century skeptics that abortion cannot be completely abolished and that asking for it to be abolished is only wishful thinking.

Abortion *will* be abolished someday. God will see to its end as he saw to the end of slavery. This is more sobering: The Church will either participate with God in abolishing it or the Church will suffer judgment for being stiff-necked. The churches in the 1800s lacked immediate abolitionists and this became a monumental problem for America. When the churches failed to rise up to lead biblically against the evils of chattel slavery, others moved in to take their place. The secular doctrine espoused by these anti-slavery incrementalists drifted America further from biblical justice and into disobedience against God on the issue of how to love their neighbors as themselves, show no legal or social partiality, and avoid injustice. The consequence of such a compromised ideology ushered in four long years of bloody warfare. McKivigan wraps up his scholarly work on slavery abolition efforts with this criticism of the apathetic Christian culture of the 1800s: "If the war had not intervened, the abolitionists might eventually have created enough anti-slavery sentiment among churchmen to bring about a more peaceful and more decisive end to slavery. Although the anti-slavery movement failed to make the northern churches into firm friends of the blacks, the ultimate responsibility for this failure rests with the churches and the northern public, not with the abolitionists."[71]

Open By Permission of the Church

Today, a similar book to Birney's could be written about 21st-century churches: There is no power outside of the church that could sustain abortion for an hour, if it were not sustained within the churches. Theologian Francis Schaeffer observed, "Every abortion clinic should have a sign in front of it saying, 'Open by the permission of the church.'"[72] Abortion thrives in America due to the participation and endorsement of progressive churches, the long-fought compromise of pro-life ideologies, the worship of states' rights over human rights, the obedience to judicial supremacy and not to Constitutional law, and the silence and lack of abolition leadership by conservative, Protestant pulpits. Abortion remains because of our churches. Very few professing Christians plead for the lives of the preborn as they are being dragged to the slaughterhouse. The sidewalks in front of abortion mills are empty of Christ's sons and daughters. As a Florida police officer observed to abolitionist Kevan Myers, who was ministering in front of an abortion clinic with a small band of believers: "Abortion must not be a big issue for Christians, because this city is full of Christians, and you are the only ones here."[73]

History names three groups involved in the slavery debacle: anti-slavery colonizers, abolitionists and pro-slavery proponents. In reality, there were only two camps: those for slavery and those against it. While countless Catholics and Protestants detested slavery, not many disliked it enough to insist on the complete and immediate end of what they claimed was evil. Their endgame was something else. Their endgame involved chipping away pieces of slavery and returning emancipated black men and women to Africa in installments.

Lee contested it was cruel for the endgame to send away black people from their native-born land. In his harsh critique of the anti-slavery colonization movement, he concluded:

> Hence, pro-slavery men tolerate the Colonization Society, and say, "it does very well as a kind of safety-valve through which to let off the morbid anti-slavery sentiment of some anti- slavery men." A kind of safety-valve through which to let off the morbid sympathy and sense of natural justice, which otherwise might burst out against the oppressor with righteous indignation, and blow up the cruel system that oppresses the innocent poor. Anti-slavery man! you have noble impulses planted by heaven, and designed for noble purposes— the elevation of your species. What a misfortune that they should be lost upon the air, sponged up in a worse than futile course.[74]

Colonizers were more anti-black than they were anti-slavery, whether or not they realized it. Their actions overshadowed anything they claimed. They could proclaim to loathe slavery but when they fought for anything less than its complete end, their words became empty. Likewise, the abortion debate affords two positions: for abortion in certain cases and against abortion in all cases. Allowing for abortion in any instance is being *for* abortion. This includes supporting rape or incest exceptions, abortion in medical emergencies, and legal immunity for women to willfully be involved in prenatal homicide. These pro-abortion elements disqualify any individual or organization from being fully and truly anti-abortion. It is cruel for the anti-abortion endgame to give some people a permanent pass in murder. The pro-life movement is more anti-preborn than it is anti-abortion.

Actions Speak Louder than Words

There are important lessons from history available to teach modern-day Christians. We should not ask *who* was against slavery but *how* was someone against it. Did the individual argue consistently and biblically for the end of all forms of slavery without exceptions? Did the person express their hatred for slavery but still allow mistreatment of black people under the law? It would behoove Christians today to ask *how* someone is against abortion for the differences will be just as telling. Many pro-life leaders care for the preborn but their commitment to the comforts of women is of higher importance, likened to the split loyalty of colonizers in their affection for slaves *and* slaveholders. Pro-life Catholics and Protestants alike uphold the biblical teaching that all humans are made Imago Dei, but implicitly consider women a superior image bearer compared to that of the preborn. Pro-life laws *always* aim to protect women and only *sometimes* protect *some* of the pre-born. Abortion exceptions, legal impunity, or pragmatic delay all reduce the passion for protecting the preborn to empty words.

The cliché quip "actions speaker louder than words" is fully applicable to the abortion fight. Just as it is hard to believe the disgust colonizers supposedly had for slavery, it is equally difficult to believe the disgust at abortion when legislators and pro-life PACs work so hard to avoid ending it. And when pro-life advocates herald preborn murder exceptions for rape, incest and health of the mother they only draw closer to the camp of the colonizationists.

The anti-slavers cried out: "We hate slavery! It must end!" The abolitionists responded, "We agree! Let's abolish it and establish equal justice and protection for our black neighbors!"

The anti-slavers drew back: "Oh no, we cannot do that. What if it negatively affects their masters? What if white society becomes Africanized? They are of an inferior race...priority must be for the white man."

Is not the same argument reflected in the pro-life philosophy? The pro-life community cries out: "We hate abortion! It must end!" Abolitionists respond, "We agree! Let's abolish it and establish equal justice and protection for our preborn neighbors!"

The pro-life movement recoils: "Oh no, we cannot do that. What if it negatively affects abortive mothers? What if women have health issues? The preborn are of an inferior class...priority must be for the woman."

In this way the pro-life movement mimics the tenets of the anti-slavery colonizers. It claims to abhor abortion yet doubts that equal protection and justice under the law for the preborn will be good for society and women. The pro-life movement, while boasting of many good intentions, will in the end fail to deliver complete abolition by its current principles. Fee noted the same thing with anti-slavery colonizers:

> Look at facts. The Colonization Society has been in existence more than thirty-seven years. It has had the sanction of church and state, the patronage of state and of the national government, the eloquence of the pulpit and the bar, the indefatigable labors of talented and good, but misdirected men. What has it accomplished?...When will it accomplish the work?[75]

The pro-life movement has been in existence for more than 50 years. It has had the support of churches, conservative political supermajorities, the Supreme Court and the pulpits. Talented men and women eager to see the end of abortion are misdirected on how they can achieve it apart from complete criminalization. When will the pro-life movement accomplish its work?

In actuality, it is not structured to abolish abortion just as colonization was not created to abolish slavery. Thankfully, the double-minded policies on the issue of slavery faded into the history books and have been replaced by the common acceptance of equal justice between differing ethnic groups. As it turns out, criminalizing slavery was not bad for white society after all.

Today, most Americans see slavery as a sin and find it unimaginable to tolerate such a system of oppression. This is due to the perseverance of immediate abolitionists and their quest to catechize culture on the sin of slavery, the need to criminalize it, and the urgency to establish equal justice and protection between ethnic groups. Nevertheless, the racism fallout that followed the end of slavery should not be ignored. If the churches had embraced the abolition call instead of the racist colonizing attitude of rejecting amalgamation (the mixing of races) and withholding legal and social equality, America could have averted a war and 100 years of racist attitudes that continue to this day in some pockets of the culture. Slavery was indeed abolished, but the unbiblical spirit of colonization lived on.

What will America's future look like if it embraces the feminist, pro-life attitude of rejecting equal justice under homicide laws for preborn humans? What mess will be left for future generations to rectify if Christians today insist on preserving the idolatry of matriarchal supremacy by a mother's right to murder? History has already shown what will unfold if the churches do not go about abolition biblically. The nation will endure even more decades of turmoil and incomplete justice for the preborn as well as God's wrath. President Abraham Lincoln ominously spoke of national sin in his second inaugural address on March 4, 1865:

> Fondly do we hope – fervently do we pray – that this mighty scourge of war may speedily pass away. Yet, if God wills that it continue until all the wealth piled by the bondman's two hundred and fifty years of unrequited toil shall be sunk, and until every drop of blood drawn with the last shall be paid by another drawn with the sword, as was said three thousand years ago, so still it must be said: "The judgments of the Lord are true, and righteous altogether."[76]

Christians can and should expect continued calamity for our generation due to our own slowness and hesitancy to end the evil of abortion. Cali writes in *The Doctrine of Balaam* a similar conclusion to Lincoln's:

> It is quite possible that God will not use us as a means to bring about repentance from our national sin of partiality in the killing of millions of children. Our calls of repentance to the state may be an indictment against our God-hating nation that is being judged by the hand of the Lord. He may see fit that the accumulated sins of our nation must now be paid as the land vomits us up.[77]

Romans chapter one demonstrates how America is already under the judgment of God. The Lord turning people over to debased minds is the consequence of persistent sin and a sign of current judgment; not the foreshadowing that judgment will come. It is time to repent and do right. Christians need not fear the current unpopularity of abortion abolition. America's ancestors already proved success can still come regardless of popularity. Gradualism should be abandoned for the call of immediatism. There is a day in the future in which abolition will be realized. Garrison declared, "The Abolitionism which I advocate is as absolute as the law of God, and as unyielding as His throne. It admits of no compromise."[78]

Lee encouraged his fellow 19th-century Christians: "Let us do our duty, if others will do wrong. Let us set a right example. That is all God requires of us."[79]

By God's grace, the American churches will cease to be the bulwark of abortion and will declare along with Garrison, "I will not go with the multitude to do evil."[80]

6

LICENSE TO KILL: RISE OF THE MOTHER ABORTIONIST

"Open is the way of Satan; many walk therein." – John Huss, martyr of Rome (1370-1415)

Matriarchal Victimhood

A YOUNG WOMAN KNEELS on a yoga mat and fans burning sage smoke around the room with a handheld fan. She inhales as the aroma of incense rises and fills the small living room. Ritualistically, she places a picture of the Virgin Mother Mary and a lit candle on an end table beside her mat. Pensive for a moment, she adds another token next to the Mary image: a Tarot card that symbolizes female fertility. The boho-chic décor, natural wood tones and bright windows of the room give the impression of a beach vacation. Her loosely braided, dark hair draped across her shoulder adds to the casual, relaxed atmosphere of the video.

She sifts through some more New Age paraphernalia spread out before her and grabs another object from the pile: a package of pills. She sets it next to the lit candle.

Satisfied with how the table is now arranged, she looks into the camera and soothes, "Building an altar for your abortion can be a really cathartic procedure. I like to always have a candle going on my altar, so there's always light within the darkness. I also really like to add the abortion pills themselves to the altar to really bless the pills that we will be taking into our bodies during this process."[1]

Unfortunately, this is not pagan satire nor is it an opening scene to a lame melodrama. Instead, this is a snippet from a YouTube video encouraging women to relish the sacredness of their abortions, worship the rise of female divinity, and commemorate the cycle of life and death. It's a tutorial on how to build an abortion altar. And this occultic practice is not relegated just to an isolated, social-media trend.

In 2023, The Satanic Temple opened an abortion clinic in New Mexico bearing the equivoque name Samuel Alito's Mom's Satanic Abortion Clinic. On its website's homepage the clinic states, "Samuel Alito's Mom's Satanic Abortion Clinic™ is an online clinic that provides religious medication abortion care. The clinic provides abortion medication via mail to those in New Mexico who wish to perform The Satanic Temple's Religious Abortion Ritual."

The abortion medication is free to anyone within New Mexico who is a part of The Satanic Temple (TST) or interested in performing the Satanic abortion rite. The ceremonial aspects of the ritual include gazing at yourself in a mirror and focusing on your personhood. After meditatively breathing and relaxing, the woman is to recite: "One's body is inviolable, subject to one's own will alone." The Satanic abortion ritual is complete after the woman has delivered the dead fetus and recites: "By my body, my blood; by my will, it is done."[2] Currently, TST has the lofty goal of expanding its abortive religious ceremonies and services to many more states.

While not every abortive woman is associated directly with TST, the ritual of recognizing the life of the sacrificed preborn is still trending on social media with thousands of women posting their stories of delivering their dead babies or sharing photos of their aborted offspring – some even dressed as newborns – to honor the late lives of their murdered children. Consider only a few examples from post-abortive women who chronicled their abortion burial plans:

> I just had my MA [medication abortion] a week ago and my babies are in the freezer waiting for me to sort my head out enough to bury them.[3]

I saw my baby when it came out...I planted her outside my house by a tree and every day I want to dig her out and hold her but I promised her dad I wouldn't.[4]

I want so badly to bury them instead of just throwing them in the garbage. I've had them wrapped in my pants in a bag for a whole day and I can't seem to bring myself to once again look at, and handle and touch them....I put on a pair of gloves and prepared a small cardboard box with tissue in it...until I can get a little wooden box...[5]

Did my abortion on the 9th this month and she came out on the 10th. She died in my hands. I had to wake up in the morning and go bury her.[6]

We saved up enough for cremation even if it's the smallest amount we could possibly get as we don't have a place to lay her. We decided to name our little and based the gender on what I believed it was through my symptoms and gut feelings.[7]

Women such as these are not great pro-life poster children for the movement's doctrine of women being hapless abortion victims. When looking at abortion statistics, essays and books by leading pro-abortion feminists, comments by pro-choice citizens, details from post-abortive women, and quotes from abortionists, the universal victim narrative becomes almost impossible to understand.

It is irrational to internalize the doctrine of never prosecuting women for their participation in preborn murder.

Is *every* woman involved in prenatal homicide culpable to the same degree? No – and that is why due process is needed instead of an unjust blanket approach that no abortive woman should ever be prosecuted, or the inverse judgment that all abortive women should receive the same punishment. All women who are not criminally forced into an abortion are guilty of murder, but the degree of their participation in homicide should be a matter for the justice system. The women in the quoted examples model a high level of criminal intent, or what the criminal justice system calls *mens rea*. While not every woman is at the level of brazenness similar to the woman in the YouTube video, most women do know what they are choosing to do when they pursue an abortion. Women know pregnancy is growing a new human life and abortion is the intentional destruction of that life.

Abortionist Dr. William F. Harrison testifies to this fact in his essay *Why I Am An Abortion Provider*: "No one, neither the patient receiving the abortion, nor the person doing the abortion, is ever, at any time, unaware that they are ending a life."[8]

How did we reach a point where people comprehend the reality of abortion yet remain unfazed by terminating human life? The pro-life movement points to dehumanizing language and deception of the abortion industry to conceal what abortion is.

Dehumanizing language such as "products of conception," "tissue" or "blobs of cells" is used to mentally comfort those who choose to kill their unborn babies, but it hardly erases the truth of what they are doing much in the same way calling 19-century slaves "chattel," "legal property" or "horses" never fully obscured the reality that they were human. Still, dehumanizing language serves an important role. It provides cognitive dissonance for people to detach themselves from what they are a part of to pursue what they want against another person without the associated guilt. It is what allows a woman to pursue an abortion without acknowledging to herself that she is killing her child and yet still knowing that is exactly what she is doing, as Harrison affirms.

While the pro-life movement identifies dehumanizing language as partly to blame for a woman's pursuit of abortion, the language itself does not remove guilt or internal knowledge of the act. It simply makes it easier to look the other way during the process. Comfortably looking the other way is not the definition of victimhood and should not be a satisfactory excuse to avoid legal consequences for preborn murder.

Brutally Honest

The other permeating pro-life belief that the abortion industry is deceptive is not an overstatement. It indeed operates on a level of deceit. Planned Parenthood has advertised it offers prenatal services when undercover journalists discovered the majority of clinics do not provide any such prenatal screenings or care.[9] Planned Parenthood has also stated, "Three percent of all Planned Parenthood health services are abortion services," when the actual number of income from abortions is more than 50 percent.[10] The pro-abortion movement also claims abortion betters the quality of life for the poor and black communities when the industry originated to eradicate those very populations. Yet there are many within the abortion industry and among leading abortion activists who are honest that abortion kills a human being. These individuals do not use cognitive dissonance as a tool to suppress truth from their actions; rather, they employ secular moralism to defend the killings. They are unashamed by the truthfulness of what abortion is:

> They [pro-lifers] accuse us of pretending we're not doing what we're doing? I'm in the business of death![11] – Joan Wright, abortion clinic owner

> I have the utmost respect for life; I appreciate that life starts early in the womb, but also believe that I'm ending it for good rea-

sons.... Life is hard enough when you're wanted and everything's prepared. So yes, I end life, but even when it is hard, it is for a good reason.[12] – Cheryl Alkon's interview with an abortionist

Abortion is killing the fetus. ... Human life, in and of itself, is not sacred. Human life, per se, is not inviolate.[13] – "Dr. Smith," abortionist

I have angry feelings at myself for feeling good about grasping the calvaria [head], for feeling good about doing a technically good procedure that destroys a fetus, kills a baby.[14] – Diane M. Gianelli's interview with an abortionist

A late termination is actually not very nice and there is no way of getting away from it. I do not feel I am doing it for any other reason than for the best of both the mother and the baby.[15] – Dr. John Parsons, abortionist

It is morally and ethically wrong to do abortions without acknowledging what it means to do them. I performed abortions. I have had an abortion and I am in favor of women having abortions when we choose to do so. But we should never disregard the fact that being pregnant means there is a baby growing inside of a woman, a baby whose life is ended. We ought not to pretend this is not happening...Sometimes a woman has to decide to kill her baby. That's what abortion is. We have to deal with that or we're abandoning these women. – Judith Arcana, abortion rights activist[16]

Nobody wants to perform abortions after ten weeks because by then you see the features of the baby, hands, feet. It is really barbaric. Abortions are very draining, exhausting, and heartrending. There are a lot of tears....I do them because I take the attitude that women are going to terminate babies and deserve the same kind of treatment as women who carry babies...I've done a couple thousand, and it turned into a significant financial boon, but I also feel I've provided an important service. The only way I can do an abortion is to consider only the woman as my patient and block out the baby.[17] – John Pekkanen's interview with an abortionist

...abortion is the taking of a life.[18] – Mary Calderone, former medical director of Planned Parenthood

I have never denied that human life begins at conception. If I have a complaint about our society, it is that we do not deal with death and dying. Do we believe human beings have a right to make decisions about death and dying? Yes we do, and those decisions are made every day in every hospital.[19] – Tim Shuck, abortion clinic counselor

...abortion is killing. Nobody can argue with that. When the fetus is inside the uterus it is alive and when the pregnancy is terminated it is dead – that by any definition is killing.[20] – Dr. Bertram Wainer, abortionist

When "pro-life" forces agitate against feticide on the basis that it is killing, pro-abortion feminists should be able to acknowledge, without shame, that yes, of course it is. When we withdraw from gestating, we stop the life of the product of our gestational labor. And it's a good thing we do, too, for otherwise the world would sag under the weight of forced life.[21] – Sophie Lewis, feminist theorist and author

I'm destroying life.[22] – William F. Harrison, abortionist

I think that it is a baby, and I use [the word] with patients...I have no problem [killing] if it's in the mother's uterus.[23] – LeRoy Carhart, abortionist

I know that throughout my own pregnancies, I never wavered for a moment in the belief that I was carrying a human life inside of me. I believe that's what a fetus is: a human life. And that does not make me one iota less solidly pro-choice.[24] – Mary Elizabeth Williams, abortion rights activist

These quotes from leaders within the abortion movement are forthcoming. Many of these statements come from magazines, books, newspaper articles and speeches, all of which have been widely circulated among hundreds of thousands

— if not millions — of Americans. None of these abortion advocates obscure what abortion does, though they do attempt to promote it as a moral good to either prevent suffering in those not wanted or to preserve the lives of the mothers.

There is another line of thinking that defends the right to kill the unborn. It relies not only on situational ethics but also on the law to determine the morality of its position. As such, those who employ both the law and situational ethics attempt to exert a more robust standing than the ideologue quotes of their colleagues:

> We know that it is killing, but the states permit killing under certain circumstances.[25] – Dr. Neville Sender, abortionist

> Is abortion murder? All killing is not murder. A cop shoots a teenager who appeared to be going for a gun, and we call it justifiable homicide – a tragedy for all concerned, but not murder. And then there's war...[26] – Don Sloan, abortionist

> The word unlawful is very important, because, because it implies that killing IS lawful in some circumstances, but when it is unlawful, it becomes murder.[27] –Miriam Claire, abortion rights activist

> It [the fetus] is a form of life.... This has to be killing.... The question then becomes, 'Is this kind of killing justifiable?' In my own mind, it is justifiable, but only with the informed consent of the mother .[28] – Anonymous abortionist, interview in *Democrat & Chronicle*

> I've thought through this issue, to do it as long as I have, and I have to sleep well at night… Is it life? Clearly it is life. Does it deserve protection? My answer is "no." The bottom line, you have two competing interests: the mother and the baby (or the embryo or the fertilized egg). And sometime during that nine month gestation, a woman's rights are going to digress. At that point, I guess, rights can be ascribed to the fetus.[29] – "Michelle," abortionist

It has been discussed in previous chapters how God's law is a tutor. When manmade laws do not reflect God's just laws, we catechize culture wrongly on good versus evil. In this situation, these abortionists and pro-abortion activists look at the law that by precedence (not constitutionality or biblicalness) allows them to kill a certain part of the population, so they conclude it must not be that bad because it is "legal." This is ultimately how culture intellectually knows what abortion does to a preborn human and yet still accepts that moral atrocity.

The dehumanizing language of the preborn and deceit by the abortion industry are mere tools used to justify the laws that already make exceptions for preborn murder. More than that, it is the idolatrous hearts of individuals in rebellion against their Creator that manufacturers the desire to kill in the first place, and the current exception laws give men's and women's hearts the endorsement to continue in this wicked desire.

While the pro-life movement views lies about the humanity of the unborn to be the *primary* cause for women falling into the trap of abortion, the reality is women have abundant access to the truthfulness of abortion. A woman who insists that the preborn are not yet human is not espousing wildly-circulated intellectual information from leading abortion advocates but is instead suppressing the truth because of a debased mind (Romans 1:18-32).

Holding to the pro-life doctrine of feminine ignorance theologically overlooks how the Bible describes the natural state of our spiritually dead hearts. Women do not need misleading information to dupe them into murder because the desire to kill already exists within every human heart. The desire to murder is the condition of a fallen, sinful flesh; and laws that restrain that natural inclination are needed. Even secularists understand that the permission or restraint provided by laws is crucial in dictating societal behavior, as evidenced by the quotes from leaders within the abortion industry. These pro-choice leaders and philosophers concluded abortion to be a morally sanctioned killing because it is legal; therefore, their ethics (moral code) is tied up in what the current laws of the land allow or disallow. This is situational ethics. Situational ethics determines the morality of an issue based on the context in which it is found. Instead of defaulting to absolute truth found in Scripture – unchanging truth for all people in all circumstances for all time – someone guided by situational ethics will use other modes as a moral baseline.

The abortion industry is not the only establishment to employ situational ethics. Another example would be a pro-life 15-week abortion ban. Author and preacher CR Cali says if one asks a pro-life lawmaker if a pro-life bill being passed is righteous, the lawmaker will not know how to answer unless the context of the law is known. In the case of a 15-week abortion ban, it would be viewed as a good bill when implemented in Vermont, Oregon or Hawaii, which allow abortion through all nine months of pregnancy; however, if a 15-week ban were implemented in Texas, Oklahoma or Arkansas, which have closed down in-clinic abortions, it would be viewed as a bad law. In either case, it is certainly not a righteous law that reflects God's standard because God's standard *never* changes: Right remains right and wrong remains wrong. While it goes against relativism inclinations, a 15-week abortion ban is a bad law according to God's word because it still allows for some babies to be legally killed. It informs society through the law that it is only wrong to kill babies *older* than that arbitrary age. It codifies partiality, the very thing God forbids lawmakers from practicing. A 15-week abortion ban can only be "good" when used within the scope of a secular, situational ethics model.

The Laywoman Abortionist

Thankfully, Christians can determine what is right or wrong on the issue of murder apart from manmade laws. Christians should know what is right due to God's revealed decrees in Scripture about murder. It is always wrong to kill an innocent person regardless of what laws are or are not written by men. The quotes from abortion workers reveal how despondently pro-life laws have failed to align with Scripture over the past 50 years. Even women have internalized the implicit messaging from pro-life laws, as evidenced by one woman comforting another on a post-abortive forum with, "it's not a sin. It's not against the law."[30]

Ben Zeisloft, editor-in-chief of the independent newspaper *UPenn Statesman*, succinctly explains this dilemma: "Anyone who has ministered in front of an abortion facility can attest that mothers often raise excuses such as 'my baby cannot feel pain yet,' 'my baby does not even have a heartbeat,' or 'my baby is only ten weeks old.' Where did they learn to speak about their babies like this? From pro-life laws. The result? Their conscience is soothed as they murder their own children."[31]

Lawyer and scholar Josh Craddock echoed this same concern in 2013 in response to pain-capable bills. Craddock's warning was that pro-life bills inform women on humane ways to end the lives of their babies, resulting in the concentrated focus of regulating abortion. Craddock said:

> The problem with so-called "fetal pain" legislation is that it obscures the real issue: the personhood of the unborn child from the moment of fertilization. Instead, it teaches that abortion is bad because it is painful. It then prescribes a remedy by allowing only abortions that are not painful for the baby, as if that is a panacea. Some "pro-life" lawmakers have even gone so far as to propose abortion anesthesia for the baby....Instead of spending years and millions of dollars pushing this shortsighted bill through Congress, let's get back to our mission: abolishing abortion....If we intend to convince legislators to end abortion, we must hold them to a higher standard. We must not be placated with bills riddled

with the bodies of "exceptions"; we must play harder to get. If we intend to educate the public about the humanity of the unborn child, we cannot raise an inconsistent standard that OKs the killing of some unborn children (those conceived in rape or incest, those prior to 20 weeks, those who cannot feel pain, etc.). That will be rejected as a defense of all unborn human life, as it was in Roe v. Wade.[32]

Today, the truth of these warnings is seen plainly. Thanks to soft abortion laws, the comfort of being an abortionist has extended from licensed medical professionals to average women – and in ways the pro-life movement may not have anticipated.

According to the Guttmacher Institute, medication abortion accounted for 39% of all abortions in 2017[33]; by 2020, it accounted for 53%; in 2022 it accounted for 54%; and in 2023 it accounted for 63%[34] of all abortions performed in the United States. Since the reversal of *Roe v. Wade,* and many states passing laws that are threatening the closure of abortion facilities, the Guttmacher Institute projects medication abortions to climb even more. Evidence shows chemical abortions are the new frontier and area increasing with no end in sight.

A chemical abortion is performed by using two different pills. The first pill is mifepristone, which blocks the production of progesterone, the hormone needed to maintain the pregnancy. Progesterone contributes to a rich, nourishing environment for the growing human; but with mifepristone, the developing baby is starved of the nutrients she needs to survive and slowly dies. The second medication, misoprostol, induces labor to force the baby from the uterus. On label, these two medications are generally used through 12 weeks of gestation but can be effective through 23 weeks of pregnancy, according to the Royal College of Obstetrics and Gynaecologists. It is important to note that misoprostol is also used for other purposes such as helping a woman who had a spontaneous abortion (also known as a miscarriage) deliver the dead baby without surgical intervention. Misoprostol by itself is not evil but the application of it can be.

At the time of this writing, all 50 states allow for medication abortion in some capacity. There may be some variance on whether it is allowed through telehealth medicine, pharmacy pick up, procured in person from a medical facility, or whether it is criminal for individuals to distribute it to others. For the states that allow telehealth consultations and prescriptions for abortion pills, abortion medication suppliers such as Just The Pill, Choix and Hey Jane are quickly moving into those states to expand the online murder pill industry.[35]

An article published on WIRED in July 2022 explores the now flourishing abortion pill market many women are turning to as abortion facilities near their homes close in many conservative states. The article reports most of these abortion pills are imported from international companies to residents of states with strict abortion access. Medside24 is the most common online provider and gets its supply of abortion pills primarily from India. While international drugs delivered by mail are technically illegal, it is a business hard to regulate. As Mary Ziegler, professor at the University of California Davis School Of Law, told WIRED, "The FDA has a policy that limits personal importation of drugs, which could cover medication abortion, but historically the FDA really hasn't done a whole lot of enforcement. There is a sense that what these companies are doing is not legal, but there's also a sense that no one is really going to do anything about it."[36] Similarly, *The New York Times* published an article covering the story of a Texas woman who went on a race against time to find abortion pills before her second trimester. By her estimation, she was around eight weeks pregnant, just past the then-Texas Heartbeat Bill cutoff for an abortion. Realizing she could no longer access an abortion clinician within Texas, the young woman, who wished to remain anonymous, admitted, "I was about to turn twenty-seven and now I had to choose: have a baby or somehow find a way to be my own abortion doctor."[37]

While the post-*Roe* Texas trigger law (Texas Health and Safety Code § 170A .002-4) made it a first-degree felony to perform an abortion on another person, "Texas women can still order abortion pills online and perform their own abortions without any possibility of legal ramifications."[38] Taking advantage of this loophole, this young woman procured abortion pills through an online site and personally performed the abortion in the privacy of her own home. She is not alone.

Online abortion forums are filled with thousands of women detailing their self-managed abortions within the privacy of their homes. Growing alongside the at-home preborn murder trend is the audacious crusade to encourage women to continue abortions despite the demise of *Roe*. Shout Your Abortion, an abortion activist group led by women, has a dedicated website and Facebook page to share women's abortion stories for comradery and encouragement in choosing abortion. It also promises to help women access abortion pills regardless of the state in which they reside. Shout Your Abortion's current tagline is "We will aid and abet abortion" and it makes no secret that its main mission "is normalizing abortion and elevating safe paths to access, regardless of legality."[39] Its goal is clear: to continue the abortion momentum post-*Roe*. This, of course, can only succeed with the cooperation of pregnant women and the protection of pro-life immunity laws.

Recent online forums show that the impetus is continuing with little dissuasion, even for women in more restrictive states. From women recounting their experience with at-home abortions to reflecting on the surreal moment of seeing the babies they killed or coaching women on how to manage their own abortions, the enthusiasm – and demand – for abortion has yet to wane. Excerpts from more abortive women detail this reality:

> I just took the pill at home…my daughter is seven months old I'm a single mom too. Sacrificing this life to save yours is PRO life. Your living daughter deserves a happy healthy mother. Hugs! I have no regrets.[40]

> I am supposed to do my abortion on Wednesday (pill method). I'm about two months, will I see my baby as I will be at home? [41]

My medical abortion happened fully yesterday…however at one point when I went to the bathroom I seen the baby…in my pants…little arms and little legs…I was not expecting to fully see it, I thought it would be covered more.[42]

My baby came out, I had to cut the umbilical cord [and] flush him. I miss him every day.[43]

I am struggling to find peace within me. This past Sunday I took my 4 pills. I was almost 10 weeks, and the worst part is seeing the baby fall in my underwear.[44]

There is no way to tell the difference between a miscarriage and an abortion. If you don't want to mention you had one, say you miscarried.[45]

… you do not need to go anywhere. Self-manage it at your home or a safe place. Take 2 days off of work, the day of and the day after. Use a heating pad, some strong ibuprofen, and some big absorbent pads.[46]

I read on the PP website that medication abortion basically mimics a miscarriage and you can tell the doctors you had a MC [miscarriage].[47]

Has anyone ever used AIDACCESS? I'm in a state where abortion is illegal so I want to use that but idk if it's legit. I'm several months pp [post-partum] and I got a positive test, and as much as it hurts me I cannot have this baby.[48]

I used Aid Access. A pharmacy in New Jersey ships them to you in discreet packaging.[49]

In 2023, the Guttmacher Institute published data that revealed 63% of all abortions were medication abortions. That means well over half of all abortions are administered and managed by the women themselves. This creates a perplexity for the pro-life movement. Its position is only *abortionists*, not women, should be prosecuted for performing an abortion. The pro-life position maintains professional abortionists understand abortion is killing a life but women seeking an abortion do not have the same level of understanding. Based on statistics, testimonies and current social trends, the majority of abortionists are the babies' mothers – and they are not surprised to deliver their dead, human offspring.

License to Kill

While some states forbid facilities from distributing abortifacients for medication abortions, one giant loophole remains: There are no laws in any of the 50 states prohibiting women from procuring the pills for themselves. Whether through national suppliers, a friend or an international pharmaceutical company, no woman is criminalized from using pills to end the life of her preborn child. There is no legal backlash for mothers who pursue abortion of any kind, at any time, or for any reason, even within states that have "severe restrictions" or "bans." In every case, the restrictions apply only to providers, not to pregnant women.

Oklahoma, much like Texas, is considered to have severe abortion restrictions; however, Oklahoma statute 63 § 1-731.4 states it does not "authorize the charging or conviction of a woman with any criminal offense in the death of her own unborn child."[50]

Arkansas used the same language in its 2021 pro-life bill Act 309 to exempt women from legal consequences, and Missouri included in its statute §188.017 titled Right to Life of the Unborn Child Act that "a woman upon whom an abortion is performed or induced in violation of this subsection shall not be prosecuted for a conspiracy to violate the provisions of this subsection."[51]

While Missouri treats abortionists who violate the law with a Class B felony, Alabama successfully made abortion a Class A felony for anyone who performs an abortion on a woman (except for cases of where the mother's life is considered at risk), yet it explicitly legalizes women to commit their own abortions by slipping in under section § 26-23H-5: "No woman upon whom an abortion is performed or attempted to be performed shall be criminally or civilly liable."

Alabama's northern neighbor Kentucky has been praised for passing recent abortion bans. Nevertheless, Kentucky pro-life representatives wrote into statute §311.772 that "Nothing in this section may be construed to subject the pregnant mother upon whom any abortion is performed or attempted to any criminal conviction and penalty."

Only the states considered the most conservative and strongest in pro-life efforts were chosen to showcase the vast amount of exemptions for women that exist. These loopholes are significant because they aid the expansion of the abortion industry by transferring the power of being an abortionist right into the hands of women.

The Centers for Disease Control and Prevention reported in its most recent publication on abortion that 93% of abortions occur before 13 weeks gestation, six percent are between 13-21 weeks, and only one percent are performed after 21 weeks gestation.[52] Since misoprostol and mifepristone can be used off-label up to 24 weeks of gestation[53] in self-managed abortions, this means the abortion pill could theoretically meet around 99% of abortion needs without women ever stepping foot into a clinic. At the minimum, 93% of abortions can occur under proper label use of abortifacient medication.

With an unregulated mail-in-abortion market on the rise and no legal deterrents for women, more mothers will replace the role of the professional abortionist in years to come.

Despite evidence proving most mothers to be the principal actors in the murder of their unborn children, Kristan Hawkins, Students for Life of America President, and Marjorie Dannenfelser, Susan B. Anthony Pro-Life America President, wrote a joint article in August 2022 once again reiterating their stance against prosecuting these women for abortion:

> Few things cause more alarm than the idea of prosecuting women for abortion, which the pro-life movement as a whole has rejected repeatedly.... Pro-life feminists have always advocated prevention and accountability from men and society.... As leaders of two national organizations operating in all 50 states and working to pass life-affirming legislation, we state again emphatically that we oppose prosecuting women for abortion.[54]

Their stance is the majority position of the pro-life movement. For decades, pro-life leaders have catechized the movement and society that abortive women are not to be viewed as guilty. In the words of these prominent pro-life leaders, accountability is expected from "men and society," not preborn murdering women:

> We know how much women suffer from abortion, and how they are lied to by the abortion industry. Any penalty for illegal abortion should fall on abortion providers, not the women who turn to them in desperation.[55] – Eric Scheidler, executive director of the Pro-Life Action League.

The pro-life position is that you protect both the baby and her mother from a procedure that is destructive of both...The punishment should be for the abortionist, not the baby's mom.[56] – Frank Pavone, national director of Priests for Life

No pro-lifer would ever want to punish a woman who has chosen abortion. This is against the very nature of what we are about.[57] – Jeanne Mancini, president of the March for Life Education and Defense Fund

While Trump has since 'clarified' his position on punishing women, his statements suggest he should spend more time with pro-life conservatives to gain a better appreciation of what their goals and objectives really are. This is why Family Research Council Action has consistently supported legislation that protects the mother and her child."[58] – Tony Perkins, president of the Family Research Council

I'm going on record in opposition to the prosecution of women. I believe we are all seeking to save the lives of babies, and we have done that in our laws. We are part of the group...that signed onto the paper that basically says we want to reach out to women, and have compassion for them, and help them to see that they have alternatives to abortion, but we don't want to prosecute them. A lot of them are being forced or coerced to have abortions and we are not going to participate in that.[59] – Susan Klein, Executive Director of Missouri Right to Life

We should stay focused as we have for decades on the abortionists and the abortion industry. It won't move the pro-life needle forward by prosecuting the mother....This is not to say the mother doesn't need to repent. But even the suggestion she should be prosecuted would create an unholy trinity of victimization: the mother, the child, and the pro-life cause.[60] – Mark Creech, Executive Director of Christian Action League

I think there is a moral, biblical and a legal case for saying that yes abortion is murder; yes we should declare it murder; yes we should make it illegal, but in the case of the mother, considering where we're at in the culture and where women are at right now, we should enact mercy on these murderers ... a special dispensation for women.[61] – Joel Berry, Managing Editor of *Babylon Bee*

An early denouncement of criminalizing abortive women can be traced back to 1989 to National Right to Life, the Catholic bedrock pro-life organization in the United States. National Right to Life president Jack Willke wrote in his book *Why Can't We Love Them Both* about his admiration for the pro-choice crowd's tactic of appealing to abortion rights as women's rights. He viewed this campaign as "clever" and "effective." This influenced his desire to shape the pro-life movement similarly.[62] Willke explored how appealing with feminist compassion could be an effective way to promote the pro-life cause. He declared that if the anti-abortion movement was to ever succeed, it needed to boast about how much it loved women. As Willke traveled the country to promote the pro-life cause, he stressed that abortion-seeking women often lived in difficult circumstances and deserved just as much compassion as the babies they slaughtered. He argued that doctors who performed abortions should be criminalized, not the women. From the beginning, it became one of the primary goals of the pro-life movement to prove it too was feminist, and eventually Willke's philosophy and book became known as the "pro-life Bible."[63]

The Wrong Compass

Feminist idolatry developed a pro-life movement that excuses women for murdering their unborn children. This is eerily reminiscent of the slavery colonization movement. While slavery colonizers mouthed compassion for slaves, their compassion for the slaves' oppressors was often greater. This disinterested them from wanting to prosecute slave owners. More than that, they offered compensation for any financial loss slaveholders would incur in the event of emancipation, and took a soft approach in expressing any opposition toward the evil of what the slave masters were doing so as not to offend them overtly. The colonization movement excused slaveholders for owning and murdering a subclass of humans. The pro-life movement excuses women for murdering the subclass of preborn humans. Racial supremacy excused slave owners from their crimes against black men, women and children, and sought to reward, not prosecute, these masters for it. Similarly, the pro-life movement's efforts shield women from the legal consequences of their culpability. Feminine supremacy has led to another human rights crisis within this nation.

Willke's feminism emphasis was nothing more than grandiose virtue signaling. The underlying motivation was not to let secular culture "outlove" the anti-abortion movement. Born from this competitive drive came the philosophy of, ironically, joining the pro-abortion crusade in its declaration of universal maternal innocence. The anti-abortion movement is now in a problematic spot. As clinical abortions decline in favor of medicated ones, the pro-life movement is forced to clarify its position on prosecuting abortionists without implicating women. The two are not mutually exclusive. Yet pro-life organizations have intensified their rhetoric and legislative actions in favor of prosecuting anyone *else* who kills the preborn.

The absurdity of this position is obvious. According to this ideology and certain state laws, if two pregnant women perform an abortion on each other both of them could be subject to prosecution. If, however, they sat together and personally performed their own abortions, nothing would legally come of it. In each case, they murder a preborn human. What exempts them from consequence is if that preborn human is their own child.

The pro-life worldview universally exempts all women from prosecution based on the belief that they are unaware of their involvement in criminal activity. Pro-life apologists argue the abortionist is the guilty one, as he or she is a trained doctor who understands the science of life and pieces baby parts back together after an abortion. The abortionist, they reason, has expert knowledge women do not and is the only blameworthy party. It is reasonable to concede most abortion doctors do have a different perspective on the murder of the preborn as opposed to the mother's perspective, but is that legal, logical, or biblical ground to excuse the other people involved? To test if this ideology falls under secular moralism and situational ethics or biblical morality, it can be applied to another issue.

Would Christians be equally comfortable saying men sexually attracted to minor girls are victims of the marketing and entertainment industries that sexualize young girls and, therefore, sexual predators influenced by these businesses should not face prosecution? After all, the advertising and entertainment industries have done research and understand the success of capitalizing upon the sexual drive of men, preying on their sexual vulnerabilities, lying to them, and feeding the lust of their eyes into a strong desire to ensure repeat customers and brand loyalty. It could be argued these sexualized industries made men feel as if they had no other choice but to act on their desires for underage children. The hyper-sexualization of culture presents the idea of desiring underage girls as normal and allowable. Society made that choice seem like the best one for these men. Would any credible Christian insist that perhaps these sexual predators are not predators but victims as well, coerced by a greedy industry into doing something wrong?

While both murder and pedophilia are sins against another person, only one is excusable by professing Christians in a female-worshipping society. Both pro-abortion and pro-life advocates give women who end the lives of their preborn children impunity because it fits the narrative of modern-day feminism, not because it is scriptural. Feminine exemption is fed from matriarchal idolatry, moral relativism and situational ethics. An unbiblical sympathy for women, and the naive belief women are hoodwinked into homicide, feeds an iniquitous concession. It is an illogical argument that holds little water when juxtaposed against the quotes of many leading feminists and abortion organizations or when the same rationalization is applied to other crimes.

Pro-life pietism assumes only anti-abortion women intellectually understand abortion is murder, while women of the other side do not yet have that knowledge. Many well-meaning individuals believe that if women considering abortion understood that it is killing a human, they would also be against it. When one evaluates the pro-abortion side, it is discovered these activists have been trying for decades to educate the pro-life movement they are not, in fact, ignorant of the nature of abortion or the humanity of the preborn. They just do not care.

Women Have Always Known

Planned Parenthood, today's abortion giant, circulated an informational pamphlet in the early 1900s which educated women on how to prevent pregnancies. While explaining birth control, it included a question titled "Is it an abortion?" It answered the question in the following way:

> "No, it is entirely different. Abortion kills life after it has begun. Birth control prevents the beginning of life. Abortion is dangerous to your life and health. Birth control, when prescribed by a doctor, cannot hurt you in any way."[64]

Another similar pamphlet published by Planned Parenthood of America Federation in 1952 listed the exact same question and answer within its content. Twenty-one years prior to *Roe v. Wade*, Planned Parenthood was transparent about the practice of abortion. The reality of the procedure would have been largely understood among the populations of which these pamphlets were distributed. Margaret Sanger, founder of Planned Parenthood, circulated many of these pamphlets primarily amongst what she called the "inferior races" and "human weeds" populace.[65] Sanger strongly believed in limiting the poor and black communities from overpopulating. These demographics would have been among the first to be educated that abortion ends a human life.

The understanding that abortion ends a human life is not relegated only to Sanger and the early years of Planned Parenthood. A 2005 *Los Angeles Times* piece followed the work of abortionist William Harrison and spotlighted different abortion stories. One interesting statement within the article reads: "Harrison glances at an ultrasound screen frozen with an image of the fetus taken moments before, against the fuzzy black-and-white screen, he sees the curve of a head, the bend of an elbow, the ball of a fist."[66]

This is definitively humanizing language of the preborn, and is used in an abortion-friendly article. A reporter, not a trained preborn killer, wrote the piece, which means at least this reporter as a lay person understood the humanity of the preborn and what abortion does. It is highly improbable no other women ever read that article's detail. Even more recent was a 2022 National Public Radio (NPR) broadcast of a woman aborting her twins. NPR published the audio of the abortion, which NPR reporter Kate Wells narrated as follows: "The lights are dimmed, there's soothing music. It actually feels a lot like a childbirth. The medical gown, the bare legs in stirrups, and a person next to you who says, 'You can do this.'" The abortive mother informed Wells that she told her children at home she was pregnant with their siblings but "would not be giving birth to them."

There are no good explanations for why pro-life leaders perpetuate the idea that women remain darkened in their understanding of the true nature and intent of abortion. Although many are unaware of the procedural specifics, most people recognize that abortion results in the termination of a human life. Understanding the precisely calibrated and surgical way an abortion is performed is a separate issue from women's understanding of the abortion's *intent*. Sixty percent of women who procure abortions already have children. This means six out of 10 women have already experienced pregnancy. They have heard the heartbeat on the Doppler, seen a tiny baby on an ultrasound, and birthed a living person. This is not a naïve group.

Libby Mitchell, a television producer and contributing editor and writer for the HuffPost, a left-leaning online news source, wrote about the insulting nature of pro-life bills meant to regulate the abortion industry. She admits it is not simply the fact that she is pro-choice and against any meddling in abortion rights, but it is the method, to which these pro-life lawmakers adhere, insinuating the idiocy of women that infuriates her. Mitchell writes:

> Because at the heart of every one of these bills is the belief that women are idiots. The sponsors of every one of these bills says they aren't trying to stop abortion, but instead are just trying to make women more "aware" of what is happening in their wombs, and what will happen if they undergo an abortion. Do they really think women who have found themselves with an unwanted pregnancy aren't "aware" of all that? I would say they are painfully aware.[67]

Not coincidentally, Mitchell's article is titled "Women are NOT Stupid." Similarly, pro-choice activist Dr. Naomi Wolf published an article in *The New Republic* where she complains about the devaluing of human life in our society while also arguing for the preservation of abortion rights. Her approach tries to take a more philosophical attitude than most pro-abortion arguments, recognizing the overuse of abortion and its detriment on society. From her perspective, there is a pious time to devalue others and an evil time to devalue others, although her arbitrary line of when degrading life becomes "overused" is unclear. She is a woman who wants it both ways – to devalue some people but not have it lead to devaluing all people. Amid her messy philosophical dilemma, she makes this assertion:

> I will maintain that we need to contextualize the right to defend abortion rights within a moral framework that admits that the death of a fetus is a real death.[68]

Several pro-abortion activists also claimed to take abortion pills on the steps of the Supreme Court as the justices heard oral arguments on Mississippi's 15-week ban in 2021, the case that eventually led to the reversal of *Roe v. Wade*. The protestors chanted, "Abortion pills are in our hands and we will not stop!" Behind them was a large sign that read: "We Are Taking Abortion Pills Forever."[69] For these women, holding the power of life and death over the unborn is the quintessence of feminism, and they are unremitting to give up that control.

Shout Your Abortion states on its website, "The Supreme Court has overturned *Roe v. Wade*, eliminating federal protections for abortion rights and setting the stage for abortion to be banned in half of the United States. Fuck SCOTUS. We're doing it anyway."[70] This does not sound like victim language. This is criminal intent.

In a recent hearing before the House Oversight Committee, on September 29, 2022, a pro-abortion witness said her abortion was "the best decision" she ever made and "an act of self-love."[71] Her testimony could not be truer. Jesus says in the gospel of Mark, "And you shall love the Lord your God with all your heart and with all your soul and with all your mind and with all your strength.' The second is this: 'You shall love your neighbor as yourself.' There is no other commandment greater than these." John 15:13 reiterates this command: "Greater love has no one than this, that someone lay down his life for his friends." According to God's standard, there is no higher definition of love than to give up your life for the betterment of someone else's. But abortion is the inverse of that. As the House Committee witness testified, her primary concern was for *herself*, not her unborn child. Her words are not original. A 2020 poem titled "This Abortion is an Act of Love" by Aimee Whittemore, a renowned author and teacher at Middle Tennessee State University, expresses all the reasons the author chose abortion. She riddled her poem with self-absorbed and worldly expressions. Themes such as killing the unborn for the sake of the planet, for fewer children to compete for their father's fortunes, for fat savings accounts, and the general sake of women's rights flow from the writing. The author sums up all the reasons to seek an abortion: "For me, for me, for me."[72]

Katha Pollit, an accomplished writer and columnist at *The Nation*, wrote in 2018, "At the bottom, abortion is about a woman's individual freedom, her (cold word) autonomy – her right, you might say, to love herself."[73] Pollit is recognized as a leading pro-abortion voice in progressive politics. Her sentiment undoubtedly has influenced many abortive women, perhaps even the House Committee witness. These honest admissions from pro-choice women that abortion kills another human, that they do not care what the law says, that they will commit abortion anyway, and that they are pursuing abortion because of self-love, are crushing blows to the pro-life dogma that states women are victims of the preborn murder industry. It is much easier for pro-abortion activists to admit they are killing a human than it is for the pro-life movement to admit of them.

No one speaks this way about other crimes. No one makes excuses for drunk drivers by saying they did not fully understand how alcohol would impair them and they are victims of the alcohol industry. Imagine a drunk driver, who killed innocent victims, standing on the courthouse steps, downing a bottle of Tequila, and shouting, "Alcohol forever! I will not stop!" It is unfathomable anyone would show sympathy to her, let alone fight for her immunity to continue driving drunk and killing others. If this reasoning is rubbish when applied to other circumstances where criminal choices are involved, then it should be time to stop using it to describe pregnant women who choose to kill. The pro-choice crowd and abolitionists agree on one thing: that it is time for the pro-life movement to stop calling women morons. As former Planned Parenthood president Faye Wattleton once said, "Women are not stupid ... women have always known that there was a life there."[74]

A Society's God

Despite overwhelming evidence that most abortive women are anything but victims in the murders of their unborn children, the pro-life movement and pro-life religious leaders still push that narrative. At the 2023 Southern Baptist Convention in Louisiana, Jason Keith Allen, President of Midwestern Baptist Theological Seminary and Spurgeon College, had this to say in response to the question if he believes homicide laws should apply to all people involved in preborn murder:

> I believe life is sacred from the womb to the tomb. From conception to natural death. I do believe that the taking of life in the womb morally speaking is tantamount to murder...If you're asking me if I believe in places where abortion has been outlawed – praise God those places are growing – do I believe...where the law has been violated if that violation criminal punishment may be brought, the answer is I do believe that may be appropriate, it is indeed appropriate. If you're asking me if the random seventeen-year-old girl or the random twenty-five year old lady, for whatever reason, had an abortion, if I believe that I am willing to say to you today before God's people that they should be prosecuted for murder like one who would take the life of someone outside the womb, if that is the exactly the same, I cannot make that commitment to you in this moment, brother.[75]

Former professor at Southeastern Baptist Theological Seminary Karen Swallow Prior also teaches that women are most likely not morally culpable for preborn homicide. Prior writes, "Yet, punishing the woman whose circumstances make her believe abortion is her best option reinforces the idea that she is a radically autonomous being acting on her own apart from the formation of culture and her culture's norms and laws."[76]

Like Hawkins and Dannenfelser, Prior pushes the ideology that society and men should be held responsible for abortion but not the women participating in it. The pro-life movement takes painstaking strides to push a universal victim narrative for all abortive women. On the other hand, Pastor Josh Buice writes, "For individuals to support the abolition of abortion but to reject the prosecution of women who murder their babies is to be woefully inconsistent. Our justice system is extremely robust and allows all layers of every case to be heard and considered individually. Every case is unique and deserving of due process under the law. However, if pro-life groups oppose abortion but refuse to hold women accountable for murder, they reject equal protection and justice for all. That is a broken ethic that should be abandoned and opposed by Christians."[77]

God's law and America's highest written law (the Constitution) both prohibit any person from murdering another human. The unfortunate reality is the pro-life movement writes in loopholes for preborn killers and participates with the abortion industry in ignoring constitutional law that is supposed to protect all humans. As church-state expert and author Reverend R.J. Rushdoony once wrote:

> In Biblical law, all life is under God and His law. Under Roman law, the parent was the source and lord of life. The father could abort the child, or kill it after birth. The power to abort, and the power to kill, go hand in hand, whether in parental or in state hands. When one is claimed, the other is soon claimed also. To restore abortion as a legal right is to restore judicial or parental murder.[78]

This is precisely what has been accomplished. For almost 50 years, *Roe v. Wade* set the precedent to recognize parental murder, and states have equally spent as much time writing laws upholding this standard. The pro-life movement displays its own cognitive dissonance when it refuses to acknowledge mothers can and do act with malice aforethought and as the primary aggressors against their preborn children. Even abortion activist Miriam Claire recognizes the premeditation involved with an abortion. She argues that abortion must be defended as a justified, legal killing for those involved; otherwise, the abortion movement has a severe dilemma. Claire lectures: "It is up to pro-choice advocates to get the message out that *abortion is not murder*."[79]

Why is it important to stress this message? Claire explains that the legal definition of murder is the "unlawful killing of another human being with malice aforethought" and that "premeditation definitely pertains to abortion because in one way or another the woman decides to have an abortion and takes steps to carry it out. That is by any definition intentional behavior."[80]

Claire and many of the abortionists she interviewed for her book acknowledge that the unborn fetus is living and human "but not yet a baby."[81] Their greatest point of defense for abortion is that is lawful killing. Is the unborn living? Yes, Claire concurs. Is the unborn a human being? Most likely, she says. Is killing the living, unborn being murder? No, she determines, because even if the unborn are human beings their demise is legally permitted as in other situations, like self-defense and capital punishment. She sums up her rationale by circling back to a common pro-life talking point:

> Just because more than 50% of the American people believe abortion is murder (according to various polls) doesn't make it true. Many of those same people also believe that abortion is justified in some cases, especially rape and incest, and should be legally available. If abortion is murder, why should there be exceptions against it?[82]

The pro-life and pro-abortion movements participate with the state in assigning ultimate authority over the preborns' right to life to the parents, and, very specifically, the mothers. The pro-life movement supports the right to life for the preborn if derived from the wishes of their mothers. It believes only theoretically and abstractly that preborn humans' right to life is derived from the doctrine of being image bearers of God and from the guarantees of the Constitution. From this bifurcated belief, the pro-life movement neglects to act with jurisprudence to adequately protect the preborn with the same laws that protect born humans because legally establishing equal protection and justice for the unborn would result in *anyone* involved in destroying that preborn human's life being liable to legal prosecution.

The pro-life movement, through its broken ethics and unbiblical morals, helped contribute to the godless matriarchal supremacy of the culture. No other demographic has the same power over another person's life the way women possess over the unborn. The only other time this nation saw such unrestricted right over another human's right to life was during the slaveholding days more than 150 years ago. Today, women are the only part of the American populace that has a license to kill with impunity.

When the legislative dust settles, women are the real ones the pro-life movement is interested in protecting. It shares that in common with the pro-abortion culture. Author Gary North asserts: "A *society's god is its publicly designated source of law*. Thus, a society's legal order will testify to the nature and character of its god."[83]

The secularism within the pro-life movement has resulted in its participation with irreligious society in elevating women above all other community members. When the pro-life movement writes laws that only and always protect a mother from the consequence of the law at the expense of preborn humans, it has established her as a god and given her sovereignty over preborn life.

All identifying details from abortive women's quotes within this chapter (and book) have been altered to protect their privacy.

7

Equal Justice: Loving Our Preborn Neighbors as Ourselves

"If it seems more horrible to kill a man in his own house than in a field, because a man's house is his place of most secure refuge, it ought surely to be deemed more atrocious to destroy a fetus in the womb before it has come to light." — John Calvin, reformer (1509-1564)

Equality under the Law

Prior to the Supreme Court's decision overturning *Roe v. Wade* and *Planned Parenthood v. Casey* on June 24, 2022, pro-abortion groups were already screaming that reversing *Roe* would lead to immediate bans and imprisonment for thousands of women. Abolitionists raised their eyebrows at this. They were not nearly as optimistic about abortion being criminalized, and they certainly had never seen such expediency in the justice system, but the abortion crowd's tantrum raised a long-ignored justice question for the general public: What *does* equal justice for preborn humans look like?

In simple terms, if someone murdered a preborn human it would subject them to the same investigation, charges, trial and prosecution as if they had murdered a born human. The Constitution prohibits any person from murdering another human, and the State cannot allow the planned execution of anyone without a fair trial and jury conviction. In today's culture, the safety measures that protect the lives of born humans are dismissed for preborn humans. In order to achieve equal protection and justice for all humans under homicide law, we should apply the same legal, judicial and moral expectation to the preborn. Cali simply explains this concept: "When we say 'without exception and without compromise', we are demanding equal justice and equal protection under the law. We want all principle actors, co-conspirators, and accomplices in all forms of homicide to be governed by the very same law."[1]

This straightforward, unbiased concept is not well-received. Leftist mantra responds to abolitionism with the accusation that all abortive women, both past and future, will be hunted down, imprisoned and executed on death row. The pro-life tone soothes women by reminding them it would never support legislation that results in abortive mothers being punished for their part in preborn homicide. The abolition movement says it is faithful to both the Constitution and Scripture to protect preborn humans with the same laws that protect born humans from murder. All three groups benefit from the truth of what would happen in a country with abortion completely criminalized.

It is worth defining terms promptly as "abolishing abortion" means different things in pro-life and abolition circles. For the abolition movement, "to abolish" means to criminalize abortion *for all people*. Criminalization means the institution of abortion is no longer accepted formally or legally in any capacity, and any willful participation on the behalf of any and each person in the act of abortion can result in legal consequences for that individual. This is entirely fitting with the laws of our land.

The Fourteenth Amendment of the U.S. Constitution states, "No state shall deny to any person within its jurisdiction the equal protection of the laws."[2] This means we are forbidden by the Constitution to show partiality to any person or group of people. This is problematic since preborn humans have experienced partiality for 50 years. We have seen this partiality before. Until the ratification of the Thirteenth Amendment in 1865, the country denied equal rights to slaves, too.

The stain of our slave history should energize Christians to quickly establish equality under homicide law for the preborn; yet this is the very thing the pro-life movement opposes alongside the pro-abortion movement. In fact, since the overturn of *Roe,* the pro-life movement is using the rhetoric "abolish abortion" more and more, yet its intention is wildly different from abolitionism. Pro-life organizations speak of abolishing or criminalizing abortion in reference to the abortion industry and paid providers. As a result, pro-life PACs and politicians have focused efforts on only criminalizing abortion for those who financially profit from it. This reality was fulfilled in Texas, Oklahoma, Louisiana, Arkansas, Missouri, South Dakota, Wisconsin, Kentucky, Tennessee and Alabama after the *Dobbs* decision. However, these states do not provide equal protection and justice under homicide law for their preborn because mothers still have full legal privilege to destroy these children in any way they desire and at any gestational age with no repercussions. For those whom abortion *is* "criminalized", they do not yet face first degree murder charges.

Conversely, attorney Bradley Pierce says abolition bills provide equal justice and protection for the preborn by removing the exceptions in state homicide statutes that allow for them to be killed. On Abolish Abortion Texas' website, an affiliate of Foundation to Abolish Abortion, it states:

> When we talk about bills to abolish abortion, we aren't really talking about creating new laws at all. Often, like in Texas, state law already defines abortion as homicide but then has an exception that allows for abortion. An abolition bill just removes or overrides that exception.[3]

This is an important distinction. Abolition bill critics routinely claim these bills will introduce unusual and cruel punishments for women. Currently, mothers are exempt from all legal punishment for killing their preborn babies, so changing the law to hold *all* people accountable for destroying the life of a preborn human would be in a sense "new;" but there is nothing unusual, cruel or novel about holding people accountable for murder.

At the time of this writing, no abolition bill introduced in any state legislation has contained new law. Each abolition bill has only required existing laws to be used impartially.

A Case of Unjust Exemptions

Kansas has been a battleground for abortion even before *Roe v. Wade* set foot in the courtroom. While a primarily conservative state, Kansas was one of the first and only states to offer late-term abortions and its abortion laws have typically been progressive even by pro-life standards. Despite that, Kansas defines killing of the preborn person as murder...but still allows for it. This paradox is not an anomaly. Many states currently function with such contradicting philosophical and legal realities. In the instance of Kansas, it recognizes the preborn as a "person" and "human being" according to one important state statute printed in its entirety below.

> Article 67. - ABORTION 65-6732. Legislative declaration that life begins at fertilization. (a) The legislature hereby finds and declares the following: (1) The life of each human being begins at fertilization; (2) unborn children have interests in life, health and well-being that should be protected; and (3) the parents of unborn children have protectable interests in the life, health and well-being of the unborn children of such parents. (b) On and after July 1, 2013, **the laws of this state shall** be interpreted and construed to **acknowledge on behalf of the unborn child at every stage of development, all the rights, privileges and immunities available to other persons, citizens and residents of this state,** subject only to the constitution of the United States, and decisional interpretations thereof by the United States supreme court

and specific provisions to the contrary in the Kansas constitution and the Kansas Statutes Annotated. (c) As used in this section: (1) "Fertilization" means the fusion of a human spermatozoon with a human ovum. (2) ***Unborn children or unborn child shall include all unborn children or the offspring of human beings from the moment of fertilization until birth at every stage of biological development.*** (d) Nothing in this section shall be construed as creating a cause of action against a woman for indirectly harming her unborn child by failing to properly care for herself or by failing to follow any particular program of prenatal care.[4] [Emphasis added.]

This statute would be a life-saving measure for all preborn Kansans if it were not for its sudden deference to Supreme Court decisions and state statutes that invalidate whether the preborn can actually enjoy the right to life. The highest court in the land can be wrong, as the country saw the Supreme Court admit in 2022 with the reversal of its *Dobbs* decision. The U.S. Constitution, as well as state constitutions, is the Law of the Land, not the judicial bench. The constitutions are clear about rights ascribed to each human. Allowing judicial opinions to override constitutionally aligned legislation is what political philosopher Hadley Arkes calls, "antijural jurisprudence."[5] It allows the judicial branch to operate in a way it was never designed. This error of judicial supremacy is clear in this Kansas statute:

> (b)...the laws of this state shall be interpreted and construed to acknowledge on behalf of the unborn child at every stage of development, all the rights, privileges and immunities available to other persons, citizens and residents of this state, subject only to the constitution of the United States, ****and decisional interpretations thereof by the United States supreme court and specific***

provisions to the contrary in the Kansas constitution and the Kansas Statutes Annotated.

The aforementioned section references *Roe v. Wade*, as well as other Kansas statutes, that effectively remove protection for the preborn when certain people want them dead. In fact, the statute reads in such a way that court opinions in conflict with the promised protections of the Constitution take precedence over the clear inalienable rights ascribed to all human life within the U.S. Constitution and state constitution.

This results in corrupt legislation that says preborn humans have personhood only so long as no one else – such as the courts – say they do not. Kansas statute 65-6732 gives lip service to the Constitution, but in practice it allows lawlessness to nullify the true law. This section of Kansas law, which grants only *partial personhood* to the preborn, came about because of a tragic event. In 2007, Kansans for Life, the largest pro-life organization in Kansas, supported and helped facilitate the passage of a new pro-life law called Alexa's Law, a statute crafted after the brutal murder of pregnant 14-year-old Chelsea Brooks. Brooks' family and pro-life organizations sought to amend the law to prosecute violent crimes committed against the preborn for a very specific reason. Brooks' family wanted to charge Chelsea's murderer with double homicide. While it sounds reasonable, Alexa's Law is grievously misguided by anti-jural jurisprudence by exempting different people involved in the premeditated deaths of preborn humans from criminal prosecution. Alexa's Law clarifies the preborn are people due protection under the law unless "specific provisions to the contrary in...the Kansas Statutes Annotated" override the preborn human's protections. The Kansas statutes being referred to are as follow:

Article 54. - CRIMES AGAINST PERSONS. **21-5419. Application of certain crimes to an unborn child.** (a) As used in this section: (1) "Abortion" means an abortion as defined by K.S.A. 65-6701, and amendments thereto; and (2) "unborn child" means a living individual organism of the species homo sapiens, in utero, at any stage of gestation from fertilization to birth. (b) This section shall not apply to: (1) <u>Any act committed by the mother</u> of the unborn child; (2) any medical procedure, including <u>abortion, performed by a physician or other licensed medical professional at the request of the pregnant woman or her legal guardian</u>; or (3) the lawful dispensation or administration of lawfully prescribed medication. (c) As used in K.S.A. 2012 Supp. 21-5401, 21-5402, 21-5403, 21-5404, 21-5405, 21-5406 and subsections (a) and (b) of 21-5413, and amendments thereto, "person" and "human being" also mean an unborn child. (d) This section shall be known as Alexa's law.[6]

This Kansas statute is filed under homicide laws and leads with "certain crimes to an unborn child." Subsection (c) under point (3) lists several other statute numbers. Those numbers reference the specific *types of murder* recognized in Kansas. Before looking at those, though, notice points (1), (2) and (3) under subsection (b). In regard to the unborn, these bulleted points exempt women, licensed medical professionals, and a girl's guardian from the homicide laws which are listed under subsection (c) of point (3). These homicide laws are:

K.S.A. 21-5401: Capital murder.

K.S.A. 21-5402: Murder in the first degree.

K.S.A. 21-5403: Murder in the second degree.

K.S.A. 21-5404: Voluntary manslaughter.

K.S.A. 21-5405: Involuntary manslaughter.

K.S.A. 21-5406: Vehicular homicide.

Per this statute, if a preborn human is not wanted and the mother either takes abortion pills or hires an abortionist to murder her baby, then both she and the abortionist are exempt from all the above homicide charges. A girl's guardians also have legal protection, which creates a perfect climate for coercion to take place. This is also clear protection for sexual abusers and human traffickers. However, if someone *outside* this protected group causes the death of a preborn child against the mother's or guardian's wishes, homicide charges may be brought against that individual. The test for whether a preborn human has the right to life in Kansas is whether the baby is wanted by the mother. And the test for whether a preborn human in Kansas can expect justice under homicide law depends on who murders him or her.

This pro-life statute smacks of Margaret Sanger's tagline and now Planned Parenthood's motto: "Every child a wanted child." This hypocritical law and flagrantly unconstitutional and unbiblical treatment of preborn humans is listed as a pro-life achievement on the website of Kansans for Life.[6]

Despite claims by anti-abolitionists, it is pro-life bills that introduce new and unfair laws, not abolition bills. It is unnatural for anyone to have special privilege to murder certain types of people under the penal codes. Impunity only happens when intentional bills excuse a demographic from legal prosecution; otherwise, the law would stand for all people equally in a society. Alexa's Law exemplifies this well, though it isn't limited to Kansas. As Pierce points out, abolition bills aim to remove these unjust exemptions in order to protect the life of the preborn human from all aggressors.

Those within the pro-life movement who are against criminalizing abortion usually bring up the fear of jails being encumbered with abortive women as their next line of defense against abolition bills. The pro-abortion movement also screams about how many abortive women will end up on death row. Both perspectives are unfounded. If state homicide laws do not imprison suspects without an investigation and trial, nor send other types of murderers to death row without due process, then it will not happen for abortive mothers accused of preborn murder either. The judicial system is purposely complicated and meant to protect both the accused and the victim. If states remove exemptions biased against the preborn, and apply existing homicide laws to abortion, then we would treat ending the life of a preborn human the same way we treat ending the life of a born person. If an arrest was made, due process would take effect for the accused to guard against false allegations. If an investigation found no evidence of a crime, the case would be closed. If the allegations were legitimate, a trial would follow. As Pierce says, "Equal protection would provide due process and would require case-by-case examination by a justice system that requires near unanimous agreement to punish anyone at all."[7]

Criminal Justice 101

Due process is a system of procedures that must be followed to ensure the innocent are not punished and that the guilty receive justice. To understand due process, it is best to look at how a case begins.

First, a crime must be reported. Usually, another citizen reports a crime to the police. Once an investigation begins, the police investigate to determine probable cause to believe a crime has, in fact, been committed. If enough evidence suggests a crime has occurred, the police present their evidence to a judge. If the evidence is compelling, the judge issues a warrant for the police to continue their investigation. If the evidence is not compelling, the police return to their work to gather more information in order to obtain a warrant. Once a warrant is in hand, the police must collect enough convincing evidence through investigation to present to a prosecutor who will determine if more evidence is needed for a case to be considered, or if there is sufficient evidence to go to trial.

The legal system considers alleged murder a felony. In most felony cases, the prosecution must first present the case to the grand jury. The prosecutor takes the evidence before a grand jury, who deliberates the evidence behind closed doors to protect the accused's reputation. If the grand jury determines there is enough probable cause to seek a conviction, they issue a true bill to indict, which is followed by an arrest. Police, judges, prosecutors and a grand jury must unanimously agree upon and clear many hurdles in order to arrest someone for a suspected homicide. Additional processes must occur before punishment occurs. Former FBI deputy assistant director of counterterrorism Stu McArthur says, "At the time of trial the defendant is presumed innocent. This places the burden of guilt upon the government to prove guilt beyond a reasonable doubt." McArthur further elaborates about preborn murder: "This part of the system would protect a woman who was 'forced' to have an abortion because the government would not be able to demonstrate the person, who is presumed innocent, had the *mens rea*, or criminal intent, to commit the crime charged."[8]

The accused is arrested if everything has gone smoothly up to indictment; the arrested person is now called the defendant and is entitled to an attorney. If the defendant cannot afford a private attorney, the state will pay for one for them. A competent attorney will look for ways to have the case thrown out before proceeding to trial, and this could occur if evidence is collected illegally or improperly.

To throw out a case, the attorney would speak with the judge assigned to the case in an effort to have it dismissed. The request to throw out the case will be denied if the judge believes everything has progressed properly. Next, a trial date is set and a jury of peers is selected. The bar is set much higher in a trial. The prosecution must prove *beyond a reasonable doubt* that a crime was committed and that *the defendant committed that crime with criminal intent*. This requirement of proof is called an "extremely high burden." In a presentation to the public, Pierce described it as, "You have to prove not just probable cause, not just preponderance of the evidence, not just what is called clear and convincing evidence, but you have to prove it beyond a reasonable doubt. That's a *very* high bar."[9]

This high – and sometimes unachievable – goal is protection for the accused. In deliberation, the jury must decide if the evidence is convincing beyond a reasonable doubt. If jurors cannot unanimously agree on a verdict, a hung jury occurs. A few options remain for the case. The judge could ask the jury to deliberate longer, but if their deliberation time already seems adequate, and the judge believes the jury is at an irreconcilable impasse, the judge can declare a mistrial and the charges are dropped. Another outcome is the prosecution may seek to retry the case or the prosecution may enter a plea bargain with the defendant to avoid another tedious and expensive retrial.

If the jury unanimously agrees on a guilty verdict, the trial proceeds to the sentencing phase. During this phase, character witnesses are called, aggravating circumstances considered, and mitigating circumstances evaluated, all of which may support leniency in the sentencing. While judges almost always decide on the sentencing for the now-convicted defendant, the one exception would be in cases involving the death penalty. When the death penalty is an option, juries are involved in deciding the sentencing for the convicted. This crucial aspect is often overlooked by those who fear abortive women on death row. In the current culture, it would be unlikely for a jury to vote unanimously to execute a woman who had an abortion. And states that do not have the death penalty enacted cannot rely on it as a legal form of punishment.

Once sentencing is issued, the defendant can appeal to another court. Appeals are typically determined by a panel of three judges, who are randomly selected. An appeal is not a retrial but a review of trial court proceedings to ensure fairness and legality. In most states, the defendant appeals to an intermediate-level appellate court, then can appeal to the state supreme court. States such as Delaware, Maine, Montana, New Hampshire, Rhode Island, South Dakota, Vermont and Wyoming do not have appellate courts; instead, a defendant appeals directly to their state supreme courts. The process for appeal for felonies is different. A defendant who is convicted and sentenced for murder is granted an automatic appeal to the state's highest criminal court, which skips the intermediate-level court. The highest court in any state is the state supreme court, and the highest court within the nation is the Supreme Court of the United States. An average state supreme court consists of nine justices, who consider the case. If an individual resides in a state that implements the death penalty, and is convicted of capital murder, they are entitled to an automatic appeal to the United States Supreme Court, which houses an additional nine justices who will evaluate the case. If the state's highest court *and* Supreme Court of the United States agree that the case is fair, there is sufficient evidence, and the law was followed, the defendant has another option for appeal called habeas corpus. In the federal court system, habeas corpus can be used to determine whether or not a state's detention of a prisoner is valid. According to Cornell Law School:

> A *habeas* petition proceeds as a civil action against the State agent (usually a warden) who holds the defendant in custody. It can also be used to examine any extradition processes used, the amount of bail, and the jurisdiction of the court.[10]

Essentially, habeas corpus allows the defendant to repeat the entire appeal phase. The fourth Chief Justice of the Supreme Court, John Marshall, wrote in a decision in 1830 that the "great object" of the writ of habeas corpus "is the liberation of those who may be imprisoned without sufficient cause."[11] Marshall believed the use of habeas corpus to be of extreme importance within the American judicial system. It is to be yet another check against wrongful prosecution and imprisonment.

Even if after a defendant makes it through the entire judicial system (twice even!) and every person involved unanimously agrees the convictions and sentencing are justified, the governor can still pardon or commute someone's sentence.

The American justice system is built to stop innocent people from false imprisonment, unjust convictions and death row. This does not mean the system works perfectly. Fallible and corrupt humans are still the principal actors in the justice system, but painstaking strides have been made to ensure justice prevails. These procedures make a complex justice system that, at every twist and turn, offers protection to a defendant through dozens of people hearing, reading and reviewing the case, evidence and law. This process does not neglect justice for the victim. Evidence is continually reviewed to determine who is truly at fault so that the judicial system can seek justice, and sometimes retribution, on behalf of those victimized.

The Protection of Due Process

When the pro-abortion crowd whines how every woman would instantly end up in jail if abortion was banned, they echo a common sentiment of progressive politics, which despises the justice system and sees it as an obstacle to Marxist goals. They often use rhetoric to undermine the judicial system and due process in order to erode certain elements of the system they see as inhibiting equity for their special interests or people groups. Keeping with this philosophy of judicial immediacy, one can see how they might believe others would operate similarly in exploiting the justice system. They envision this exploitation to manifest by rounding up post-abortive women and throwing them in the slammer with little to no vetting of the crime or situation. This ignores how the justice system actually works, and how most citizens support the time needed for adequate and accurate conclusions from due process. Judicial impulsivity could certainly result in oppression, and progressives seem to fear their own version of "justice" being used against them. Despite the risk to individuals with eliminating due process, many progressives still petition for, at least, a watered-down version of it.

In 2017, President Barack Obama published in the *Harvard Law Review* a commentary expressing his views on criminal law and justice. His commentary only focused on *mens rea* once, the fundamental principle within the justice system that distinguishes between an accident and a crime, and is a foundational element for criminal trials and sentencing. Of *mens rea*, Obama said it was a "proposal....that could undermine public safety and harm progressive goals."[12] Spending time to determine if someone meant to commit a crime, or did so accidentally, is apparently a waste of time in the progressive's mind. However, many law scholars argue that good law has clear *mens rea* outlined so it is obvious when someone has transgressed a law. John-Michael Seibler, former legal fellow at the Heritage Foundation, writes:

> Mens rea safeguards everyone equally from unwarranted prosecution — from drug offenses to white-collar crime. Yet Congress and federal agencies routinely produce criminal laws and regulations with weak or no intent standards, often prohibiting conduct that no one would assume is illegal. As a result, honest people have

been criminally prosecuted for morally innocent mistakes or accidents.[13]

Obama is not alone in his frustration by due process. Due primarily to progressive politician Senator Kristen Gillibrand, Marxist politics eroded due process protections on college campuses for the accused of sexual crimes. Gillibrand and her progressive colleagues helped pass Title IX, the rigid federal regulation system on how schools are to handle sexual allegations.[14] Under the Obama Administration's Title IX regulations, hundreds of schools were subjected to federal investigations for, according to the administration, not taking sexual allegations more seriously. This is a prime example of poor *mens rea*. What is meant by "more seriously?"

In a reflexive action, campuses across the United States established campus court systems, which in reality were merely mock trials. These "courts" omitted due process and instead relied on the proceedings to show on paper that they addressed the sexual abuse complaints. On most college campuses, it became the norm to see the accused as guilty without any proof, witnesses or corroborated evidence, and to swiftly and quietly impose punishment to get it over with. At alarming rates, students accused one another of sexual crimes, and, without a thorough investigation or the safeguards of due process, hundreds of students' lives were ruined. Many were later proven innocent, but the damage was irreversible. A lack of poor *mens rea* and a disregard for due process created a bubble culture where people of ill-intent quickly learned they could use false narratives for their advantage. Those truly victimized were denied justice, as their perpetrators were also hurried through the erroneous college court environment with many cases never making it to the criminal justice system.

Shortcuts around due process are devastating to society and individuals. Anne Hendershott, Professor of Sociology and Director of the Veritas Center for Ethics in Public Life at Franciscan University, wrote in 2017 about Title IX:

Schools responded by building a campus court system that venerated victims, villainized the accused and often disallowed evidence pointing to the innocence of the accused. On most campuses today, there is no presumption of innocence when an allegation is made. And, in the moral panic surrounding sexual assault, any allegation is considered credible as punitive policies were implemented infringing on the civil rights of those accused.[15]

Following the lead of her progressive mentors, socialist sweetheart U.S. Representative Alexandria Ocasio-Cortez admitted in an interview with CNN that due process and justice "must center on the victim."[16] In the progressive world, justice has not been served if retribution is not immediately imposed upon individuals suspected of guilt. Due process is an obstacle to their philosophy of secular justice.[17]

Contrary to Ocasio-Cortez's viewpoint, we must have due process for the accused *and* the victim. If justice were to be limited for one group, the entire system would suffer from partiality in *every* criminal case.

Biblically, we are to treat all people with justice, both victims and the guilty. Progressives argue only those they see as victims should have access to justice. Ominously, abortion is the instance in which we permit the death penalty for someone (the preborn) without due process. By stipulating legal loopholes for the murder of preborn humans, we deprive them of much more than just life. Their right to life, liberty and the pursuit of happiness is removed by denying them the protection of due process, habeas corpus and a justified death penalty. Their deaths, while permitted by state statutes, are actually unconstitutional executions. This flagrant disregard of inalienable rights is not something we should seek to expand through progressive politics.

There may be a tendency for readers to assume this chapter implies the criminal justice system is perfect and without corruption. This is certainly not the case nor the point. Corrupt players in the system can sometimes distort justice. When a broken cog throws off the entire mechanical workings in a machine, we replace the broken cog. If a system that was founded to seek justice to the utmost possible in a fallen world is susceptible to corruption, how much worse will it be if we accept less-than-just standards, statutes and bills? Do we think we, too, will not slide from those subpar expectations?

Unfortunately, there is a common thread between the progressive's views of the justice system and the pro-life movement's views of the same system. Pro-life leaders who oppose equal justice are expressing the same progressive sentiment toward the judicial system: the belief that the justice system is incapable of rightly handling the case of abortive women, so we must shield women from that system. Whereas progressives look to work around due process to achieve the results they desire, or hack away at the system (i.e. defund police, catch-and-release, criminal sanctuary cities), pro-lifers look for ways to exempt abortive women from the system altogether. This is a damaging message the pro-life movement pushes when it preaches abortive women should not be legally liable. While these pro-life leaders may look at exempting women as an issue of philanthropy and mercy, the subliminal message is that the American justice system cannot be entrusted with doing right by women who are involved with preborn homicide (though it can be trusted to rightly judge and prosecute abortionists and those who coerce women).

Managing Editor of the *Babylon Bee* Joel Berry said in a debate with founders of Abolitionists Rising, Russell Hunter and James Silberman, that it is too difficult to determine the guilty intent in abortive women. While Silberman explained how proving intent is part of due process – and if it cannot be established beyond a reasonable doubt, then a conviction cannot follow – Berry replied, "Considering where we're at, I would not trust that decision to a jury or a prosecutor at this point in time in our culture ... determining the level of heinousness of a crime, whether the mother knew what she was doing, all of those things, I would not trust that to a judge, a jury, or a prosecutor at this point in time. I would prefer to build something in legislatively to make sure that these women are protected."[18]

If the justice system cannot do right by that group of citizens, then it follows logically to distrust it in other circumstances. It is too common to see conservative pro-life influencers link arms with progressive Marxist ideology to tear down faith and honesty within the justice system. Concerns about justice for abortive women reveal an ignorance of the judicial process and abolition bills, and perpetuate dangerous ideology that will undermine justice in other criminal categories and bolster the progressive's position of dismantling due process and law enforcement.

A Special Class of Murderers

Webster's Dictionary 1828 defines partiality as "biased to one party; inclined to favor one party in a cause more than the other" or "not indifferent." Opponents of abolition argue that criminalizing abortion would subject abortive mothers to discriminatory treatment. Of course, this is completely false and a diversion of the extreme bias present in all pro-life rhetoric, education and written laws. Equal justice does not imply equal outcomes or equal punishment, nor does it mean prejudice against abortive women. Abolish Abortion Texas succinctly explains the function of an abolition bill:

> The point is that abolition bills do not control the investigation of a crime. Abolition bills do not control the decisions of law enforcement or district attorneys as they decide what (if any) charges to bring. Abolition bills do not control the verdicts of judges or juries as they consider the evidence and determine whether to give maximum or minimum penalties or no penalty at all. Abolition bills do not control how appellate courts examine the record of trials and sentences. Abolition bills do not control whether a governor chooses to shorten someone's sentence or even pardon them altogether. Abolition bills do not dictate or control the outcomes at all.[19]

Abolition bills merely remove or override abortion exceptions, ensuring that the same laws prohibiting the homicide of a born person will also prohibit the homicide of a preborn human, thereby subjecting all individuals to the same laws preventing homicide.

A unique class of citizens is created by pro-life laws that exclude guilty mothers from punishment: those who are permitted by law to commit murder. Abolition bills would change our laws to stop this prejudice against preborn humans. This is not an unfair process if we genuinely confess that abortion is murder.

Pro-life leaders teach that pro-abortion discourse has led abortive women to believe the preborn are not fully human. The pro-life movement believes this justifies a special dispensation for all abortive women, which leads to codified bias. Many consciences would be informed against killing their preborn children if the law taught that abortion is murder. The pro-life movement ignores this, instead working to create its own version of dehumanizing laws against the preborn, which merely teach women there is a right and wrong time to kill their preborn children, rather than it is always wrong.

During a hearing for the Abolition of Abortion in Texas Act (HB 896) in 2019, Jason Storms, a pastor and member of the pro-life group Operation Save America, gave the following heart wrenching testimony:

> I was guilty as an accomplice in the murder of my own child, and I should have been prosecuted accordingly... Mothers and fathers – parents – right now in Texas can be charged with parental neglect, parental abuse, and even parental homicide when we see the tragedy of parents taking the lives of their own children. It is because mothers and fathers have a duty to love and protect their children. That responsibility doesn't start when they're born, but it starts when they're conceived. Here's a fact: my girlfriend and I, if we knew we would've been facing homicide charges, would never have aborted that child. That child would be alive today. I'd have a 22-year-old little child that I could celebrate life with right

now that's not here. The law is a deterrent to crime. We shouldn't think of this only as a matter of putting a woman on the stand. We should think of this as a great deterrent. Men and women would not think of doing this if we stood firm on the law and provided equal protection for these children.[20]

Despite what pro-abortion and pro-life critics argue, millions of women will not be imprisoned if abortion is criminalized. Most parents will not pursue preborn murder if immunity is not an option. The vast majority will consider raising a child to be less risky and unpleasant than incarceration or the death penalty. The notion that criminalizing abortion will not deter millions of women from seeking it implies one of two ominous conclusions: first, that the majority of women who seek abortions today are not law-abiding citizens who will continue their lives of lawlessness despite the criminalization of abortion; or second, those who believe women will not be deterred by homicide laws are not law-abiding people themselves and do not understand how the law would deter other individuals from homicide any more than current laws do not deter their own current criminal behavior. Both are preposterous scenarios and should cause any pro-life or pro-abortion advocate to balk and reexamine their line of thinking. Most women who have abortions *are* law-abiding citizens, and choose abortion as a sanctioned option to avoid parenthood.

Ex Post Facto Laws

For pro-life individuals who do support punishing women involved in preborn homicide, they are often fearful that past abortive women will also be prosecuted. This fear is largely founded on the myth that says women from 20, 30 or 50 years ago will be pursued and prosecuted for previous abortions. Retroactive punishment is troubling no matter the law passed. Fortunately, the Constitution prohibits retroactive punishment or *ex post facto law*, which translates as "out of the aftermath" or "from a thing done afterward."[21] There are two clauses within the Constitution that prohibit ex post facto laws. Article 1, Section 9 says Congress cannot pass any ex post facto laws. And Article 1, Section 10 dictates, "No state shall...pass any bill of attainder, ex post facto law..."[22] Both federal and state governments are forbidden from enacting laws that punish people for acts performed when those actions were lawful. Further, ex post facto law might be employed to increase the severity of penalties that were not in effect at the time the offense was committed. This is also forbidden.

One example of ex post facto law being prohibited, even in a gruesome crime, was the case of Dennis Rader, infamous American serial killer known as "BTK." The acronym Rader endearingly dubbed himself stood for "bind, torture and kill," a sinister description of how he committed his murders. A jury found Rader guilty of killing 10 people through torturous means in Wichita, Kansas, from 1974 to 1991. Following his 2005 conviction, Rader received 10 consecutive life sentences without the possibility of parole. Many people were confused by what they considered a lenient sentencing, especially since Kansas had reinstated the death penalty in 1994. And this is the importance: The last known BTK killing was committed in 1991, three years *before* the death penalty became an official sanction in Kansas. Because of the limitation of ex post facto laws, Rader was spared death row. The state was prohibited from adding to his punishment what was not permissible at the time he committed his crimes. The same would hold true for criminalizing abortion. In this situation, only abortive women moving forward from criminalizing abortion could be held liable under the law. Strangely, pro-life lawmakers have been some of the loudest voices espousing the lie of retroactive punishment.

During the Louisiana House vote on the abortion abolition bill HB 813, Representative Tanner Magee asked Representative Alan Seabaugh if the abolition bill passed if the state could go back in time and arrest every woman who had sought an abortion. Seabaugh answered, "There's some language in the bill that attempts to prevent that, but I do not believe it would be effective. So the answer to your question, I think, is yes." What is astounding about Seabaugh's response is Section 5 of the abolition bill explicitly prohibited retroactive enforcement as stated: "This Act applies to crimes committed on or after the effective date of this Act." Even the Louisiana Constitution prohibits retroactive enforcement (Art. I, § 23) as does the U.S. Constitution (Art. I, § 9 and 10).[23] Even more stunning is the fact that Seabaugh is a lawyer who grades the Louisiana bar exam's constitutional law section. He *knows* better – he knows even if the bill did not expressly ban retroactive punishment the state and federal constitutions do; thus, ex post facto law could not emerge through an abolition bill or any other bill.

Remarkably, Seabaugh did not take advantage to educate his colleagues on this misconception. Instead, he allowed Magee's misinterpretation of ex post facto law to stand to promote opposition to the abolition bill. For a self-proclaimed pro-life Republican, it was a deceptive move. As he implored a nay vote on the bill, he boasted, "If this bill would save even one baby's life I would vote on it. But it will not."[24]

Professing Christians should be passionate about justice. We must also be honest and transparent in our interactions with the world. Abolition bills promote justice for all humans and clearly outline what that means. Only the foes of equal protection and justice cloud the issue with lies, myths and hysteria. Seabaugh further declared, "I think Roe v. Wade is one of the worst decisions that has ever come out of the U.S. Supreme Court: Up there with Dred Scott and a few others. It is an abomination, in my opinion. But it is the law. Like it or not, it is the law. It has been the law for almost fifty years."[25] Seabaugh was wrong again. *Roe* was never the law but a court decision that both pro-abortion and pro-life groups were willing to follow even though it contradicted the Constitution. When Seabaugh could rescue all preborn Louisianans from murder, he opted to blame the Supreme Court for his shortcomings.

The Constitution already contains what we need to protect all human lives from unwarranted death. When the Thirteenth and Fourteenth Amendments were ratified, it was widely understood to include the once slave population, even though it does not call out white or black ethnic groups as qualifying for those particular protections. Likewise, it is understood that noncitizens have the right to freedom of speech, freedom of religion, protection against unreasonable searches and seizures, the right to due process, and the list goes on. Pro-abortion and pro-life political philosophy operates, however, on not recognizing the protection of preborn humans because *their* personhood is not specifically called out in the Constitution. On this notion, no one is safe under secular and pro-life logic of following egregious court rulings. If an unjust court ruling can grant the privilege to kill other humans and disregard the right to life, then any group of humans could be just one Supreme Court decision away from genocide. Rita Lowery Gitchell, defense litigator and contributing writer for Thomas More Society, had this to say about such a dangerous judicial standard:

> When weighing rights, should Lady Justice ask if the litigants are dependent on others for survival? Many who read this blog are aware of the dependency of the disabled, the elderly, infants, and children. Continuation of permitting dependency on another as a reason to deny unalienable rights is a dangerous precedent that allows a slippery slope to undermine the endowed human dignity of each person that deserves equal protection under the law.[26]

Practicing – not merely professing – constitutionalists understand that these rights are applied to all humans regardless of race, sex, age or location. This logically includes those within the womb. When politicians and judges are sworn into office, they swear to uphold the Constitution, not court opinions. All governing powers pledge allegiance to the Constitution, which is the supreme Law of the Land. The Supremacy Clause of the Constitution provides, "This Constitution and the Laws of the United States which shall be made in Pursuance thereof…shall be the supreme law of the land…"[27] (U.S. Const. Art VI, Clause 2.) To be deemed a legit law, a law must adequately reflect constitutionally guaranteed rights. Any declared legislation or court opinion must pass the litmus test of correctly and plainly reflecting what is in the Constitution. What is the purpose of the Constitution if it is ignored whenever a court declares something contrary to it? It is lawless for any person or entity to ignore or subvert the Constitution.

A Shield for Abusers

Lawlessness has repercussions. Giving women amnesty to commit or participate in preborn murder contradicts God's standard for holding murderers accountable, destroys justice for preborn victims, and mocks God's command to not show favoritism. It also provides the groundwork to protect other human rights abusers.

In 2011, the Journal of Midwifery and Women's Health published an article stating that 400,000 American minors are trafficked every year. This report also exposed that the "United States is one of the largest market[s] for trafficking in the world, second only to Germany."[28] On the heels of that finding, a 2014 study published by the Beazley Institute for Health Law and Policy provided even more startling statistics. The institute revealed that, on average, sex trafficked survivors "reported being used for sex by men approximately 13 buyers per day" with the median commercial sexual act being with 10 buyers each day.[29] This obviously results in unplanned pregnancies.

Out of the women interviewed for the Beazley study, 55 percent reported at least one abortion and around 30 percent of the trafficked women reported multiple abortions. The overwhelming majority of women revealed that they were either forced to have abortions or so forcefully coerced that there seemed to be no other option. Many more women had repeated miscarriages as a result of physical violence inflicted on them during sex work, either by buyers or pimps. Traffickers also use threats against people the women and girls cared for, starvation, being tied up and psychological abuse to maintain control over their victims. According to the study, 92% of trafficked survivors "reported being the victim of at least one form of physical violence," and threats were commonly used to control them. Survivors, predictably, displayed substantial mental trauma. Depression, multiple personality disorder, borderline personality disorder, and suicide ideation were among the psychological concerns encountered. The survey found that 98% of the women examined "reported at least one psychological issue during their captivity."

While these are extreme circumstances, it should go without saying that identifying all post-abortive women as victims obscures the reality of the women and children who are actually victims of the most heinous abuses. The woman who is starved, beaten, strangled and threatened to abort is a far cry from the woman who aborts to salvage her relationship, avoid her family's shame, or dodge financial responsibility. This calls for re-evaluating the use of the term "abortion victim."

The American Heritage College Dictionary defines victim as "one who is harmed or killed by another." According to this definition, women who are criminally forced into having an abortion are abuse victims; the abortion was the means by which she and her child were victimized. The person forcing harm upon her body and her child's body would be the victimizer. This definition, however, excludes women who schedule their own abortions, call their insurance to find out what coverage is offered for abortion, use their own money to pay for preborn murder, take time off work to travel to another state for an abortion, or search the Internet for ways to perform their own abortions covertly.

When we generalize all post-abortive women as abortion victims, it devalues the harm being done against the truly victimized woman or child. It also causes anti-abortion society to view the abortion process as the evil thing and not the abuser behind it. The phrase "abortion victim" is often a misnomer and has been marketed by the pro-life movement as a rhetorical tool to promote its doctrine of partiality and feminist favoritism, not as a universal categorical reality. While some pro-life advocates may use the term "abortion victim" to signify the horrors committed against some women, it still detracts from the issue at hand that led to the abortion: abuse. Understanding that forced or coerced abortion is the outcome of physical abuse, sexual abuse, or both, it should inform Christians all the more as to why abortion should be entirely criminalized. It should also inform Christians to not overuse or misuse the abortion victim terminology when discussing abortive women in general.

By not abolishing abortion, the gate is left open to provide cover for pimps and other sexual abusers. The Beazley study, as well as the Journal of Midwifery and Women's Health research, reported that "pimps and traffickers generally exercise nearly complete control of their victims."[30] In light of this, as instructed by their abusive controllers, women will lie about the reasons for their abortions. When any woman caught in an abortion is granted immunity, it gives legal cover for her abuser who uses the legal loophole of women being immune from prosecution to continue fueling his tyrannical treatment of his victims. Because pimps and traffickers have such power over their victims, it is conceivable that a woman will lie if caught in an illegal abortion by claiming it was her choice. Fear of her abuser and of being abandoned without support creates obedience to her oppressor.

On the other hand, if abortion was illegal, any woman caught in preborn homicide could face criminal charges, and a criminal inquiry may expose trafficking operations. In addition, the abusers behind any coerced or forced abortion may face conspiracy, coercion and murder charges. An examination into a duress situation may be the only way to free a woman or child enslaved in human trafficking. Overlooking this potentially life-saving legal framework, pro-life apologists frequently argue that subjecting women to an investigation would be cruel because they have been through enough trauma with an abortion.

Frank Pavone, Director of Priests for Life, once said that since abortion causes enough suffering for women, prison is not necessary.[31] No other person in society is granted such a gracious treatment by the law. Most Americans would not provide this same sympathy to mothers who drown, stab or strangle to death their born children, even though many of these mothers also grieve and regret their actions. This position also overlooks the fact that innocent people in society are often investigated but never charged. For example, when a family loses a child in a drowning accident, law enforcement typically conducts a preliminary investigation to rule out foul play. A parent who brings their child to the emergency room with a suspiciously broken bone can face questioning and a possible visit from Child Protective Services to rule out abuse. This is standard procedure. There is no rational justification to protect abortive women from the same treatment that everyone else in society must endure. What ensues from this pro-life act of compassion may trap a woman in perpetual abuse and impede her rescue.

Co-Conspirator Confusion

Like inadvertently protecting abusers through immunity law for abortive women, there is another misunderstanding that prevents people from embracing abolition. This complaint against total criminalization claims that convicting abortionists would be near impossible because they would be regarded as co-conspirators with the woman in the preborn's murder, discrediting their testimonies against one another. Matthew Franck, professor and chairman of political science at Redford University, discussed this in a *National Review* article:

> ...if the woman were a criminal co-conspirator with the abortionist, in the common law tradition the abortionist could not be convicted on the basis of the woman's uncorroborated testimony — and all too often there were no other witnesses and no other evidence. This problem was also solved by treating the woman as a victim rather than as a co-criminal.[32]

Franck maintains that before *Roe v. Wade*, there were no other witnesses to abortions other than the woman and the abortionist. There is a hole with this assertion. The woman would have to find out the name of the abortionist somehow, most likely from another individual aware of the operating abortionist. Even if no one witnessed the crime being committed other than the woman and the abortionist, her claim that an abortionist killed her preborn child could be corroborated by other women who also had used that abortionist, or the individuals who provided the woman the abortionist's contact information, thereby showing that the abortionist was indeed actively committing preborn murder.

Working from the same angle as Franck, Ana Brennan, Vice President of the Society of St. Sebastian, believes "if women are charged as co-defendants their ability to testify against the abortionist would be compromised, thereby hindering prosecutions and convictions"; therefore, the main strategy should be to leave women alone – even those with criminal mens rea – in order to prosecute only abortionists as this is thought be the most pragmatic tactic that will "save the most lives."[33]

Senior writer Joe Carter for the popular evangelical blog *The Gospel Coalition* concurs with the damage abolition would purportedly cause. Carter argues for universal legal immunity for women by concluding:

> Even if we reject the view that the woman who chooses an abortion can also be a victim, there's a compelling reason to avoid holding her legally culpable: we want to prosecute abortionists. The purpose of forgoing prosecution of the mother is not to let them evade the moral consequences of their actions, but to help ensure the principal criminal—the abortionist—would be identified, prosecuted, and brought to justice.[34]

The question at hand is whether to forgo prosecuting women for prenatal murder because it would be "too hard" to prove the crime and convict abortionists if abortive women were also liable under the law as co-conspirators. The major flaw with this objection is that there must be corroborating evidence in addition to one witness when seeking to charge someone with *any* crime, whether co-conspirators are part of the equation or not. For McArthur, this is simply not a problem. Investigators routinely work cases involving co-conspirators ranging from gang violence, bank robberies, drug rings, kidnapping, human trafficking and murder. "The justice system regularly uses the testimony of one co-conspirator to convict another," McArthur explains. "Sammy the Bull was the Mafia underboss of the Gambino crime family. He committed 19 murders on behalf of the Mafia. We used him to testify against the boss John Gotti, obviously with extensive corroborating evidence."[35]

Whether or not a woman was a co-conspirator with an abortionist, her testimony as an eyewitness would still need corroboration. In a murder case, no statement is taken seriously without heavy vetting. Women who are granted legal protection for abortions do not automatically become trustworthy eyewitnesses. A single witness to a crime is not considered reliable until their testimony is verified. Similarly, accusations against the prime suspect – in this case, the abortionist – are not rendered void by the evidence of the co-conspirator. Corroborating evidence can include DNA samples, other eyewitnesses that place the woman at the abortionist's location, bank records, phone calls, texts, GPS tracking information, friends or family who knew the woman's plans, journal entries, forensic evidence (which shows the woman was pregnant but no longer is), physical damage or evidence left by an abortion, and so on. All those examples would support her testimony against an abortionist, whether as an "innocent" eyewitness or a co-conspirator. As McArthur says, "Whenever a crime occurs, there are literally 100 more variables, out of the ordinary, that can be accounted for to corroborate the witness."

McArthur acknowledges that obtaining evidence against an abortionist may take time, but there are ways to investigate. To obtain incriminating evidence against the abortionist, law enforcement may wait a few months, then have the woman get in touch with them once more and film the entire conversation. If the abortionist was apprehended with the abortion instruments, they would be admitted into evidence as the means of committing the murder. Ideally, this would work best if the woman *was* a co-conspirator. It would be challenging to look into even suspected illegal abortionists if abortion were outlawed for everyone but mothers. There would be little compelling reason for a woman to reveal the abortionist's identity if the law protects her. Often times, law enforcement will use the threat of judicial punishment to convince suspects to give up "the bigger fish" in exchange for reduced sentencing. This is not the case for women who have legal immunity for prenatal homicide. There would already be no punishment for her involvement in this type of murder. What sentence would be commuted for her? It is possible she could be charged with obstruction of justice if she refused to help police in their investigation of a suspected illegal abortionist, or she could be issued a subpoena for a trial against an abortionist and forced to testify (if enough evidence was gathered to warrant a trial). A woman could be charged with perjury if she lied under oath about her knowledge of an illegal abortionist. Aside from these lesser felonies, there would not be much else with which to persuade her cooperation. It seems that the pro-life movement would support women being imprisoned for perjury or obstruction of justice, but not for preborn murder. Arguing against abolishment because the justice system cannot convict co-conspirators is "naïve to the way law enforcement truly works,"[36] as McArthur puts it.

People should rightly care about justice and desire proper use of the law for women who are victims of abuse or duress. While many pro-lifers and abolitionists share this moral and biblical concern, the solutions offered by the pro-life movement actually undermine justice for women and preborn humans rather than advancing it. McArthur expounds on the need for criminalizing abortion to protect abused women:

> If a woman was being pressured to have an abortion, she's not in a conspiracy with whoever is pressuring her because she does not share the same criminal objective as the person pressuring her. But she could be used to testify against that person for the fact that the person is pressuring her. That would be the crime, which resulted in the murder of the pre-born child. The charge would be the boyfriend or the husband was forcing someone to try and commit a crime.... If she was being pressured by the boyfriend and didn't share the object of the conspiracy, and the boyfriend forced her and she had the abortion, she would not have any mens rea and so would not be a co-conspirator with the abortionist or boyfriend, but rather a witness against them. She would just be a witness of their crime; their crime of conspiring to kill the child.

> That's how she would escape prosecution because she was truly a victim-witness.[37]

The strawman arguments used to oppose abolition do not stand up to scrutiny. Not every single woman would be charged with abortion; not every single woman is legally guilty of abortion; no retroactive punishment can be applied against women who sought abortion before it was criminalized; millions of women will not end up on death row because not every state utilizes that as a criminal penalty; it is unlikely juries will use execution as a constant punishment against abortive women; and co-conspirators are routinely caught and prosecuted in many crimes across the nation every year.

There is no excuse to continue delaying equal protection and justice for preborn humans. A Christian ethos forbids us to sanction the destruction of some image bearers based on their gestational age, how they were conceived, the mother's life circumstances, or the possibility of a challenging prosecution. Furthermore, respect for God's law does not allow us to hold some murderers accountable yet not others under judicial law, because partiality is unjust and biblically forbidden.

8

THE COST OF PARTIALITY

"My brothers, show no partiality as you hold the faith in our Lord Jesus Christ, the Lord of glory." –James 2:1

Black and White Yet Gray All Over

WHILE WOMEN STILL HAVE legal protection to murder their unborn children at any stage of development, for any reason, and in any state, there are other miscarriages of justice occurring throughout the Union.

Heartbeat bills, 15-week bans (or the like), pain-capable limits, born-alive protections, restrictions against abortion for fetal abnormality, and prohibition of sex-selective abortions are all laws that innately discriminate against babies who do not fall within these categories. By extension, these restrictions also rely on an operator-dependent ultrasound to determine whether a baby falls within the allotted category for murder. Once these laws are established, it is the abortionist's discretion whether he or she followed these requirements. If abortion is truly murder, then individuals who habitually perform abortions are hired assassins, and entrusting them with the honor system of self-governance is foolish.

Other instances of discrimination exist under permitted exclusions for rape and incest conceived children, and prioritization of the mother's health above her baby's life. These, too, are prejudicial, enabling a death sentence for the preborn in these circumstances while protecting the right to life for their peers who do not fall within these limitations.

These factors are used to evaluate whether a preborn human has the right to life, thereby abdicating the protection already provided by the Constitution in the Fourteenth Amendment to all humans. More importantly, establishing laws that favor some preborn humans over others directly violates the Bible. If we are not permitted to show a judicial preference for the poor over the rich (Leviticus 19:15; Deuteronomy 1:16-17), or societal preference for the rich over the poor (James 2:1-13), and we are warned to not be partial to anyone lest God "soon take us away" (Job 32:21-22), because Christians are to do "nothing in a spirit of partiality" (1 Timothy 5:21) since showing partiality "is not good" (Proverbs 24:23), for God shows no partiality (Romans 2:11; Acts 10:34) and those in Christ are to imitate him (Ephesians 5:1-2; Romans 8:29; 1 John 2:6; Matthew 5:48), then what is informing 21st-century American Christians that we *can* write laws that partially protect some preborn while permitting the slaughter of others?

Is murder not more severe (Genesis 9:6) than desiring to sit next to a well-dressed aristocrat (James 2:1-13)? If God calls a person's religion worthless because that person desires the company of some people over others, what is God's holy disposition toward laws that Christians write, financially support, or vote for that allow the murder of some humans while protecting others, and showing collective favoritism to all women over the preborn? Although it is a biblically black-and-white matter, many Christians prefer to see anti-abortion legislation as a gray area.

The legislative process of drafting laws to address preborn homicide lacks biblically founded ethics. The pro-life movement has rarely explored if proposed legislation will result in immoral law. Most Christians do not ponder whether they should celebrate a conservative-supported law or not. For most, the question whether a law is ethical boils down to whose political party passed it. As such, most Christians do not view any anti-abortion legislation as immoral unless it is expanding abortion access, though even that is becoming a new point of compromise for the pro-life movement as pro-life elites such as National Right to Life

Vice President Tony Lauinger push to expand abortion within trigger-law states and pro-life groups and representatives write resolutions such as H.R. 464 that seek to enshrine constitutional protection for women to murder their preborn children freely.

These pitfalls are the consequences of the fruit of being anchored in situational ethics rather than biblical principles. Situational ethics leads us to conclude there are murky moral areas in which God does not expect us to know his will. R.C. Sproul wrote that with God "there is a definite and absolute black and white" and the problem for fallible humans is to discern "which things belong where."[1] The gray area does not reflect an autonomous zone where people can operate without conviction of conscience or guilt before God, but shows the ethical issues that we have yet to fully grapple with. If we cannot determine whether a law belongs in the black zone, which represents sin and unrighteousness, or the white zone, which represents virtue and holiness, we are not exempt from interpreting its category by simply declaring it a gray issue. Instead, we have demonstrated our ignorance and ethical confusion, subjecting ourselves to operating in unknown guilt before God. Sproul contends: "Finding the black and white areas is a noble concern.... Only within the context of atheism can we speak of there being no black and white. We desire competent and consistent theism, which demands a rigorous scrutiny of ethical principles in order to find our way out of the confusion of the gray."[2]

Every Christian should seek to find their way "out of the gray." It should trouble us when we don't know what pleases our Savior and what does not. Cultural theologian Joseph Boot echoes Sproul when he says there is an urgent need "for a comprehensive, scripturally rooted development of the Christian mind, and the application of this perspective to all of life, including the sphere of the state and political life."[3] It is not enough to know what evils God would have us oppose; we must also understand *how* he has guided us to oppose those evils.

God, the supreme lawgiver, has made it clear on what we must do to live holy lives that please him. It is ignorant to believe that God has abandoned us to moral relativism and secular, political pragmatics to govern the nation and individual lives. The outcome of our biblical carelessness on abortion legislation has been the publication of good-on-paper-only pro-life decrees. While lots of money is spent on fundraising to solicit politicians' support, write pro-life bills, and establish new abortion-restrictive laws, little money is spent on the backend to uphold these same initiatives.

A massive example of this is the federal Born Alive Infant Protection Act (BAIPA), which was passed in 2002. The statute was intended to provide legal protection for infants who were born alive due to a botched abortion. Limited documentation shows that the pro-life movement raised more than $250 million to pass this Congressional act, but the total value of contributions is suspected to be substantially higher.[4] During the fundraising campaign, pro-life organizations boasted that the statute would save countless lives and discourage doctors from participating in the heinous practice of leaving born-alive infants to die. What resulted was worse fall-out from our legislative injustice and prejudice.

The Failure of Born-Alive Acts

Representative Trent Franks (R-Ariz) once stated boldly that there are "forty-four thousand abortion survivors living in the country today."[5] Other sources provide far more conservative estimates. Some estimate the annual abortion survivor rate at roughly 430 babies, totaling a little more than 20,000 survivors since the issuance of *Roe v. Wade*.[6] Willard Cates, former chief of the Abortion Surveillance Branch of the US Centers for Disease Control and Prevention (CDC), estimated 400-500 abortion live births occur each year. All these sources reach the same conclusion: The majority of initial survivors die shortly after a failed abortion.[7]

Any of these figures mean it is an everyday occurrence somewhere within the country. BAIPA passed with bipartisan support due to the reality of these figures. Yet in the 21 years after its passage, no doctor has been convicted, even where they were proven to routinely kill infants born alive. During a testimony before the House Judiciary Committee on May 15, 2013, Attorney General Eric Holder admitted to this reality, stating that he was unaware of BAIPA ever being enforced in the 11 years since it was enacted.[8]

Besides law enforcement and the judiciary failing to press charges against individuals who violate BAIPA, there is also the issue of reporting. Cates testified, "It's like turning yourself in to the IRS for an audit. What is there to gain? The tendency is not to report because there are only negative incentives."[9] Despite the failure of the 2002 Born-Alive Infant Protection Act, Republicans and pro-life organizations are trying to pass yet another born alive act. On January 9, 2023, H.R. 26, known as the Born-Alive Abortion Survivors Protection Act (BAASPA), was introduced into the U.S. House. It passed the House on January 11, 2023.[10]

Patrina Mosley, FRC's Director of Life, Culture and Women's Advocacy, argues "the 2002 law lacks adequate enforcement mechanisms" and that BAASPA is important as it "would require health care practitioners to exercise the same degree of skill, care, and diligence that would be offered to any other child born at the same gestational age and ensure that the child be transported and admitted to a hospital."[11] BAASPA sponsor Senator Ben Sasse (R-Neb.) declared of the bill:

> In 2002, Republicans and Democrats came together to ensure that children born alive are recognized as persons under federal law, but unfortunately federal law does not criminalize the denial of care to babies that survive an abortion.... This hearing is about making sure every newborn baby has a fighting chance whether she's born in a labor and delivery ward or whether she's born in an abortion clinic. That's what the Born Alive Abortion Survivors Protection Act does. That's all it does. It makes sure that a baby born alive during a botched abortion would be given the same level of medical care that would be provided to any other baby at the same gestational stage.[12]

Hadley Arkes, a political scientist, author and founder and director of the James Wilson Institute, is the architect and legal mind behind the born-alive legislation. Arkes says of the born-alive 2.0 version, "The new bill, the Born-Alive Survivors of Abortion Protection Act, was brought forward to restore the serious penalties, criminal and civil, which had been stripped from that earlier bill.... The telling point here is that the intentional killing will be treated as a homicide under federal law."[13]

Without knowing the background of the original born-alive act, the assurances appear credible; however, the promises of BAASPA bear a striking resemblance to language used to enact the original Born-Alive Act in 2002, which pro-life leaders now regard as inadequate legislation. More than 20 years ago, the praises for BAIPA were just as convincing:

> Enactment of this bill [BAIPA] is necessary to ensure that all infants who are born alive are treated as legal persons for purposes of federal law.... Therefore, H.R. 4292 is proposed to codify (for federal law purposes only) the traditional definition of "born alive" that is already found in the laws of most states: complete expulsion from the mother, accompanied by heartbeat, respiration, and/or voluntary movements. The bill would also codify the traditional principle that the legal term "person" and equivalent terms "shall include every infant member of the species homo sapiens who is born alive at any stage of development.[14] – National Right to Life

> Upon the president's signature [of BAIPA], there will be no legal distinction between a 50-year-old, a 15-year-old, a 5-year-old or a 5-minute-old. Between them, their worth as individual people should bear no distinction, either.[15] – Rick Santorum, pro-life United States Senator

> The Administration strongly supports enactment of H.R. 2175, a bill that would ensure that infants who are born alive, at any stage of development, are individual human beings who are entitled to the full protections of the law. H.R. 2175, which is similar to laws in a majority of States and the District of Columbia, would provide guaranteed legal protection whether or not the infant's delivery was natural or the result of an abortion.[16] – Executive Office of President George W. Bush

> This important legislation ensures that every infant born alive – including an infant who survives an abortion procedure – is considered a person under federal law. This reform was passed with the overwhelming support of both political parties, and it is about to become the law of the land.[17] – President George W. Bush

BAASPA advocates believe the new version is necessary because it attempts to strengthen prosecution of abortionists who permit a born-alive infant to die. Under the new initiative, BAASPA defines criminal consequences for refusing or ignoring medical care to an abortion survivor as up to five years in prison, fines, restitution up to three times the cost of the abortion, and punitive damages paid to the woman.[18] These are the same criminal and civil sanctions that were purposefully excluded from BAIPA because pro-life advocates believed it would be easier to pass and avoid a veto from then-President Bill Clinton. Arkes said, "My own sense was that Bill Clinton would not veto a bill as modest and disarming as this one."[19]

While President Joseph Biden is equally likely to veto such a new act, pro-life groups have not given up hope of passing it this time. Even if Biden were to sign off on it, BAASPA does not consider born-alive killings as first degree murder.

The penalties outlined are equal to those imposed for some of the least serious offenses listed in state penal codes.

Most states classify felonies as A, B, C, D and E, with a few states adding letters past Class E felonies. Class A Felony is the most severe. It includes offenses such as aggravated rape with a weapon, first-degree murder, first-degree kidnapping and the use of weapons of mass destruction. The further down the alphabet the less severe the penalties become. Class E Felonies are often considered lower-level crimes and carry a maximum sentence of five years in jail and a fine, ranging from $5,000 to $10,000. Class E Felonies also include stalking, involuntary manslaughter, making a false bomb report, perjury, forgery and abandonment of a child.[20] In light of this, BAASPA equates the fault of an abortionist who refuses treatment for a born-alive infant with perjury. Worse, if an abortionist purposefully killed the baby after delivery, he or she would not be charged with first-degree murder under these criteria.

Arkes' allegation that BAASPA would treat a born-alive abortion victim's death as a homicide is only partially true. It would classify that child's horrific death as involuntary manslaughter at the most, which is a far cry from a first-degree murder charge if someone attempted the same crime on a born person. Under BAASPA, punishment is more aligned with involuntary manslaughter than malice aforethought, and individuals who mercilessly kill preborn humans would only receive slaps on the wrist. Even though pro-life leaders knowingly removed the criminal sanctions from BAIPA, it was sold as the "Law of the Land" with "no legal distinction between a 50-year-old, a 15-year-old, a 5-year-old or a 5-minute-old." If pro-life leaders are attempting to revive the born-alive movement, the clear divide in these age groups must be recognized.

The response to the failure of born-alive acts has resulted in more of them. Individual states have attempted their own versions of born-alive acts with limited success. Despite efforts to clarify criminal sanctions, there is no reason to expect the enforcement and strength of a new born-alive statute to differ from that of the first iteration. Even if prosecution suddenly is upheld and pursued, there is another issue with born-alive edicts. A Regent University Law Review article (like Cates' observation) highlights the apparent reasons why born-alive laws are doomed to fail:

> No one involved in an abortion attempt, save the child, gets what he wants unless the child is killed. And once an abortion procedure begins, the entire life experience of the child from that point on is under the sole observation and direct control of those who want him dead. This presents an exceptional conflict of interests: the only people in a position to enforce the rights of a child born alive through an abortion attempt—a legal person due the full protection of the law—are the same people who want him dead and have acted to kill him. Moreover, under the normal circumstances of a child born alive through an abortion attempt, the only witnesses to the birth—and thus the only people in a position to report a BAIPA-related violation of EMTALA or CAPTA—are the potential violators themselves.[21]

Born-alive protection laws are useless and distract anti-abortion individuals from the more meaningful fight to criminalize *all forms* of abortion. Born-alive laws have failed and will continue to fail because the principal purpose is to provide preborn killers self-governance to function on the honor system and protect their victims' right to life. This is a repeated and grave error in pro-life born-alive campaigns.

The Not-So-Rare Occurrence of Born-Alive Murders

Frank's assertion, together with testimony from within the abortion industry, reveals partial-birth and born-alive murders continue to occur regularly. In 2012, pro-life organization Operation Rescue gathered evidence against Texas abortionist Douglas Karpen. Several of his former employees, Deborah Edge, Gigi Aguilar, Krystal Rodriguez, and another who remained anonymous, confessed what was happening behind the scenes. The evidence presented by these former employees proved that Karpen performed born-alive abortions. Besides the photographic evidence to back up their claims, the informants revealed something else shocking: Karpen habitually killed babies beyond the legal age limit as a regular component of his business.

The informants' cell-phone images revealed the aborted babies had their necks slashed open, indicating that they were most likely born alive. The babies were also found to be well past the Texas 24-week gestational age limit for abortion. Edge stated in an interview she often saw babies born alive and then slain by Karpen. She stated that she "wasn't aware that it was illegal" at the time to kill children born alive.[22]

Delivering newborns alive only to dismember them, stab them or strangle them is unfathomable, and yet Karpen employed all those techniques to do the job. Rodriguez admitted that "as long as the patient had cash, he was going to do it past 25 weeks."[23] Edge confessed, "He does a lot of huge abortions. A lot of the times, we would bring the big fetus that were over age, we would re-open the bag and just look at it and be like, 'Oh my gosh, it's so big.' Sometimes he couldn't get the fetus out. He would yank pieces – piece by piece – when they were oversize. And I'm talking about the whole floor dirty. I'm talking about me drenched in blood."[24]

Karpen wasn't deterred by the Texas laws, which forbade abortion beyond 24 weeks of gestation, prohibited killing a born-alive baby, and was governed by the federal Born Alive Infant Protection Act. He also violated informed consent law, the 24-hour waiting period, ignored cases of child abuse, and coached minors across state lines to avoid parental consent. Karpen was charged with many first-degree murders for the born-alive deaths, but a grand jury chose not to indict him in 2013. Tragically, he is not the only example of this.

Kermit Gosnell was the poster-example of infamy prior to the Karpen saga. No one could have predicted what would be discovered when Pennsylvania authorities first began investigating allegations of Gosnell's abortion clinic. What began as a police raid to seize evidence of unlawful prescription sales and distribution ended in a horrifying discovery. Those who entered the crime scene described it as filthy and covered in dried blood. It reeked of cat urine "courtesy of the cats that were allowed to roam (and defecate) freely"[25] and housed dozens of unsterilized medical supplies. Life-saving devices such as the defibrillator, pulse oximeter, EKG machine and blood pressure cuff were rarely (if ever) in working order, and "the emergency exit was padlocked shut."[26] The more investigators probed, the worse the situation became.

Severed baby parts were discovered in cabinets, random places in the basement, a freezer, jars, bags and plastic containers. One 28-week-old intact baby boy was frozen inside a gallon water bottle, clear evidence of Gosnell's dismissal of his state's law outlawing abortion after 24 weeks of age. Through the evidence, it was concluded that hundreds of late-term babies were unlawfully terminated or born-alive and then mutilated to death. Gosnell's crime scene and place of work infamously became known as "a baby charnel house."[27]

At the time of Gosnell's trial, he was the lone doctor at his abortion facility, Women's Medical Society, alongside two key employees who were unlicensed medical school graduates. Stephen Massof was taught by Gosnell how to sever the spines of born-alive babies by using scissors to jab into the backs of their necks and snipping through the cervical part of the vertebra. Massof testified he witnessed this barbaric method performed 100 times at the clinic. He was sentenced to six to 12 years in prison for third-degree murder.

Likewise, employee Lynda Williams joined Massof and Gosnell in their gruesome operation, having personally witnessed Gosnell behead born-alive babies by snipping the upper spinal cord in at least 30 cases. She, too, severed the spine from the brain of a baby born alive, who she believes was between 26 and 27 weeks old. In a demented ritual, Williams said Gosnell would "sometimes give her just the feet of a fetus to place in formaldehyde." Williams pleaded guilty to third-degree murder and conspiracy.

In addition to the bloodbath at Gosnell's clinic, a jury found him guilty of 211 misdemeanor counts, including violating the 24-hour informed consent law, destroying evidence, conspiracy and corrupt organization charges, conspiracy to distribute controlled substances such as oxycodone, alprazolam and codeine, and maintaining a location for the illegal distribution of these drugs. After the grisly details of how he murdered born-alive children and kept their body parts as trophies, illegal drugs almost appear to be a non-issue. Gosnell himself appeared to believe the charges against him were made up and that he would be exonerated someday for his "innocence." Gosnell's attorney stated after the sentencing, "Dr. Gosnell, he believes that what he did was not commit homicide. He believes he never killed a live baby."[28]

While Gosnell was found guilty of three counts of first-degree murder and the involuntary manslaughter for the death of former patient Karnamaya Mongar, justice was only considered for a few of his victims. Countless others were never recognized as victims, either because they fit within the legal parameters of when and how to kill a preborn human or because there was insufficient evidence. Gosnell was sentenced to three consecutive life terms without parole and an additional 30 years on federal drug charges.

As the Gosnell case came to a close, the grand jury was presented with considerable evidence indicating that Gosnell's former boss, Leroy Brinkley, had also engaged in similar illegal activities. Brinkley was accused of distributing illegal narcotics, hiring unqualified personnel, failing to report cases of minors and suspected cases of sexual abuse, rarely documenting procedures and complications, failing to sterilize medical equipment, and even using rusted equipment in routine procedures. While Brinkley did not collect trophy baby parts, he conducted his multiple abortion facilities in unethical ways, resulting in the deaths of at least two known abortive mothers at his Delta Clinic in Baton Rouge, Louisiana. Like Gosnell, Brinkley specialized in late-term abortions. He was accused of helping in multiple illegal late-term abortions at Gosnell's clinic, and a former Delta employee admitted Brinkley charged an under-the-table "premium price" for late-term abortions. Despite his illicit behavior, Brinkley was never charged with a crime.

Early 2022 saw the discovery of yet another case of late-term abortions in Washington, D.C. Progressive Anti-Abortion Uprising (PAAU) Founder and

Executive Director Terrisa Bukovinac, along with PAAU Director of Activism Lauren Handy, went to Dr. Cesare Santangelo's abortion facility, the Washington Surgi-Clinic, "to engage in anti-abortion advocacy."[29] A truck from Curtis Bay Medical Waste Services was parked at the abortion clinic that day, ready to load the aborted children and other medical waste for disposal. The women engaged the driver in conversation and asked if they could have one of the boxes marked with a biohazard symbol. They sensed his discomfort and told him they wanted to give the babies a proper burial. He agreed, and the ladies left with the box of tiny human parts, unaware of the package's contents.

When Handy and Bukovinac opened the box, they discovered around 115 small humans who were most likely aborted in the first trimester. A red, wrapped package laid beneath those bodies. Opening this package revealed five near-term babies, some dismembered and others entirely intact . The majority of their injuries reflected the illegal practice of partial-birth abortion or allowing born-alive victims to die. While not the medical description of the process, partial-birth abortion is the practice of delivering a substantial part of the living child from the mother's body and then killing it. Medically, the procedure is called dilation and extraction, or D&X, which involves removing the fetus intact through the cervix.[30] Dr. Daniel Grossman, director of Advancing New Standards in Reproductive Health (ANSIRH) at Bixby Center for Global Reproductive Health at the University of California, San Francisco, says of D&X, "The procedure is no longer legal unless medication is used to stop the fetal heartbeat first,"[31] the very thing Santangelo said he *did not* do in an undercover Live Action video. Rather, Santangelo cuts the umbilical cords of second and third trimester babies, allowing them to bleed out and go into cardiac arrest before delivering them.[32]

Partial-birth abortion and leaving born-alive infants to die were both illegal at the time Santangelo committed his crimes. Senators from the Senate Homeland Security and Governmental Affairs Subcommittee on Government Operations and Border Management requested that Washington, D.C. Mayor Muriel Bowser, Chief of the D.C. Metropolitan Police Department Robert Contee, and U.S. Attorney General Merrick Garland investigate the circumstances of the deaths of these five babies. The subcommittee demanded autopsies because "evidence suggests one or more of them may have lost their life through an illegal partial-birth abortion or may have been born alive and later killed."[33] To date, no charges have been brought against Santangelo. And unfortunately, such depraved work does not end with Santangelo.

The annals of history recall LeRoy Carhart, one of America's most notorious late-term abortionists. Trained by the late Dr. George Tiller of Wichita, Kansas, Carhart carried on the legacy of murdering second and third trimester children after Tiller's own murder in 2009. His professional and personal legacy is tainted by instances of animal abuse and neglect, bloodied medical instruments, improper licensing, illegal drug use by employees, untrained staff administering drugs and starting IV lines, altering patient charts, falsifying gestational age to work around legal restraints,[34] maiming multiple women in 2016, 2017, 2018 and 2020, and medical malpractice that claimed the lives of 19-year-old Christin Gilbert and 29-year-old Jennifer Morbelli. Gilbert had Down Syndrome and her family took her to Carhart at 28 weeks pregnant because of sexual assault. Due to the severity of her Down Syndrome condition,[35] a confidential family source believes Gilbert would not have agreed to have sex *or* kill her child. If true, Gilbert would have been the victim of an illegal forced abortion.

American Family News published an article in August 2022 citing Carhart is "named in a complaint that lists 27 medical emergencies and two medical malpractice cases."[36] Unfathomably, Carhart not only continued operating his business, but, shortly after the *Dobbs* decision in June 2022, set up a GoFundMe page to raise half a million dollars for a new clinic in Pueblo, Colorado.[37] Even with such a jaw-dropping rap sheet, Carhart successfully remained in business and out of prison. He justified his career of killing by claiming, "I don't think any of us know when life begins; certainly the scientists don't. I don't believe the religious scholars do."[38] Carhart died in 2023 at the age of 81.

Another abortionist, Stephen Brigham, ran a multi-state abortion scheme in which he began illegal late-term abortions in his home state of New Jersey and then transferred patients across the border to Elkton, Maryland, where the procedure could be completed legally, despite the fact that he was not licensed to practice medicine in Maryland. When his assistant, Nicola Irene Riley, botched an abortion and perforated a woman's bowels on her second day on the job, resulting in an emergency drop-off at Union Hospital, Brigham's scam began to unravel. Riley told a nurse she was a physician and worked at the "secret clinic that performs second-trimester abortions in town."[39] This tidbit of information surprised Union Hospital staff, who were unaware of any abortion facilities in Elkton. This resulted in a prompt call to the authorities. When Brigham's clinic was raided following the whistleblower's report, 35 aborted babies up to 36 weeks of gestation were discovered in the clinic's freezer, as well as copious amounts of falsified paperwork, the illegal use of using another doctor's Maryland license to write prescriptions, insurance fraud, and lying to the New Jersey Deputy Attorney General about not performing late-term abortions. Brigham and Riley were each charged with multiple counts of first and second-degree murder, but the charges were ultimately dropped.

Abortionist Ulrich Klopfer left behind a more mysterious legacy. Questions surrounding his disreputable career were taken to the grave with him when he died of natural causes in 2019. Until his death, even those closest to him had no idea he was hoarding the remains of aborted babies in his home garage. The final attorney general report on the investigation of Klopfer stated:

> Upon conducting a thorough search of the property over the course of two days, utilizing nearly the full resources of the Will County Sheriff's Department, 2,246 medically preserved fetal remains were found among boxes of personal items, rusting cars, multitudes of soda cans, and other random garbage stacked high to the ceiling in Dr. Klopfer's garage. The Will County Coroner's Office took possession of the 2,246 remains found on the Klopfer family property at the conclusion of the search. The fetal remains were in various states of decay. The remains were mostly found inside molding boxes and old Styrofoam coolers containing large

red medical waste bags. It appeared as though each remain had been placed in a small clear plastic specimen bag for purposes of being medically preserved in a chemical suspected to be formalin, a formaldehyde derivative. However, many of the bags had degraded over time and/or suffered damage, resulting in leakage from the individual bags into the outer bag, box, or cooler.[40]

A week after the disturbing discovery at Klopfer's place of residence, 165 additional fetal remains were discovered in an abandoned vehicle that Klopfer owned. This brought the final count to 2,411 hoarded baby parts.[41] While the extent of his hoardings of murdered babies was unknown until his death, during his lifetime it *was known* that he chose not to report multiple instances of sexual abuse and rape involving minors under the age of 14, maintained incomplete reports, failed to keep medical records, and did not provide women with information or counseling prior to their abortions. His license was suspended indefinitely in 2016 as a result of these crimes, yet no justice was pursued for the thousands of his preborn victims.

Tip of the Iceberg

This is not an exhaustive list of offenses. Pro-life leaders estimate these high-profile cases are merely the tip of the iceberg, as AUL's vice president of legal affairs Denise Burke once remarked.[42] Life News, National Catholic Register and Operation Rescue also admit that Gosnell is only a glimpse of what is frequently occurring, and the American Life League said, in light of the Gosnell case, that "regulating abortion mills or the act of abortion will not solve this terror against the innocent. Abortion is a filthy business, and shiny clean abortion chambers do nothing to change the grievous crime to the most innocent."[43]

These incidents demonstrate the heinous and tolerated nature of abortion within the United States and the impossibility of fully regulating and monitoring a murder enterprise. Unless task forces routinely inspect the medical waste, paperwork and insurance filings of every abortion facility within a state, or law enforcement officers hold a post inside every clinic to monitor for trafficking and abuse victims, there is no way to enforce pro-life laws like partial-birth abortion bans, arbitrary gestational age restrictions, heartbeat bills, reports of abuse cases and so forth.

Despite annual pro-life "victories," abortion regulations are mostly unenforced. Representative Tim Johnson (R-Kan.) said of his state's abortion industry, "There are less regulations on these abortion clinics that are set up in some areas ... than there are for veterinarian clinics..."[44] The juxtaposition of the preborn murder industry to veterinarian services is grossly unsettling. There is no comparison. One is a legitimate business that does not violate any of God's laws or the U.S. Constitution, whereas the second violates all of them. It is common for pro-life advocates to argue from this position, however, to demand more regulation of preborn murder. This position's serious moral error is ignored, as is the continuous failure of pro-life legislation. In the rare instance an abortionist is charged with a crime, he or she usually receives citations, fines and a temporary suspension of medical licenses; none of which are punishments for premeditated murder. Gosnell remains a rare case of an abortionist being tried and jailed for murder after being caught in illegal born-alive killings. And of course, he was not charged under the BAIPA, which was the pro-life policy aimed at preventing cases like Gosnell's, Karpen's and the others from ever occurring in the first place.

The attempt to restrain some of the most gruesome evil through prejudiced legislation has largely failed. According to those in the industry, it is easy for them to ignore the law, falsify paperwork, and do whatever they want despite any pro-life laws in place.

BAIPA was intended, as indicated by pro-life promises, to ensure any infant born alive after a failed hit on his or her life is treated under the law as any other individual. Recent violation of BAIPA, however, was documented when Santangelo disclosed, "[if a woman] delivered before we got to the termination part of the procedure here, then we would do things – we would – we would not help it. We wouldn't intubate...You let nature take its course."[45] Other abortion employees confirm similar violations. Edge confessed babies born alive were such a common occurrence she witnessed abortionist Karpen on multiple accounts "actually twisting the head off the neck with his own bare hands" to end the life of delivered babies.[46]

An employee at Gosnell's "House of Horrors" estimated more than 40 percent of abortions that Gosnell performed were *after* 24 weeks' gestation, the Pennsylvania cutoff window for when a woman could murder her preborn child.[47] In 2018, nine Indiana abortionists were caught failing to report suspected child sex abuse. Abortionists Caitlin Bernard, Cassandra Cashman, Carol Dellinger, Mandy Gittler, Jeffrey Glazer, Kathleen Glover, Martin Haskell, Resad Pasic and Sarah Turner failed to report 48 abortions in girls as young as 12, despite Indiana law's explicit requirement to report the procedure for anyone under the age of 14. According to a comprehensive Americans United for Life (AUL) report, 115 abortion facilities in at least 26 states failed to staff with licensed personnel and get informed consent from a licensed medical professional.[48] AUL's investigative 195-page report showed that abortion providers in all 50 states were operating illegally. Some of the more common offenses included a lack of informed consent, unlicensed and unqualified staff, unsafe handling of medications and testing, and a refusal to report suspected sex traffickers or incidents of rape and incest.

The illegal issues found within the regulated abortion industry are profuse. While officials and the public are not aware of every dishonest transaction, the fact that they occur regularly is widely known. Besides AUL's report, groups such as Live Action, Center for Medical Progress and Operation Rescue have all released multiple undercover videos exposing Planned Parenthood and other unaffiliated abortionists who lie about sex-selective abortions, gestational age, illegal tissue harvesting, partial-birth abortion practice, botched abortions, underage minors, protection for sex traffickers and concealed born-alive babies.

Unfortunately, these fact-finding initiatives have replaced long-term and effective pro-life enforcement of their own laws. Anti-abortion investigations have only served to strengthen the pro-life movement's case for further abortion regulation. In comparison, antislavery investigative work during William Wilberforce's time was utilized to advocate for *the complete criminalization* of slavery. It is noteworthy that the pro-life movement does not respond to the gruesome human rights crisis of abortion in the same manner that slavery abolitionists responded to the ghastly nature of the slave crisis. Antislavery investigation led to the public's demand of criminalizing the industry. Pro-life investigation has only led to more regulation of the preborn murder industry.

There is little to show for all the pro-life marketing, lobbying and money. BAASPA will most likely follow the same path if it makes it past the Senate floor and Biden's desk. Even if every pro-life regulation was enforced and offenders prosecuted, it does not change the fact that preborn humans are still murdered. Much wickedness flourishes under partiality.

The Pro-life Way to Kill

Roughly 88 percent of abortions occur within the first trimester, with the remaining 11 percent occurring in the second and third trimesters.[49] In general, a late-term abortion is one that occurs after the first 12 weeks of pregnancy.[50] There is a problem with precisely calculating how many late-term abortions occur. As previously established, not every late-term abortion – or every abortion, for that matter – is documented. Women who commit abortion in the privacy of their own homes account for the discrepancy in statistics, but another problem is that each state has its own abortion reporting criteria. Some states require fetal age to be documented, while others rarely ask for any data. In fact, some states do not require *any* abortion reporting to their health departments, and no state is compelled by federal law to submit abortion statistics to a national database. States voluntarily submit abortion data to agencies such as the Centers for Disease Control and Prevention (CDC).

While both the CDC and the Guttmacher Institute strive to measure state and national abortion rates using any available data, they employ distinct research approaches and occasionally report differing results.[51] These reasons explain how the CDC reported 629,898 abortions for 2022, but the Guttmacher Institute believes the figure is closer to 886,000.[52] Because there are few other options, statistics from these agencies will be used within this chapter; but no figures are absolute and there is an error margin on either side of any reported number. Despite efforts to report, track and record abortion statistics, all efforts fail to capture *every abortion* due to state reporting discrepancies, the rise in DIY abortions, and covert illegal abortions.

Interestingly, it is not just anti-abortion individuals interested in the annual number of abortions, and it is not just pro-abort fanatics or abolition critics that decry the worthlessness of partial-birth bans. Not only is it very difficult to track down numbers of that type of abortion occurence, but even pro-life activists acknowledge that laws prohibiting partial-birth abortion bans are ineffective in general.

In 2007, Dr. James Dobson with Focus on the Family admitted, "Ending partial-birth abortion, which would more accurately be named 'late-term murder,' does not save a single human life."[53] Agreeing with Dobson's conclusion, Judge Roy Moore issued the following confession regarding the partial-birth abortion ruling through *Gonzales vs. Carhart*:

> Things aren't always as they seem. And when this ruling came out, many praised the ruling; in fact I was one of them. I had not fully read the ruling... But then when you read the Carhart opinion, you realize what they have done is atrocious. ... When I heard someone say, 'this opinion does not save a single human life,' they are correct... I likened this Carhart opinion, to... just like in Germany, a court in Germany, during the Holocaust coming out and saying, The Congress has just passed a rule that we couldn't gas these Jews but it certainly allows us to put them in a deep ditch and cover them with dirt while they are still breathing. You see, that is how atrocious this Carhart opinion is. It says you can still kill them, you just have to do it a different way. Now if anybody

doesn't believe that that is what this opinion says, I invite them to read it.[54]

In the *Gonzales vs. Carhart* case, the conservative-led Supreme Court demonstrated how easy it was to navigate around a partial-birth abortion ban. The alleged pro-life justices instructed how an abortionist could better murder a preborn human to avoid a ban without compromising the procedure's original purpose: the death of the child. Some of the recommendations written in the majority opinion to legally kill were "an injection that kills the fetus is an alternative under the Act that allows the doctor to perform the procedure," as well as advising doctors to "find different and less shocking methods to abort the fetus in the second trimester, thereby accommodating legislative demand."[55] The opinion did not stop there, as it further explained how "the Act excludes most D&Es in which the fetus is removed in pieces, not intact" and that the partial-birth ban established anatomical landmarks, which clarify "that the removal of a small portion of the fetus is not prohibited" so long as the baby is dismembered before being delivered up to the naval or, in the case of a head first position, the baby must be killed before the entire head is delivered. The justices also wrote:

> If a living fetus is delivered past the critical point by accident of inadvertence the Act is inapplicable. In addition, the fetus must have been delivered "for the purpose of performing an overt act that the [doctor] knows will kill [it]."[56]

The Supreme Court explained if a baby is *"accidentally"* delivered past the anatomical landmarks, the restriction does not apply. Furthermore, a doctor must be proven to have purposely delivered the baby up to the naval or the entire head with the objective of violently killing it. The scapegoat for abortionists was so neatly laid out: simply claim it was an accident and you will be fine. Better still; devise a more effective method of killing the baby before it is delivered. Problem solved.

Pro-life initiatives that dictate how a preborn human *can* be killed contradict the pro-life position that abortion is wrong. The pro-life movement attempts to change the way preborn humans are executed by prohibiting born-alive, partial-birth or dismemberment abortions but allows for the injection of feticide, dismemberment in utero, and suction. It is hard to see how these efforts align with the pro-life concept that every life is valued.

What Are Pro-Life Laws Accomplishing?

All of this leads one to ask the obvious: What exactly *are* pro-life laws accomplishing? As early as three years after the 1973 *Roe* decision, many began wondering what – if anything – influences the abortion rate within the United States. According to certain statistics, the abortion rate has been steadily declining since the inception of *Roe*. The pro-life movement claims that its policies have helped lower the number of abortions. Pro-abortion advocates claim it was decreasing prior to the barrage of regulations. Both sides are still interested in determining if there is a decline in abortion rates and what might be driving that.

Evidence suggests that pro-life laws have some impact on the overall abortion rate. It is not wholly moot, as many pro-abortion advocates maintain. Several types of pro-life laws have lowered the number of abortions despite being written in a way that contradicts God's Word. At the same time, it does not appear that these laws are as important as the pro-life side claims. It appears pro-life laws, such as parental notification, reduced public funding, and two-day wait requirements lowered the abortion rate by 10 to 15 percent before the trend of self-managed abortions hit the market several years ago.[57]

One of the challenges of accurately presenting the success rate of pro-life laws is a lack of accountability and consistency. First, there is no state task force or rigorous oversight committee for abortion facilities. This permits violations to occur.

Second, state reporting rules differ, which contributes to an incomplete picture of the data. Abortion can be tracked in 50 different methods throughout the

50 states. Forty-six states and the District of Columbia require abortion facilities to submit annual reports to their state health departments; however, the criteria of those reports vary significantly. For instance, both Florida and Louisiana require the reporting of patients' health, instances of rape, incest, fetal abnormality and parental involvement, but Florida allows for "other" reasons for abortion, whereas Louisiana requires mandatory counseling to be recorded. Neither Florida nor Louisiana requires the *type* of abortion to be reported, whether surgical or medication abortion. In contrast, Hawaii merely requires information about the type of abortion performed and if it was for a fetal abnormality. Kansas requires abortionists to report fetus viability, reasons for an abortion *after* fetal viability, and parental involvement. Oklahoma, its neighboring state, required significantly more data before it closed its clinics, such as the type of payment made for an abortion, any complications from the abortion, whether it was a medication or surgical abortion, reason for the abortion, and other criteria. California and Maryland require no reporting, while Colorado, Connecticut, Delaware and the District of Columbia require reporting to state agencies but do not define what information is required, leaving that to the discretion of each individual abortion facility.[58]

Third, society has fluctuated tremendously in substantial areas, such as women in the workforce, socioeconomic situations, wide access to contraceptives and the rise of over-the-counter abortion medication. Even with much diversity and cultural variables, there are numerous theories on how pro-life laws impact abortion rates. The studies keep coming, and the interest in the data has not waned.

One of the most referenced sources on this topic is the work of Professor Michael New at the University of Michigan-Dearborn. His peer-reviewed study *Analyzing the Impact of U.S. Antiabortion Legislation in the Post-Casey Era: A Reassessment*, published in 2014, has helped both pro-abortion and antiabortion activists understand the impact that legislation can have on abortion. In his research, New reports:

>...empirical results add to the substantial body of peer-reviewed research which finds that public funding restrictions, parental involvement laws, and properly designed informed consent laws all reduce the incidence of abortion.[59]

New's 2014 data was published in response to Marshall Medoff and Christopher Dennis's National Abortion Rights Action League's (NARAL) data. In Medoff and Dennis's research work, they point out a few errors found in New's 2011 examination of anti-abortion laws and their effect upon the abortion rates. New corrected those errors and republished it as his now widely used 2014 study. The corrections made in the 2014 study actually change very little from the initial study. As New points out, "Most of the errors identified by Medoff and Dennis in my data set ... were due to relatively small differences ... Overall, these errors fail to substantively affect my findings."[60] The purpose of New's research was to examine the potential effects of specific anti-abortion legislation on the prevalence of abortions. To be clear, New only examined a few pro-life laws, so his work only reflects a small portion of anti-abortion legislative efforts.

In their published work, Medoff and Dennis argue that birth control, not pro-life efforts, is one driving force behind the declining abortion rate. In recent years, a study published in the "Journal of Adolescent Health" suggested that the birth control pill and other contraceptives lower fertility rates, which lower abortion rates. If fewer "unwanted" children are conceived, one may expect there to be fewer abortions. This study examined adolescent birth rates and pregnancy from 2007 to 2014 and found that "Improvements in contraceptive use ... appear to be driving recent declines in adolescent birth and pregnancy rates."[61] New raises several issues with this conclusion. He initially argues that focusing on the birth control perspective is faulty since "academic literature paints a very mixed picture of the relationship between contraception use and the incidence of abortion."[62] In fact, one of the studies Medoff and Dennis use to support their assertion that contraceptives reduce abortion rates actually proves the contrary. New explains:

...the data that Medoff and Dennis cite showing increases in contraception use since the early to mid-1980s ... also show consistent increases in contraception use from the early 1970s to the late 1980s. This finding was consistent among all groups of women, regardless of age, marital status, or race. However, the increase in contraception use did not reduce the number of abortion performed in the United States during either the 1970s or 1980s.[63]

He then cites research published by the National Center for Health Statistics indicating that birth control usage increased "between the mid-1990s and the period between 2006 and 2010."[64] In addition to those findings, a Guttmacher Institute analysis revealed higher use of contraceptives *and* abortions, as did a study in Spain that observed "significant increases in both contraception use and abortion rates."[65] Second, according to New, his study did not seek to answer the question of what was driving down the overall national abortion rate. Rather, the primary objective was "to analyze the impact of a group of anti-abortion laws that received greater constitutional protection after the Supreme Court's 1992 *Casey* decision."[66] This is not to suggest that New neglected other possibilities for abortion rate decline. In his 2011 analysis, New discussed nine other factors that could have contributed to overall declining abortion rates *alongside anti-abortion laws:* (1) a strong economy, (2) declining fertility rates, (3) emphasis on lowering teenage pregnancy, (4) changes in sex education curricula, (5) reduced sexual activity among minors, (7) improvements in the reliability of contraceptives, (8) greater adult use of contraceptives, and (9) fewer physicians performing abortions.[67]

Regardless of other variables that may impact the rise or fall in abortion rates, New's 2014 research concluded several key issues. First, a lack of public funding is specifically tied to the abortion rate. When funds were limited abortion rates were reduced by 10 to 15 percent.[68] Second, informed consent laws, which require at least two visits before having an abortion, also had a "statistically significant impact on the adult abortion rates." Third, parental involvement laws produced "significant declines in minor abortion rates."[69] It is widely accepted at this point that New's research did, in fact, answer the questions he set out to answer. The specific pro-life laws he examined do help reduce the abortion rate. In response to the evidence of pro-life laws reducing how many babies are murdered, pro-life director of the Center for Human Dignity at the Family Research Council Arina Grossu exclaimed:

> All of this is to say that pro-life laws save lives by reducing abortion rates — and the pro-life movement is on a roll. States have passed a whopping 226 pro-life laws since 2011. Between 2011 and 2013, more pro-life bills were signed into law than in the entire previous decade. They include parental involvement laws in 38 states, physician and hospital requirements in 39 states, gestational limits in 42 states, public funding limits in 17 states, mandated counseling in 17 states, and waiting periods in 26 states. States should continue adopting *common-sense laws* that protect the health and safety of women and their children. They are literally life-saving.[70]

Other well-known pro-life leaders celebrated the accomplishment of legislative and incremental pro-life efforts. Executive director of Center for Bio-Ethical Reform Greg Cunningham declared in a debate with Hunter, "The political scientists are telling us babies' lives are being saved as a consequence of all of this."[71] Pro-life legal "victories" continued from the time of New's published work into the early 2020s. In 2021 alone, more than 530 pro-life bills were introduced into state legislatures, with 61 already signed into law. Dannenfelser celebrated such achievements in a press release: "The unprecedented surge of pro-life activity in state legislatures this year proves life is winning in America ... the pro-life movement will never rest until unborn children and their mothers are protected in the law."[72]

What Should the Christian Response be to Pro-life Laws?

It is easy to become engrossed in a spirit of celebration over incremental gains while ignoring the atrocities that occur under these same laws. While pro-life laws have reduced the number of preborn humans being murdered by a small margin, the tragic reality is that *more* preborn children have died under pro-life initiatives than if complete and immediate abolition had been pursued from the moment the *Roe v. Wade* opinion was announced. The focus on regulation has prolonged the fight. This focus has detracted from the question every professing Christian should ask about pro-life incremental laws: What does the Bible have to say about this method of law?

When Christians celebrate a 10- or 15-percent reduction in preborn murder through legislative incrementalism, they are celebrating the effectiveness of laws that God despises. The correct response is to praise God for bringing good out of wicked laws, but Christians should not purposefully seek to establish unjust laws. Most Christians, however, choose to celebrate the unjust law itself – the very kind of law God warns against establishing. Even if a law that God forbids Christians from adopting had a 100 percent success rate, Christians should refuse to support it since it is against God's law. Legislation should be supported based on its obedience to God's Word rather than only its potential effectiveness. This is the key distinction between the pro-life and abolitionist worldviews. The pro-life movement focuses on saving babies while the abolitionist's focus is on glorifying God.

Pro-lifers are committed to success; so the pro-life argument is that "if it works, it is acceptable." This pragmatism can lead to entrapment. If the goal is to reduce the abortion rate, and the only criterion for determining whether something is "good" is whether it works, then there should be no moral objection to a law that forces hysterectomies upon child-bearing women. This would also reduce the abortion rate and eventually eliminate it. The only way to claim that such a law is heinous is if its immorality is grounded in God's Word. The reason pro-life and abolition activists do not enact such draconian measures to achieve a net-zero abortion goal is that both movements understand that God has forbidden people from abusing others' bodies, and that God calls good his design for women to bear children. It would be against both biblical truths to force a woman's sterility. Why, then, is there hypocrisy and duplicity toward God's instructions forbidding laws of partiality?

On the other hand, abolitionists are committed to Scripture. There is no option for legal and moral compromise within abolitionist ideology. When inconsistencies present, it is not a reflection on the soundness of abolition ideology but rather on the individual who may still have some gray areas in their own worldview that need to be aligned with Scripture and consistent logic.

God's Word is explicitly clear on what *types* of laws can and cannot be written. Scripture outlines categories: unjust vs. just; partial vs. impartial; wicked vs. righteous. God is not nuanced. The role of Christian men and women in politics and lobbying is to determine in which category to place a law. Christians have access to wisdom from above (James 1:5) and should be well-equipped to determine such a task. Would we truly say that we are unsure in which category to place a law forcing women to have hysterectomies in order to prevent abortions?

People have only two choices in life: to obey God or disobey God. Yet some religious leaders have promoted arbitrary guidelines when it comes to formulating public policy, which has negatively influenced Christian political and legal thought:

> The Bible tells me that abortion is a sin and great evil, but it doesn't tell me the best way to decrease or end abortion in this country, nor which policies are most effective. The current political parties offer a potpourri of different positions on these and many, many other topics, most of which, as just noted, the Bible does not speak to directly.[73] – Timothy Keller, Presbyterian theologian and author

> The messy middle is where the [political] problems are solved.[74] – Andy Stanley, evangelical pastor and author

I will say it's not my role to bind anyone's conscience in terms of how to vote.[75] – Brent Leatherwood, President for the Ethics and Religious Liberty Commission

Murder laws aren't analogous, since a murder is, by definition, an unlawful killing. The convo is all about what sort of killing should be unlawful. Doctor-assisted suicide? Abortion? Drone strike? An overwhelming majority of Christians believe abortion is a nuanced topic.[76] – Phil Vischer

It's the incremental approach. It's forced upon us by circumstances of our politics and our political system. We have to take the battle constantly in defense of the unborn and take what ground we can.[77] – Scott Klusendorf, founder and president of Life Training Institute

Scripture provides a separate set of instructions from these religious influencers. God's Word counsels us to "not be partial in judgment" (Deuteronomy 1:16-17), "do no injustice in court" (Leviticus 19:15), only "do what is right and just" without doing any "wrong or violence to the fatherless" (Jeremiah 22: 3), that the Lord requires justice of us (Micah 6:8), while we "seek good and not evil" (Amos 5:14); to refrain from doing "evil so that good may come" (Romans 3:8), that we mimic our Lord when we "hate evil, and love good, and establish justice in the gate" (Amos 5:15), and to not become partners with the wicked and fools (Ephesians 5:11). This short list of instruction does indeed restrict what type of legislation Christians may advocate for, write and enact. While Keller was correct that the Bible does not specify every detail that must be included in an anti-abortion bill, it does provide a standard by which such legislation must be judged. Contrary to Klusendorf's assertion, we cannot take "what ground we can" if it is done so in rebellion to God.

Sproul wisely counseled, "We are not free to do what is right in our own eyes. We are called to do what is right in His eyes."[78] If a proposed law favors some preborn humans over others, allows violence against the fatherless, gives legal protection to the principal actors in preborn homicide, and fails to establish justice for all preborn humans, then the answer is obvious: It does not align with Scripture and should be rejected. This is the ethical dilemma with pro-life legislation. When the pro-life advocate asks, "Isn't it good that *some* lives are saved by this law?" the biblically-minded Christian must counter, "Is the method good by which the saving has come?" God's enemy has marketed his own version of "good." It began with the question, "Did God *really* say?" followed closely with the promised fruit of disobedience, which is what still entices people today: "You will be like God, knowing good and evil (Genesis 3:4)." The hiss is clever: "Did God *really* say you cannot pass a heartbeat bill? You will save many lives if you just take that deal!"

Regardless of what incremental anti-abortion laws temporarily produce or promise to generate, they fail to address the moral issue of abortion, create more injustices, stall medical developments to save ectopic lives, depart from God's legislative standard, mock God's holiness, and leave the nation still guilty of bloodshed. A.W. Tozer chided the rebellious Christian when he said, "Most Christians don't hear God's voice because we've already decided we aren't going to do what he says."[79] This appears to be why professing Christians refuse to abandon pro-life allegiance in favor of biblical abolition. They have determined not to hear God's voice on the matter. As statesman Alan Keyes put it in response to the partial-birth abortion ban:

> Why on earth am I called upon to rejoice in a decision that in every single line, in every single word, in every bit of logic in the whole decision, painfully shows its regard for a concept that vio-

lates the law of God, the law of man, Constitutional law, and every sane concept of decency that anyone in this country can come up with?[80]

Every professing Christian should ask why he or she is required to rejoice in biblically disobedient legislative efforts. Pro-life laws have accomplished their intended purpose of regulating abortion. Regulation results in enshrined favoritism toward some preborn humans over others. Pro-life laws of partiality cannot and will not abolish abortion. Incremental politics cannot police the abortion industry nor eradicate any part of it. Conservative commitment to regulating prenatal homicide has only prolonged it. Our partiality has been costly.

9

RECOVERING PROTESTANT ETHICS

"Pray like it all depends on God, then when you are done, go work like it all depends on you." – Martin Luther, reformer (1483-1546)

The Protestant Ethic

"THE PROTESTANT WORK ETHIC promotes excellence," concluded Dr. Gene Edward Veith from the work of 20th-century sociologist Max Weber.[1] Weber was intrigued by the moral transformation, social reforms and economic growth driven by Protestant ethics that blossomed from the Reformation. Though he hated capitalism and Calvinism, Weber could not help but notice the remarkableness of Protestant economic trends and wrote of it in his book *The Protestant Ethic and the Spirit of Capitalism*.

Centuries before Weber, 17th-century French political philosopher Montesquieu admitted that English Protestants "had progressed the farthest of all peoples in the world in three important things: in piety, in commerce, and in freedom."[2] Montesquieu observed that Protestantism's ethics accelerated society's progress toward human rights reform and greater degrees of freedom than had ever been seen in Europe and abroad. Author Dr. James Kennedy records, "Prior to the coming of Christ, human life on this planet was exceedingly cheap. Life was expendable prior to Christianity's influence."[3]

Since Christ's resurrection, Christianity changed much of that, and the Reformation accelerated the value of theology, ethics and human worth even more.

The abolition of slavery is a recent example of Protestant moral and social reforms. It explicitly addressed the issue of "expendable human life." Slavery abolition was a distinctly Protestant Christian burden and movement, and their conviction challenged the age-old belief that slaves were less valuable than other human beings. As already discussed within this book, Catholics believed that challenging the Constitution and states' rights was more reprehensible than owning slaves. This ethos essentially prompted them to "wash their hands" of the peculiar institution. Orestes Brownson penned this perspective of his fellow Catholics:

> We deny, and always have denied, the right of congress to legislate on the subject...We always regarded the so-called "Missouri compromise" as unconstitutional. Slavery with us is purely a STATE institution, deriving from state sovereignty alone, and there is under our system no power to authorize or to abolish it, but the state itself, that is, the people in their state as distinguished from their federal capacity.[4]

The Catholic-led pro-life movement is once again advocating for state sovereignty on the issue of crimes against preborn humanity. Yet Protestant abolitionists have an even stronger case for abolishing the human rights injustice of prenatal homicide because now the nation exists under the Fifth and Fourteenth Amendments, and the overturning of *Roe v. Wade* has removed all legal excuses for not completely abolishing abortion. But history serves as an intense tutor, shedding light on why pro-life Catholic leaders will not pursue abortion abolition even when given the opportunity.

Though Catholics detested slavery, they were not in the business of changing the laws to consider slaves as equal image bearers of God. Their ethics differed greatly from those of 19th-century Protestants. Brownson said of Catholics and anti-slavery colonizers:

> For ourselves personally, we would not emancipate the slave population at the South, if we had the power, not, indeed, because we like slavery, but because with all the study we have been able to give to the subject, we can discover no condition possible at present for the mass of that population superior to that in which they now are. Humanity towards that population, if nothing else, would prevent us from being an abolitionist.[5]

Christians must fight this same ethos against the preborn. In the secular culture, abortion is commonly referred to as a charitable action that prevents "unwanted" children from bad living conditions such as abuse or poverty. Equally as common is the preaching of the Catholic-led pro-life position that humanity toward abortive women, if nothing else, prevents them from being abolitionists. Hence why there are legal protections for abortive women that the pro-life movement is unwilling to relinquish.

In his 1900 study, Weber's student Martin Offenbacher emphasized the differences between Catholics and Protestants in Baden, Germany:

> The Catholic is quieter, having less of the acquisitive impulse; he prefers life of the greatest possible security, even on a smaller income, to a life of risk and excitement, even though it may bring the chance of gaining honour and riches. The proverb says jokingly, 'either eat well or sleep well.' In the present case the Protestant prefers to eat well, the Catholic to sleep undisturbed.[6]

Offenbacher focused on the industrial impetus between Catholics and Protestants, and both groups behaved similarly during the slave years. Catholics were more concerned with the comfort of the Union than the comfort of the slaves, thus preferring that the problem remain mostly unresolved. Protestant abolitionists despised this complacency and worked tirelessly to change it, despite the fears that moral revolution would unleash. According to Bryan Caplan, Professor of Economics at George Mason University, Catholics and Protestants have similar moral convictions (for example, both oppose slavery and abortion), but they are executed differently. Caplan observes:

> I've often heard people distinguish between two distinct ethical outlooks. They usually call them the "Catholic" approach and the "Protestant" approach ... The "Catholic" approach has extremely high moral standards (e.g. Be celibate; give everything you have to the poor; love everyone), but enforces them loosely... The "Protestant" approach has moderate moral standards (e.g. Don't commit adultery; prudently give to the deserving poor; don't hate people who've never done you wrong), but enforces them strictly... As a moral realist, I think the most important question is "Which ethical view is correct?" And as a moral intuitionist, I judge the Protestant approach plainly superior. The moral case against adultery is easy to grasp; the moral case for celibacy, not so much. The moral case against hating people who have done you no wrong is easy to grasp; the moral case for loving total strangers, not so much.[7]

As Caplan mentions, Catholicism primarily deploys ambiguous ethics and loosely holds people accountable to those standards, whereas Protestants apply scriptural standards with greater rigor. This heralds back to earlier chapters where the importance of Scripture between Catholics and Protestants were discussed. Each views Scripture through a different lens. As a result, their behavioral systems differ. One is evasive and plays it safe while the other is direct and resolved. It explains why the Catholic-influenced pro-life movement can proclaim abortion as taking innocent life but will not call it murder like its Protestant abolitionist counterpart. It also explains why the pro-life movement is more willing to overlook murderous intent in women, whereas the abolitionist movement finds it impossible to ignore such motive. This is precisely why the momentum to reform our nation's morals and laws on child sacrifice continues to falter under the dominion of Catholic pro-life ethics.

Christians have long sought to reform societal laws and morals. As biblical Christianity spread throughout the world, many countries abolished abuses such as infanticide, Roman patriarchal killings of their children, female feet binding, forced child temple prostitution, *suttee* practices of burning widows alive on their deceased husbands' caskets, tribal executions of elderly community members, chattel slavery and cannibalism. This is quite a resume. Twenty-first-century Protestants should be eager to carry on this legacy of striving for change in the face of opposition. One specific opportunity for such ethical reform is the ectopic pregnancy issue.

Ectopic Pregnancies: A Taboo Dilemma?

While the pro-life movement works hard to pass born-alive laws to theoretically protect second and third trimester developing humans, the movement simultaneously works (perhaps unintentionally) to maintain the unethical treatment of humans who are developing from ectopic pregnancies. To date, abortion advocates, pro-life advocates, and even some abolitionists have all agreed that ectopic pregnancies have a high fatality risk and can only be treated by terminating the life of the preborn human to save the life of the born person. Often, those within the anti-abortion movement would say that terminating the life of the preborn human in a pregnancy emergency is not an elective abortion but intended to save the most life possible (the mother's). This logic is used to justify pregnancy termination in cases like ectopic pregnancies.

It is a unique legal exception in the medical industry. The right to intentionally end the life of one patient to better the odds of another is only allowed between preborn children and their mothers, specifically in this section concerning ectopic complications. Pro-life leaders frequently argue in favor of this strategy under duress law, which protects and permits physicians to prioritize which patients to focus on in an emergency. The application of duress legislation is only partially valid in ectopic pregnancies. The steps taken during an ectopic pregnancy differ from how a doctor would treat two patients in another triage situation. This is because one common method of "treating" ectopic pregnancies is to administer methotrexate, which inhibits cell growth and destroys the life of the developing human. This drug is so effective in ending pregnancies less than 49 days' gestation that it has been used for elective chemical abortions, with a success rate of more than 90 percent when combined with vaginal misoprostol.[8] According to the Mayo Clinic, methotrexate is administered early in an ectopic pregnancy that does not have unstable bleeding. The dosage is administered by injection and a woman's hCG levels are evaluated to determine whether the pregnancy has been ended or if more medication is required.

Salpingostomy is another common method for dealing with ectopic pregnancies. This laparoscopic procedure involves making an incision in the fallopian tube to either repair the damaged tube or remove the ectopic human. The third most common medical procedure is salpingectomy, which is the surgical removal of one (unilateral) or both (bilateral) affected fallopian tubes. In this case, if the preborn human is still alive in the fallopian tube, he or she will be removed with the tube. Many claim that the death of the preborn human is inadvertent in this procedure because it is caused by removing the tube in which he or she is developing. For many pro-life individuals, this third option is the preferred "ethical" approach. Pro-life influencer Abby Johnson had this to say about salpingectomy:

> I had no idea how little people knew about the treatment of ectopic pregnancies in a pro-life and ethical way. So let me attempt to flesh this out.... If the Hcg levels are increasing and the baby is still growing, then the ethical and moral way to treat the ectopic pregnancy is to remove that section of the tube where the baby is implanted.... So basically, it is all about intent in these circumstances. Any direct

attack on the unborn baby is unacceptable and unethical. While yes, the baby will die if you remove the tube, it is an indirect result of removing part of the fallopian tube.[9] – Abby Johnson

Johnson emphasizes the purpose of intent in the developing human's death because, as previously established, criminal intent is fundamental to due process and is utilized to determine an individual's guilt, prosecution and sentencing. Anti-abortion advocates often claim that terminating the life of an ectopic developing human is not the same as an elective abortion. The claim is that if the ectopic complication was not present, there would be no intent or desire to end the life of the preborn human; however, just because the intent is not the same as in an elective abortion does not mean that the ectopic issue is handled correctly. It is possible for our current response to an ectopic crisis to *also* be unethical. What needs to be addressed is whether the current model of care is the most biblical approach to ectopic emergencies.

We can already see that there are some serious issues with managing ectopic pregnancies because the death of the preborn human is currently the standard outcome. The key issue with each of the three treatment scenarios is that the intention is not to provide life-saving interventions on behalf of the developing human. "Treatments" such as methotrexate and salpingostomy are an intentional assault on the life of the preborn human without any lifesaving attempts. The focus is to remove and discard the developing child. Similarly, while salpingectomy does not directly cause death to the unborn patient, it does remove and leave the preborn human to die on his own after being cut off from the mother's body. No efforts are made to save his life once he is removed from his mother. This is ironic given what the born-alive initiatives attempt to subvert. Born-alive laws were enacted to prohibit the removal of a live preborn human from the mother's body without providing life-saving services, and to punish those who leave preborn humans to die without such medical intervention. This is an ethical quandary for the pro-life movement.

First, any sympathy for born-alive abortion victims is abandoned for ectopic preborn humans. Second, in standard care during pregnancy, the mother and preborn child are both routinely viewed as patients. Dr. Diana W. Bianchi, director of the Eunice Kennedy Shriver National Institute of Child Health and Human Development and head of the Prenatal Genomics and Therapy Section for the Medical Genetics Branch at NHGRI, says of this in her collaborative book *Fetology: Diagnosis & Management of the Fetal Patient*:

> We wanted this book to be more than a mere collection of facts; we wanted a cohesive approach to diagnosis, management, and in some cases, treatment of the fetal patient....After much debate, we selected the title *Fetology: Diagnosis & Management of the Fetal Patient* to indicate that the focus of this book is on the diagnosis and the overall management of the fetal patient. No one medical specialty is devoted to the care of the fetus. By definition, therefore, *fetology* requires a multidisciplinary team approach.[10]

While fetal medicine has been widely used since the mid-1900s, the dispute today is primarily over whether anyone owes a human in the embryonic stage any rights, protection or medical aid. Of course, this is an arbitrary position and introduces ethical sloppiness. If humans suddenly gain rights at a certain age, then it follows logically that line can be moved forward or backward to suit the needs of those in power. This would expose all humans at any age to potential danger. The logically consistent position is that the moment a human comes into existence (which is the point of fertilization) he or she is due protection to the best of our ability and deserves the right to life. Since it is accepted in medical literature that a human embryo is, obviously, a human being in the embryonic stage of development, the squabble remains over what constitutes as legal responsibility to a human being at that age. This stems not from confusion over who is human but from refusal to apply unbiased constitutional, ethical and biblical logic to equal treatment of all humans. It's an issue of semantics. There is a reason the fight is intense on this point.

According to Cornell Law School, manslaughter is defined as killing another human being *without* malice. Specifically, manslaughter under criminal law is defined by 1) the defendant owing a legal duty of care to the deceased victim; 2) The defendant committed an act or omitted to do a specific act; and 3) The act committed or the omission of a certain act substantially caused or accelerated the death of the now deceased victim. Since doctors legally owe their patients care without negligence or malice, one can see why both pro-abortion and anti-abortion advocates skirt around whether embryos should be considered patients. If they were, based on this legal information, a doctor who decides to remove a developing preborn human and abandons him to die without providing lifesaving, intervening care is, by definition, committing manslaughter.

While Johnson is correct that methotrexate and salpingostomy are unethical because both procedures directly inflict fatal harm upon a preborn human, Johnson avoids the ethical dilemma that arises from allowing routine use of salpingectomy as a "reasonable" treatment for ectopic pregnancy without requiring an effort to save both lives involved in this medical emergency. While malice is absent, so is the intent to offer medical help for the preborn patient. In this approach, treating an ectopic pregnancy is unlike treating born patients in other life-threatening situations. The priority for such patients would be to provide the best care possible to save *both* their lives; at the very least, there would be no attack on one of them, nor predetermined negligence resulting in one of their deaths.

While duress law has been applied to ectopic procedures for decades, purposefully neglecting the preborn patient does not fall neatly into this legal category. While these procedures may be an effective way to reduce the mother's health risk and complications, they are not an ethical treatment plan for the *two human patients* involved, as one of them is never given a chance to survive. Manslaughter should not be an acceptable treatment plan for ectopic patients.

Ectopic Transfers: A Best Kept Secret

Of course, the popular notion is that there is nothing that can be done for the ectopic patient. Christian philosopher and historian Bill Fortenberry debunks some of the most common fallacies about ectopic pregnancies and discusses the miraculous discoveries on how to treat both child and mother. In his book *Ectopic Life: What Your Doctor Doesn't Know About Ectopic Pregnancy,* Fortenberry describes dozens of cases in which doctors from more than 150 years ago successfully transplanted ectopic babies into their mothers' uteruses. In one particular 1917 case, Dr. C.J. Wallace reported on his successful ectopic transplant in the journal of *Surgery, Gynecology and Obstetrics*. In his report, Wallace enthusiastically declared:

> In this day of advanced surgery, with the art of transplanting different parts, and in fact organs of the body, I wonder at the escape of so important a procedure, entailing so little danger, as the transplanting of an ectopic pregnancy from the fallopian tube into the uterus...we should make a supreme attempt to save the life of the growing child by opening the tube carefully and transplanting it into the uterus where nature intended it should go. It can be very quickly done. It does not endanger the life of the mother and may be her only chance to bear a child ... I have not the least doubt that many such transplanted ectopic pregnancies will be reported in the near future.[11]

More than 60 years later, Dr. J.F. Clark also made a revolutionary discovery in 1982. Clark's study, "Embryo Transfer In Vivo," showed that a ruptured fallopian tube does not always result in a baby's death. In fact, Clark's research found that 42% of babies from a ruptured fallopian tube will implant in another abdominal space with enough blood supply to carry the baby to at least 28 weeks gestation.[12] Given that most infants born after 26 weeks of gestation have a high survival rate nowadays, expectant management would significantly improve the survival rate of these misplaced babies.[13] Expectant management is the practice of not intervening if there is not an urgent necessity.

Expectant management is used in other pregnancy situations for women with severe placenta previa, preeclampsia and gestational diabetes. Expectant management closely monitors the mother and the child in hopes that the anticipated complications will resolve through medications, diet, therapeutic treatments or natural reimplantation. Pregnancies suffering from placenta previa, preeclampsia or gestational diabetes frequently result in labor induction or surgical delivery. This would also be the case for any baby developing outside of the uterus; at some point there would come the need to deliver that child surgically. A recent example of this occurred in December 2023, when a French woman was admitted to a hospital with abdominal pain. Doctors discovered a 23-week-old baby growing in her abdominal cavity. The medical team monitored the woman for another six weeks before delivering the child surgically at 29 weeks of gestation.

Based on current published data detailing successful ectopic transfers (some dating back to the early 1800s), Fortenberry concludes that 24% percent of all tubal pregnancies could result in a live birth[14] if the medical community dedicated genuine interest in developing this life-saving care for preborn humans. Astoundingly, this figure applies only if current knowledge and procedures from the 20th century or earlier are used. With today's technological advancements, the number is certain to be substantially higher.

Dr. Stephen Sammut, a behavioral neuroscientist and professor and researcher for Franciscan University of Steubenville, is conducting one such modern-day study. Sammut's research over the last few years has primarily focused on ectopic transfers using laboratory rats as models. Because rats have a multi-chambered uterus, Sammut successfully transferred implanted rat embryos from one uterine horn to the other. His transfer and reimplantation efforts have produced many born rat offspring.[15] This is just the beginning of groundbreaking research. Rats are not the closest animal to mimicking human conditions, so the path forward may still take time.

"It's not really that we are utilizing or creating an animal model of ectopic pregnancy; we are creating an animal model of the potential surgical technique that could be used in the case of an ectopic pregnancy, where the hope is we would be able to transfer the embryo from the ectopic site into the uterus to allow both the baby and the mother to grow healthy, be born, and the mother remains healthy," Sammut said in an interview with Bonnie Coffey Cannone with Abolish Abortion Florida.[16]

While the trials in rats were effective, further research is needed before it can benefit humans. Part of the delay is due to lack of funding and interest from other researchers in continuing Sammut's work in other animal specimens and, eventually, human clinical trials.

Sammut's ectopic study, as well as his work on other abortion-related issues such as the abortion pill reversal, is funded by private donations from individuals and grants from the Watson Bowes Research Institute. In his research, Sammut collaborates with his research assistant, Christina Camilleri, and Dr. Cara Buskmiller, a board-certified OBGYN who is a consultant for the research team. He emphasizes the importance of a multi-disciplinary team of scientists and doctors in advancing this research into human clinical trials.

"As a scientist, you always have to know your limitations," Sammut explained. "And my limitations, the little that I do know – it has to be stated 'as little' when it comes to the human and uterine pregnancy aspect – you literally need an expert who is an OBGYN who is assisting with their knowledge in their field and bringing the two fields together so we can apply the methodology and the technique that we feel will work not just in the rat, but has the potential of also working in the human."[17]

For now, most ectopic pregnancy deaths are caused by early misdiagnosis, complete unawareness, and expectant management incompetence. These hurdles impede life-saving options for both patients. The mother dies because of untreated and uncontrolled blood loss and organ stress, not the unconventionally implanted baby. Still, the preborn human in an ectopic pregnancy is often depicted as the major threat against the mother. As a result, even well-meaning people abandon their concern for the preborn human and focus solely on the mother, whom they see as an unfortunate victim of her child.

While successful ectopic transplants are not secretive, the truth of their existence is suppressed in modern culture. Abortion advocates have no incentive to push the medical industry to find new ways to save the lives of ectopic-developing humans. Though many members of the abortion movement support women who want to keep their babies, the movement's foundation is built on the ability to discard difficult pregnancies or preborn humans who pose a threat to the mother's way of life. This key principle of the abortion movement conflicts with devoting resources and efforts to scientific research and revolutionary remedies for ectopic pregnancies. This is because abortion supporters already have a "treatment" for ectopic pregnancies. There is no ethical concern that the abortion industry must address in terms of how ectopic pregnancies are managed.

The anti-abortion movement should have a different ethical stance from that of the abortion movement. Instead, plenty of anti-abortion individuals share this space with pro-choice advocates. Many within the pro-life movement fear that serious interest in attempting to save the preborn in an ectopic pregnancy that poses a risk to the mother will be used by pro-abortion smear campaigns to portray the pro-life movement as anti-woman. Both pro-abortion and anti-abortion advocates argue that saving the baby is ineffective or too risky. This is due to ethical laziness and the idolatry of women. Both parties reject the documented methods for managing an ectopic pregnancy, which attempt to save both patients' lives rather than murdering the youngest. Fortenberry writes, "... the doctor who accepts that a prenatal child is a person with an unalienable right to life will recognize that, in cases of ectopic pregnancy, he is responsible for the well-being of two patients, the mother and the child, and he will take the course of action that he thinks will most likely result in the life of both."[18]

All of this reveals that even the anti-abortion community struggles with viewing humans in the embryonic stage of development as truly human. Neither the abortion industry nor the pro-life movement shows any interest in insisting that ectopic patients deserve medical care.

Protecting Ectopic Developing Humans with the Law

There is an inconsistency in the anti-abortion movement with prioritizing one human's right to life over another; not in a case-by-case analysis, but as a blanket response to all ectopic cases. Choosing the mother's life over the life of the preborn human is a persistent pro-abortion stance, and many pro-life advocates practice this principle with ectopic pregnancies. It is the confession and belief that women should have the legal option to terminate a growing human being inside of them in certain circumstances. Pro-life legislation that includes exceptions for ectopic abortion implicitly instructs that anything done to save the mother's life is ethically acceptable, even if direct attacks are levied against the preborn patient.

Abolitionists have tried to be more careful with the wording of their legislative bills so that doctors and parents do not have the freedom to kill ectopic patients and neglect attempts to save their lives. This does not mean doctors cannot treat ectopic emergencies under abolition legislation.

In 2022, Gunter sought to prevent the spread of false information regarding the Louisiana abolition bill. Pro-life leaders declared that abolition bill HB 813 would prohibit ectopic treatment. Gunter fired back: "HB 813 does not ban the removal of an ectopic pregnancy, but simply requires that doctors do everything medically possible to save the life of the preborn child."[19] Foundation to Abolish Abortion, which had organization members involved in helping write HB 813, published this in response to unwitting claims against the abolition bill:

> The bill does not alter existing Louisiana case law, which provides that "[a] person is excused from criminal liability if he acts under a duress of circumstances to protect life... in a reasonable manner and with no other acceptable choice." *State v. Recard*, 704 So.2d 324, 328 (La. App. 3 Cir. 11/26/97). *See also State v. Smith*, 777 So. 2d 584, 587 (La. App. 4 Cir 12/20/00) ("This doctrine has been

applied in circumstances other than those enumerated in La. R.S. 14:18").[20]

Oklahoma abolition bill SB 1729 introduced in the 2024 legislative session by Senator Dusty Deevers (R), contains the following wording in regard to pregnancy emergencies:

> This chapter shall not apply to: 1. The undertaking of life-saving procedures to save the life of the mother when accompanied by reasonable steps to save the life of the unborn child; or 2. A spontaneous miscarriage.[21]

In the 2023 legislative session, Kansas abolitionists submitted HB 2181, which explicitly defined intent as an important factor in determining whether the death of an unborn child was malicious, negligent or justified. Section 4(e) of the bill explained:

> (e) This section shall not apply to any surgical procedure performed *with the intent* to: (1) Save the life or preserve the health of the unborn child; or (2) remove a dead, unborn child whose death was caused by spontaneous miscarriage, stillbirth or ectopic pregnancy. [Emphasis added.]

This bill's distinctions are of notable importance. The authors of the bill intended to clarify the duty to act in such a way that good-faith efforts are made to save both the mother's and the preborn child's lives in emergency pregnancy situations. It also outlined that the removal of an already deceased preborn human would not be considered an elective abortion, regardless of whether the unborn human died from implanting outside of the uterus or another tragic event. The purpose of this bill's restrictive wording was to prohibit the use of medications or surgical procedures as the preferred first response in an ectopic pregnancy with the only outcome being the child's death when other alternatives in care are available.

These three bills are just a sampling of the dozens of abolition bills introduced over the years and they highlight the moral standard abolitionists have for ensuring protections for the preborn human in every circumstance. Christians should not cower on the ectopic dilemma. Instead, we should be leading the ethical fight. We must recognize it is one thing for a doctor to prioritize care during duress and another thing to enter a triage situation already set on destroying the life of one of the patients. We should not accept that unethical standard. If preborn humans had equal rights and justice under the law, doctors would consider them patients in need of care, and medical treatment for them would be scientifically advancing. Removing the ectopic developing human should only occur if he or she has already died or a uterine implantation is being attempted. Because we would never sanction the intentional neglect or killing of born humans in triage situations, the same attention and protection should be extended to our preborn neighbors.

Two Different Paths of Response

Expectant management is currently the ethical response to most ectopic situations. The question with an extrauterine pregnancy is whether it is necessary to remove the child *immediately* once an abnormal pregnancy is diagnosed, or if more time can be given to see if that pregnancy results in a scenario similar to what Clark documented: that the child be left alone until after 20 weeks' gestation, delivered by cesarean surgery, and given a fighting chance at life. The Protestant Christian ethic should be the latter. Even in the case of a ruptured tube, expectant management could occur alongside triage efforts to repair the fallopian tube and treat any major blood loss in the mother without removing the child as he or she attempts reimplantation elsewhere within the abdominal cavity.

The anti-abortion movement would condemn doctors who rush into pregnancies diagnosed with diabetes or preeclampsia to kill the preborn child as the preferred treatment method. Likewise, the ectopic developing human deserves the same discretion, critical thinking, expectant management and goodwill as are given to preborn humans in other high-risk pregnancies. Instead, developing humans in ectopic pregnancies face opposition from the abortion industry and much of the anti-abortion movement. It even seems trendy to compare a pregnancy complication to an act of aggression by the preborn human, attempting to justify the use of self-defense in taking that human's life to save the "victimized" mother. This mindset significantly impedes efforts in life-saving research.

Mark Creech, Executive Director of the pro-life Christian Action League of North Carolina and former president of the Ethics and Religious Liberty Commission of the Southern Baptist Convention, said of pregnancies with health risks to the mother:

> Whenever two lives are at stake because of some complication in the pregnancy, if the baby is a threat to the mother's life, there is no evil in protecting her life by taking the child....That's the decision of the mother, the father, or other family members, if the mother can't make it for herself. They may choose to save the baby and allow the mother to die or let the baby die to save the mother. But if the baby were aborted to save the mother's life, that's a form of self-defense and there is no sin in it.[22]

Acyutananda, a pro-life blogger and frequent writer for Secular Pro-Life, asserts the same thing in his writings on health complications for a pregnant woman:

> The answer is: we [pro-lifers] do believe that the unborn is an innocent human being, but we feel that society has no right to legally prevent a woman from saving herself, even if it is by use of lethal force against an innocent human being, from a very serious

developing threat which would not exist without the participation of her own body.[23]

These beliefs are consistent with those of infamous abortionists such as LeRoy Carhart, Neville Sender and Don Sloan, who claim that abortion is state-permitted killing and justifiable like a self-defense killing. Of course, self-defense, as described by the law, involves using lethal force against someone who is believed to harbor the intent to harm someone else. Cornell Law School explains self-defense as "a defense to a number of crimes and torts involving force, including murder, assault and battery." For obvious reasons, a developing human being does not intend to murder or assault his or her mother. Because criminal mens rea is such a central part of the justice system to prove whether someone meant to commit a crime, and it cannot be proven through a trial that a developing preborn human would have such malicious intent, then the taking of his or her life would be illegal, unjustified and an unconstitutional execution per the Fourteenth Amendment. Acyutananda's conclusion to use "lethal force against an innocent human being" is not the legal definition for self-defense but for murder. The argument is self-defeating and should be discarded. There is no biblical, logical or legal basis for such a philosophy.

Reforming Current Mindsets and Medical Practices

For Christians, the conflict over sacrificing a preborn human to save a born person should not be confusing. There is no scriptural reason to continue ectopic killings for the goal of "treating" someone else. Even on pragmatic, legal grounds, there is no compelling argument for fighting for this medical abortion right. Fortenberry writes:

> This does not in any way mean that a doctor should allow a woman under his care to die from a ruptured ectopic pregnancy. The realization that the doctor has two patients in such cases should

remind us of two important legal and ethical facts. First, it is important to remember that a doctor is not held liable for the death of a patient that he tried to save. Every state in America already has laws protecting doctors from prosecution if they make a good faith effort to save the life of a patient and are unable to do so. These laws apply to both born patients and prenatal patients. They apply to both the mother and the child. As long as the doctor legitimately attempts to save both lives, he is not liable if one of his patients does not survive.[24]

Under the law, a doctor "should make a good faith effort to save both the mother and the child, but he is not responsible if one of them dies despite his efforts to prevent that death, nor is he responsible if one of them dies because he had to decide to save the life of the other first."[25] The solution is not to give doctors the legal authority to do what they know would undoubtedly kill one patient to focus on the more socially valuable patient. Rather, the abolitionist ethic views the child as a person with an unalienable right to life; thus, the medical community should work to save that preborn person in crisis instead of marking him for death, as is the current treatment protocol. This means that the use of medication such as methotrexate and surgical procedures like salpingostomy should be abandoned. Despite the widely available literature from scientists declaring hope for ectopic children, many anti-abortion leaders use old talking points, unbiblical ethics and outdated misunderstandings of successful ectopic transfers. This deadlocks the ectopic issue, traps it in the past, and promotes the idea that where we are now is morally acceptable:

> There are medical cases, known as ectopic pregnancy, where the embryo implants on the inner wall of the fallopian tube. If you do not remove that embryo, as that embryo grows in that narrow tube, the danger to the mother is clear: that embryo grows, the tube bursts, the mother hemorrhages to death. You're a pro-life

doctor. What are you going to do? Do you do nothing and let two humans die? Or do you act in such a way that you save one life even though the unintended but foreseen result is the death of the human embryo...we act to save the mother...when a doctor acts to save a mother's life, he is not intentionally killing an innocent human being. He can foresee the death of the embryo in the case of ectopic pregnancy, but he does not intend it. So I don't even call that abortion. That's a life-saving surgery that any physician who's pro-life would do, and no legislation has ever forbid that kind of surgery.[26] – Scott Klusendorf, pro-life apologist and founder of the Life Training Institute

What should a pregnant woman do if her physician advises her that carrying her baby to term will place her own life at serious risk (as is the case in many instances of ectopic pregnancy)? Our initial reaction would be to tell this mom to seek a second opinion about her condition from a different doctor, preferably one with strong pro-life convictions. If the diagnosis remains unchanged, then we would have to concede – though sadly and reluctantly – that this *may* be a case in which it would be morally acceptable for the mother to opt for treatment that may end the life of her preborn child.[27] – Focus on the Family

Ectopic pregnancies pose a serious threat to the life of the mother and are unsurvivable for the improperly implanted child. Removing an ectopic pregnancy is done in the interest of preserving as much life as possible and is critical for the mother's survival. Neither of these things are legally or morally classified as abortions.[28]
– Students for Life

For example, consider the falsehood that pro-life laws prohibit medical intervention for ectopic pregnancy or miscarriages. Not a single state law in effect does this – all contain exemptions to save the life of the mother, something the pro-life movement has supported all along. Ectopic pregnancy cannot result in a live birth and can be fatal to the mother if not addressed.[29] – Marjorie Dannenfelser, president of Susan B. Anthony List, and Kristan Hawkins, president of Students for Life of America

Treating an ectopic pregnancy is not an abortion. The child cannot survive to term in a tubal pregnancy. And the mother can die if not treated. Abortion is the intentional killing of an innocent human. The heartbreaking loss of the child is unintended.[30] – Lila Rose, founder and president of Live Action

In an ectopic pregnancy treatment, the goal is to save as many lives as possible. We are able to save the mother's life, but lack the medical technology needed to save the baby. We mourn the baby's death. In an abortion, the goal is to end the life of the baby. In this case, we intend the baby's death. This makes abortion wrong.[31] – Created Equal

For these reasons the American Association of Pro-Life Obstetricians recognizes the unavoidable loss of human life that occurs in an ectopic pregnancy, but does not consider treatment of ectopic pregnancy by standard surgical or medical procedures to be the moral equivalent of elective abortion, or to be the wrongful taking of human life.[32] – American Association of Pro-Life Obstetricians

The baby always dies. We treat ectopic pregnancies to ensure the mother lives.[33] – Dr. John Bockmann, author of *Reconsidering Fetal Pain*

In this regard, pro-life leaders promise to preserve the status quo ectopic treatment. In the age of artificial intelligence, organ transplants, in vitro fertilization, touch sensation in prosthetics,[34] and 3D printed skin for burn victims, the pro-life movement acts as if what doctors were able to achieve more than a century ago with saving ectopic children is impossible to replicate or improve upon today. Instead, the pro-life movement, like the abortion industry, insists that sacrificing the preborn human is the only way in which to save the mother's life. On this premise, the pro-life movement clings to a woman's choice to discard an ectopic human, claiming that this differs from a woman's choice to discard the preborn in other situations. This is tragic hypocrisy. In both cases, the one being discarded is considered the lesser human. Pro-abortion advocates genuinely believe abortion saves the lives of women in other medical emergencies, abuse situations, mental crises or poverty. What makes the pro-life position on destroying ectopic preborn life more justifiable?

The pro-life argument to "save the most life" is viewed as an acceptable position on when to end preborn life, despite its glaring duplicity. The two main pro-choice arguments for abortion rights are ending a preborn child's life because it is not viable, and ending a preborn child's life to save the life of the mother. The squabble is over which scenarios constitute destroying an unborn human, and the pro-life movement claims to have the upper hand. It is delusional for the pro-life movement to adopt the same line of reasoning as the pro-abortion industry, while claiming to hold a morally superior position.

Many within the anti-abortion community would welcome innovation that would save babies in ectopic pregnancies, but it insists on withholding equal protection until such technology or routine procedures exist. There is plenty of room for ethical reformation. Positive change should start now to save more lives of ectopic or extrauterine humans, while technological advancements continue until research results in a routine surgery to transfer a developing human into the mother's uterus. Legislation that grants doctors immunity to destroy ectopic children stifles technological and medical advancement by cementing the status quo. Vague medical abortion protections for "health of the mother" also do the same damage to the right-to-life movement.

Reforming Unjust Legal Exceptions

Every piece of pro-life legislation to date contains exemptions for the life of the mother and are ambiguously worded such as Texas post-*Roe* trigger law § 170A.0 02-4 which states: "The prohibition [against abortion] under Subsection (a) does not apply if ... in the exercise of reasonable medical judgment, the pregnant female on whom the abortion is performed, induced, or attempted has a life-threatening physical condition aggravated by, caused by, or arising from a pregnancy that places the female at risk of death or poses a serious risk of substantial impairment of a major bodily function unless the abortion is performed or induced..."

Or Kansas statute § 65-6721 which reads as: "No person shall perform or induce a partial birth abortion on an unborn child unless ... the partial birth abortion is necessary to save the life of a mother whose life is endangered by a physical disorder, physical illness or physical injury, including a life-endangering physical condition caused by or arising from the pregnancy itself." Similarly, South Dakota's trigger law §22-17-5.1 states that "Any person who administers to any pregnant female or who prescribes or procures for any pregnant female any medicine, drug, or substance or uses or employs any instrument or other means with intent thereby to procure an abortion, unless there is appropriate and reasonable medical judgment that performance of an abortion is necessary to preserve the life of the pregnant female, is guilty of a Class 6 felony."

These definitions are so broad that almost any ailment can (and does) fall under the medical abortion category, including mental health, hyperemesis gravidarum, preeclampsia, eating disorders, cancer and anything else a doctor will ascribe for a woman to abort her baby to preserve her own physical or mental health. For the anti-abortion individuals who want to be consistent in their defense of protecting the lives of unborn humans, views on the ectopic crisis must change. It is unjust to deny certain humans legal protection simply because defending their right to life will disrupt others' comfort or challenge the current medical routine. There should be no exception to the unconstitutional killing of human beings under any circumstance. We must not perpetuate 19th-century sentimentality. Establishing the humanity of currently oppressed people will always be costly for a time; yet, it is a worthy cause to endure.

If the anti-abortion movement wants to be distinguished from the abortion movement on this point, it must renounce its compromised, shared stance with the pro-choice camp. Influential anti-abortion leaders must stop siding with abortion advocates in favor of prioritizing the mother over the unborn child as the simple solution. Anti-abortion advocates must also stop opposing equal protection and justice for ectopic babies as evidenced by Southern Baptist Convention President Bart Barber's rant against legislative protection for unborn humans in health crises:

> He [abolitionist Dusty Deevers] doesn't just think it isn't necessary to have an exception to save the life of the mother; he thinks it is necessary NOT to have an exception for cases where the life of the mother is in danger.[35]

Barber was partially correct in his accusations. Abolitionists are against "health of the mother" exceptions when it permits doctors to legally and intentionally abort the unborn patient in emergencies without being required to provide life-saving care or treatment for that human being; however, the abolitionist position does not nullify the ability of a doctor to treat a mother in an ectopic pregnancy. It simply dictates that a doctor must remember he has two patients to care for and that there is no right to purposefully or negligently destroy one of them. Both are patients; both are image bearers; both have the right to life.

As the country moves further away from *Roe*, the anti-abortion movement must urgently press the medical community to address this apparent tragedy of failing to routinely save ectopic developing humans. Crowd-funding and the formation of nonprofits to offer a cash reward to the first person who successfully transplants an ectopic human embryo into the mother's uterus are a couple of ways average citizens can become involved in societal reform. Legislative efforts should continue to clarify the law to demonstrate that a reasonable attempt to save the life of the ectopic developing baby is required, rather than the default approach of cutting out the baby and throwing her away or poisoning her to death with methotrexate.

Arguably, there is still much work to be done. The Protestant proclivity to reform is undeniably needed. This is a rapidly evolving ethical issue that many Christians will need to invest in to grapple with, define and refine. The goal should be to have the technology and capabilities in place to save both mother and child. In the meantime, we should not deny legal protection for ectopic developing humans until that goal is accomplished. We should insist that doctors use the lifesaving measures afforded them to attempt to save both mother *and* her child.[36]

10

Reforming Judicial Dogma

"God has no glory from that zeal that has no scriptural warrant." – Matthew Mead, Puritan (1629-1699)

The Conservative Trojan Horse Court

When the Virginia Supreme Court stated in 1858, "in the eyes of the law...the slave is not a person,"[1] one can almost imagine the fist pumps, high-fives and whoops and whistles that broke out in celebration south of the Pennsylvania line. This dehumanizing, unjust law was like honey to the slave owner's soul. The ruling validated the licentious behavior of the slave industry and set in motion a fierce battle ahead for abolitionists who would insist that such a lawless court decision be ignored and not enforced.

Twenty-first-century Americans cringe at such blatant disdain for human life. It is hard to envision how slavery was as normalized then as it is now normalized to share a classroom, office, or bus with people of different ethnicities. It is easy to dismiss the effort made to debate the case of the slave's humanity, change laws to guarantee equal justice, and reject abhorrent conclusions such as that of the 19th-century Virginia court. Most Christians today see comparable shortcomings by our present Supreme Court. Those who oppose abortion rightly point their fingers and shake their heads at the Court, saying, "*Roe* was the worst decision ever!" Yet the sentiment that follows this proclamation makes little sense. In fact, the pro-life movement speaks frequently of the unconstitutional and atrocious ruling of *Roe* yet turns around and urges loyalty to the Court and that very decision.

Consider something from a somewhat ironic perspective: What do we get when we have a Republican president, a Republican House majority, and a conservative-appointed Supreme Court majority (1973)? *Roe v. Wade*!

What do we get when we have a Republican president, a Republican House majority, Republican Senate majority, and a conservative-appointed Supreme Court majority (2016)? Still *Roe v. Wade*!

What do we get when we have a Democratic president, Democratic House majority, Democratic Senate majority, and a conservative-appointed Supreme Court majority (2022)? The reversal of *Roe v. Wade*!

Logistics and riddles aside, there was one consistent factor from 1973 until 2022: The rise, sustain and fall of *Roe* was in the hands of the United States Supreme Court's *conservative majority*. For five decades, the Court felt little compulsion to address the abortion crisis it perpetuated, despite the country being led by prominent political conservatives at nearly every level of government.

One of most publicized pro-life dogmas was to fill the court with conservatives who would overturn *Roe v. Wade*. Nonetheless, this court precedent stood unchallenged for half a century under the watchful eyes of these very conservatives tasked with fixing the mess. Worse, a conservative-appointed Supreme Court gave America *Roe v. Wade* in the first place. Examining this fact is unsettling because it demonstrates how clearly misled and disillusioned conservative America has been on this issue. Using the courts to influence and enforce pro-life policy is not a side issue; it is a key strategy of the pro-life cause. It is an illustration of the pro-life movement's dedication to judicial supremacy. In short, judicial supremacy entails expecting, accepting and obeying court opinions as if they were laws issued from the bench. This produced problems in the 19th century and it still causes problems. CR Cali wrote prior to *Roe's* reversal:

The idea is to support Republican Pro-Life presidential candidates who would nominate Republican Pro-Life justices. Once the court has been filled with Republican Pro-Life appointed justices, then Roe v. Wade can be reversed. This strategy itself feeds the myth of judicial supremacy and enshrines the expanding power of SCOTUS, bowing to the court and unjust rulings.[2]

The pro-life movement has mistakenly declared the Court to be one of the best methods by which to win the abortion debate while ignoring the Court's repeated sins. Relying solely on the courts should have been one of the final tactics employed. Instead, it was heralded as the key hero. Today, the majority of pro-life supporters have no clue that the conservative-appointed Supreme Court was the birthplace of legalized preborn murder. To explain the folly of citing the Supreme Court as one of the primary weapons in the arsenal against abortion, it is necessary to review a bit of its history.

50 Years of Abortion under Conservatives

In 1973, the entire country was in suspense as the Supreme Court heard the infamous case that transformed the face of the nation. Despite a conservative-appointed majority on the Supreme Court, the *Roe v. Wade* case resulted in a 7-2 judgment in favor of the plaintiff, Norma Leah Nelson McCorvey, best known by her legal pseudonym "Jane Roe."

McCorvey lived in Texas where abortions were only permitted in cases where the mother's life was at risk. Though McCorvey's life was not in jeopardy, she still desired to kill her preborn child. With the assistance of Texas attorneys Linda Coffee and Sarah Weddington, she challenged the Texas legislation that allowed abortion in limited circumstances. Interestingly, six of the seven conservative-appointed justices ruled in favor of McCorvey/Roe. The only dissenting justices were Republican-appointed Justice William Rehnquist and Democratic-appointed Justice Byron White. Republican-appointed Justices Harry Blackman, William J. Brennan, Warren Burger, Lewis F. Powell and Potter Stewart along with Democratic-appointed Justices William O. Douglas and Thurgood Marshall, ushered in the pro-abortion era of *Roe* that indelibly reconstructed America. The following table helps to visualize the 1973 Supreme Court bench (Democratic appointed justices are italicized):

1973 Supreme Court	Appointed By
Warren Burger, Chief Justice	President Nixon (R)
William O. Douglas, Justice	*President Roosevelt (D)*
William J. Brennan, Justice	President Eisenhower (R)
Potter Stewart, Justice	President Eisenhower (R)
Byron White, Justice	*President John F. Kennedy (D)*
Thurgood Marshall, Justice	*President Lyndon Johnson (D)*
Harry Blackmun, Justice	President Nixon (R)
Lewis F. Powell Jr., Justice	President Nixon (R)
William Rehnquist, Justice	President Nixon (R)

Things altered slightly during Gerald Ford's (R) presidency when he appointed John Paul Stevens to succeed Douglass. This increased the number of Republican-appointed justices. By time Ronald Reagan (R) entered the political scene, it had become the official pro-life agenda to appoint conservative judges to the Supreme Court in order to rectify *Roe*. Reagan campaigned strongly on this strategy. He attempted to make good on that promise by appointing Justices Sandra Day O'Connor, Antonin Scalia and Anthony M. Kennedy to replace Stewart, Powell and Burger. Under Reagan, the Supreme Court bench looked as follows:

1989 Supreme Court	Appointed By
William Rehnquist, Chief Justice	President Nixon (R)
John Paul Stevens, Justice	President Ford (R)
William J. Brennan, Justice	President Eisenhower (R)
Sandra Day O'Connor, Justice	President Reagan (R)
Byron White, Justice	*President John F. Kennedy (D)*
Thurgood Marshall, Justice	*President Lyndon Johnson (D)*
Harry Blackmun, Justice	President Nixon (R)
Antonin Scalia, Justice	President Reagan (R)
Anthony M. Kennedy, Justice	President Reagan (R)

Amazingly, the conservative appointment of Supreme Court justices continued under President George W. Bush's (R) administration when he appointed Justices David Souter and Thomas Clarence to replace Brennan and Marshall. At this moment, Rehnquist, White and Blackmun were the only remaining justices from the original *Roe v. Wade* decision. This left just Blackmun as the remaining justice who had supported *Roe,* and, coincidentally, wrote the majority opinion in the case. In 1991, the Supreme Court bench boasted the following:

1991 Supreme Court	Appointed By
William Rehnquist, Chief Justice	President Nixon (R)
John Paul Stevens, Justice	President Ford (R)
David Souter, Justice	President George H. W. Bush (R)
Sandra Day O'Connor, Justice	President Reagan (R)
Byron White, Justice	*President John F. Kennedy (D)*
Thomas Clarence, Justice	President George H. W. Bush (R)
Harry Blackmun, Justice	President Nixon (R)
Antonin Scalia, Justice	President Reagan (R)
Anthony M. Kennedy, Justice	President Reagan (R)

Over the course of 19 years, the number of Democrat-appointed justices steadily decreased until the early 1990s when the court became 8-1 Republican appointed. This was an astonishing conservatively-achieved goal. The pro-life strategy had been successful. There was widespread belief that the end of *Roe* was imminent. Given the pro-life movement's advantage following these judicial victories, few pro-life leaders and citizens were prepared for what transpired in 1992.

Buckling Down on Abortion Rights

In the late 1980s, Pennsylvania Governor Robert Casey (D) sponsored a new abortion-restricting law. Several abortion providers and doctors represented by Planned Parenthood sued Casey, arguing that abortion restrictions were unconstitutional. The case had the potential to overturn *Roe v. Wade*, which conservatives expected. Instead, in a shocking 5-4 betrayal, the Supreme Court's conservative majority upheld the legitimacy of *Roe* by ruling in favor of Planned

Parenthood. While the Court upheld several pro-life laws in question, it struck down the husband notification provision, which was one of the plantiffs' contested Pennsylvania laws. This decision shifted the scope of *Roe v. Wade* from a trimester framework to a fetal viability standard. This redefinition helped expand abortion access and the abortion industry.

Previously, *Roe* allowed abortion exclusively during the first trimester (as a decision between a woman and her doctor) and was mostly untouchable. *Roe* allowed states to regulate (but not prohibit) abortion in the second trimester and possibly prohibit abortion when a fetus was viable, unless the mother's life was at risk. *Planned Parenthood v. Casey* broadened the first trimester framework to include an "undue burden" requirement for all nine months of gestation. While this allowed states to regulate abortion in the first trimester, it also meant that states would face greater difficulty restricting or banning abortion in later trimesters because they would have to prove that their restrictions would not create "substantial obstacles" for a woman before the fetus is considered viable. Several key questions were considered by the court when deciding *Casey*:

> So in this case we may inquire whether *Roe*'s central rule has been found unworkable; whether the rule's limitation on state power could be removed without serious inequity to those who have relied upon it or significant damage to the stability of the society governed by the rule in question; whether the law's growth in the intervening years has left *Roe*'s central rule a doctrinal anachronism discounted by society; and whether *Roe*'s premises of fact have so far changed in the ensuing two decades as to render its central holding somehow irrelevant or unjustifiable in dealing with the issue it addressed.[3]

The 1992 conservative-appointed Supreme Court ultimately found *Roe* was "in no sense proved 'unworkable,'" that it was relied upon heavily as "customarily chosen as an unplanned response to the consequence of unplanned activity or to the failure of conventional birth control," and that "no evolution of legal principle has left *Roe's* doctrinal footings weaker than they were in 1973."[4] Based on these conclusions, *Roe* not only remained standing but was fortified. Not only did these supposedly conservative justices fail the entire pro-life movement's expectation to overturn *Roe*, but several of the justices made statements that indicated they were not at all interested in ever overturning *Roe*.

Roberts confessed that overturning a precedent "is a jolt to the legal system," as it plays an important role in "promoting stability and evenhandedness." Even if the court ruling is clearly erroneous, Roberts said, "It is not enough that you may think the prior decision was wrongly decided."[5] Overturning a prior decision appears to be based on popularity more than constitutionality. This concern with safeguarding precedent was shown in *Planned Parenthood v. Casey,* which discussed *stare decisis*, the doctrine of precedent, which is the legal approach used to determine points in litigation based on previous court decisions. As the *Casey* decision articulated:

> ...without explaining why overruling *Roe*'s central holding would not only reach an unjustifiable result under principles of *stare decisis,* but would seriously weaken the Court's capacity to exercise the judicial power and to function as the Supreme Court of a Nation dedicated to the rule of law.... The root of American governmental power is revealed most clearly in the instance of the power conferred by the Constitution upon the Judiciary of the United States and specifically upon this Court. As Americans of each succeeding generation are rightly told, the Court cannot buy support for its decisions by spending money and, except to a minor degree, it cannot independently coerce obedience to its decrees. The Court's power lies, rather, in its legitimacy, a product of substance and perception that shows itself in the people's acceptance of the Judiciary as fit to determine what the Nation's law means and to declare what it demands.[6]

Roberts feared that overturning *Roe* would undermine the Supreme Court's legitimacy; so even in instances where the Court was wrong, he believed it should be determined whether a reversal is in the best interest of the nation and rule of law, or if undermining the Supreme Court's authority would be more detrimental. As the case opinion continues, "Thus, the Court's legitimacy depends on making legally principled decisions under circumstances in which their principled character is sufficiently plausible to be accepted by the Nation."

Roberts and the majority in the *Casey* ruling are not unique in these perceptions. Alito stated similar sentiments on *stare decisis*:

> Roe. V. Wade was an important precedent of the Supreme Court. It was decided in 1973. So, it's been on the books for a long time. It has been challenged on a number of occasions. The Supreme Court has reaffirmed the decision; sometimes on the merits; sometimes – in *Casey* – based on stare decisis.[7]

Of course, the irony of these jurists' concerns is that an unlawful decision already undermines the Court's authority. These justices ruled against the very Constitution that gives them power. Nothing destabilizes the Supreme Court more than this point. Furthermore, Roberts veers far beyond the bounds of judicial authority by claiming that court decisions need "to be accepted by the Nation." *Roe* was not accepted by a sizable part of the nation in 1973. Even if it had been, our nation is not governed by simple majorities who could have embraced that landmark abortion case as law. If the people of the United States wanted abortion legalized, they had to amend the Constitution by three-fourths of the States. Instead, the Court established its own illegitimate version of abortion "law", bypassing both the Executive and Legislative branches. And just about everyone has played along.

The justices reluctantly admit their error but deflect it by asking whether the country could manage being realigned with the Constitution after so many decades of deviating from it. The Supreme Court bench should have asked themselves: Is our job to uphold the Law of the Land or to rule favorably with popular culture? The concern with saving face, rather than upholding the Constitutional right to life for all humans – weighs heavily in the judicial sphere and has only strengthened oppression against the preborn.

The Conservative Legacy of Pro-Abortion Rulings

The Court's violations of the Fifth and Fourteenth Amendment rights of the preborn are not isolated incidents. In fact, the conservative-appointed Supreme Court's record on abortion cases does not look that "conservative." While most Americans are likely familiar with the *Roe v. Wade* decision, the majority is unlikely to be familiar with other landmark abortion cases such as *Doe v. Bolton*, *Bellotti v. Baird*, *City of Akron v. Akron Center for Reproductive Health*, or *Stenberg v. Carhart*, to name a few.

In the history of the United States, the Supreme Court has never extended portions of the Fifth or Fourteenth Amendments to preborn humans. The Court has consistently ruled against the Fifth Amendment, which states that "No person shall be...deprived of life, liberty, or property, without due process of law..." and the Fourteenth Amendment, which states in Section One, "...nor shall any State deprive any person of life, liberty, or property, without due process of law; nor deny to any person within its jurisdiction the equal protection of the laws."

The Court, established to assist in determining difficult legal issues, has ignored the most fundamental constitutional provisions designed to safeguard all human life from unjust, unfounded assault and death. Instead, the Court used "penumbra and emanations" of the Constitution to creatively interpret the right to prenatal homicide. Rusty Lee Thomas, former national director for Operation Rescue and Operation Save America, wrote in his book *Biblical Strategies to Abolish Abortion*:

> "Historically, penumbra was first introduced by astronomer Johannes Kepler in 1604 to describe the shadows that occur dur-

ing eclipses. Legally, it is the shadow areas of the Constitution ... Justice William O. Douglas claimed that the right of privacy happens in the Constitution within 'a penumbra' (a limited shadow where light from a given source is not entirely excluded, as in an eclipse) 'that is an emanation' (something which flows from another source) such as the Bill of Rights."[8]

Since abortion is not explicitly stated in the Constitution, the Court incorporated it into existing liberties to make it fit. This inventiveness has led to a Court and state-directed assault on preborn humans' safety, thus enabling their unconstitutional executions. An overview of some of the Court's decisions demonstrates this despotic treatment of the preborn.

In *Doe v. Bolton*, considered *Roe's* companion case and decided on the same day, the Supreme Court ruled that Georgia had too many abortion-restricting laws interfering with a woman's right to choose to terminate her child based on health concerns. The Court's majority wrote: "We agree...that the medical judgment may be exercised in the light of all factors – physical, emotional, psychological, familial, and the woman's age – relevant to the wellbeing of the patient. All these factors may relate to health. Based on the Court's broad definition, "health of the mother" swiftly grew to justify abortion up to birth for nearly any reason, and the Court acknowledged this consequential impact of its decision in its opinion writing. Despite the expected consequences of its decision, the Court ruled against applying the Fifth and Fourteenth Amendments to preborn humans.

Six years later, in 1979, the Supreme Court overturned a Massachusetts law requiring women under the age of 18 to obtain parental consent before having an abortion. This *Bellotti v. Baird* case upheld women's autonomy regardless of age, ruling that all minors could get court consent for abortions without parental knowledge. This made it easier for minors to seek the unconstitutional death of their preborn children.

Seven years after *Bellotti v. Baird*, the conservative-appointed majority once again struck down parental consent in its 1986 case *City of Akron v. Akron Center for Reproductive Health;* but parental consent was not the ruling's only casualty. It prompted the challenge of many Ohio statutes, including the requirement for doctors to provide women with information about the abortion process, a 24-hour waiting period after signing a consent form, and necessitating that second trimester abortions be performed only in hospitals. At no time during this trial was the Court concerned with preserving the constitutional protection of life for the preborn.

Stenberg v. Carhart demonstrated the most egregious and blatant disregard for preserving the application of due process under the Fifth and Fourteenth Amendments. Instead of ruling to establish equal constitutional protections for all humans, the Court overturned a Nebraska law that prohibited partially delivering a late-term fetus alive and then executing it. Ironically, the Court stated: "Under the Fourteenth Amendment, a state cannot pass an anti-abortion law that does not include an exception for the health of the mother. It also cannot pass a law that criminalizes partial-birth abortions unless it is thoroughly clear that it does not extend to other forms of abortion."

Here, the Fourteenth Amendment was narrowly applied to protect only the lives of select humans, namely born women. The focused interpretation of not "depriving any person of life" was used to justify women ending the lives of their unborn children (without due process for the preborn) in order to preserve their own lives in whatever capacity seemed fitting to them. The Court was more concerned with consistent precedent and the health of the mother than it was with showing impartial, constitutional protection to all humans, born or preborn.

Unfortunately, the Supreme Court has never moved to constitutionally protect all preborn humans; thus, it has never been "pro-life" in the sense of protecting everyone's right to life and providing justice when others do them harm. The Court has not met the standards of either pro-life or abolition ideologies. The chart below proves helpful in showing that, according to pro-life standards, the Court has ruled in favor of pro-life legislation only a handful of times since 1973, but never enough to equate such loyalty and trust in it.

Pro-Abortion Decisions	Pro-Life Decisions	Year
Roe v. Wade	–	1973
Doe v. Bolton	–	1973
Bigelow v. Virginia	–	1975
Bellotti v. Baird	–	1979
–	Harris v. McRae	1980
City of Akron v. Akron Center for Reproductive Health	–	1983
Bolger v. Youngs Drug Products Corporation	–	1983
Thornburgh v. American College of Obstetricians and Gynecologists	–	1986
–	Webster v. Reproductive Health Services	1989
Hodgson v. Minnesota	–	1990
–	Rust v. Sullivan	1991
Planned Parenthood v. Casey	–	1992
Schenck v. Pro-Choice Network of Western New York	–	1997
Stenberg v. Carhart	–	2000
Ferguson v. City of Charleston	–	2001
Ayotte v. Planned Parenthood of Northern New England	–	2006
–	Gonzales v. Carhart; Gonzales v. Planned Parenthood	2007
Whole Women's Health v. Hellerstedt	–	2016
–	Dobbs v. Jackson Women's Health Organization	2022

This chart summarizes some of the most prominent abortion cases heard by the Supreme Court. From this list of 20 high-profile cases, there are just five pro-life "wins," which hardly seems celebratory. This table is generous in classifying even those five cases in favor of the preborn.

In *Harris v. McRae*, the Court rejected a challenge to the Hyde Amendment and upheld the pro-life law that prohibits Medicaid funding for abortions except when a mother's health is jeopardized. The verdict provided no protection for preborn children; rather, clarification was given that those who desired to kill their preborn children must do so without using Medicaid funds.

In *Webster v. Reproductive Health Services*, the ACLU represented the plaintiffs in a case challenging a Missouri law that required doctors to run diagnostic tests on a fetus' viability after 20 weeks of gestation, prohibited "the use of public employees and facilities to perform or assist abortions not necessary to save the mother's life",[9] and restricted the use of public funds to counsel a woman to have an abortion. The Supreme Court affirmed the Missouri law, keeping all three requirements intact, in what the pro-life movement hailed a grand victory. More importantly, the Court rejected the United States Solicitor General's request to use this case to overturn *Roe v. Wade*. Instead, the Court declined, delaying *Roe's* reversal by 14 years and failing to do what pro-life leaders had fought so hard to have those justices appointed to do.

The *Rust v. Sullivan* trial introduced a challenge to Title X, which barred abortion counseling or referrals from family planning centers funded by this government program. The Court upheld Title X regulations, which, like the Hyde Amendment, did not impose limits on women seeking abortions but rather controlled how federal funds may be utilized by pregnancy centers around the nation. It left all preborn execution methods and allowances undisturbed.

As discussed in the previous chapter, the Court upheld the pro-life dismemberment ban (also known as the partial-birth abortion ban) in the last two *Gonzales* cases while also providing creative suggestions to abortionists on how to still successfully kill a preborn human before he or she was halfway delivered alive.

The *Dobbs v. Jackson Women's Health Organization* received worldwide recognition when SCOTUS overturned its previous *Roe* and *Casey* decisions, declaring that there is no guaranteed Constitutional right to abortion. While the pro-life movement held out hope for more than 50 years, it arguably fell short. The Court had the authority to declare and clarify that the Fourteenth Amendment applies to all humans, both born and unborn, yet it chose to leave the applicability of the Fourteenth Amendment or continuation of unconstitutional execution of preborn humans to the states.

The moral and legal reality is these court decisions should be regarded as pro-abortion simply because they permit abortion for some or all preborn humans. It is important to remember these cases were only classified as wins according to pro-life standards, not by abolitionist standards. For those committed to the pro-life, incremental philosophy, these "pro-life" SCOTUS decisions do not outweigh the pro-abortion ones. There is little evidence to justify such trust and hope in the Supreme Court for protecting all human life.

Despite the Court's terrible track record, many people are pleased when miniscule victories in favor of pro-life legislation occur every few years or decades. The bar for pleasing most anti-abortion Americans is extremely low.

The scope of the conservative-appointed Court's hesitation to overturn *Roe* and *Casey* has not been fully explored here, but it is nothing short of miraculous. God can and will change the hearts of leaders. This is the providential truth upon which abolitionists base their hope. Yet even after *Roe's* reversal, marketing any court system as the best hope for ending abortion is a costly mistake. In fact, the irony of pro-life judicial supremacy becomes more apparent as time passes.

A Legacy of Misplaced Hope

If an accounting department embezzled money and the entire company was aware, how rational would it be for the board to explain to its employees that they will continue to support and pay those same accountants in the hopes they will one day correct their infraction? Should those who are to provide checks and balances within a corporation remain loyal to the lawbreakers, even though they ignored the law, created the crisis, and put the entire company at risk? Why would anyone go that route when the corporation has alternative options to address such a legal grievance? The most obvious response would be to fire the accounting team, press charges against them, and then reconvene to discuss the next steps in resolving the disaster.

This is the incredulous situation Americans have with the Supreme Court on the matter of abortion. There were additional legal options available to address SCOTUS' error. Instead, the branch of government that created the problem that pro-life conservatives have spent decades fighting to fix is the same institution to which conservatives chose to outsource the solution. The Court ruled against the law on purpose. This was not a mistake. Rather, it hints at something sinister. If the most distinguished jurists in our country can misinterpret the unambiguous language of the Fifth and Fourteenth Amendments, what other areas of more complex litigation are they also blundering? Just as someone knowingly embezzles money, the Court went against the sensibility of the Constitution. These scenarios defile the trust of the public by intentionally transgressing simple laws designed to either restrain or protect all people. This is not a call to anarchy;

this is a time for checks and balances. Not only is judicial supremacy dangerous because it distorts the basic structure of a constitutional republic, but in this case it has turned the culprits into heroes and endangered an entire demography of humanity (the preborn). Tragically, judicial supremacy is practiced by both conservatives and progressives.

A 2018 *Politico* article quoted Carol Tobias, president of National Right to Life Committee, as saying, "Like many conservative organizations, National Right to Life puts a huge emphasis on the impact the courts can have on the future of abortion policy." The issue at hand was Kennedy's retirement and his vacancy, giving Trump an opportunity to appoint yet another conservative justice to the Supreme Court. Of this, Marjorie Dannenfelser, President of Susan B. Anthony List, said, "Justice Kennedy's retirement from the Supreme Court marks a pivotal moment for the fight to ensure every unborn child is welcomed and protected under the law." Forty-five years after *Roe* and 26 years after the *Casey* decision (and the massive national expansion of abortion that followed), the pro-life movement continued to pitch its main strategy as filling the Supreme Court with "its" justices.

Trump said in a 2016 Presidential debate, "The justices that I'm going to appoint will be pro-life, will have a conservative bent…they are great scholars in all cases and they are people of tremendous respect." Once elected, he fulfilled his promise to seek out conservative justices. Following Trump's campaign pledges and marching to the beat of the judicial drum, pro-life organizations reiterated their belief that the Supreme Court is a primary way to fight abortion:

> This 2016 Presidential election is critical; the stakes have never been higher. Our next president holds the prolife fate of our country in his or her hands. We applaud Mr. Trump's list of pro-life candidates for Supreme Court justices.[10] – Susan Smith, Pro-Life Council of Connecticut President

> Donald Trump has completed a candidate questionnaire with 14 of 14 pro-life answers. He has put out a list of possible Supreme Court candidates that have been widely praised as those who will uphold the Constitution, not legislate from the bench.[11] – Dr. Wanda Franz, president of West Virginians for Life Political Action Committee

> President Trump has made another outstanding choice in nominating Judge Brett Kavanaugh to replace Supreme Court Justice Anthony Kennedy, keeping his promise to nominate only originalist judges to the Court. Judge Kavanaugh is an experienced, principled jurist with a strong record of protecting life and constitutional rights, as evidenced by his opinions in *Garza v. Hargan* and *Priests for Life v. HHS*.[12] – Marjorie Dannenfelser, Susan B. Anthony List President

The excitement over Trump's future justice appointments was comparable to that shown over Bush's, Reagan's and Nixon's. These praises were sung during the era of *Roe v. Wade* and *Planned Parenthood v. Casey*. The payoff from conservative justices had yet to materialize, despite the numerous opportunities within the Court's reach.

These knocks against SCOTUS are not meant to undermine its importance. This is pivotal: The Supreme Court serves a vital role in the framework of American governance, and the integrity of the judicial system must be maintained. Worshiping a rogue bench erodes civil integrity, however. When the Court errs, the Constitution gives the authority to check the Judicial Branch by impeaching judges who breach their office, whether due to personal scandal, illegal operations or in violation of the Constitution.

Congress can also ignore an unconstitutional decision. If the Court can issue opinions that clearly contravene the rights guaranteed by the Constitution, then what is the point of constitutional protections in the first place? Is it not more binding than just a pleasant, albeit subjective, sentiment? In reality, every state and U.S. representative takes an oath to "support and defend the Constitution"[13] as does the president and jurists. In the event one of those institutions is corrupted, the other governmental branches must address the issue in order to preserve constitutional integrity.

Why was impeaching a Supreme Court justice never used as a conservative strategy correction, despite the fact that the majority of Congress was conservative during the life of *Roe v. Wade*? While impeaching justices is uncommon, the mere threat of impeachment may have prompted the Court to reverse its previous decision, or forced the justices involved in *Roe* and *Casey* to resign, as with Justice Abe Fortas.

Who Was Fortas?

Fortas is a figure who has been largely forgotten, but his story should serve as an important admonition. Fortas was a gifted lawyer with a promising career as a justice. From 1963 to 1969, his early career legacy included landmark cases such as *Gideon v. Wainwright*, which established the right of those accused to have access to an attorney regardless of their ability to pay, as well as First Amendment cases such as *Tinker v. Des Moines Independent Community School District*, which helped establish First Amendment rights for students and teachers, and *Epperson v. Arkansas*, in which the court overturned the right to prohibit the teaching of evolution. Fortas also established one of Washington's most prestigious law firms, Arnold, Fortas and Porter; it exists today as Arnold and Porter.

By 1948, Fortas had befriended a young senator from Texas, Lyndon B. Johnson, who eventually served as vice president to President John F. Kennedy and inherited the presidency after Kennedy's assassination in 1963. When Johnson was elected to the presidency for a single term, Fortas and Johnson remained close friends. Eventually, Johnson appointed Fortas to the Supreme Court bench in 1965, where Fortas served a brief but highly impactful term as one of the country's highest justices. He enjoyed a brief period of success, but when Johnson nominated Fortas to become Chief Justice things began to fall apart for the brilliant scholar.

The Senate must approve any nomination for the position of Chief Justice, and, through the scrutiny process, some serious questions were raised. For one, while Fortas' close relationship with President Johnson was not a secret, just how close they were quickly became apparent through Senate proceedings, leaving much integrity to be desired. The U.S. Senate revealed in its second Fortas nomination hearing:

> [a]s a sitting justice, he regularly attended White House staff meetings; he briefed the president on the secret Court deliberations; and, on behalf of the president, he pressured senators who opposed the way in Vietnam.[14]

The separation of power between the Executive Branch and the Judicial Branch grew more difficult to discern, with Fortas acting more as a presidential advisor and Cabinet strongman than a Supreme Court justice. Just one year after this ethical disaster, Fortas unwisely accepted $20,000 from the Wolfson Foundation. Though it seems trivial, the donation came from the family foundation of Louis Wolfson, who had been indicted for securities fraud. A secretly recorded conversation between Wolfson and Fortas revealed that the judge "was very heavily involved in advising Wolfson on legal difficulties he had with the Securities and Exchange Commission."[15]

When news of Fortas' close relationship with a suspected criminal became public, it proved too much for his career to overcome. Not even Johnson's devoted nepotism could save him. Despite returning the $20,000 to the Wolfson Foundation, irrevocable damage was already done to his reputation and, in light of impeachment rumors, Fortas resigned voluntarily in disgrace from the Supreme Court bench.

If Fortas' blurring of the lines between his professional duty and his close association with a suspected criminal was enough cause for the Senate to consider impeachment, then impeachment should most definitely be on the table for justices who side against the Law of the Land, especially when subjecting a group of humans to unconstitutional execution.

Fortas is just one example of a justice who has been threatened with removal from office for failing in his duty. It is worth noting the pro-life movement's silence on potential impeachment as a remedy for jural constitutional violations. There is scant evidence that this has ever been seriously considered by the pro-life movement as an antidote to a court that rules against constitutional protection for preborn humans.

In 1997, Willke declared that the pro-life movement's "ultimate human rights goal remains an amendment to the U.S. Constitution, which will guarantee equal protection by law for all living humans from the time their life begins at fertilization until natural death."[16] Currently, the pro-life movement's goal is diluted, as it seeks to enshrine legal protection for mothers who commit preborn murder, as evidenced by H.R. 464. This obviously negates the personhood of the unborn. Furthermore, a personhood amendment is redundant because the Constitution already provides specific protections of life to all humans. It also introduces future ethical battles as personhood is not solely limited to human beings as mentioned at the beginning of this book. In the end, a personhood amendment would only serve to undermine other immediate solutions for enforcing existing preborn protections.

Despite personhood murmurings, the pro-life focus has clearly centered on maintaining – not disciplining – the Supreme Court. As Willke clarified, "The intermediate goal remains the complete reversal of the 1973 Roe vs. Wade and Doe vs. Bolton decisions by the Supreme Court."

Today, both rulings have been reversed, and the pro-life political action committee leaders and conservative politicians should be pressured to pursue abolition bills that provide equal justice and protection for preborn humans *with no exceptions* to their right to life.

One Trick Ponies

Another option in response to *Roe* was nullification. This, however, violates the ideology of judicial supremacy for both the pro-life and abortion movements. Even after many politicians admitted that *Roe* was an unlawful decision, state legislators continued to pass laws that aligned with *Roe*. Instead, the Legislative Branch should continue to pass laws that it believes are aligned with the Constitution. It can do so with the expectation that those laws may challenge an existing, unlawful court precedent, initiate a new court case, and provide an opportunity to overturn a previously incorrect judicial ruling.

The *Dobbs v. Jackson Women's Health Organization* case provided the opportunity for the Supreme Court to correct its errors with *Roe*, which it finally (though partially) did. To have fully rectified its error, the Supreme Court should have denounced *Roe* and ruled under the Fourteenth Amendment of the U.S. Constitution that all people, born and preborn, are guaranteed protection of their lives under the law. The route that SCOTUS chose, however, was to restart a war on states' rights. The Court partially corrected its erroneous ruling and, much like Pontius Pilate washed his hands of any sinful decisions made by Jewish leaders regarding Jesus, SCOTUS delegated the decision to state leaders to either continue or cease killing preborn humans while the Court washed its hands of the results.

Pro-life legislators worship the judicial system because they only pay lip service to the Constitution but honor the lawlessness of the courts. When a court says, "Women have a right to abortion," and the Legislative Branch, along with pro-life PACs say, "Then we'll just regulate it like any other industry," lawlessness is honored and upheld. Christians should consider whether partnering with and supporting such policymakers is ethical. The American Anti-Slavery Almanac for 1841 had harsh words to say about such alliances:

> Remember, that by voting for a man to fill an office you make him your agent, and if you vote for him knowing that his principles are wrong, when he puts forth those principles in his official acts, those acts are your acts, you are just as guilty as if you had performed them yourself. By voting for him, with the knowledge you have, you assume the responsibility of his acts; you become a partner in his sin, and shall be partaker of his plagues.[17]

Sometimes when Christians vote for politicians, those lawmakers can surprise or disappoint their constituents; but a politician who pulls off a plot twist is not the same as one who promises voters he will only support laws that are based on unbiblical values and unconstitutional ideas. The one-trick pony politician who has his hands tied to the altar of the Supreme Court bench should be avoided by voters. Christians should flee from collaborating with a politician who is knowingly involved in or supportive of such wickedness. A wise ruler would nullify unlawful court rulings. As will be explored in upcoming sections, many states have no problem ignoring the Supreme Court's ruling on marijuana. And interestingly, while progressives were judicial supremacists under *Roe v. Wade*, the moment it was reversed their rhetoric and doctrine changed to support "nullification," or, more accurately, insurrection.

On the day of SCOTUS' ruling, Congresswoman Alexandria Ocasio-Cortez (D-NY) stood in front of the Supreme Court, yelled "Illegitimate!" and urged people to get "into the streets." Representative Maxine Waters (D-CA) declared women will continue to do with their bodies what they want and will defy the Supreme Court saying, "You ain't seen nothing yet...The hell with the Supreme Court."[18] Dozens more attorneys joined the frenzy, refusing to prosecute anyone involved in an abortion, believing it to be an act of nullification. In a joint letter released in August 2022, 92 district and state attorneys and attorney generals stated:

> Not all of us agree on a personal or moral level on the issue of abortion. But we stand together in our firm belief that prosecutors have a responsibility to refrain from using limited criminal legal system resources to criminalize personal medical decisions. As such, we decline to use our offices' resources to criminalize reproductive health decisions and commit to exercise our well-settled discretion and refrain from prosecuting those who seek, provide, or support abortions.... Our criminal legal system is already overburdened. As elected prosecutors, we have a responsibility to ensure that these limited resources are focused on efforts to prevent and address serious crimes, rather than enforcing abortion bans that divide our community, create untenable choices for patients and healthcare providers, and erode trust in the justice system. Enforcing abortion bans would mean taking time, effort, and resources away from the prosecution of the most serious crimes — conduct that truly impacts public safety.[19]

Because the Declaration of Independence and the U.S. Constitution both recognize the individual right to life of *every* human, these protestors are actually practicing lawlessness, not nullification. Conservative politicians and the pro-life movement are well aware of the practice of nullification. Conservative politicians and the pro-life movement have proven two things. First, they recognize the use of nullification and impeachment in other political areas but refuse to apply it to the unborn holocaust. Second, they will endure decades for their desired incremental outcomes but willfully choose not to apply that tenacity to total abolition.

Tenacity is demonstrated in the pro-life movement's unrelenting fight for Republican-elected presidents to appoint conservative Supreme Court justices in blind faith hoping their allegiance would one day pay off. When pro-life advocates fail to support abolition legislation with the same fervor, arguing that they are unlikely to succeed, it is clear they are operating under a double standard. After all, it took 50 years for overturning *Roe* to succeed.

The abolitionist movement desires for anti-abortion organizations to fight for equal protection and justice for the preborn with the same zeal as the pro-life movement fights for their preferred judges. When abolitionists repeatedly attempt to pass laws that provide equal protection and justice, the pro-life movement steps in to stop them, claiming that it wastes time and money. They believe the nation is not ready to fully end abortion and that abolition legislative efforts will end up enjoined in court and never work. As Live Action NEWS once published, "Total abolition is not what this country is ready for right now. With how our country is, baby steps and gradualness is what we can do and are trying to do."[20]

This concept of gradual compromise trickles down from top conservative leaders. During the first Republican debate of the 2024 presidential primary in Milwaukee, Wisconsin, candidate and former Vice President Mike Pence declared he is "100 percent pro-life" and then went on to explain that a 15-week ban should be the official platform of the GOP since 70 percent of Americans support it. He clarified this position at the Faith and Freedom Coalition conference in Washington, D.C., where he stated, "Every Republican candidate for president should support a ban on abortion before 15 weeks as a minimum nationwide standard." The irony of Pence's statement was not lost on his critics. One hundred percent pro-life means choosing to protect the preborn life only in agreement with what is the current popular position of society. This means if the current national threshold against abortion is 15-weeks' gestation, then that limit should be suffice for the run-of-the-mill conservative.

Not all agree with a federal ban. Current Presidential candidate Donald Trump says abortion should not be criminalized at a federal level but should be left to the states to decide what to do with it. Speaker of the House Mike Johnson, former trustee for the SBC Ethics & Religious Liberty Commission, says he also would not pass a nationwide abortion ban if Republicans gain majority in the House and Senate, stating explicitly, "And so I believe in the sanctity of human life. It's also an important article of faith for me. But I have 434 colleagues here. All of us have our own philosophical principles that we live by, but you have to have a political consensus."[21]

The pro-life movement only asks for what it thinks society will allow. Abolitionists ask for what God has required. The vigor and propulsion of the pro-life movement has insisted that the cure for the abortion crisis largely rests with the Supreme Court (and lower courts), despite the clear rejection of the Court to do what pro-life leaders desired.

However, as SCOTUS recently proved, it was nowhere near ready to overturn *Roe* until 50 years after its occurrence, and yet the pro-life movement still clung to its judicial strategy. The dogma of trusting the courts to police its own unconstitutionality is chancy and unnecessary. The founding fathers were far more visionary than to create a governmental system with only one way to address tyrannical leaders, laws and court opinions. The concept of limited government served as the foundation for the American Experiment.

Unlimited Authority Means Limited Obedience to God

Many of America's founding men and women believed in limited civil obedience. In the early years of this nation, Americans worked under the conviction that civil government could only operate and govern in conformity with God's law. The Declaration of Independence models this belief by affirming all men "are endowed by their Creator with unalienable Rights, that among these are Life, Liberty and the pursuit of Happiness." This well-known phrase undoubtedly ensures an individual's protection in these areas, but also suggests that the government is not allowed to violate these rights. This is further clarified in the following sentence, which states, "That to secure these rights, governments are instituted among men."

The founders took great care to distinguish a government instituted *among* men from a government instituted *by* men. The first denotes something outside of men causing the effectual institution, while the second instance implies men as the originators and creators of authoritative systems. Consider the first verse from Romans 13 which states, "For there is no authority except from God, and those that exist have been instituted by God." As far back as 1159 AD, John of Salisbury wrote in his famed work *Policraticus*, "All power [authority] is from the Lord God; the power which the prince has is therefore from God, for the power of God is never lost nor severed from Him, but He merely exercises it through a subordinate hand."[22]

Government is a concept created by God and designed to be occupied by man to help in ruling the earth that God entrusted to human caretaking. To rule poorly or unbiblically is to rebel against God and to be an enemy toward the good of the people.

Yet most modern-day Christians have been raised under the doctrine of statism, which conveniently teaches that the government has unrestricted and limitless power. It refers to a political structure "in which the sphere of civil government exerts substantial, centralized control over much of society"[23] and is frequently used synonymously with communism or totalitarianism. Rather than acknowledging a person's right to exist and thrive, statism grants *permission* for an individual to do so. With statism, the government seeks to uphold *its* authority over people's rights. In a republic, the government works to protect people's rights from itself.

Reading Romans 13 in the context of a statist political system, modern-day Catholics and Protestants interpret the passage to suggest that a citizen's subordination to a civil government is unrestricted, thus limiting their submission to God. The anti-slavery movement encountered this same double-mindedness. People cannot serve two masters. If Christians attempt to honor God's command to establish justice and love their preborn neighbors as they love themselves, while simultaneously following the pro-life and pro-abortion edicts that allow for the unconstitutional execution of preborn people, they end up like their 19th-century anti-slavery counterparts who found themselves fighting to preserve slavery. The fight wasn't because they morally supported it; they believed the laws permitted the institution and should be upheld at all costs. Matthew Trewhella wrote in *The Doctrine of the Lesser Magistrates*:

> God is the ultimate Law-Giver and Ruler. God has established four realms of government which He delegates authority. They are: (1) self- government; (2) family government; (3) church government; (4) civil government. Each has its own role function, and jurisdiction. If one invades the jurisdiction of the other, chaos or tyranny ensues.[24]

Judicial supremacy flirts with dictatorship. The numerous abortion cases heard by SCOTUS established such unorthodox and unlimited jurisdiction that has resulted in an American holocaust. While many pro-life advocates express contempt for these unconstitutional rulings, the actions of pro-life organizations and legislators prove their willingness to engage in lawless decrees by enacting legislation that corresponds to the Court's declaration of who qualifies for the right to life. When nullification is mentioned, the pro-life movement attempts to delegitimize it as a rational approach, or accuses people who support nullification of failing to obey God's command to submit to authority.

It must be considered how the pro-life movement's approach and submission to the Court would never be used in any other form of government. It would not advise a physically-abused wife to endure the abuse and submit to her husband because he has unrestricted authority over her. Similarly, the pro-life Christian community would object to church leaders who verbally or sexually abuse their members. Little (if any) advice would be given to those church members to toughen up and take it like "good Christians." Similarly, a faithful conservative would not instruct children who were being starved by their mothers that they deserved it and should be better children. If Christians do not give unlimited force to other forms of authority to exploit those under it, then they should not do so with the civil magistrates. All forms of government have a legitimate obligation to others and all are accountable before God. As Thomas Jefferson once said, "The care of human life and happiness, and not their destruction, is the first and only legitimate object of good government."

Deferring to Lawlessness and the Selective Use of Nullification

When the 19th-century Supreme Court ruled that slaves were not actually citizens and, therefore, could not expect any protection from the federal government or courts, many northerners disagreed with that constitutional interpretation. An article published by the southern news outlet *Fayetteville Observer*, wrote, "The decision [Dred Scott v. Sanford] has produced a sensation in the North. The Republicans in the N.Y. Legislature have already a resolution 'to consider the decision.' We suppose they will resolve that it is not law, and should be nullified."

The south's expectation that the northern states would refuse to abide by the Dred Scott case was not wrong. Pro-slavery laws and court decisions, such as the Fugitive Slave Act, which required all citizens to assist in apprehending and returning runaway slaves to the south, were disregarded for years by a number of northern states.

Nullification is the process of ignoring unconstitutional rulings and laws. It is an age-old practice that predates the American Revolution, although Thomas Jefferson and James Madison may have been among the first to officially introduce and formalize it in the United States.

Nullification is a philosophical conviction, political process and physical action that demands an authority figure, state, court or federal government to realign with true law. Madison said a state is "duty bound" to interpose and "to arrest the progress of evil." This theory of interposition holds that states are obliged to intervene on behalf of their citizens when the federal government abuses its constitutional authority and discriminates against the people. Given the balance of power on which our country was formed, the founders strategically planned for tyranny to be difficult to achieve.

While no state has jurisdiction over another individual state, interposition allows a state to retaliate against the federal government if it behaves as a bully. The same holds true against a tyrannical judicial branch. Jefferson declared that when the federal government "assumes undelegated powers, its acts are unauthoritative, void, and of no force." He further explained: "[W]here powers are assumed which have not been delegated, a nullification of the act is the rightful remedy."[25] In this context, the states should have enacted nullification against the *Roe v. Wade* decision to protect the lives of unborn humans within their jurisdictions. Instead, the exact opposite occurred, with the states acquiescing with such a tragic court interpretation.

In the 14th-century, John Wycliffe wrote in his book *Civil Dominion* that those who rule unjustly and unlawfully, whether in the government or the church, should not be obeyed because they have "breached the terms of which God delegates authority."[26] Because Wycliffe believed the role of civil government and the church was to promote the prosperity of the people and reflect God's moral law, he wrote that any actor who violated those terms should be viewed as a lawless rebel and resisted. As many as 600 years ago the principle of nullification was understood and practiced by Christians as an act of protection.

Critics of nullification liken it to secession or speculate that it could cause another civil war. Both nullification and secession are legal and political solutions to a totalitarian government but with one major difference. Nullification appeals to a higher law in defiance of a lawless figure without running from the fight. Secession is the act of removing oneself from the tyrannical authority; it is to declare complete independence such as the United States did toward England and southern states attempted prior to the Civil War.

Other opponents fret that nullification promotes anarchy. They caution that disobeying even illegitimate law leads to more lawlessness. Arkes discovered this level of criticism when he challenged the legal positivism (which is moral relativism applied to law) of conservative politics. Arkes wrote:

> "Head for harbor," said one of our friends, "not start a revolution" – not urge people to the threshold of insurrection. But we had sought, in several ways, to direct people away from the course of lawlessness... I was struck in contrast with the notable want of prudence shown by our erstwhile allies: Their reactions seemed to

me out of scale, for they seemed to be taking far more offense at us than at the offenses that we had sought in detail to describe."[27]

The "offenses" Arkes warned of was judicial supremacy. In 1996, the journal *First Things* organized a symposium on judicial usurpation titled "The End of Democracy?" Arkes, along with several of his friends and like-minded intellectuals such as Chuck Colson, Robert George, Russell Hittinger, Robert Bork and Richard Neuhaus, participated in the symposium. As these men began to explain the dangerous territory the conservative-appointed court – referred to as the "regime" by Arkes – was taking the country, the pushback was not against the rogue court but against the prophetic voices heralding the warning. Bewildered, Arkes penned his thoughts on such misplaced opposition:

> ...we never thought we were repudiating the American regime. Quite the reverse: We were seeking to vindicate the principles of the regime, to restore them in the face of a political class that was artfully replacing that regime with something else. Our friends seemed to take as gravely serious the threat that we writers were posing, and yet they could not take with the same seriousness the warning set forth by Lincoln: namely, that a regime quite republican in its outward forms could be converted, in its substance, into something else, something radically different.[28]

In his book *Natural Rights and the Right to Choose*, Arkes cautions that even decent regimes can and do fall into corruption, and, when that happens, law-abiding, freedom-loving people should resist and push back against the lawlessness of that regime. This is nullification. And it is urgent Americans practice it sooner rather than later in an effort to curb the power-trip of SCOTUS. It has been the conservative-appointed court that has transformed the moral face of the nation by ushering in same-sex marriages, deeming IVF embryos as property, and floundering to define and protect the value of all human life. Arkes laments:

Step by step the federal courts had shown a willingness to challenge, at their root, the laws that restrained the taking of human life at the beginning (with abortion) and at the end (with euthanasia and assisted suicide). With the same sweep, the judges were willing to think anew, and map anew, the begetting of human life, in mechanical fertilization or the storing of embryos. But then again, the courts became willing to pronounce anew on the meaning of sexuality as they took the first steps in altering the understanding of marriage. What the judges were doing, virtually on their own, was remodeling the very matrix of the laws on birth, death, sexuality, and marriage.... It was a record that reached into the deepest premises of our law and the meaning of "the human person."[29]

Conservatives have long complained about such rulings, but, rather than demanding that the balance of powers address those grievances, they remain caught in their own trappings of legal positivism. While abolitionists would disagree with Arkes on incremental initiatives such as partial birth abortion bans or born-alive protection laws, he was correct in his stance against the lawless overreach of the Court. His warnings against the antijural unraveling of the Court came in the early 2000s, and more than 20 years later, few conservatives have bothered to heed his forewarnings and steer the ship back toward the Constitution. Instead, the shrill cry against nullifying lawlessness persists from conservatives because of their unfounded fears of anarchy and their legislative and judicial ignorance. Few Americans understand that nullification is the furthest thing from anarchy. Dissent from a declared "law" is only nullification if it appeals to a higher or true law.

If a mayor orders his town to stop celebrating the Fourth of July or face a $2,000 fine, citizens should remind him of their First Amendment right to peacefully assemble, continue celebrating, and refuse to pay the fine. They may even choose to sue or impeach him. The city council could be petitioned to take disciplinary action against the mayor as well. These actions would nullify his unjustified, unfounded declared authority and realign him with constitutional law.

When some slavery abolitionists believed the Constitution included provisions for slavery, they justified nullifying it on the grounds that Scripture is the superior authority. They subordinated the most supreme Law of the Land to God's Word, which says all people are made in his image and we are to treat others how we desire to be treated. In this regard, nullification differs significantly from anarchy, which recognizes no law superior to an individual's will. An anarchist defies rules simply because that person dislikes what he or she is told to do, not because they respect the law of God or laws of the land. Nullification is much different. Nullification acts as a whistleblower for treasonous behavior. It says to the lawless, "We will not go along with you as you violate the laws of the land. We will continue recognizing those true laws and abiding by them as an indictment against your disloyalty."

Anarchy could not care less about treason because it does not see law as sacred or superior to which one must comply. Anarchism is a dystopian political theory that is skeptical of the legitimacy of authority and power.[30] It elevates individual liberty above all else and pursues freedom from all forms of domination. This is entirely antithetical to Christianity. According to Scripture, governing authorities come from God. Christ's headship, as well as the structure of the church and family, continue to paint a picture of clear, meaningful and intentional authority in every person's life.

Nullification is consistent with Christianity. Because Christians recognize authority as from God, it is appropriate to not follow in the footsteps of someone who deviates from both the Bible and the Constitution (where it's in agreement with biblical principles). Nullification declares, "You are transgressing the law and I will not also become a transgressor with you." As Exodus 23:2 states, "You shall not fall in with the many to do evil."

Men such as Jefferson and Madison were among those who believed that states had an obligation to resist evil, even when that evil was within the federal government or the courts. The concept of state sovereignty was born from this concern. Opponents will argue that nullification is a lofty ideology that is not practical in today's world. This is especially ironic given the recent years of COVID restrictions, lockdowns and mandates. American citizens, organizations, school districts, cities and even entire states practiced nullification against stringent federal and state overreach.

In California, churches such as Grace Community Church refused to stop meeting due to lockdown measures, and while the state sought to take punitive action against the church, where John MacArthur pastors, the church responded by filing its own case against the state, which it won.[31] In New York, thousands of workers, especially police officers and firefighters, refused the mandatory COVID vaccine, citing that being forced to undergo a medical procedure violated their rights. They continued to show up for work until they were strong-armed into unemployment. While initially their acts of nullification resulted in their job loss, they had the final say. The workers filed a lawsuit against the state and in October 2022, the New York State Supreme Court reinstated all fired, unvaccinated workers and awarded retributive back-pay, demonstrating that the workers' acts of nullification were indeed legally valid and were recognized as such by the state's highest court.

Likewise, Florida Governor Ron DeSantis ignored restrictions enacted to limit the spread of COVID. DeSantis nullified local ordinances by barring cities and counties from collecting fines imposed on citizens who violated social distancing rules or face mask mandates, and a Florida U.S. District judge overturned and nullified the unlawful Centers for Disease Control and Prevention travel mask mandates.[32]

At the time of this writing, 40 of the 50 states are defying the Federal Controlled Substances Act (FCSA), which outlaws the possession of marijuana. These states believe they are nullifying the Supreme Court decision *Gonzales v. Raich*, which ruled in favor of the FCSA.[32] What distinguishes this case as special interest is that it is debatable whether the states have the constitutional authority to defy the federal government on this controlled substance issue. Stu McArthur, former Federal Bureau of Investigation Deputy Assistant Director for Counterterrorism, believes the Constitution allows the federal government to enact drug laws "because of its enumerated power to regulate inter-state commerce." He goes on to stress, "If my premise of enumerated power is correct, then I think the states are acting unlawfully in nullifying [*Gonzales v. Raich*] and they are the ones not submitting to the governing authority – the Constitution. But, nonetheless, this shows the States' willingness to defy the federal government in matters they believe in."[33]

If McArthur's assessment is accurate, it should be extremely alarming that states are willing to ignore laws that they *should* be upholding while refusing to ignore illegitimate laws that warrant no faithful observation and allow for the unlawful execution of humans. Nullification is alive and well. Conservatives simply do not apply it to preborn murder. Instead, judicial supremacy is taught in regard to preborn murder, which holds that states and citizens must adhere to court abortion decisions no matter what. This obedience is expected even when a court's rulings are blatantly unconstitutional. It represents a fundamental skew of the judicial branch's function. It is also in direct opposition to the founding fathers' beliefs. The founders established the Constitution as Law of the Land (U.S. Const. Art VI, Clause 2.), not court opinions.

The (Historically) Lesser Power of the Judicial Branch

Robert Lowry Clinton is Professor Emeritus of political science at Southern Illinois University Carbondale and has written multiple books on the legal system, as well as articles in the academia sphere. Clinton explains, "The Constitution is clear on the judicial role, and, while it authorizes judicial review, it does not authorize judicial supremacy."[34] Nevertheless, the Supreme Court acts similarly to the constitutional revision council, which was explicitly rejected by the founders at the Philadelphia Convention in 1787. The Council of Revision would have endowed the President and a panel of Supreme Court justices to veto Congressional bills. Elbridge Gerry, former vice president under President James Madison, strongly opposed the measure saying it mixed "together the Legislative and the other departments" and that it would result in "making Statesmen of the Judges; and setting them up as the guardians of the Rights of the people" instead of relying on "the Representatives of the people as the guardians of their Rights and interests."[35]

Similarly, Alexander Hamilton was a prolific author on government issues who was likewise critical of the habit of elevating the Judicial Branch above the Executive and Legislative. This may sound strange to most people. Many of us were taught in school about the balance of powers, in which the Executive, Legislative and Judicial branches exist peacefully as equal components. This, however, is not how our government was originally structured. Rather, the Executive and the Legislative branches were to have equal power, with the Judicial Branch serving as a subordinate authority. As Hamilton wrote in Federalist Paper #78:

> Whoever attentively considers the different departments of power must perceive, that, in a government in which they are separated from each other, the judiciary, from the nature of its functions, will always be the least dangerous to the political rights of the Constitution; because it will be least in a capacity to annoy or injure them. The Executive not only dispenses the honors, but holds the sword of the community. The legislature not only commands the purse, but prescribes the rules by which the duties and rights of every citizen are to be regulated. The judiciary, on the contrary, has no influence over either the sword or the purse; no direction either of the strength or of the wealth of the society; and can take no active resolution whatever. It may truly be said to have neither FORCE nor WILL, but merely judgment; and must ultimately depend upon the aid of the executive arm even for the efficacy of its judgments. This simple view of the matter suggests several important consequences. It proves incontestably, that the judiciary is beyond comparison the weakest of the three departments of power...[36]

The judicial position is one of interpretation only. Its role is to offer expertise and clarification on disputed issues, but it cannot issue rulings that contradict the Constitution, which it is bound to uphold. In matters of contradiction, the founding fathers ensured that states have the freedom to challenge grievous court rulings though nullification, impeachment, amendments and court of appeals. (Similar safeguards exist to limit executive or legislative overreach.)

While Hamilton understood the court's inability to injure the Constitution due to its politically weak design, this is not the case today. Instead, the Supreme Court participates in trampling preborn individuals' Constitutional rights and pro-life and pro-abortion advocates give it free rein to do so. Clinton echoes Hamilton's viewpoint that, "in the early days" of the American republic, the Court "was widely considered the 'least dangerous branch' of government." Clinton stresses the Court did not always claim to "possess such a power to make final pronouncements on the meaning of the Constitution" and the other branches of government did not expect it to either. "Our present conception of judicial supremacy is a recent development in American constitutional history," Clinton states.[37] Progressives and conservatives each want to stack the Supreme Court because they believe the bench has the final say. Again, Clinton remarks about this departure from our political foundation:

> Instead of the powerful Congress, the energetic but carefully checked executive, and the "least dangerous branch" envisioned by the Framers, we now have a weak (if not dysfunctional) Congress, a powerful and relatively unchecked executive, and a Court that claims for itself final, ultimate, and exclusive authority to determine the scope and range of power possessed by the other branches of government.[38]

Despite the founders' belief that they would not submit to tyrannical rule that opposed the basic freedoms found within the U.S. Constitution, the pro-life movement has consistently deferred to *Roe v. Wade* as the "Law of the Land" alongside pro-abortion apologists. And contrary to Jefferson's assertion that a good government cares about protecting all of its citizens, today's American government does not care about protecting all human life. Instead, word wars are used to obscure what constitutes human life and who is entitled to protection. The most alarming trend, however, is how many professing Christians advocate offices, politics and Supreme Court decisions that either support or perpetuate lawlessness against the preborn.

Considering the average 21st-century professing Christian rarely holds a biblical worldview, it should come as no surprise that the Bible is rarely used to evaluate political opinions. If the FRC's 2021 survey is correct, only nine percent of American Christians actually possess a biblical worldview, and out of 67 percent of professing Christian parents with preteens polled, only two percent had a biblical worldview.[39] The urgency to reclaim the mind of Christ is at an all-time, perilously high point. Trusting in authoritarian regimes and judicial supremacy was enabled by a lack of scriptural, logical and historical understanding. And it has resulted in the oppression of preborn humans.

Those who are committed to preserving and promoting the right to life for all people must refrain from engaging in judicial supremacy. Christian citizens and legislators must forsake judicial supremacy, not just in rhetoric but also in action. Legislators must pass laws that they believe are consistent with the Constitution, not questionable court opinions. When error is obvious, Congress has the authority to remove any disreputable jural actors, which must be done seriously and swiftly. They must not disregard the Constitution's univocal protections. Professing Christians should urge their legislators to do nothing less than herald the complete and immediate criminalization of abortion, nullify illegitimate court rulings, and impeach unlawful justices. The preborn have waited far too long for Christians to reform and make this right.

11

Unthinkable

"Now where temporal government or law alone prevails, there sheer hypocrisy is inevitable, even though the commandments be God's very own. For without the Holy Spirit in the heart no one becomes truly righteous, no matter how fine the works he does. On the other hand, where the spiritual government alone prevails over land and people, there wickedness is given free rein and the door is open for all manner of rascality..." – Martin Luther, reformer (1483-1546)

Making Abortion Unthinkable

WITH ROE IN THE rearview mirror, anti-abortion individuals are asking, "Now what?" For the pro-life movement, a major goal is to make abortion culturally unthinkable. Forty years ago, Catholic pro-life influencer Frank Pavone pushed the "unthinkable" rhetoric among other anti-abortion pioneers. Pavone explains, "This is our mission! In the late 1980s, I began circulating among pro-life leaders the language that we want to make abortion unthinkable. It is now a common expression in our movement."[1]

From a brief survey of headlines, tweets and quotes, it is apparent this is now a main agenda for the pro-life movement:

> Pro-lifers must unite in 2021 to make abortion unthinkable.[2] – Nancy Flanders, Live Action

...we aim to make abortion illegal, unthinkable, and unnecessary.[3]
– Elizabeth Graham, The Southern Baptist Ethics & Religious Liberty Commission

Making abortion illegal and unthinkable[4] – *National Review*

Early Feminists would view abortion as unthinkable. – *Clarion Herald*[5]

Our role is to systematically eliminate the root causes that drive women to abortion, through education and advocacy.[5] – Serrin Foster, president of Feminists for Life

The goal to overturn Roe – that's always been a hope...but a much deeper and harder and loftier goal has been to make abortion unthinkable.[6] – Jeanne Mancini, president of March for Life

Now it's time for the pro-life movement to get refocused and to get recommitted to getting involved at that grassroots level. I sort of have this feeling that when we had a pro-life administration, a lot of people got complacent in that. But the reality is that no president can stop abortion, it's up to us to really create and build up a culture to make abortion unthinkable and to build up a culture that values life.[7] –Abby Johnson, pro-life activist

Save the Storks (@savethestorks): "It is through #lovecompassionaction that we will one day make abortion unthinkable." 8:04 PM • 01/20/20

Students for Life (@StudentsforLife): "We will make abortion unthinkable." 3:40 PM • 05/17/22

March for Life (@March_for_Life): "We march to stand against the greatest human rights violation of our time. We march to give a voice to the voiceless. We march to proclaim the dignity of every human being. We march to make abortion unthinkable." 1:02 PM • 12/09/22

Human Coalition Action (@HuCoAction): "The best gift you can give this season is life. Visit our website today and donate to help make abortion unthinkable." 5:00 PM • 12/11/22

Youth for Life NI (@YouthforLifeNI2): "The mission of Precious Life is to make abortion unthinkable. To do this, we must offer abortion-vulnerable women real tangible help & this is why we witness and reach out to women at abortion killing centers." 9:18 AM • 12/18/22

This "unthinkable" goal is to be realized primarily through educational programs and social awareness with the loosely attached biblical concept of human value. The aim to make abortion unthinkable is a necessary component of the pro-life movement since it promotes the doctrine of maternal impunity. The pro-life movement knows the law will not be a deterrent to women because it will not apply to women. Something else must stand in the gap. That something else is the social construct of ongoing literature, education and welfare programs all designed to encourage a woman to choose life and dissuade her from murder.

Essentially, it is colonization's voluntary manumission and amelioration programs repackaged for the 21st century. Much like slave masters who chose not to release their slaves under manumission programs, a mother who does not choose life for her child faces no consequences aside from the burden of a seared conscience. Like the colonizers' vain wish for a slave-free nation apart from the law, the pro-life movement hopes to achieve an abortion-free utopia also despite the law. They envision a world in which pro-life persuasiveness prevents women from abortion. However, enrichment programs are limited in scope. Ultimately, licentious behavior must be curbed by the law.

The emphasis on social initiatives to dissuade women from having abortions will not make abortion immoral and unthinkable for the vast majority of the culture. This is also supported by an argument from Secular Pro-Life. Ironically, this organization opposes prosecuting women for prenatal homicide and rejects scriptural authority, but it nevertheless recognizes the importance of the law in transforming society's minds on moral matters. Secular Pro-Life author Acyutananda writes:

> Improving conditions for pregnant women, mothers, and children is a moral imperative, and not only because it will decrease the number of abortions. It will not only decrease the number of abortions, it will increase the number of healthy and empowered women and children. So we should pursue that goal for its own sake. But we should face the fact that improving conditions in that way would do nothing at all to make abortion unthinkable. Nothing. Such progress would cause some women to think less

about abortion, but that is not what we mean when we say "unthinkable." When we say we want to make abortion unthinkable, we are using "unthinkable" to mean "so shocking that it cannot be imagined as possible."[8]

Acyutananda describes how social programs influence people's behavior but not necessarily their beliefs. He uses the hypothetical example of the government lavishing gifts on people who choose to raise their babies rather than murder them, resulting in a plummeting abortion rate. Things look good; then the economy worsens and financial incentives are removed. The once-declining abortion rate rises again because society has not been transformed morally but only situationally. Acyutananda ends the scenario by stating, "Couples will go back to baby-killing as usual, because their valuation of the preborn had not changed. They had given life because it was convenient to do so. Their consciousness about preborn life had not changed. Abortion had become situationally unnecessary for a year, but couples had not learned to perceive the preborn (at any stage of development) as full-fledged members of their family, and society had not learned that the preborn (at any stage) are our little sisters and brothers, whose protection is imperative for us."[9]

Situational ethics cannot be used to transform the country's morality about abortion. That will never lead to a significant, long-term shift in cultural conviction. Laws of equal protection and justice will humanize the preborn far more quickly and permanently than social and educational programs and will have a greater impact on supporting the moral claim that abortion is murder and therefore wrong. Classifying abortion as homicide would restrain the greatest number of people from committing preborn murder. Otherwise, legislation misinforms women about what is moral or immoral regarding abortion.

A *Los Angeles Times* article demonstrates just how morally deluded society gets when unjust laws govern people's consciences. The article highlighted several women and the reasons for their abortions. One such patient was "Amanda," of which the article states:

> She regrets having to pay $750 for the abortion, but Amanda says she does not doubt her decision. "It's not like it's illegal. It's not like I'm doing anything wrong," she says. "I've been praying a lot and that's been a real source of strength for me. I really believe God has a plan for us all. I have a choice, and that's part of my plan."[10]

Rebecca Hotovy, with the pro-life organization Justice for All, has found similar sentiment in her advocacy work for the preborn. In a *Life Report* podcast episode, Hotovy admitted the difficulties in educating college students that abortion is murder because the legal codes do not match that rhetoric. On the podcast, she admitted:

> I've talked to students on campus, though, when we talk about abortion – their reasoning for why abortion is okay is because the law says it's okay. And I ask them, "Should the law be what determines what is right and wrong?" and they'll be like "Well, yeah, it does." And then I cringe and I say, "Well, have we ever had laws that have been unjust?" And then they go, "Yeah, we have. [But] the law . . . influences people's thoughts."[11]

According to author and philosophy professor Stephen Schwarz, "If a person will not respect the integrity of another for moral reasons, let him at least do so for practical reasons, the avoidance of punishment."[12] If abortionists, women, men, abusers and human traffickers will not respect the life of the preborn from moral conviction, then they should have the consequence of the law to restrain them from doing harm. Helen M. Alvaré, law professor at George Mason University's Antonin Scalia School of law, agrees that the effect of law alongside social programs is needed for setting a moral barometer. As she stated in a 1996 debate with abortion activist Naomi Wolf: "The basis for the [pro-life] moral position is that it is the taking of a human life. In other arenas in society where the taking of a human life is concerned, the law also enters. If it doesn't enter, that is the anomaly, that's the strange thing! So the very basis for the moral position leads in order to avoid hypocrisy. . . . I'm not saying the legal struggle will solve everything. The moral and legal have to go in tandem."[13]

Alvaré advocates for legal provisions to support anti-abortion moral claims. Without the strength of law, rhetoric fades into dismissive opinion. Individuals, nonprofit organizations and churches can only go so far in affecting moral reform since God has structured the government to be the final arbiter in society of what is good and just. This is why it is critical that the civil government rules rightly. Jon Speed, pastor of missions and evangelism for By the Word Baptist Church in Texas says of this: "The church ministers grace. But the government ministers justice. Romans 13 is clear: It bears the sword against the evildoer. If we expect the government to know the difference between good and evil, the standard is the same as it was in Josiah's day: the Law of God."[14]

The Church and other well-meaning institutions can start changing society's beliefs and morals, but only the government can enforce what is right or wrong. God established the government to restrain evil and reward good. When this precept is reversed (either through tyranny or negligence), the Church's work increases but never replaces the sword of the magistrates. In this fallen world, both the work of the Church and the restraint of the law are required to govern and guide the wicked hearts of humankind.

This is not to imply that amelioration efforts are intrinsically wrong. The Church should be engaged in such works. Caring for the poor, the sick, the downtrodden, the disabled, the orphans, the widows and the homeless are all biblically designated jobs for the Church. But pro-life PACs are not the Church. Problems arise when pro-life political entities fundraise and advertise for things such as fetal development awareness, abortion procedure educational programs, state-funded pregnancy centers, or ultrasound laws, blurring the distinction between what the civil government and the Church should be doing.

Should the state punish abortion facilities for not offering ultrasounds to women before they slaughter preborn humans? Or should the state punish abortion facilities for slaughtering humans? Ultrasound services, pregnancy centers, food services, financial help and the like should be left to the Church to manage and offer. The civil authorities should pursue and execute the weightier matter of protecting all humans' right to life and bringing justice against those who violate homicide laws.

Ultimately, the law makes committing an act unthinkable because of the potential legal consequences. Our country did not make slavery unthinkable before abolishing it. Rather, the law abolished it first, and it is now unthinkable 200 years later. Because the law now stands as a barrier to subjugation, abolishing slavery aided in reforming people's perspectives of what they can and cannot do to another human being. The pro-life principle of following lawless court opinions, promoting amelioration rather than abolition, and resisting nullification is dangerous dogma. Following unconstitutional rulings and supporting lazy magistrates could see no end.

During a conversation at the Kansas Capitol building with abolitionist pastor Kevan Myers, pro-life Representative Clarke Sanders admitted that even if the Supreme Court ruled that prepubescent humans were no longer legally protected and did not have a guaranteed right to life, "the Court is the Law of the Land and cannot be ignored."[15] Myers argued that if the Court suddenly ruled that children aged 10 and under could be murdered by their caregivers, it would be the duty of every state to defy such an atrocious error and protect the children in their midst. Sanders stood firm on his conviction that Kansas could not ignore such a ruling. He maintained we would have to accept it until the courts remedied the error. Joe Pojman, Executive Director of Texas Alliance for Life, concurs with Sanders. "We could no sooner ignore SCOTUS than the force of gravity," Pojman said in his dissent of the 2019 Abolition of Abortion in Texas Act (HB 896).[16]

There should be little comfort to any citizen when representatives – who are elected to pass laws in compliance with the Constitution and who are the only political source entrusted with creating laws by both the U.S. Constitution and state constitutions – delegate their responsibilities to an unelected jurist bench. The consequence of granting the judicial branch legislative power to override existing, written laws may someday result in worse human rights oppression than what we see today, especially when legislators – and the lobbyists who support them – claim to be pro-life but concede there is little they will do to defend life if the courts declare that some humans no longer have certain inalienable rights.

If this is the permeating belief among both pro-life *and* pro-abortion politicians, then any group of people is just one court opinion away from having their constitutional right to life rescinded. Arkes soberly reflects on the dire situation of allowing the courts to redefine personhood and natural rights apart from the binding authority of the Constitution:

> Aristotle recognized that political life began with the understanding of that creature who was suited distinctively *by nature* for the polis. But what was once the predicate of political life, and a government by consent, has been converted into a question. Men and women in judicial office now profess to regard the question of "What is a human being" as an inscrutable, religious matter. The question then of "what beings are protected by the law now as human beings" is a question that must turn entirely on positive law, for there are apparently no objective standards that yield an answer objectively true .... The question, "What is human life?" becomes a question for political authority, and the question will have to be answered then without the consultation of any standards of moral judgment outside of the opinions held by those who exercise power.[17]

As Acyutananda concludes, "Laws importantly influence culture, just as culture influences laws. If we are not continually and actively demanding legal protections for unborn persons similar to those we would demand for born persons, we will appear to believe that the unborn are not really persons, which will undermine even our efforts at moral suasion."[18]

An Unthinkable Rebranding

Given the ideological commitment to make abortion unthinkable through various programs, it will prove difficult to achieve as the pro-life movement struggles with a political identity crisis. There is wide-reaching fallout from catechizing politicians to be soft and unresolved on abortion. It prevented conservative culture from rushing in to strongly and immediately abolish abortion in the wake of *Roe's* reversal, but it has also conveyed puzzling and counterintuitive messages to representatives. With polls now showing that most Americans disagree with *Roe's* overturn, some within conservative politics are evaluating whether to abandon the pro-life label altogether.

In September 2023, *NBC News* published an article highlighting how the Republican Party is shifting away from its pro-life stance. The temptation to drop the pro-life label is largely inspired by a recent poll conducted by an unnamed conservative Super PAC at the time of this writing. According to the poll results, respondents either no longer identify with the pro-life movement or they misunderstand what it represents.

Senator Kevin Cramer (R-N.D.) commented of the poll: "What intrigued me the most about the results was that 'pro-choice' and 'pro-life' means something different now, that people see being pro-life as being against all abortions...at all levels."[19] Senator Josh Hawley (R-MO) reiterated the same perplexity about misconceptions of pro-life goals when he stated, "Many voters think [pro-life] means you're for no exceptions in favor of abortion ever, ever..."[20]

Cramer and Hawley, both dedicated pro-life politicians, state unequivocally that the pro-life movement is not interested in criminalizing all types of abortion for everyone. This is also reflected by the National Republican Senatorial Committee (NRSC) encouraging Republicans to oppose a national abortion ban and instead give their "support for reasonable limits on late-term abortions when babies can feel pain with exceptions for rape, incest and life of the mother."[21] As usual, the lawmakers are listening to these pro-life PACs.

In the first 2024 Republican primary presidential debate, Nikki Haley, presidential candidate and former United Nations Ambassador, summed up the pro-life position by proclaiming, "Can't we all agree we should ban late-term abortions ... and can't we all agree that we are not going to put a woman in jail or give her the death penalty if she gets an abortion?"[22] Campaign Life Missouri director Samuel Lee boasted about upcoming Missouri abolition bills: "Any bills to authorize murder charges against women who undergo abortions are dead on arrival. I've killed lots of bills in my 40 years as a pro-life lobbyist and I guarantee they'll be LOTS of pro-life lawmakers in both chambers who'll kill these."[23] Pro-life Representative Tony Lovasco (R-MO) reinforced Lee's anti-abolition position by declaring, "Charging women with murder for having an abortion may be an intellectually consistent position. It's also a horrible idea. Compassion saves more lives than threats of vengeance, which only pushes more folks to the pro-choice camp. I won't support these bills."[24]

The opinions expressed by Cramer, Hawley, Lee, Haley, Lovasco and the NRSC are also shared by the entire pro-abortion movement; it, too, does not want to imprison women for abortion and would be mostly satisfied with legalized first and second-trimester abortions. Polls continue to reveal that the supermajority of Americans are comfortably in the middle with allowing abortions in certain circumstances, though built-in bias in these polls may be skewing the true sentiment of those surveyed, as will be seen below. Still, pro-life politicians have no expectations, goals or desires to abolish abortion. They are shocked that any American would want to criminalize prenatal homicide without some exceptions in place.

According to Tarrance Group's 2023 poll, 77% of voters support at least some abortion restrictions. When the polling is evaluated, the assumed bias is evident. In every question, the poll included abortion exceptions for rape, incest and life of the mother. There were no questions available for prohibiting abortion completely, for all people, and without any exceptions. All individuals surveyed had to choose an option that included some allowance for abortion. Each question from the poll is as follows:

> 1) Abortion should be prohibited throughout pregnancy, *with exceptions for life of the mother, rape, and incest.*
>
> 2) Abortion should be prohibited after a baby's heartbeat can be detected at 6 weeks of pregnancy, *with exceptions for life of the mother, rape, and incest.*
>
> 3) Abortion should be prohibited after a baby can feel pain at 15 weeks of pregnancy, *with exceptions for life of the mother, rape, and incest.*
>
> 4) Abortion should be allowed throughout all 9 months of pregnancy, *without any restrictions.*[25] [Emphasis added.]

The polling by the Tarrance Group on behalf of SBA Pro-Life America reveals a significant amount of bias and confusion. For one, the use of the term "prohibits" was used ambiguously. Does prohibition mean homicide charges for those who commit the act of abortion or does it mean misdemeanor charges? And who is prohibited from committing this type of crime anyway; all citizens or everyone but the mothers of preborn children?

What *is* clear from the survey is that SBA Pro-Life America is passionate about exceptions for abortion. It is also apparent this poll is being used to further catechize politicians and voters to think a certain way about how to be anti-abortion. Namely, how being anti-abortion means allowing abortions in instances of rape, incest and preference for the mother's life. This is counterintuitive to making abortion unthinkable.

An Unthinkable Evolution

The abortion industry owes much to the pro-life movement. Not only has the pro-life movement blurred the philosophical lines between what it means to be pro-life or pro-choice, but it has also benefited the pro-abortion movement in other ways. Today's abortion industry is so wealthy and adaptable that it is creating mobile abortion clinics to travel the country in order to avoid increasing pro-life state regulations. According to abortion provider Dr. Julie Amaon, medical director of Just One Pill, no one will ever know what is inside the nondescript vans.[26] Much detail, care and money are being spent on developing these vans to function like an in-clinic procedure room, all while avoiding obvious attention to the vehicle. Besides mobile murder clinics, abortion pill sales are skyrocketing in all 50 states. Telehealth providers plan to expand swiftly into states where abortion pills can still be prescribed via telehealth. Other distributors are devising new, conniving ways to distribute the product in states that have banned telemurder, allowing women to commit prenatal homicide alone.

In states such as Texas, which the Guttmacher Institute lists as "banning" telehealth abortion, there are still exceptions that allow women to commit preborn murder without consequences. A Texas woman can purchase abortion pills, have them delivered to her home, poison her unborn child to death, discard its corpse into the public sewer system, landfill or her backyard, and walk away scot-free. In Texas, or any other state with supposed abortion "bans," a mother cannot face penalties. A storefront in central Texas brazenly allowed a "pop-up abortion information store" to instruct women on how to order abortion pills. The advertisement explained how it was legal for women to acquire abortion pills within their state.[27] Likewise, a full-page ad by Mayday.Health in an Idaho newspaper read, "Hey Idaho: You can still get abortion pills in all 50 states," followed by a QR code to take the reader directly to its website to be legally connected with abortion pills.

These examples trend with a research letter The Journal of the American Medical Association (JAMA) published at the end of 2022, which revealed startling results. The study examined abortion pill demand a year before the *Dobbs* decision, shortly after the leaked *Dobbs* decision, and again after the judgment was released. Regardless of state policy on abortion, "every state ... showed a higher request rate during the periods after the leak and after the formal decision announcement" with the largest increase in abortion pill demand reflected in the five states enacting the strictest bans. Louisiana, Mississippi, Arkansas and Alabama tripled in online abortion pill requests. Oklahoma showed the greatest surge in abortion pill requests with a six-fold jump.[28] While recorded clinic abortions have decreased in these five states because the facilities mandated to report are currently closed, abortion pill demand and usage are proving to be a successful substitute. While pro-life politicians and political action committees claim to have eliminated abortions in these five states, thousands of preborn children are now being murdered in the privacy of their mothers' homes. To add to this dismal situation, 2022 also showed the largest shift of citizens from pro-life to pro-abortion, most likely resulting in the *Dobbs* decision and the reversal of *Roe v. Wade*.[29]

For the past 19 years, roughly 50% of Americans have identified as pro-life. In 2022, however, Statista recorded that the percentage of professing pro-life Americans plummeted to 39%, the lowest it has been in 20 years. Polling results came up again in 2023 to 44%, though it is still lower than the historical average. This swing may indicate that when the majority of Americans believed abortion to be somewhat protected, they were comfortable identifying as cultural pro-lifers; but when the safety net of *Roe* was removed, what they genuinely cherished emerged. Or maybe the pro-life brand becomes less attractive when people can identify with the more socially acceptable label of pro-choice and still profess much of the same convictions they once held under the pro-life banner. Whatever the cause, the numbers reveal that people on both sides of the aisle are more committed to the idea of women's rights than equal rights.

The abortion industry has effectively and consistently marketed its doctrine of matriarchal supremacy. It has worked hard to foster a culture of pro-choice supporters. The abortion movement makes no excuses when it says women matter more than "potential people" or "a fetus." Similarly, the pro-life movement contributes to this feminist idolatry by elevating women's health over the preborns', allowing abortive exceptions for rape and incest-conceived children, and teaching that all women involved in preborn homicide should have the legal protection to commit such crimes.

These pro-life doctrines are inconsistent with confessing the sanctity of life for preborn humans. These ideals act against all social goals to make abortion unthinkable. When the pro-life movement promotes laws to protect women who commit prenatal homicide from punishment, it leaves the preborn legally vulnerable. When it claims that all lives matter but then proclaims the lives of children conceived through rape and incest do not deserve protection, it loses credibility. Because of this doublespeak, pro-life efforts to catechize the culture on the value of preborn humans have failed. When the pro-life movement sends contradictory messages, supporters are left with broken ethics, shallow logic and divided loyalties. It has taught the culture to be pro-choice.

As much as professing Christians may not like to admit it, the pro-life movement has fed the abortion monster. Fifty years of incremental bills gave this beast the time it needed to become completely adaptable to any obstacle. This is not an unreasonable, harsh blame to place on mainstream pro-life influencers and organizations. They have been the leaders of the campaign for life. They claimed this for themselves in the National Right to Life Open Letter, which was addressed to all United States lawmakers. These prominent pro-life organizations claim to represent "tens of millions of pro-life men, women and children across the country," with National Right to Life dubbed as the "flagship of the pro-life movement."[30]

Citizens have also played a willful and ignorant role in compromise. Every Christian concerned with establishing justice should be alarmed by the current situation. Abortion has never been in higher demand than after *Roe*'s death. Abortion rights are currently constitutionally protected in many states, including California, Michigan, Ohio and Vermont. Many more states are expected to follow suit in the future, as pro-life politicians continue to oppose abolition efforts and gradually guide the culture toward secular justice. It is truly unthinkable how pro-choice the anti-abortion movement has become.

The Unthinkable Effect of Gradualism

Garrison once warned, "How has the slave system grown to its present enormous dimensions? Through compromise. How is it to be exterminated? Only by an uncompromising spirit. This is to be carried out in all the relations of life—social, political, religious."[31]

Christians must put an immediate end to child sacrifice. The longer it is tolerated, the greater the risk that abolition will fail as more enemies join the pro-life movement to stall the cry for criminalization, and more Christians become acclimated to our cultural decadence. Abortion rights leader Frances Kissling's instruction that "we need more responsible and compassionate state policies" and "sensible balanced legislation and regulation of abortion" to maintain the abortion industry was a brilliant move. With pro-life politicians and organizations now employing this very rhetoric, it is evident that Kissling's advice was achieved.[32] This is nothing new. Infiltration is the oldest trick in the book. Nearly 200 years ago, 19th-century abolitionist Elizabeth Coltman Heyrick observed the same tactic to preserve the slave industry:

> The enemies of slavery hitherto ruined their cause by the senseless cry of *gradual* emancipation. It is marvelous that the *wise* and the *good* should have suffered themselves to have been imposed upon by this wily artifice of the slaveholder, for with him must the project of gradual emancipation have first originated. The slaveholder knew very well that his prey would be secure, so long as the abolitionists could be cajoled into a demand for *gradual* instead of *immediate* abolition. He knew very well that the contemplation of a *gradual* emancipation, would beget a *gradual indifference to emancipation itself*. He knew very well, that even the wise and the good, may, by habit and familiarity, be brought to endure and tolerate almost any thing.[33]

Wilberforce reiterated Heyrick's observation of underhanded policies advertised as the means to combat cultural evils but intended to extend those very evils:

> The gradual abolitionists have been, in fact, the only real stay of that system of wickedness and cruelty which we wish to abolish; though that assertion is unquestionably true; it is trying beyond expression that they should be the real maintainers of the slave trade.[34]

Garrison, echoing the English abolitionists, lamented that "gradualism in theory is perpetuity in practice." How is gradualism perpetuated? Christians are taught to always vote for the lesser of the two mainstream evils, which only ensures that someone evil wins. The expectation of a wholesome, moral candidate is discouraged in conservative circles as impractical and childish. Those who refuse to vote for a compromised nominee face mockery and shame. Slavery abolitionist Birney addressed this attitude in the 19th century. Birney reasoned that "if there was but one election to be decided, then go for the best candidate of the two" but, in fact, "an election occurs every few years," churning out new contenders, so the expectations of candidates should be higher. *The Voice of Freedom* printed in 1839 the following caution of the "lesser evil" strategy:

> It would almost happen that of two candidates set up, one would be rather more favorable to the principles of abolitionists than the other; but yet, when elected, he might not do a single legislative act to forward their cause. It was plain they might go on forever voting for such men, and accomplish nothing toward the destruction of slavery. As long as it was found that they would be thus put off with a single grain of abolition in a candidate, and even that mixture too small and weak to show itself in action, the parties would never set up a genuine abolitionist.[35]

Two months later, another newspaper ran an article written by former U.S. Representative Gerrit Smith. Smith scathingly reminded voters what they gain when they settle for unbiblical candidates:

> ... a man may do "many things" that a Christian does, and yet not have the heart of a Christian – and yet totally reject Christianity. He may, for instance, be honest in his dealings in property, he may drink no intoxicating liquors. He may read his bible daily. He may daily call to God in prayer; and yet if he refuses to forgive his enemies, he has not a particle of Christian religion in his heart. Analogous to his case is that of the member of Congress, who is in favor of ... the abolition of the inter state slave trade – and of a dozen other anti-slavery measures – and yet be opposed to the abolition of slavery ... His heart is an entire stranger to the principles of abolition. The anti-slavery measures, which he supports, are not espoused by him in answer to the principle of abolition ... To vote then for a "five-sixths abolitionist" – or even for one "who will vigorously support nine" anti-slavery measures out of ten, and thus make himself a nine-tenths abolitionist ... is to be guilty of voting for an anti-abolitionist; for one who is not in principle opposed to the crime of slavery.[36]

We, too, have continued to vote for politicians and policies that accomplish nothing to end abortion and favor the abortion industry above the preborn. As Smith points out, a candidate who will not even vocalize support for complete abolition will ultimately be the enemy of abolition. But we potentially have a greater dilemma. The political enemies of the preborn are not predominantly gradual abolitionists who want to take their time accomplishing what they know is right. Today's pro-life politicians are not comparable to the 19th-century "villainous" gradualists. Slavery gradualists promised to abolish slavery albeit slowly. Today's conservative politicians flatly refuse to abolish abortion.

In a heated rebuttal to anti-abortion constituents who wanted a hearing for abolition bill HT 2256, Representative Steve Holt (R-IA) scathingly remarked, "I wonder if those advocating for this legislation are aware that this legislation would allow mothers who abort their children to be prosecuted and jailed. This is something that no credible person in the pro-life community that I have spoken to believes is acceptable. In fact, I have been advised that numerous pro-life groups across the country believe this is a dangerous and horrible approach, and I agree with them...It has never been the goal of the pro-life community in the years I have fought for life to prosecute mothers...I will not ever advance legislation that jails women who have an abortion."

The same week, Southwestern Baptist Theological Seminary alumnus and pro-life Representative Marcus McEntire (R-OK) was asked in a recorded interview if he would support a bill of abolition, to which he responded, "No, I will not support a bill for abolishing abortion in Oklahoma."[37] Instead, McEntire authored HB 1656, which would legalize abortion once again in Oklahoma for rape and incest-conceived children. Just days before his anti-preborn comments, McEntire was awarded roses at Rose Day, the annual Oklahoma pro-life rally, to celebrate his efforts on their behalf. This two-facedness is evident throughout the country and at all levels of politics.

The most notable 2024 Republican presidential candidates all stated they are against completely criminalizing abortion. Ron DeSantis, governor of Florida and former presidential candidate, said he is "absolutely not" in favor of any legislation that would allow women to be prosecuted for prenatal homicide, and that such laws "will not happen in Florida" under his watch.[38] Former U.S. President Donald Trump said he "is strongly pro-life, with the three exceptions – rape, incest and protecting the life of the mother."[39] Haley said she is "unapologetically pro-life," but has made it clear she opposes legislation that holds women accountable for preborn murder. Former presidential candidate Vivek Ramaswamy claims to be pro-life but says, "I don't believe a federal abortion ban makes any sense."[40]

Conservative America's top presidential candidates are not gradual abolitionists – they are anti-abolition pro-choicers. Despite the atrocious options, anti-abortion voters are told that a six- or 15-week ban is good enough and we should gladly embrace such a generous offer. Christian America even claims that if a person's conscience prohibits them from voting for a lesser evil, they are self-righteously damning the country to a greater evil. Yet to accept evil – whether much or little – preserves evil. It does not combat it. Slavery abolitionists endured the same taunts and reasoning. An excerpt from the debate in the 1839 Anti-Slavery Convention reveals Birney's response to such excuses:

> The Rev. brother had asked whether they [abolitionists] were going to insist upon perfection before they could vote for a candidate presented to them: certainly not. But would that gentleman vote for a man to be Professor in a college who would openly avow himself to be for a little lying, a little stealing, a certain amount of drunkenness, though not the very utmost amount possible? He knew he would not. Would he vote for a man as a pastor of a church who advocated slavery to the slightest degree? He would not. So neither did abolitionists demand perfection, but they did demand for their cause what was reasonable, and what all admitted, theoretically, to be right...all Mr. B. [Birney] asked was, that those who admitted these things to be wrong, and wished to bring them to an end, should act according to their own principles.[41]

Are we willing to act on the values we confess? Will we keep saying one thing while voting for another? Things get better by demanding better. Yanking away candidates' electoral support when they compromise on child sacrifice sends a resonating message. Pollsters and election statisticians take note of any major changes within a party's base. The threat of political loss means something to them. On the other hand, shaming voters with the accusation of "you will just throw away your vote" or "if you don't vote for such-and-such then the country will be handed over to the party of death" are pleas to maintain the moral degradation that exists in our current political climate. They are appeals to worldly strategy rather than trust in the supernatural capabilities of God and obedience to infallible Scripture.

The first instructions God gave his people for choosing leaders is found in Exodus. God's people are to select men who fear God, are men of truth, and hate covetousness (Exodus 18:21). Psalm 94:20-21 says, "Can wicked rulers be allied with you, those who frame injustice by statute? They band together against the life of the righteous and condemn the innocent to death."

On the other hand, civil magistrates are to be God's ministers to all people for their good (Romans 13:4) and are to rule over men justly, "ruling in the fear of God" (2 Samuel 23:3). How is a voter rejecting a politician who has announced he will negotiate with child sacrifice in more sin than the politician who refuses to fulfill his God-ordained duty to protect life? Conservatives mistakenly blame cultural erosion on those who reject the compromised magistrates who have permitted such moral concessions to occur under their political watch.

Christians should exercise caution when those who profess to oppose abortion urge us to continue supporting the politicians, legislation and policies that preserve it. Many people in the pro-life movement are only interested in regulating abortion from an abortion-friendly sentiment, self-preservation or sheer ignorance. The seduction of humanist, anti-god relationships poses an immediate danger to Christians who foolishly link arms with the wicked with the hope of achieving good. It introduces corruption and compromise, not righteousness and justice. While Scripture instructs Christians to flee from the presence of evildoers, influential pro-life leaders and organizations continue to urge the opposite:

> With the millennial and the Gen Z experience, more people than ever are identifying as LGBT, nonpartisan, no affiliation even religiously, I think we realize—if this cause really is for everyone—we need to be inclusive. [42] – Aimee Murphy, founder of Rehumanize International

> The very explicitly religious tone of some of the stuff at the March for Life has a place, but as the major key, I think a lot of these new

pro-life organizations would want to see a move toward more secular arguments being the baseline. If we're serious about this being a human rights issue, then it's essential to build as broad a coalition as possible.[43] – Ben Conroy, member of Minimise Project

You're critical of the pro-life movement because we're willing to work with secularists, and we're willing to work with ungodly people. We're willing to work with people who don't claim the name of Christ, and we're willing to work with people of other religions, and other political persuasions, and on and on and on. That's absolutely true. I'll work with anybody. I don't care who it is. If it will save a baby's life, I will work with that person. They could be the embodiment of evil and I'll cooperate with them if doing so saves a baby's life.[44] – Greg Cunningham, Executive Director of Center for Bio-Ethical Reform

It should be unthinkable to partner with the wicked on any project. Psalms 26:4-5 says, "I do not sit with men of falsehood, nor do I consort with hypocrites. I hate the assembly of evildoers, and I will not sit with the wicked." If sinners entice us to ignore God's precepts, we must reject their ideas because their feet run to do evil (Psalms 1:10-15). We are to leave the presence of the fool because knowledge will not be found on their lips (Proverbs 14:7) since goodwill is only found among the upright (Proverbs 14:9). Proverbs 1:7 says, "The fear of the Lord is the beginning of knowledge; fools despise wisdom and instruction."

We acquire knowledge of how to navigate the things of this world by first rightly understanding God's holiness and what our position toward him should be. The fool in the Bible is the one who does not fear the Lord; it is the one who worships someone or something other than God. Fools take no pleasure in understanding the things of God but only in expressing their own corrupt opinions (Proverbs 18:2). Establishing equal protection and justice for preborn humans is a divine mandate; therefore, fools will fail to understand how to go about it. This is why working closely with morally foolish people on anti-abortion efforts is treacherous. They will only drag us away from biblical principles. The folly of secularists has led many Christians to unwittingly support the abortion industry through unbiblical, incremental concessions or outright rejection of biblical abolitionist principles.

God despises when his people whore after false ideas, religions and gods. No biblical precedent exists for "trying our best" in opposition to God's Word. Any "good" we may perform apart from God's commands are seen as filthy rags (Isaiah 64:6), and will continue to provide opportunity for the abortion industry to thrive. Author Gary North points out:

> ... the question remains: Which is truly "barbaric," mass murder through legalized abortion or the required judicial sanctions revealed in biblical law? The Christian antinomians of our day - that is to say, virtually all Christians - have voted for the barbaric character of biblical law. They are faced with a choice: Minimal sanctions against abortion or the civil enforcement of biblical law? Their answer is automatic. They shout to their elected civil magistrates, "Give us Barabbas!" Better to suffer politically the silent screams of murdered babies, they conclude, than to suffer the theocratic embarrassment of calling for the public execution of convicted abortionists.[45]

No More Unthinkable Compromise

There should be no more compromise with the lives of the unborn. Heyrick's appeal applies to 21st-century Christians:

> Had the [gradual] abolitionists preserved a single eye to their great object; had they kept it distinct and separate from all extraneous considerations; had they pursued it by a course more direct, through means more simple; had they confided more in the goodness of their cause, and dreaded less the opposition of its adversaries; had they depended more upon Divine, and less upon human support, their triumphs, instead of their defeats, would long since have been recorded. Surely their eyes must at length be opened; they must perceive that they have not gone the right way to work, that the apprehension of losing all by asking too much, has driven them into the danger of losing all by having asked too little; that the spirit of compromise and accommodation has placed them nearly in the situation of the unfortunate man in the fable, who, by trying to please everybody, pleased nobody, and lost the object of his solicitude into the bargain.[46]

Compromise on murder will never yield desirable results. That's the point. Each side gives up some of their desired outcome. The pro-lifer gives up complete obedience to God's law and true justice. The pro-abort gives up the ability to transgress as much as she wants. Who of these is righteous before God? Neither, as both violates his law. The pro-life movement has been effective in gradually managing the preborn homicide industry. The abolitionist's goal is to criminalize preborn murder and refuse to move the goalpost for lesser victories.

From a material perspective, the pro-life movement has the money, power, influence and support required to win the fight. The problem is not with resources but with principles. Most pro-life organizations are not the righteous standard by which to set our compass. To continue abiding by their playbook reveals us as tolerant of lukewarm policies, which God tells us in Scripture he despises. North informs:

> The vast majority of Christians hate God's revealed law far more than they hate abortion or abortionists. They would far rather live in a political world that is controlled by humanists who have legalized abortion than in a society governed by Christians in terms of Biblical law. So, God has answered the desire of their hearts. He has done to modern Christians what He did to the Israelites in the wilderness: 'And He gave them their request, but sent leanness into their soul (Ps. 106:15).'[47]

Those who are satisfied with simply regulating preborn murder can continue to do things as they have for the past 50 years. It has not been a failed strategy; it has been fruitful. For those who desire to see the criminalization of abortion and live in a society free from legalized child sacrifice, then an abrupt change of course is vital. We can have different flavors on cultural and legal solutions when it comes to issues such as paid family leave, child tax credits, construction of pregnancy and family resource centers, how to spend taxes, and so forth, but we cannot have multiple paths for writing partial or impartial laws to protect all human life. Scripture gives permission only for impartial laws to govern a land and that is what Christ followers must demand, promote and support. Ecclesiastes 8:11 says, "Because the sentence against an evil deed is not executed speedily, the heart of the children of man is fully set to do evil." Christians should heed this warning and seek to establish just laws that do not allow or instruct certain people to commit heinous crimes against preborn humans. The pro-life objective of making abortion unthinkable apart from God's law and constitutional law is unreasonable, impossible and unaware of the spiritual battle at hand. Famed preacher Charles H. Spurgeon acknowledged the depravity of the human heart when he said, "You cannot slander human nature; it is worse than words can paint it." The law is needed to restrain all types of people from all types of murder.

There is no reason for those ready to abolish abortion and include it in the history books with slavery to wait for the pro-life movement to change course. Scripture outlines God's commands to do justice, hold evildoers accountable, forbid murder, not acquit the wicked, and care for orphans. If we ignore these commands, do we actually believe we will escape the same judgment that was poured out upon Nadab and Abihu, the ten Israelite spies, Uzzah, Ananias and Sapphira, and the entire nation of Israel? They failed to honor what God's holiness required, denied God's promises, imagined themselves purer than they were, mocked the Holy Spirit, and whored after pagan rituals. Puritan preacher Timothy Cruso wrote, "All willful disobedience to our Lord's revealed will is destructive, if persisted in, and admits of no excuse. To suspend our practice of any duty, until we understand the reason of the precept, is indeed worthy of an everlasting hell."[48]

This is precisely what 21st-century Christians have done. The appeal for equal justice has been delayed until it makes sense to us and there is a more opportune time to pressure politicians and society for it. Today, we are reaping the consequences of a weak Christianity that aligns more closely with pagan practices than biblical precepts. American preacher Matthew Trewhella writes:

> He is judging the form of Christianity prevalent in our nation. He will reform and purify His bride. And when you have a form of Christianity that is incapable of reforming itself, He uses judgment to reform and purify. Judgment begins in the house of the Lord.[49]

Christians must abandon their compromise with the world. It is unthinkable that we would wait until we understand how God will bring about abolition before committing to its cause. Scripture implores us to act in faith and obedience *today*. The examples for us to return to God's ways and immediately cease our disobedience are clear:

> And that servant who *knew* his master's will but did not get ready *or act according to his will*, will receive a severe beating (Luke 9:47). [Emphasis added.]

He will render to each one according to his works: to those who by patience in well-doing seek for glory and honor and immortality, he will give eternal life; *but for those who are self-seeking and do not obey the truth, but obey unrighteousness, there will be wrath and fury.* There will be tribulation and distress for every human being who does evil, the Jew first and also the Greek, but glory and honor and peace for everyone who does good, the Jew first and also the Greek. For God shows no partiality (Romans 2:6-11). [Emphasis added.]

"On that day many will say to me, '*Lord, Lord, did we not* prophesy in your name, and cast out demons in your name, and *do many mighty works in your name?*' And then will I declare to them, 'I never knew you; depart from me, *you workers of lawlessness*'" (Matthew 7:22). [Emphasis added.]

Are we counted among these faithless categories? Are the works we do to regulate child sacrifice accepted by God? It is unthinkable how professing Christians refuse to conduct things in the way that God has commanded. Augustine said it is "necessary to have our hearts subdued by piety, and not to run in the face of Holy Scripture, whether when understood it strikes at some of our sins, or, when not understood, we feel as if we could be wiser and give better commands ourselves. We must rather think and believe that whatever is there written, even though it be hidden, is better and truer than anything we could devise by our own wisdom."[50]

God has wisely given us all the commands necessary to combat abortion. When the Church once again sees these scriptural precepts as good, we can be sure that repentance and reformation are on the horizon. For now, Puritan Thomas Watson's words hold true: "The further the soul goes from God, the nearer it approaches to misery."[51] Both anti-abortion and pro-abortion Americans have strayed far from God on the issue of child sacrifice, and misery abounds within the nation.

12

Ecclesia Reformata, Semper Reformanda

"There are some, in these apostate days, who think that the church cannot do better than to come down to the world to learn her ways, follow her maxims, and acquire her 'culture.' In fact, the notion is that the world is to be conquered by our conformity to it. This is as contrary to Scripture as the light is to the darkness."
– Charles Spurgeon, English preacher (1834-1892)

A Functional Papacy

SOMETHING HAS TO CHANGE. The pro-life movement has shown it is not biblically qualified to lead the post-*Roe* fight against abortion. It works too hard to straddle the line between pro-abortion and abolition. It writes prejudicial laws that protect some preborn humans but not others. It employs situational ethics to determine what is right instead of scriptural commands. It insists that only hired abortionists are the guilty parties in prenatal homicide instead of all accomplices involved in the act. It teaches that to love women we must grant them a license to murder their preborn children. It sees no problem with being unequally yoked to unbelievers or sitting with the scoffers and heretics in pursuit of secularly defined justice. It shrinks from battles in court while simultaneously heralding the court as a major strategy for victory. It spends money on the front end to achieve its legislative goals, but little money on the back end to enforce those laws. It seeks to achieve gains in morality apart from God's precepts. It practices lawlessness alongside progressives by yielding to unconstitutional court opinions instead of the actual, written Law of the Land. It proclaims it will end abortion but then sabotages legislative efforts that would do so. It attempts to misalign, slander and silence anti-abortion individuals who deviate from the pro-life script. Ultimately, the pro-life movement trusts and boasts in what man can do and not in what God will do.

The effectiveness of Christ's Bride has been hindered by following the edicts of Roman Catholicism and humanists on what it means to oppose the evil of preborn murder. Similarly to how the papacy governs the Roman Catholic church's doctrines and administrative body, today's pro-life movement has morphed into a regulating body that dictates a specific way to oppose abortion, and those who fall outside its declared doctrines are labeled as dangerous heretics. Catholicism's anti-abortion leadership has mingled with a healthy dose of secular moralism from other anti-abortion forces, resulting in a movement that seeks to ostracize, silence or condemn those who insist on addressing preborn murder through sola Scriptura. This has manifested in how Christians in the pro-life movement evangelize, develop policy, elect politicians, establish justice, and educate society.

When anti-abortion Christians preach that abortive women must turn from the sin of murder and seek forgiveness in Jesus Christ, they are often met with a hostile, canceling "shush" from pro-life influencers. Calling abortion murder offends many within the pro-life movement. Lizzie Marbach, former communications director for Ohio Right to Life, attests to this: "The organization often told me not to use terms like 'murder' or 'evil' when describing abortion and to frame messaging more positively instead. I pleaded for us not to prioritize politics over ending abortion during board meetings, which upset some."[1]

Former professor at Southeastern Baptist Theological Seminary Karen Swallow Prior, who claims to be pro-life, once said, "Referring to…women who obtain abortions as 'murderers' is worse than inflammatory: it is unchristlike."[2]

This is common sentiment shared across the political aisle. Many pro-life leaders, abortionists and pro-choice activists say that abortion is not murder because it is "legally" allowed. This, of course, is off-base.

As already explored within this book, the United States Justice Department defines murder under 18 U.S.C. § 1111 as "the unlawful killing of a human being." Because the Fourteenth Amendment prohibits the execution of any human being without due process of law, abortion is, in fact, illegal and conclusively murder. Unconstitutional statutes, however, have misled both Christians and non-Christians into believing that women are not guilty in these homicide cases. This is one reason the pro-life movement does not find the biblical truth about abortion necessary, comfortable or undisputable. On the one hand, the gospel destroys the pro-life unbiblical assertion that women are victims of the abortion industry and are not accountable as murderers; and the gospel challenges the pro-life's ill-conceived understanding of American law and its proper application to all image bearers. Therefore, the gospel is suppressed or softened in the debate in order to preserve these progressive dogmas.

In many ways, the leading pro-life organizations act as a governing authority that determines what is scripturally needed or relevant with abortion. It decides the anti-abortion's position on how to respond to prenatal homicide; it concludes what is moral or immoral when it comes to abortion and its exceptions; it absolves abortive women of their guilt; it convenes special council meetings with the largest pro-life organizations and influential politicians to determine policy, catechizing methods and responses to anti-abortion dissenters. Pro-life entities even threaten politicians with excommunication through primarying someone against them in the next election or pulling their funding if the politicians deviate from the movement's contrived anti-abortion ideologies. Ultimately, the pro-life movement reveals that it is a type of functional papacy. Its resistance to what is biblically commanded for believers to follow, intolerance of anti-abortion reformers, and outrage at adhering solely to Scripture is reminiscent of the Reformation. Its guide is moralism, not God's Word; its dogmas are worldly, not godly; its commitment is to itself, not the headship of Christ.

It should come as no surprise that the Catholic-led and founded pro-life movement would be structured similarly to its head, the Roman Catholic church and its religious beliefs. This poses a significant problem. Catholicism teaches people are fundamentally good. On May 19, 2024, Pope Francis said in a *60 Minutes* interview, "And people are fundamentally good. We are all fundamentally good. Yes, there are some rogues and sinners, but the heart itself is good." Scripture, however, instructs that the heart is deceitful above all things and desperately wicked (Jeremiah 17:9) and is held captive by a love of sin (John 3:19; John 8:34). In fact, our heart won't seek God on its own (Romans 3:10-11) because we love the darkness (John 3:19). This depravity is so thorough that the unregenerate heart will suppress the truth of God (Romans 1:8) because the mind is "hostile toward God; for it does not subject itself to the law of God, for it is unable to do so" (Romans 8:7).

Catholicism's unbiblical belief about human nature fuels the movement to view all abortive women as victims and its expectation that culture will morally change with the right education and marketing tools. The pro-life papacy is ignorant of a depraved culture that does not care if the preborn are human. It has no recourse for a civilization that employs the same apathy used by Nazis toward "parasite" Jews, Hutu militants toward Tutsi "cockroaches," the Khmer Rouge against "worm" citizens, and Europeans and North Americans toward "chattel" slaves. With today's increasing acknowledgment that the preborn are human but not as significant as born humans, the pro-life papacy faces a severe dilemma as it continues to preach that people merely need to realize the humanity of the preborn before they will stop murdering them. This simply is not the case. The world has demonstrated an extraordinary ability to ignore people's humanity. Our culture is becoming more aware of preborn humanity and they are telling us *they don't care*. Most Americans, while perhaps unsettled by it, support abortion in most cases in the first trimester – or at any point for rape and incest image bearers. We must listen to what our culture is saying and respond biblically appropriate. Pro-abortion activist Mary Elizabeth Williams forthrightly opines:

> Here's the complicated reality in which we live: All life is not equal. That's a difficult thing for liberals like me to talk about, lest we wind up looking like death-panel-loving, kill-your-grand-

ma-and-your-precious-baby storm troopers. Yet a fetus can be a human life without having the same rights as the woman in whose body it resides. She's the boss. Her life and what is right for her circumstances and her health should automatically trump the rights of the non-autonomous entity inside of her. Always .... I would put the life of a mother over the life of a fetus every single time – even if I still need to acknowledge my conviction that the fetus is indeed a life. A life worth sacrificing.[3]

Pro-choice author Miriam Claire agrees with Williams and writes in her book *The Abortion Dilemma: Personal Views on a Public Issue*, "It is important that pro-choice advocates understand that terminating a pregnancy is killing something that's human and alive, but not yet a 'baby.'"[4]

The protection of life should apply to all humans, not just babies, toddlers, young adults or other developmental categories. For far too long, the anti-abortion movement has attempted to convince the public that the preborn are babies, which is neither the importance nor the focus of the fight. At what point do the preborn become babies? At what hour does toddlerhood cease? At what precise moment does someone become an adult? This is an arbitrary argument that only strengthens the pro-abortion movement.

The pro-life argument that the preborn are babies is an emotional appeal to make it more difficult to harm someone who society (usually) considers cute and innocent. This argument, however, ignores the anthropology of why any human being is valuable enough to defend and protect. This is where the abolition and pro-abortion movements collide. So what if the preborn are not yet "babies"? The pro-abortion movement acknowledges they are living and human, which lands right into the court of the abolitionists. The importance of protecting the preborn is because they are *human*, not categorically babies. We must approach the anthropology of the preborn from an Imago Dei position. This easily dispels the objection from pro-abortion advocates that not all human life is equal, and from there it is simple to point out the hypocrisy of their human rights virtue signaling and discuss biblical theology on the value of humankind. Pro-life philosophy has few compelling responses to pro-abortion callousness toward human beings. Still, the optimistic façade endures.

Hawkins declared after the reversal of *Roe v. Wade*, "...we know when we get America talking about abortion, it always becomes more pro-life."[5] Mary Owens for Susan B. Anthony Pro-Life America wrote in 2022, "In this new era, life is winning, and we look forward with great hope to saving countless lives."[6] Pence boasted at the 2020 Life Wins! event, "I believe the rising generation is the pro-life generation" and that the pro-life movement "is winning because of the compassion and love that have been shown to women facing crisis pregnancies across this country for decades."[7] Greg Cunningham, Executive Director of the Center for Bio-ethical Reform (CBR) claimed the same in 2015: "I'm committed to saving every baby I can at every point of gestation, every day of the calendar, and praise God it works."[8]

Previous pro-life leaders disagree with such optimism. Don Cooper, former Operations Manager for CBR, said that CBR was one of the few pro-life groups that were honest about the failing efforts of the pro-life position. Cooper's work included traveling the country with Cunningham to give presentations on how the pro-life movement is losing ground, which contradicts Cunningham's comment above. Cooper issued fundraising letters throughout his time at CBR, explaining the precariousness of the pro-life movement in today's society where the vast majority of people believe abortion should be "lawful and without restrictions." Cooper expresses perplexion by Cunningham now preaching that the pro-life movement is winning. He observes:

> I don't understand why the resistance to change when it is clear after 42 years and 57 million children dead, and an increasing support of abortion, and an increasing number of ways to kill babies, and an increased access to abortion, an increasingly sexed up culture, an increasingly violent culture, that there needs to be a change.[9]

The pro-life movement's current strategy of resisting change and demanding that dissenters recant and return to worn-out anti-abortion efforts is indeed confusing. The only way in which America has become more "pro-life," as Hawkins claims, is if we conclude that the pro-life movement shares a vast number of ideologies in common with pro-abortion culture.

America has largely unified on allowing certain abortions at certain times for specific actors in certain conditions, giving the perception of a rising number of people who adhere to pro-life ethics (and simultaneously pro-choice ethics). Only within this context might Hawkins be correct. According to Catholic pro-life political analyst and *New York Times* columnist Ross Douthat, "The general principle of legal protection for human life in utero may or must understandably give way in extreme cases, extreme burdens: the conception by rape, the life-threatening pregnancy."[10]

This framework explains the uneasy shift away from the term "pro-life" because many people recognize its inaccuracy if they allow the execution of some preborn lives. If, however, the intended meaning behind the concept of a more pro-life America is that Americans oppose abortion more today than they did 50 years ago, this claim must be refuted. The evidence does not support it.

Instead the demand for abortion has increased over the decades, more people are accepting of it, and the only antidote to such depraved bloodlust within the culture is to teach the public all that Christ has commanded (Matthew 28:20), to proclaim the call of the gospel to repent from murder, and to require lawmakers to uphold just laws for both born and preborn humans. These are tandem goals. Laws to protect the preborn already exist. The pro-life exceptions must be removed from statute law so that existing laws will be enforced impartially. This is an ongoing battle in conservative culture. Marbach remarks on the tug-of-war between conservatives on the anti-abortion frontier:

> From Matt Walsh getting criticized by right-wingers for being "mean" to Dylan Mulvaney to Christians declaring we should "love our neighbors" by taking an experimental vaccine and staying

home, the last few years have been a non-stop battle between traditional conservatives afraid to appear offensive and the new brazen brand of conservatism that welcomes a struggle for our future.[11]

This "new brand" of conservatism should include the abolition of abortion. The abolition movement embodies the logic and morals required to oppose the hardened culture. In contrast to the functional pro-life papacy, abolitionists believe there should be no special protection for women, doctors or anyone else involved in the intentional, uncoerced murder of preborn humans. The abolition movement believes Scripture is clear that all people involved in the act of murdering another human being are guilty and must answer to the law. Abolitionists push for the current laws to extend to and equally protect *all* preborn humans as they already should. They desire to use God's Word for guiding legal ethics in the fight and are not afraid of fighting in the courts until there is a criminalization win. Abolitionists believe the justice system is equipped to handle cases of prenatal homicide as it is equipped to handle other crimes. The abolition movement believes God requires justice and can bring it where man cannot.

There are tangible ways for each Christian to help move this country away from child sacrifice. The work of reformation is not limited to political activists or street evangelists. Each believer reading this has a role to play.

Leaving Rome

Reformation does not imply remaining within the political pro-life papacy and attempting to change it. This book describes a reformation in which people coming out of "Rome" establish a separate, biblically founded movement. A post-*Roe* reformation is necessary to align the anti-abortion movement with Scripture. The Church must spearhead this transformation. The abolitionist movement, while still in its early stages, represents the realization of the anti-abortion revolution needed to guide this country. This requires the intentionality of the Church. The churches largely failed during the slave years. Pride, ignorance and apathy held back most pastors and professing Christians from joining the slavery abolition movement. Salmon P. Chase, former Chief Justice of the Supreme Court, lectured:

> The churches made a great mistake with respect to their duty on the subject of slavery then; they made confessions for the sake of peace, but their hopes in that respect were disappointed as those of all compromises ever will be. Now the churches in one half the land are beginning to defend slavery as not an evil but a good thing to be preserved and cherished; and, at the present time, it must be admitted that the American religious theory is exactly the reverse of what it was at the outset of our existence as a nation.[12]

Slavery was not fully abolished under the immediate abolitionists' terms. Rather, how "justice" was granted to former slaves was determined by the colonizer's secular aspirations. Segregation, racism and widespread black poverty followed on the heels of criminalizing the slave industry. Most of this was a self-fulfilling prophecy. Anti-slavery colonizationists claimed that the black population was intellectually and economically inferior, unable to sustain themselves as freed men and women. These same anti-slavery, anti-abolition Americans contributed to the plight of ex-slaves by refusing to pay reparations to help establish them as free citizens, and by prohibiting their access to certain stores, churches, schools, legal protection and civil rights. Even once slavery was criminalized, it would take another 100 years for black Americans to achieve the legal equality and protections that immediate abolitionists envisioned from the beginning. Pro-life legislation puts the preborn in danger of facing similar injustice for another century or more.

When maternal immunity is incorporated into the laws, the justice system becomes a game of Russian roulette for the preborn. Every pregnancy carries the risk that the preborn child may lose his or her right to life. Because the pro-life and the abortion movements have heavily indoctrinated culture to never consider women guilty in the act of abortion, there is a high probability the justice system will fail to do its job, even if abortion is criminalized under homicide law. Attorney generals and district attorneys have already announced that they will not prosecute abortive women, giving us a glimpse of this coming reality. Is Christian America prepared to get it wrong again with the oppression of another group of humans? Abolitionists are warning that we must end this human rights crisis immediately, completely and justly – and it cannot be done on the terms of the anti-abortion, anti-abolition movement. To change history, we must change our beliefs, practices and behaviors. We must leave behind the grip of the pro-life papacy and cling to biblical abolition.

As G.K. Chesterton asserted, "There are only two kinds of people; those who accept dogma and know it, and those who accept dogma and don't know it." Christians should accept only the anti-abortion dogma that comes from the Bible and not from secular and Catholic-influenced agendas. Abolition dogma is the gospel-consistent position for dealing with child sacrifice.

Coming out of Rome means trusting God – not man – to win the fight. It means no longer voting for die-hard, committed pro-life representatives who do not believe in equal protection and justice for the preborn or supporting judicial supremacy. It means contacting your local and state representatives to exhort them to fulfill their duty to protect all human lives within their jurisdictions. It means no longer supporting laws that show explicit or implicit favoritism toward some preborn humans over others. It means not giving money to pro-life organizations that do not champion the immediate and complete criminalization of the abortion industry. It means speaking up against the unfairness of the pro-life movement toward preborn humans and forsaking the misguided belief that all abortive women are also victims of their abortive decisions. It means calling your pro-life family and friends to repent of preborn prejudice alongside you. Abolition means living radically opposed to the culture as the Bible commands that we do.

When you vote, seek out candidates who would support immediate abolition and cast your vote only for them. It is not a wasted vote. Your vote represents your morals, ideologies and convictions – not someone else's. Your vote represents your expectations of an authority figure that is to rule under God's will. If a candidate has raised his or her fist against God's decrees and the Constitution, then, like the slavery abolitionists counseled, do not partner with them in their evil. The drop in polling will eventually damage established pro-life politicians who may be humbled and willing to re-examine their compromised positions in order to remain in office.

For individuals who are politically or legally minded, consider running for office as an abolitionist or lobbying policymakers. It is one thing for individual citizens to do all within their sphere of power to rescue babies by pleading at abortion mills, adopting children, sharing the gospel, and offering resources to women. But the citizen cannot abolish abortion; only the lawmakers can. To wield the sword against the evildoer and offer protection for the vulnerable is the civil magistrate's job. They can do more than average citizens. They *can* save all the babies – not just some. Legislators should not be endorsed to neglect their jobs and allow the wicked to continue in prenatal homicide.

For those who are researchers and readers, learn your state laws so you will know how and where to put pressure on your representatives. Educate those in your social circles so they can do the same. If your local politicians use the excuse they cannot end abortion, you will discern whether that is spoken from deception or ignorance. In either case, correct them.

If you have a passion for evangelism, form relationships with your legislators (particularly your district representative) and disciple them on the council of God. Provide a counter message to the Catholic and secular pro-life PAC's indoctrination. Preach in your state capitols. Speak truth into the darkness, where the spiritual strongholds are mighty.

For mission-minded individuals, organize sidewalk ministries or join existing abolition groups at abortion facilities. Interpose on behalf of your preborn neighbors and preach the Good News, which is salvation unto all men. Your presence outside the murder mills will bring glaring attention to the atrocities taking place in your city, and may be how God works to turn the hearts of men and women toward him and away from slaughter.

If you are currently in a pro-life organization or pregnancy resource center that is biblically jeopardized, examine whether you have the influence or authority to align things biblically. If not, be realistic and join or develop an organization already poised to serve from a scriptural standpoint.

For those with the ability to teach or who are gifted in rhetoric, use your words at your state capitols, church meetings, college campuses, social gatherings, and anywhere there is an audience to practice remonstration for your preborn neighbors. Educate on the need for abortion abolition. Implore people to turn to Christ and his Word alone on this issue.

For those with the gift of encouragement, find out which of your state representatives support, or would support, abolition, and motivate them to continue running the race. They shouldn't have to run alone, but they often do. Encourage Christian or conservative politicians who seem resistant to total abolition to repent, follow Christ, and pursue justice for their preborn constituents. Hold them lovingly accountable to this charge. Encourage your local pro-life groups to follow God's counsel without compromise; remind them of their duty before Christ the King.

If there are no non-ecumenical anti-abortion groups in your state that are committed to Scripture, then entrepreneurs and driven individuals should consider forming one to serve as an umbrella under which your fellow state abolitionists can exert change from a godly position.

Regardless of one's gifts and talents, take time to contact your state pro-life groups to find out if they stand for equal protection and justice for the preborn. If not, tell them you can no longer support their efforts. Push back on their excuses and call out publicly their hypocrisy so others will see. Perhaps your local pro-life organizations that may be compromised will repent and realign with God's sovereign Word. Until they are held accountable, this most likely will not happen.

Turning the Tide

The involvement of pastors and their role in this fight is the most vital or detrimental to turning the tide. Slavery abolition in Europe came on the heels of the Great Awakenings. As tens of thousands across 18th- and 19th-century America and Europe repented of sin and once again found life and truth in the Word of God, the institution of slavery crumbled. Revivalists such as George Whitefield, Charles and John Wesley, Jonathan Edwards, David Brainerd and Samuel Davies left behind a wake of conversions. From these revivals, the political and social landscapes of their days changed. That was not a coincidence. That was the byproduct of the inward work of the Holy Spirit. North acknowledges this phenomenon:

> Unless we see revival in terms of at least a century-long process, we will be planning for a false revival. We will be planning for short-lived ecstatic outbreaks that are followed by cynicism...We have had enough of these before in church history. We do not need another. A revival should be a sharp and unexpected breaking into history by God's Spirit which subsequently blends into an extended period of institutional transformation. The revival should launch the process of transformation, but the subsequent social transformation is to be a direct heir of the revival itself.[13]

Nothing contained within this book will cause any change apart from the repentance of God's people first. Repentance and revival both start in the house of the LORD. Tragically, so many pulpits remain silent on today's holocaust, or worse yet, are apologists for the Catholic-led, secularized pro-life model. Just as slavery abolition was congruent with the repentance of God's people, we have no reason to believe we will be successful in our abolition efforts today without revival. Theologian Richard Owen Roberts encourages expectant hope for revival:

> As the Church has approached the end of its twentieth century, it has been increasingly common to hear the clamoring voices of self-appointed prophets declaring that the days of revival are forever past. Among them are those who have gone so far as to predict that the next event on God's calendar is the end. Some among them appear to believe that things have never been so bad before and that they can do nothing, at this late date in human history, but get worse and worse. Are they right? Not if history speaks truthfully![14]

When 65 percent of American adults describe themselves as Christian, and more than 80 percent of Americans favor abortion in at least some circumstances,[15] the landscape for revival looks bleak. These categories overlap and show an abysmal state of biblical-mindedness among professing American Christians. Rather, the majority of professing Christians subscribe to pagan beliefs and practices regarding the preborn. The annual polls continue to reflect this. Reverend Vernon Higham writes in *The Turn of the Tide*:

> When we look at the desolation and irreligion, our hearts almost faint within us thinking we could never change anything even if we knew where to start, what to say, or what to do....Yet, we still hold to this conviction with our very lives – change can again happen, wrought in that time when we enter into that arena of God's blessing, when God again gives Himself afresh to be with His people.[16]

The temptation to expect less than God's miraculous works invites us to do busy work to pass the time until either Christ returns or our death approaches. We lower our expectations of holiness in the culture to protect ourselves from disappointment, or to stave off the feeling of foolishness. Higham continues:

It is so easy to look at the present need and say, "Revival? It has been such a long time, and the tide has gone out so far. Surely it will never come back in again. This is an advanced century: the age of the video, television, and computers. The tide has gone out too far, and it will go out still further; sin will become bolder; heresy and confusion will reign supreme. The world already behaves as if God is dead and His children forsaken. Can we still believe that it is God's intention not to leave us desolate, that we are indeed the delight of His soul, and that He desires for us to be revived from the depth of His innermost being, far more so than that degree which we desire for ourselves?" What is our verdict in these things?[17]

What is *our* verdict? If it is abortion cannot be abolished and revival will never recur, we should repent of that doubt for the one who doubts is like a wave tossed about and should not expect anything from God (James 1:5-7). God is capable of revival and restoration when his people humble themselves and turn from their rebellion. And God's people have been in rebellion to him in the way in which we have fought abortion. We profess too easily Christ is our LORD and then live in direct opposition to that proclamation in our private lives, the political arena, and the public square. We have trusted in man's works instead of God's work. Every believer in Christ should fervently hope for and pray for revival. We must avoid and reject mediocrity and disbelief. Sandlin articulates, "Christians who do not pray with a lot of faith and confidence never fail to get what they do not expect."[18]

The Impact of the Church

Minister Albert Barnes published in 1857 a reminder to the American churches of their duty before God and to the culture in the presence of evil: "... though the churches located in the midst of slavery may be wholly free from any direct participation in it, it is still true that the church is designed to influence all surrounding institutions."[19]

Your church may not participate in abortion directly, but does child sacrifice flourish in your city because of the absence of the churches on the battlefield against it? If a city is blood-stained from hosting an abortion mill that slaughters hundreds (or thousands) of image bearers in your community each year, then pastors should prepare their flocks to do battle on that front as they and their congregants have been established at their posts in that city for such a time as this.

In cities with closed abortion facilities, how many women near your church (or in your church) are sacrificing the lives of their children in the privacies of their own homes by abortion pills? Pastors must not lead their congregants astray in the guilt of being absent on the mission field when their preborn neighbors' blood was crying out on the day of their slaughter. Pastors should equip their congregants to put on the armor of God and wage war at city council meetings, from behind the pulpit, by discipling neighbors, the mayor, city council or county commissioners, by imploring state legislators to do their duty and protect all human life under the authority of Scripture and the Fourteenth Amendment, and warning moms and dads bringing their children to die at abortion clinics to run from sin and find reconciliation in Christ Jesus.

Ezekiel 33:8-9 warns the one who knows the truth but does not warn the wicked "to dissuade them from their ways", and the wicked die in their sins, that God "will hold you accountable for their blood." If, however, the wicked are warned about the peril of their ways and they ignore the warnings, then "they will die for their sin, though you yourself will be saved." We are not permitted to remain silent while we watch the culture rush toward spiritual and physical death. God is watching and judging us.

You can warn the culture and frustrate the business of your local abortion facilities with a constant presence interposing on behalf of the voiceless. Preach, teach, plead and pray on the streets of butchery. It becomes difficult for these places to retain employees as few desire to subject themselves to conviction every day that they step into work. More importantly, abortion workers need to hear the gospel and be ministered to as well.

Preach on the street corners, at markets or large events so that women who have secretly committed murder in their homes – or are tempted to commit murder – will be warned, convicted and given the hope of the gospel.

These recommendations of action are not exhaustive. There is little doubt God will bring to the mind of many people ways in which they can effectively fight for abortion abolition that were not outlined within this book – perhaps not even imagined as of yet. We should be eager to see the creativity of the Holy Spirit in guiding hundreds (maybe thousands) of individuals to become involved with abolition. Perhaps you will be one of them.

If this book has impacted you to maintain a biblical worldview on what it means to be anti-abortion, then pray for pro-life leaders, politicians and those within your social sphere that God will turn their hearts toward him in humility and repentance. With much sincerity, we should desire the leaders of the pro-life movement to repent and use the resources at their disposal without compromise for the righteous, complete criminalization of prenatal homicide.

If the pro-life papacy will not turn from its obstinate partiality, then may God remove its lampstand and rise up others to finish the work. We must rightly instruct our posterity so that each generation is warned about the peril of compromising with evil. Each generation must catechize their children about God's commands to his people in response to child sacrifice, just as our abolition forefathers catechized their successors against slavery.

May God graciously send revival to America and create an army of abolitionists so that we may someday declare along with our predecessor Wilberforce, "How popular abolition is just now! God can turn the hearts of men."[20]

Abortion must be abolished.

Resources

Abolish Human Abortion
www.abolishhumanabortion.com

Abolitionists Rising
www.abolitionistsrising.com

End Abortion Now
www.endabortionnow.com

Foundation to Abolish Abortion
www.faa.life

Free the States
www.freethestates.org

The Imago Dei Ministry
www.theimagodei.org

Not A Victim
www.notavictim.org

Rescue Those
www.rescuethose.com

IN VITRO FERTILIZATION

While this book did not go into the topic of creating human beings through the laboratory process of in vitro fertilization (IVF), it is worth mentioning that it is merely an extension of the abortion industry. All embryos created are graded before offering the highest quality to the clients for implantation. The embryos that do not make the grading cut are destroyed due to eugenics.

Furthermore, the average IVF client rarely gives life to and raises all the children they create through the IVF process. Instead, the majority of these image bearers are destroyed, donated for scientific experimentation, or indefinitely frozen. Some parents choose to give up for adoption the unwanted children they created, though this is the minority.

Speed, a leading Protestant voice opposed to creating image bearers in petri dishes says:

> Everyone that has gone through it to get a child has basically justified the process in one way or another. The most common justification is to say, 'We made sure that our extra embryos were made available for adoption.' The problem is it's the clinics that really own those embryos — your children. It's the clinics that have final control of that because they're the ones that have all the technology in place to preserve their lives. Basically, they're in cryogenic freezers.... The other issue is not only are they in control of it but if anyone adopts they have to pay the clinics exorbitant money for the process. You're essentially trafficking human life.[1]

This section is meant to be a springboard for the Christian conscience. To learn more about how God ordained children to be procreated, check out the IVF booklet *Loving Your IVF Neighbor: In Vitro Fertilization, Assisted Reproductive Technologies, & Loving Your Neighbor as Yourself* by Dusty Deevers, which can be found at www.rescuethose.com.

For a short film depicting the unscrupulous nature of the eugenic IVF industry, check out "Build-A-Baby" at www.choice42.com.build-a-baby.

While this is an older site, it provides a good starting place for those wanting to research the IVF industry and the amount of destruction that takes place behind the scenes of our frozen neighbors: https://abolishhumanabortion.com/the-untold-millions/

Endnotes

Secularism versus Sola Scriptura

1. Students for Life. "The Future is Anti-Abortion – Kristan Hawkins University of Texas San Antonio." *YouTube*, April 13, 2022, www.youtube.com/watch?v=REsqZpJO3gs&t=2906s.

2. Green, Emma. "Science Is Giving the Pro-life Movement a Boost." The Atlantic, 18 January 2018, https://www.theatlantic.com/politics/archive/2018/01/pro-life-pro-science/549308/?utm_source=copy-link&utm_medium=social&utm_campaign=share, 1 January 2023.

3. Ibid.

4. Willke, Barbara and John C. Willke. *Why Can't We Love Them Both*. 2nd ed., Hayes, 1997.

5. Ibid.

6. Sproul, R.C. *How Should I Live In This World*, Reformation Trust, 2009.

7. "Facts About Abortion." *Students for Life of America*, Students for Life of America, www.studentsforlife.org/learn/.

8. "Who We Are." *Live Action*, Live Action, www.liveaction.org/who-we-are/.

9. "About The March For Life." *March for Life*, March for Life, marchforlife.org/about-the-march-for-life/.

10. "About Susan B. Anthony Pro-Life America." Susan B. Anthony Pro-Life America, Susan B. Anthony Pro-Life America, www. sbaprolife.org/about.

11. "Joint Open Letter: Criminalizing Women Who Have Abortions is Not Pro-Life." *National Right to Life*, www.nrlc.org/communications/releases/2022/051222openletter/.

12. Apologia Studios. "Exposing A Pro-Life Leader & Training To Defend the Christian Faith." *YouTube*, October 6, 2022, www.youtube.com/watch?v=0tJ-4z-F8zA.

13. Ibid.

14. Matthew Henry commentary on Ephesians 6.

15. Brett Baggett, Abolition NOW! Conference, Wichita, Kansas, March 1-4, 2023.

16. K.S. "Should Women Face Murder Charges for Abortion? If You're Pro-Life, The Answer is Yes." *Defending Feminism*, June 29, 2022, defendingfeminism.com/2022/06/29/should-women-face-murder-charges-for-abortion-if-youre-pro-life-the-answer-is-yes/.

17. Ibid.

18. Scarfone, M. "If you're pro-life, you might already be pro-choice." *The Conversation*, September 23, 2020, theconversation.com/if-youre-pro-life-you-might-already-be-pro-choice-146654.

19. "Would you consider yourself pro-choice or pro-life?" *Statista*, Statista, www.statista.com/statistics/225975/share-of-americans-who-are-pro-life-or-pro-choice/.

20. *Foundation to Abolish Abortion*, Foundation to Abolish Abortion, www.faa.life.

21. "Our Beliefs." *End Abortion Now*, Apologia Church Ministry, www.endabortionnow.com/about-the-movement/our-beliefs/.

22. "Bringing the Gospel Into Conflict with the Evil of Our Age." *Abolish Human Abortion*, Abolish Human Abortion, www.abolishhumanabortion.com.

23. "As Christ Has Rescued Us, We Must Rescue Others." *Rescue Those*, Wordpress, www.rescuethose.com/as-christ-has-rescued-us-we-must-rescue-others/.

24. #NotAVictim. "FAQ," April 29, 2022. https://notavictim.org/faq/.

25. "Our Mission is to Free the States From Participating in the American Abortion Holocaust." *Free The States*, Free The States, www.freethestates.org/who-we-are/.

26. Cali, C.R. *The Doctrine of Balaam*, Wrath and Grace, 2019.

27. *The 1689 Baptist Confession of Faith*, Founders Press, 2017.

Eroding Ecumenicalism

1. White, James R. *The Roman Catholic Controversy*, Bethany House, 1996.

2. *The 1689 Baptist Confession of Faith*, Founders Press, 2017.

3. Ouweneel, Willem J. *The World is Christ's*, Ezra, 2017.

4. Fourth Session, *Decree Concerning the Canonical Scriptures*.

5. Allison, Gregg R. "Two Views on the Church Authority." *9 Marks*, September 26, 2017, www.9marks.org/article/two-views-on-church-authority-protestant-vs-roman-catholic/.

6. Mirus, Jeff. "The Catholic Approach to Scripture." *Catholic Culture*, March 14, 2011, www.catholicculture.org/commentary/catholic-approach-to-scripture/.

7. John Paul II, *Encyclical Letter, Redemptoris Missio, John Paul II on the permanent validity of the Church's missionary mandate*, Vatican City: Libreria Editrice Vaticana.

8. Ibid.

9. Pius XII, *Encyclical Letter, Mystici Corporis Christi, Pius XII on the mystical body of Christ*, Vatican City: Libreria Editrice Vaticana.

10. Allison, Gregg R. "Two Views on the Church Authority." *9 Marks*, September 26, 2017, www.9marks.org/article/two-views-on-church-authority-protestant-vs-roman-catholic/

11. White, James R. *The Roman Catholic Controversy*, Bethany House, 1996.

12. Ibid.

13. Catholic Church. *Catechism of the Catholic Church: Revised in Accordance with the Official Latin Text Promulgated by Pope John Paul III*. United States Catholic Conference, 2000.

14. Wells, Christopher. "Pope: Peace document born of faith in God, the Father of Peace." *Vatican News*, February 5, 2019, www.vaticannews.va/en/pope/news/2019-02/pope-francis-uae-press-inflight-press-conference.html.

15. Pope Paul VI. "Dogmatic Constitution on the Church - Lumen Gentium." Vatican: the Holy See. Rome, 21 Nov. 1965. Web. 17 Jan. 2023.

16. Henry, Matthew, 1662-1714. Matthew Henry's Commentary on the Whole Bible : Wherein Each Chapter Is Summed up in Its Contents: the Sacred Text Inserted at Large in Distinct Paragraphs; Each Paragraph Reduced to Its Proper Heads: the Sense given, and Largely Illustrated with Practical Remarks and Observations. Peabody, Mass.: Hendrickson Publishers, 1991.

17. Ibid.

18. White, James R. *The Roman Catholic Controversy*, Bethany House, 1996.

Catechizing Politics

1. Barna, George. "Perceptions about Biblical Worldview and Its Application." Center for Biblical Worldview, May 2021. Accessed January 29, 2023. https://downloads.frc.org/EF/EF21E41.pdf.

2. President James Garfield, speech on the 100th anniversary of the Declaration of Independence, July 4, 1876.

3. Hollingsworth, Barbara. "Pro-Life Leaders Say Abortionists Should Be Punished, Not Their Women Victims." *CNSNews.com*, 31 Mar. 2016, https://www.cnsnews.com/news/article/barbara-hollingsworth/pro-life-leaders-abortionists-should-be-punished-not-their-women.

4. Ibid.

5. Ibid.

6. Ibid.

7. Ibid.

8. Baptist Press. "ERLC: Preparing for Post-Roe World, Seeking Post-Abortion One | Baptist Press," n.d. https://www.baptistpress.com/resource-library/news/erlc-preparing-for-post-roe-world-seeking-post-abortion-one/.

9. Miller, William Lee. *Arguing about Slavery: John Quincy Adams and the Great Battle in the United States Congress.* New York: A.A. Knopf, Inc., 1996, pg. 33.

10. Silberman, James. "Uncovered Letter Exposes Plan to Keep Abortion Legal in Oklahoma." *Free The States*, 9 March, 2019, https://freethestates.org/2019/03/uncovered-letter-exposes-plan-to-keep-abortion-legal-in-oklahoma/.

11. Ibid.

12. Ibid.

13. LegiScan. "Oklahoma SB834 | 2023 | Regular Session," n.d. https://legiscan.com/OK/text/SB834/id/2650275.

14. "Defund National Right to Life | #DefundRightToLife You Want to Help Abolish Abortion? One Way to Help Is by Telling Your Friends to Stop Donating to National Right to Life. | by Free the States | Facebook." n.d. Www.facebook.com. Accessed May 16, 2023. https://www.facebook.com/AbolitionistsRising/videos/1720056271761167/.

15. Oklahomans for Life email to author.

16. Ibid.

17. Review of *Oklahoma Supports Life with Exceptions*. 2023. *wpaintel.com*. WPA Intelligence.

18. Hartig, Hannah. 2022. "Wide Partisan Gaps in Abortion Attitudes, but Opinions in Both Parties Are Complicated." Pew Research Center. May 6, 2022. https://www.pewresearch.org/short-reads/2022/05/06/wide-partisan-gaps-in-abortion-attitudes-but-opinions-in-both-parties-are-complicated/.

19. Faught, Jamison. March 10, 2023. "Rep. Olsen: The Wrong Kind of History Is Being Made in the Pro-Life Movement." Accessed May 16, 2023. https://www.muskogeepolitico.com/2023/03/rep-olsen-wrong-kind-of-history-is.html.

20. Faught, Jamison. March 20, 2023. "Rep. Olsen: Fallacies Abound in Pro-Abortion Bill – Senate Bill 834." Accessed May 16, 2023. https://www.muskogeepolitico.com/2023/03/rep-olsen-fallacies-abound-in-pro.html.

21. Oklahomans for Life email to author, May 22, 2023.

22. Fortier, Jackie. "California Voters Enshrine Right to Abortion and Contraception in State Constitution." *NPR*, November 9, 2022. https://www.npr.org/2022/11/09/1134833374/california-results-abortion-contraception-amendment-midterms.

23. Rick Pluta, Michigan Public Radio Network. "Michigan Voters Approve Amendment Adding Reproductive Rights to State Constitution." *NPR*, November 9, 2022. https://www.npr.org/2022/11/09/1134834724/michigan-abortion-amendment-midterm-results.

24. Lefrak, Mikaela. "Vermont Votes to Protect Abortion Rights in State Constitution." *NPR*, November 9, 2022. https://www.npr.org/2022/11/09/1134832172/vermont-votes-abortion-constitution-midterms-results.

25. Congress.gov. "H.Res.464 – 118th Congress (2023-2024); Acknowledging that unborn children are legal and constitutional persons who are entitled to the equal protection of the laws." June 5, 2023. https://www.congress.gov/bill/118th-congress/house-resolution/464.

26. https://www.congress.gov/bill/118th-congress/house-bill/431/text

27. Pierce, Bradley [@bradleypierce]. "This is neither an equal protection bill nor a personhood bill. It says the Constitution shall not be construed to permit any woman to be prosecuted for murdering her own preborn child, which declares self-managed abortions as a constitutional right. This would be Roe 2.0." Twitter, June 6, 2023.

28. Ibid.

29. William Wilberforce, speech in the House of Commons, May 12, 1789.

30. Clapper, Benjamin. "Forward for Life, HB 813 Explained." Louisiana Right to Life, 13 May, 2022, https://prolifelouisiana.org/forward-for-life-hb-813-explained/.

31. "LIVE video stream regarding Louisiana HB 813, the Abolition of Abortion in Louisiana Act," *Facebook*, May 12, 2022. www.facebook.com/watch/live/?ref=search&v=425078146129229.

32. Ibid.

33. Klassen, Laura. "PRO-LIFE LEADERS TESTIFY AGAINST A BILL THAT WOULD ABOLISH ABORTION." *Facebook*, May 9, 2023. Accessed May 16, 2023. https://fb.watch/kySyyZ8PlW/.

34. Ibid, 02:48.

35. Ibid, 04:04.

36. Ibid, 05:14.

37. "Defund National Right to Life | #DefundRightToLife You Want to Help Abolish Abortion? One Way to Help Is by Telling Your Friends to Stop Donating to National Right to Life. | by Free the States | Facebook." n.d. Www.facebook.com. https://www.facebook.com/AbolitionistsRising/videos/1720056271761167/.

38. Pierard, Richard. n.d. "William Wilberforce and the Abolition of the Slave Trade: Did You Know?" Christian History | Learn the History of Christianity & the Church. Accessed June 28, 2022. https://www.christianitytoday.com/history/issues/issue-53/william-wilberforce-and-abolition-of-slave-trade-did-you.html.

39. Silberman, James. "Uncovered Letter Exposes Plan to Keep Abortion Legal in Oklahoma." *Free the States*, 5 March, 2019, https://freethestates.org/2019/03/indiana-pro-life-leaders-kill-protection-at-conception-act/.

40. Green, John and Scott, Heather. "Idaho Abortion Human Rights Act Released." *Rep. Heather Scott*, 22 January, 2019, http://repheatherscott.com/wp-content/uploads/2019/02/iahra_press_release.pdf.

41. Abortion Human Rights Act Idaho. Fred Martin says pro-life groups oppose AHRA. *Facebook*, 3 March 2019, www.facebook.com/watch/?ref=external&v=465990577267828.

42. Clowes, Brian. "How Rich is the Pro-Life Movement?" *Human Life International*, 23 March 2022, www.hli.org/resources/rich-pro-life-movement/.

43. *Hodes & Nauser, MDS, P.A. v. Schmidt*, 440 P.3d 461 (Kan. 2019).

44. WeThePeopleLVN. "WtP Leavenworth- Value Them Both Discussion Forum-July 2022," YouTube video, 54:10. July 26, 2022. https://www.youtube.com/watch?v=ljV0t1Lwa5g.

45. "'Value Them Both' Constitutional Amendment; HCR 5003." n.d. Accessed June 16, 2023. http://kslegislature.org/li_2022/b2021_22/measures/documents/summary_hcr_5003_2021.

46. AIM KS – Abortion Is Murder. "Kim Borchers (Republican Committeewoman) Tells the Truth on Value Them Both Amendment." YouTube, 27 January 2022, www.youtube.com/watch?v=5vKhhEQmy0s.

47. WeThePeopleLVN. "WtP Leavenworth- Value Them Both Discussion Forum-July 2022," July 26, 2022. https://www.youtube.com/watch?v=ljV0t1Lwa5g.

48. "Vote Yes for Value Them Both Amendment." Restoration Action, radio ad, 29 July 2022.

49. Witnessed by author, July, 2022.

50. WeThePeopleLVN. "WtP Leavenworth- Value Them Both Discussion Forum-July 2022," July 26, 2022. https://www.youtube.com/watch?v=ljV0t1Lwa5g.

51. April Cromer interview, text message to author, November 29, 2022.

52. Kim Borchers statement to author, Zoom Meeting, April 26, 2022.

53. Wilberforce, William, and Bob Beltz. *Real Christianity*. Revised and Updated, Bethany House Publishers, 2006.

Recant: The Pro-Life Cancel Culture

1. Hannula, Richard. *Trial and Triumph*, Canon, 1999.

2. Ibid.

3. Ibid.

4. Ibid.

5. Ibid.

6. John Wycliffe quote.

7. "Martin Luther's Achievements." *Britannica*, Encyclopedia Britannica, Inc., www.britannica.com/summary/Martin-Luthers-Achievements.

8. Dias, Elizabeth. "Inside the Extrme Effort to Punish Women for Abortion." *The New York Times*, 1 July 2021, The New York Times Company, www.nytimes.com/2022/07/01/us/abortion-abolitionists.html.

9. "AHA: The Anti-Abortionists Who Fight Other Pro-Lifers." *YouTube*, uploaded by Equal Rights Institute, May 12, 2021. www.youtube.com/watch?v=0SvNYXQqvuM.

10. Ibid.

11. Silberman, James. "Jonathan Van Maren and Josh Brahm. Yikes." *Free The States*, 17 May 2021, https://www.freethestates.org/2021/05/jonathan-van-maren-and-josh-brahm-yikes/; www.thebridgehead.ca/2021/05/18/the-scandal-of-the-abolitionist-mind/.

12. Equal Rights Institute, "AHA" The Anti-Abortionists Who Fight Other Pro-Lifers (with Jonathan Van Maren – Part 1)." YouTube video, 32:36. May 12, 2021. www.youtube.com/watch?v=0SvNYXQqvuM.

13. Schomburg Center for Research in Black Culture, Manuscripts, Archives and Rare Books Division, The New York Public Library. "The speech of William Wilberforce, esq., representative for the county of York, on Wednesday the 13th of May, 1789, on the question of the abolition of the slave trade" New York Public Library Digital Collections. Accessed May 25, 2023. https://digitalcollections.nypl.org/items/510d47e3-a708-a3d9-e040-e00a18064a99.

14. Equal Rights Institute, "AHA" The Anti-Abortionists Who Fight Other Pro-Lifers (with Jonathan Van Maren – Part 1)." YouTube video, 32:36. May 12, 2021. www.youtube.com/watch?v=0SvNYXQqvuM.

15. Wilberforce, William. *A Letter on the Abolition of the Slave Trade*, London, 1807.

16. Clarkson, Thomas. *An Essay on the Comparative Efficiency of Regulation or Abolition As Applied to the Slave Trade*, London, 1789.

17. Pitt, William. "The speech of the Right Honourable William Pitt, on a motion for the abolition of the slave trade : in the House of Commons, on Monday the second of April, 1792." *Oberlin College Library*. Pg. 19. www.archive.org/details/89c00c68-9c91-4a23-a152-a8d9f2bd8659/mode/2up.

18. Garrison, William Lloyd. "No Compromise with the Evil of Slavery." *Internet Archive*, 1854, www.archive.org/details/cu31924032775383/page/136/mode/2up. Transcript.

19. Burk, Denny, Alan Branch, Andrew T. Walker, Steve Lemke, Daniel Heimbach, C. Ben Mitchell, Jeffery Riley and Richard Land. "Why We Opposed an Anti-Abortion Resolution at the Southern Baptist Convention." *Public Discourse*, 22 June 2021, www.thepublicdiscourse.com/2021/06/76465/.

20. Ibid.

21. Silberman, James. "Against Pro-Life Compromise: Responding to Denny Burk, Andrew Walker, Et Al." *Free The States*, 2 July 2021, www. freethestates.org/2021/07/against-pro-life-compromise-responding-to-denny-burk-andrew-walker-et-al/.

22. "Resolution on Abolishing Abortion Floor Debate: Southern Baptist Convention 2021."

23. Klusendorf, Scott. "Saving Some, Standing for All: A Defense of Pro-Life Incrementalism." *The Gospel Coalition*, 23 September 2021, www.thegospelcoalition.org/article/defense-prolife-incrementalism/.

24. "Sanctity of Life Sunday." *YouTube*, uploaded by BethelOwasso, 19 January 2020, www.youtube.com/watch?v=IA44ePa2yWE.

25. Newman, Marc, and Scott Klusendorf. "Trading Live for Prophets." Townhall, 23 June 2021, www.townhall.com/columnists/marcnewman/2021/06/23/trading-lives-for-prophets-n2591417.

26. Kissling, Frances. "Abortion rights are under attack, and pro-choice advocates are caught in a time warp." *Washington Post*, 18 February 2011, www.washingtonpost.com/wp-dyn/content/article/2011/02/18/AR2011021802434.html.

27. Ibid. Pgs. 9-10.

28. Wear, Michael. n.d. "This Is How to End Abortion Politics as We've Known It." Wearweare.substack.com. Accessed May 12, 2023. https://wearweare.substack.com/p/this-is-how-to-end-abortion-politics.

29. Ibid.

30. "National Right to Life Praises House Action on The Born-Alive Abortion Survivors Protection Act | National Right to Life," n.d. https://www.nrlc.org/communications/nrlc-praises-house-action-on-the-born-alive-abortion-survivors-protection-act/.

31. Ibid.

32. Lee, John Gregg. *Colonization: the present scheme of colonization wrong, delusive, and retards emancipation*. 1857, pg. 9. www.archive.org/details/ASPC0001949200.

33. "Kim" Value Them Both volunteer. Text Message to author. 2 Aug. 2022.

34. "Jane" Value Them Both volunteer. Text message to author. 1 Aug. 2022.

35. Keller, Timothy [@timkellernyc]. "…every year. I know abortion is a sin, but the Bible doesn't tell me the best political policy to decrease or end abortion in this country, nor which political or legal policies are most effective to that end. The current political parties will say that their policy most aligns morally with the Bible, but we are allowed to debate that and so our churches should not have disunity over debatable political differences." Twitter, 29, April 2022.

36. Birney, James Gillespie. *The American Churches, the Bulwarks of American Slavery*. Newburyport: Charles Whipple, 1842, pg. 32.

37. Barber, Bart [@bartbarber]. "How? Why? Because unless you 100% agree with every jot and tittle of Deever's obsession with sending 16-year-old girls to prison for succumbing to the coercion of their parents to have an abortion, he will label you "against the innocent preborn." Twitter, 15 September 2022, twitter.com/bartbarber/status/1570377794529497090.

38. Sproul, R.C. Jr. "What is pietism and what are some concrete examples?" RC Sproul Jr, 7 August 2020, rcsprouljr.com/ask-rc-what-is-pietism-and-what-are-some-concrete-examples/.

39. Henderson, Roger (2008) "Kuyper's Inch," *Pro Rege*: Vol. 36: No. 3, 12-14. https://digitalcollections.dordt.edu/pro_rege/vol36/iss3/2.

40. North, Gary. *When Justice Is Aborted: Biblical Standards for Non-Violent Resistance*. Fort Worth: Dominion, 1989, pg. 20.

41. Sandlin, P. Andrew. Pietism leads to worldliness. *Facebook*, 10 February 2022, www.facebook.com/p.andrew.sandlin/posts/pfbid02KfgfQp6VaVis9LAF9MGLPQmGnXd8kCFPFk7wH6bqQCFcqJxtvafNdzHm9TUiHbzrl. 18 January 2023.

42. Sproul, R.C. Jr. "What is pietism and what are some concrete examples?" RC Sproul Jr, 7 August 2020, rcsprouljr.com/ask-rc-what-is-pietism-and-what-are-some-concrete-examples/.

43. Ibid.

44. Boot, Joseph. *Ruler of Kings*, Wilberforce Publications, 2022.

45. Ibid.

46. Keating, Karl. *Catholicism and Fundamentalism*, San Francisco: Ignatius Press, 1988, p. 127.

47. White, James R. *The Roman Catholic Controversy*, Bethany House, 1996.

48. Birney, James Gillespie. *The American Churches, the Bulwarks of American Slavery*. Newburyport: Charles Whipple, 1842, pg. 41.

Repeating History: Protestant Resistance and Catholic Opposition to Abolition

1. Douglass, Frederick. "What to the Slave Is the Fourth of July?" *Lee, Mann, & Co.*, July 5, 1852. Pg. 30. www.archive.org/details/Douglass_July_Oration/mode/2up.

2. McKivigan, John R. *The War Against Proslavery Religion: Abolitionism and the Northern Churches*. Ithaca: Cornell University Press, 1984, pg. 15.

3. Ibid.

4. Reinders, Robert C. "The Churches and the Negro in New Orleans, 1850-1860." *Phylon (1960-)* 22, no. 3 (1961): 245. https://doi.org/10.2307/274198.

5. Miller, William Lee. *Arguing About Slavery*. New York: Alfred A. Knopf, 1996, pg. 65.

6. Birney, James Gillespie. *The American Churches, the Bulwarks of American Slavery*. Newburyport: Charles Whipple, 1842, pg. 41.

7. Ibid. Pg. 21.

8. Ibid. Pg. 38.

9. Ibid. Pg. 39.

10. Brownson, Orestes. "Slavery and the Church." *BQR* (October, 1862); Brownson, Orestes. "The Slavery Question Once More." *BQR* (April 1857).

11. Birney, James Gillespie. *The American Churches, the Bulwarks of American Slavery*. Newburyport: Charles Whipple, 1842, pg. 17.

12. McKivigan, John R. *The War Against Proslavery Religion: Abolitionism and the Northern Churches*. Ithaca: Cornell University Press, 1984, pg. 13.

13. Miller, William Lee. *Arguing About Slavery*. New York: Alfred A. Knopf, 1996, pg. 38.

14. Carey, Patrick W. "Political Atheism: 'Dred Scott', Roger Brooke Taney, and Orestes A. Brownson." *The Catholic Historical Review* 88, no. 2 (2002): p. 213. http://www.jstor.org/stable/25026143.

15. Garrison, William Lloyd, African American Pamphlet Collection (Library of Congress) DLC, and Harvard University. 1854. *No Compromise with Slavery: An Address Delivered in the Broadway Tabernacle, New York, February 14, 1854. Internet Archive.* New York : American Anti-Slavery Society ... https://archive.org/details/nocompromisewit00garrgoog/page/n4/mode/2up.

16. Brownson, Orestes. *Emancipation and Colonization*, BQR (April, 1862).

17. Garrison, William Lloyd, African American Pamphlet Collection (Library of Congress) DLC, and Harvard University. 1854, pg. 5. *No Compromise with Slavery: An Address Delivered in the Broadway Tabernacle, New York, February 14, 1854. Internet Archive.* New York : American Anti-Slavery Society ... https://archive.org/details/nocompromisewit00garrgoog/page/n4/mode/2up.

18. Carey, Patrick W. "Political Atheism: 'Dred Scott', Roger Brooke Taney, and Orestes A. Brownson." *The Catholic Historical Review* 88, no. 2 (2002): p. 215. http://www.jstor.org/stable/25026143.

19. "The Colonization Movement." Indiana Historical Bureau. https://www.in.gov/history/for-educators-all-resources-for-educators/resources/underground-railroad/gwen-crenshaw/the-colonization-movement/.

20. Miller, William Lee. *Arguing About Slavery.* New York: Alfred A. Knopf, 1996, pg. 15.

21. Ibid.

22. McKivigan, John R. *The War Against Proslavery Religion: Abolitionism and the Northern Churches.* Ithaca: Cornell University Press, 1984, pg. 25.

23. Brownson, Orestes. "Emancipation and Colonization." *BQR* (April, 1862).

24. Miller, William Lee. *Arguing About Slavery.* New York: Alfred A. Knopf, 1996, pg. 10.

25. Southard, Nathaniel ed., and Child, Lydia Maria, 1802-1880 comp. "The American Anti-Slavery Almanac, for 1841," 1841, pg. 16.

26. Ibid.

27. Miller, William Lee. *Arguing About Slavery.* New York: Alfred A. Knopf, 1996, pg. 12.

28. Brownson, Orestes. "Emancipation and Colonization." *BQR* (April, 1862).

29. McPherson, James M. *Abolitionist and Negro Opposition to Colonization during the Civil War.* Phylon (1960-) 26, no. 4 (1965): 391–99. https://doi.org/10.2307/273703.

30. Fee, John Gregg. "Colonization: the present scheme of colonization wrong, delusive, and retards emancipation." 1857, pg. 9-10. www.archive.org/details/ASPC0001949200.

31. Crouthamel, James L. "James Watson Webb: Mercantile Editor." *New York History* 41, no. 4 (1960): 418. http://www.jstor.org/stable/23153652.

32. McKivigan, John R. *The War Against Proslavery Religion: Abolitionism and the Northern Churches.* Ithaca: Cornell University Press, 1984, pg. 19.

33. Whitehead, Kaye Wise. "'The Long Arm of Justice' Swings from the Emancipation Proclamation to the March on Washington." *Black History Bulletin* 75, no. 2 (2012): 24–30. http://www.jstor.org/stable/24759674.

34. Miller, William Lee. *Arguing About Slavery.* New York: Alfred A. Knopf, 1996, pg. 11.

35. Birney, James Gillespie. *The American Churches, the Bulwarks of American Slavery.* Newburyport: Charles Whipple, 1842, pg. 12.

36. McKivigan, John R. *The War Against Proslavery Religion: Abolitionism and the Northern Churches.* Ithaca: Cornell University Press, 1984, pg. 86.

37. "Image 1 of Declaration of the Anti-Slavery Convention Assembled in Philadelphia, Dec. 4, 1833. Philadelphia. 6th December 1833." n.d. Library of Congress, Washington, D.C. 20540 USA. Accessed May 26, 2023. https://www.loc.gov/resource/rbpe.15302500/?sp=1&st=text.

38. Ibid.

39. Schomburg Center for Research in Black Culture, Manuscripts, Archives and Rare Books Division, The New York Public Library. "The speech of William Wilberforce, esq., representative for the county of York, on Wednesday the 13th of May, 1789, on the question of the abolition of the slave trade" New York Public Library Digital Collections. Accessed May 25, 2023. https://digitalcollections.nypl.org/items/510d47e3-a708-a3d9-e040-e00a18064a99.

40. Ibid. Pg. 64.

41. Brownson, Orestes. "Slavery and the Church." *BQR* (October, 1862); Brownson, Orestes. "The Slavery Question Once More." *BQR* (April 1857).

42. Brownson, Orestes. "Home Politics." *BQR* (Slavery, Government) 1875.

43. Zanca, Kenneth J. "The Lion Who Did Not Roar . . . Yet: The Editorials of James A. McMaster — May 1860 to May 1861." *American Catholic Studies* 122, no. 3 (2011): 1–29. http://www.jstor.org/stable/44195355.

44. Brownson, Orestes. "Slavery and the Church." *BQR* (October, 1862).

45. Campion, Owen F. "The Uncomfortable History of Catholics and Slavery." Our Sunday Visitor, January 17, 2023. https://www.oursundayvisitor.com/the-uncomfortable-history-of-catholics-and-slavery/.

46. Birney, James Gillespie. *The American Churches, the Bulwarks of American Slavery.* Newburyport: Charles Whipple, 1842, pg. 5.

47. Ibid. Pg. 7.

48. McKivigan, John R. *The War Against Proslavery Religion: Abolitionism and the Northern Churches*. Ithaca: Cornell University Press, 1984.

49. Ibid. Pg. 13.

50. Ibid. Pg. 7.

51. Ibid. Pg. 13.

52. *The Liberator*, August 13, 1831.

53. Digital Commonwealth. "The Liberator. V.28:No.11(1858:Mar.12) - Digital Commonwealth." *Www.digitalcommonwealth.org*, The Liberator, 12 Mar. 1858, www.digitalcommonwealth.org/book_viewer/commonwealth:5h742g15b#?&cv=2&h=Disunion. Accessed 30 Dec. 2022.

54. Fee, John Gregg. *Colonization: The Present Scheme of Colonization Wrong, Delusive, and Retards Emancipation. Internet Archive*. 1857, pg. 9. https://archive.org/details/ASPC0001949200/page/n13/mode/2up.

55. Heyrick, Elizabeth. *Immediate, Not Gradual Abolition, Or, an Inquiry into the Shortest, Safest, and Most Effectual Means of Getting Rid of West Indian Slavery*. Philadelphia: Philadelphia Ladies' Anti-Slavery Society, 1836, pgs. 24-25.

56. Miller, William Lee. *Arguing About Slavery: the Great Battle in the United States Congress*. New York: Alfred A. Knopf, 1995, pgs. 9-10.

57. Brownson, Orestes. "Emancipation and Colonization." *BQR* (April, 1862).

58. Brownson, Orestes. "Slavery and the Church." *BQR* (October, 1862).

59. *Eleventh Annual Report of the Indiana Colonization Society*, 18-19.

60. *Freeman's Journal*, April 4, 1863.

61. Dickey, JD. *The Republic of Violence*. Pegasus Books. 2002.

62. Willke, Dr. and Mrs. J.C. *Abortion Questions & Answers*. Cincinnati: Hayes Publishing Company. 1985, pg. 16.

63. "Are Pro-Lifers Wrong to Support Incremental Pro-Life Legislation?" October 24, 2020. Facebook video, 01:02. www.facebook.com/watch/?v=402432981126092.

64. Equal Rights Institute. "AHA: The Anti-Abortionists Who Fight Other Pro-Lifers (with Jonathan Van Maren – Part 1)." YouTube video, 30:25. May 15, 2021. www.youtube.com/watch?v=0SvNYXQqvuM.

65. Barber, Bart (@bartbarber). "And it is THAT—this Faustian bargain with the devil of politics, this gossipy accusing of the brethren, this focus-group-tested rabble-rousing that tramples truth in the quest for quote-tweets—that represents one of the gravest threats to the work of the SBC today." Twitter, September, 15, 2022. twitter.com/bartbarber/status/1570377800120664070.

66. Kaake, Andrew. "Abolitionists are going to get people killed, and the SBC just helped them." *Equal Rights Institute*, June 25, 2021. blog.equalrightsinstitute.com/abolitionists-are-going-to-get-people-killed-and-the-sbc-just-helped-them/.

67. Klusendorf, Scott. *Facebook*, July 17, 2021. www.facebook.com/scottklusendorflti/posts/pfbid02KjPMggLsg99x5Vv4YURQMxeRoUPTMVYB2gsXwuyAg7dBsom3rrNS5FtTUgeVrY9vl.

68. McCain, Dana Hall. "Southern Baptist Convention's problematic abortion resolution." *AL.com*, June 22, 2021. www.al.com/opinion/2021/06/dana-hall-mccain-southern-baptist-conventions-problematic-abortion-resolution.html.

69. Hayes, Steve. "Making babies poker chips." *Triablogue*, May 29, 2015. triablogue.blogspot.com/2015/05/making-babies-poker-chips.html.

70. Silberman, James. "Abby Johnson says she cares more about federal programs than abolishing abortion." *Free the States*, May 24, 2020. freethestates.org/2020/05/abby-johnson-says-she-cares-more-about-federal-programs-than-abolishing-abortion/.

71. McKivigan, John R. *The War Against Proslavery Religion: Abolitionism and the Northern Churches.* Ithaca: Cornell University Press, 1984, pg. 200-201.

72. BRIGHTRIDER. "A Storm Comes Rolling down the Plain." *YouTube*, May 16, 2022, 00:23, https://www.youtube.com/watch?v=VPu59scsBA8.

73. Kevan Meyers interview with author, May 24, 2023.

74. Fee, John Gregg. *Colonization: the present scheme of colonization wrong, delusive, and retards emancipation*. Oberlin College Library, 1857, pgs. 15-16. archive.org/details/ASPC0001949200/page/n5/mode/2up.

75. Ibid.

76. Smithsonian: National Museum of American History. "America's New Birth of Freedom." Accessed May 26, 2023. www.americanhistory.si.edu/documentsgallery/exhibitions/americas_new_birth_of_freedom_5.html.

77. Cali, C.R. *The Doctrine of Balaam*, Wrath and Grace, 2019, pg. 137.

78. Garrison, William Lloyd. *No compromise with slavery: an address delivered in the Broadway Tabernacle, New York*. New York: American Anti-Slavery Society, 1854.

79. Fee, John Gregg. *Colonization: the present scheme of colonization wrong, delusive, and retards emancipation*. Oberlin College Library, 1857, pg. 45.

80. Garrison, William Lloyd. *No compromise with slavery: an address delivered in the Broadway Tabernacle, New York*. New York: American Anti-Slavery Society, 1854.

License to Kill: Rise of the Mother Abortionist

1. Abolish Abortion Texas. "DIY, Modern Day Child Sacrifice," July 28, 2022. https://www.youtube.com/watch?v=Y3x57ntUrhs.

2. Domb, Arielle. "The Satanic Abortion Clinic That's Pissed Off Pretty Much Everyone...and Might Beat the Bans Anyway." *Cosmopolitan*, November 14, 2023.

3. Text message to author, supplied by The Imago Dei Ministry, March 10, 2023.

4. Ibid.

5. Ibid.

6. Social media post kept anonymous to protect poster's privacy.

7. Social media post kept anonymous to protect poster's privacy.

8. NRL News. "Abortionists Agree – Abortion Is Killing." *NRL News Today* -, March 26, 2015. https://www.nationalrighttolifenews.org/2015/03/abortionists-agree-abortion-is-killing-2/.

9. American Center for Law and Justice. "How Much Prenatal Care Does Planned Parenthood Really Provide?" January 25, 2017. https://aclj.org/pro-life/how-much-prenatal-care-does-planned-parenthood-really-provide.

10. Clark, Matthew. "WAPO: Three Pinocchios for Planned Parenthood's '3 Percent' Abortion Lie." American Center for Law and Justice. August 13, 2015. https://aclj.org/pro-life/wapo-three-pinocchios-for-planned-parenthoods-3-percent-abortion-lie.

11. The Ottawa Citizen. "Abortion Wars." May 28, 2000, sec. Letters.

12. Alkon, Cheryl. "Confessions of an Abortion Doctor." *Boston Magazine*, May 15, 2006. Accessed January 18, 2023. https://www.bostonmagazine.com/2006/05/15/confessions-of-an-abortion-doctor/.

13. Wang, Leo. "The Abortionist." *Berkeley Medical Journal Spring*, 1995.

14. Gianelli, Diane M. "Abortion Providers Share Inner Conflicts." *American Medical News*, July 12, 1993.

15. Terzo, Sarah. "Abortionist Admits: 'I Will See the Squashed Face... of the Baby I Just Killed.'" *Live Action News*, June 29, 2022. https://www.liveaction.org/news/abortionist-admits-killing-baby-abortion/.

16. "Feminist Politics and Abortion in the USA." *CWLU HERSTORY*, September 21, 2016. https://www.cwluherstory.org/jane-articles-media-articles/feminist-politics-and-abortion-in-the-usa.

17. Pekkanen, John. *M.D.: Doctors Talk About Themselves*. Dell, 1990, pgs. 90-91.

18. Mary Steichen Calderone "Illegal Abortion as a Public Health Problem", *American Journal of Public Health* 50, no. 7 (July 1, 1960): pg. 951. https:// ajph.aphapublications.org/doi/epdf/10.2105/AJPH.50.7.948.

19. Korn, Peter. *Lovejoy: A Year in the Life of an Abortion Clinic*. 1st ed. New York: Atlantic Monthly Press, 1996, pg. 94.

20. Claire, Miriam. *The Abortion Dilemma: Personal Views on a Public Issue*. New York: Insight Books, 1995, pg. 59.

21. Lewis, Sophie. "Abortion Involves Killing–and That's OK!" *The Nation*, August 15, 2022. https://www.thenation.com/article/society/abortion-ethics-gestation-reproduction/.

22. Simon, Stephanie. "Offering Abortion, Rebirth." *Los Angeles Times*, March 2, 2019. https://www.latimes.com/archives/la-xpm-2005-nov-29-na-abortion29-story.html.

23. Andersson, Hilary. "America's Abortion War." *One Panorama*, July 27, 2019. Podcast, website, 29:00. www.bbc.co.uk/programmes/m00071k9; Students for Life. "Late-Term Abortionist Stuns BBC in Harsh Interview." YouTube, August 27, 2019. https:/www.youtube.com/watch?v=W8WkOybCObE.

24. Williams, Mary Elizabeth. "So What If Abortion Ends Life?" *Salon*, January 23, 2013. https://www.salon.com/2013/01/23/so_what_if_abortion_ends_life/.

25. Powell, John Joseph. *Abortion the Silent Holocaust*. Tabor Pub., 1981, pg. 66.

26. Haugen, David, Susan Musser, and Kacy Lovelace. *Abortion (Opposing Viewpoints)*. Farmington Hills: Greenhaven, 2010.

27. Claire, Miriam. *The Abortion Dilemma: Personal Views on a Public Issue*. New York: Insight Books, 1995.

28. Smith, T. "Abortionist 'This Has to Be Killing.'" ClinicQuotes, April 24, 2019. https://clinicquotes.com/abortionist-this-has-to-be-killing/.

29. Slack, James. *Abortion, Execution, and the Consequences of Taking Life*. Routledge, 2011, pg. 49.

30. Social media post kept anonymous to protect poster's privacy.

31. Zeisloft, Ben. "A Biblical Alternative to the Pro-Life Movement." *End Abortion Now*, December 9, 2022. https://endabortionnow.com/a-biblical-alternative-to-the-pro-life-movement/.

32. Craddock, Josh. "Why Fetal Pain Hurts (the pro-Life Cause)." *LifeSite*, June 18, 2021. https://www.lifesitenews.com/opinion/why-fetal-pain-hurts-the-pro-life-cause/.

33. Jones RK, Witwer E and Jerman J, *Abortion Incidence and Service Availability in the United States, 2017*, New York: Guttmacher Institute, 2019, www.guttmacher.org/report/abortion-incidence-service-availability-us-2017.

34. Guttmacher Institute. "Medication Abortion Accounted for 63% of All US Abortions in 2023—An Increase From 53% in 2020," March 19, 2024. https://www.guttmacher.org/2024/03/medication-abortion-accounted-63-all-us-abortions-2023-increase-53-2020.

35. Moscufo, Michela, and Brad Mielke. "Mobile Abortion Clinics Ramp up Operations as Roe v. Wade Is Overturned." *ABC News*, June 30, 2022. https://abcnews.go.com/US/mobile-abortion-clinics-ramp-operations-roe-wade-overturned/story?id=85789069.

36. Meaker, Morgan. "Abortion Pill Demand Is Driving an Underground Network." *WIRED*, July 18, 2022. https://www.wired.com/story/the-wild-abortion-pill-supply-chain/.

37. The New York Times. "How I Had an Abortion at Home in Texas | NYT Opinion." YouTube, June 29, 2022. https://www.youtube.com/watch?v=tjIgYs81mB8.

38. Abolitionists Rising. "Texas - Abolitionists Rising," March 16, 2023. https://abolitionistsrising.com/texas/.

39. "Shout Your Abortion — Normalizing Abortion and Elevating Safe Paths to Access, Regardless of Legality.," n.d. https://shoutyourabortion.com/?fbclid=IwAR351FfJ7XZkXtz1YHRstMoW6AK2uAleKjsKOT1aTiYJgg7k_wi4luDF-PQ.

40. Social media post kept anonymous to protect poster's privacy.

41. Ibid.

42. Ibid.

43. Ibid.

44. Ibid.

45. Ibid.

46. Ibid.

47. Ibid.

48. Ibid.

49. Text message to author, supplied by The Imago Dei Ministry, March 10, 2023.

50. 2022 Oklahoma Statutes :: Title 63. Public Health and Safety :: §63-1-731.4. Abortion prohibited – Exception - Penalties. www. law.justia.com/codes/oklahoma/2022/title-63/section-63-1-731-4/.

51. Revisor of Missouri :: Title XII. Public Health and Welfare :: §188.017. Right to Life of the Unborn Child Act. www.revisor.mo.gov/main/OneSection.aspx?section=188.017

52. Kortsmit, Katherine. "Abortion Surveillance — United States, 2020." Centers for Disease Control and Prevention, November 23, 2022. https://www.cdc.gov/mmwr/volumes/71/ss/ss7110a1.htm.

53. Royal College of Obstetricians and Gynaecologists. "Making Abortion Safe." *Www.Rcog.Org.Uk/Mas*. Royal College of Obstetricians and Gynaecologists, 2022. Accessed March 21, 2023. https://www.rcog.org.uk/media/geify5bx/abortion-care-best-practice-paper-april-2022.pdf.

54. Dannenfelser, Marjorie, and Kristan Hawkins. "We're Two pro-Life Women Who Say 'no' to Prosecuting Women for Abortions." *Fox News*, August 3, 2022. https://www.foxnews.com/opinion/two-pro-life-women-say-no-prosecuting-women-abortions.

55. CNSNews.com. "Pro-Life Leaders Say Abortionists Should Be Punished, Not Their Women Victims," n.d. https://www.cnsnews.com/news/article/barbara-hollingsworth/pro-life-leaders-abortionists-should-be-punished-not-their-women.

56. Ibid.

57. Ibid.

58. Ibid.

59. Klassen, Laura. "PRO-LIFE LEADERS TESTIFY AGAINST A BILL THAT WOULD ABOLISH ABORTION." *Facebook*, May 9, 2023. Accessed May 16, 2023.

60. Williams, L.A. "Southern Baptists Divided Over Right Way to Oppose Abortion." Christian Action League. May 20, 2022. www.christianactionleague.org/southern-baptists-divided-over-right-way-to-oppose-abortion/.

61. Abolitionists Rising, "Should Women Be Prosecuted?: A Debate with Babylon Bee's Joel Berry." *YouTube*, December 9, 2023. https:// www.youtube.com/watch?v=eOYyrOiu2kQ&t=10268s.

62. Willke, Barbara and John C. Willke. *Why Can't We Love Them Both*. 2nd ed., Hayes, 1997.

63. Ibid. Pg. iv.

64. Birth Control Federation of America. "Plan Your Family for Health and Happiness." Pamphlet, Data set. Sophia Smith Collection, Smith College (Northampton, Massachusetts), n.d. https://libex.smith.edu/omeka/items/show/440.

65. Sanger, Margaret. *The Pivot of Civilization*. Oxford/New York: Pergamon Press, 1922.

66. Simon, Stephanie. "Offering Abortion, Rebirth." *Los Angeles Times*, March 2, 2019. https://www.latimes.com/archives/la-xpm-2005-nov-29-na-abortion29-story.html.

67. Mitchell, Libby. "Women Are NOT Stupid." *HuffPost*, May 23, 2012. https://www.huffpost.com/entry/women-are-not-stupid_b_1371414.

68. Wolf, Naomi. "Our Bodies, Our Souls." *New Republic*, October 16, 1995.

69. Cruz, Caitlin. "Activists Swallowed Abortion Pills on Steps of the Supreme Court." *Jezebel*, July 28, 2022. https://jezebel.com/activists-swallowed-abortion-pills-on-steps-of-the-supr-1848143679.

70. "Shout Your Abortion — Normalizing Abortion and Elevating Safe Paths to Access, Regardless of Legality.," n.d. https://shoutyourabortion.com/.

71. Congress.gov. "House Oversight and Accountability Recorded Stream: 07/13/2022 at 6:00 a.m. Recorded Video." January 19, 2023. https://www.congress.gov/committees/video/house-oversight-and-accountability/hsgo00/bIhcUCh1d5M.

72. Whittemore, Amie. "This Abortion Is an Act of Love | Brevity: A Journal of Concise Literary Nonfiction." *Brevity*, January 22, 2020. Accessed January 19, 2023. https://brevitymag.com/nonfiction/act-of-love/.

73. Pollitt, Katha. "Abortion and Love." *The Nation*, June 7, 2018. https://www.thenation.com/article/archive/abortion-and-love/.

74. Donahue, May 15, 1989, Transcript #3288 NBC.

75. McArthur, Stu [@stumc910]. "@jasonkeithallen, President of MWBTS, cannot commit "in this moment" to providing equal protection to all human beings created in the image of God..." Twitter, June 14, 2023.

76. Prior, Karen Swallow (@KSPrior). "Yet, punishing the woman whose circumstances..." *Twitter*, March 25, 2024. https://x.com/KSPrior/status/1772339353307509006

77. Buice, Josh. "Why Christians Should Support the Abolition of Abortion." G3 Ministries, January 12, 2023. https://g3min.org/why-christians-should-support-the-abolition-of-abortion/.

78. Rushdoony, Rousas. *The Institutes of Biblical Law*. P&R, 1973, pg. 186.

79. Claire, Miriam. *The Abortion Dilemma: Personal Views on a Public Issue*. New York: Insight Books, 1995, pg. 54.

80. Ibid. Pgs. 55-56.

81. Ibid. Pgs. 60, 63.

82. Ibid. Pg. 57.

83. North, Gary. *When Justice Is Aborted: Biblical Standards for Non-Violent Resistance*. Fort Worth: Dominion, 1989, pg. 20.

Equal Justice: Loving Our Preborn Neighbors as Ourselves

1. Grace Life Church. "Ending Abortion Without Exception (Pro-Life Is Not Enough Conference-2021): CR Cali," *YouTube*, 05:05, December 7, 2021. www.youtube.com/watch?v=XGsdY-DktfQ.

2. U.S. Const. amend. XIIII, section 1.

3. Abolish Abortion Texas. "What about the Death Penalty?" April 19, 2022. https://abolishabortiontx.org/what-about-the-death-penalty/.

4. Legislative declaration that life begins at fertilization, published L. ch. 119, § 2; Stat. 65-6732 (2013); Application of certain crimes to an unborn child, published L. ch. 136, § 54; Stat. 21-5419 (2010).

5. Arkes, Hadley. "Natural Rights and the Right to Choose." New York: Cambridge University Press, 2002. Pg. 146.

6. "Pro-Life Legislation Successes in Kansas." n.d. Kansans for Life. Accessed May 19, 2023. https://kfl.org/legislation/pro-life-legislative-successes/.

7. Abolish Abortion Texas. "Equal Protection: How the Justice System Works," *YouTube*, October 6, 2022. https://www.youtube.com/watch?v=8j3X6eVWFqA.

8. Stu McArthur, interview by author, March 25, 2023.

9. Abolish Abortion Texas. "Equal Protection: how the justice system works." *YouTube*, October 6, 2022. www.youtube.com/watch?v=8j3X6eVWFqA.

10. LII /Legal Information Institute. "Habeas Corpus," n.d. https://www.law.cornell.edu/wex/habeas_corpus.

11. Roberts, John. "ON PETITION FOR AN EXTRAORDINARY WRIT OF HABEAS CORPUS TO THE UNITED STATES DISTRICT COURT FOR THE DISTRICT OF OREGON." *Supreme Court*, November 10, 2021. Accessed January 20, 2023. https://www.supremecourt.gov/DocketPDF/21/21-715/199908/20211116093323030_20211116-092314-00002024-00006677.pdf.

12. Obama, Barack. "The President's Role in Advancing Criminal Justice Reform." *Harvard Law Review* 130, no. 3 (January 5, 2017). https://harvardlawreview.org/2017/01/the-presidents-role-in-advancing-criminal-justice-reform/.

13. Seibler, John-Michael. "As 'Law and Order' President, Trump Can Improve Criminal Justice for Everyone." *The Heritage Foundation*, n.d. https://www.heritage.org/crime-and-justice/commentary/law-and-order-president-trump-can-improve-criminal-justice-everyone.

14. "Kirsten Gillibrand | U.S. Senator for New York," n.d. https://www.gillibrand.senate.gov/campus-sexual-assault.

15. Hendershott, Anne. 2017. Review of *Progressive Politicians Two-Faced over Due Process Rights*. *Crisis Magazine*, December 4, 2017. https://www.crisismagazine.com/opinion/progressive-politicians-demand-due-process-protections.

16. CNSNews.com. "Ocasio-Cortez: Due Process and Justice 'Must Center on the Victim,'" n.d. https://www.cnsnews.com/news/article/susan-jones/ocasio-cortez-due-process-and-justice-must-center-victim.

17. Payton, Bre. "How Progressives Changed The Way We View Our Rights And The Constitution." *The Federalist*, April 27, 2018. https://thefederalist.com/2018/04/28/progressives-changed-way-view-rights-constitution/.

18. Abolitionists Rising, "Should Women Be Prosecuted?: A Debate with Babylon Bee's Joel Berry." *YouTube*, December 9, 2023, 02:42:30, https:// www.youtube.com/watch?v=eOYyrOiu2kQ&t=10268s.

19. Abolish Abortion Texas. "What about the Death Penalty?" April 19, 2022. https://abolishabortiontx.org/what-about-the-death-penalty/.

20. "FULL HEARING: The Abolition Of Abortion In Texas Act, HB 896 (8 Hours)," April 8, 2019. https://archive.org/details/FULLHEARING-The-Abolition-of-Abortion-in-Texas-Act-HB-896.

21. LII / Legal Information Institute. "Ex Post Facto Laws," n.d. https://www.law.cornell.edu/constitution-conan/article-1/section-9/clause-3/ex-post-facto-laws.

22. Article I Section 9 | Constitution Annotated | Congress.gov | Library of Congress.

23. Constitution Annotated. "Article I Legislative Branch," n.d. https://constitution.congress.gov/browse/article-1/section-9/.

24. "LIVE video stream regarding Louisiana HB 813, the Abolition of Abortion in Louisiana Act," *Facebook*, May 12, 2022. www.facebook.com/watch/live/?ref=search&v=425078146129229.

25. Ibid.

26. Gitchell, Rita Lowery, *Who is entitled to the Right to Life, Liberty, and the Pursuit of Happiness?* July 4, 2021. https://www.thomasmoresociety.org/news/who-is-entitled-to-the-right-to-life-liberty-and-the-pursuit-of-happiness.

27. "Article vi Section 2 | Constitution Annotated | Congress.gov | Library of Congress." n.d. Constitution.congress.gov. https://constitution.congress.gov/browse/article-6/clause-2/.

28. Dovydaitis, Tiffany. "Human trafficking: the role of the health care provider." *Journal of midwifery & women's health* vol. 55,5 (2010): 462-7. doi:10.1016/j.jmwh.2009.12.017.

29. Levin, Jamie, and Serj Mooradian, eds. "The Health Consequences of Sex Trafficking and Their Implications for Identifying Victims in Healthcare Facilities." Loyola University Chicago School of Law, 2014. Accessed March 23, 2023. https://www.globalcenturion.org/wp-content/uploads/2014/08/The-Health-Consequences-of-Sex-Trafficking.pdf.

30. Ibid. Pg. 77-78.

31. Hollingsworth, Barbara. "Pro-Life Leaders Say Abortionists Should Be Punished, Not Their Women Victims." *CNSNews.com*, 31 Mar. 2016, https://www.cnsnews.com/news/article/barbara-hollingsworth/pro-life-leaders-abortionists-should-be-punished-not-their-women.

32. NR Symposium, "One Untrue Thing." *National Review*, August 1, 2007, www.nationalreview.com/2007/08/one-untrue-thing-nro-symposium/.

33. Brennan, Ana, "Love Them Both: Why Abortionists Should be Prosecuted for Abortions, Not Women." *Life News*, December 6, 2018. www.lifenews.com/2018/12/06/love-them-both-why-abortionists-should-be-prosecuted-for-abortions-not-women/?fbclid=IwAR3LqgahYyBD2HJIEEZWxuy2jVVAcXUBfNUmey0T3Hiow-zbVxwt9PM4MAs.

34. Carter, Joe, "Should Women Be Prosecuted for Self-Induced Abortions?" *The Gospel Coalition*, April 14, 2022. www.thegospelcoalition.org/article/women-prosecuted-abortions/.

35. Stu McArthur, interview by author, March 25, 2023.

36. Ibid.

37. Ibid.

The Cost of Partiality

1. Sproul, R.C. *How Should I Live In This World*, Reformation Trust, 2009, pg. 8.

2. Ibid, pg. 10.

3. Boot, Joseph. *Ruler of Kings*, Wilberforce Publications, 2022. Pg. 23.

4. "Estimate of Funds Raised by the PBA Ban." 2007. https://www.americanrtl.org/sites/default/files/Documents/pba-fundraising.pdf.

5. *Washington Post*. "Eric Holder Testifies before House Judiciary Committee." *YouTube*, May 15, 2013. 2:40:30 https://www.youtube.com/watch?v=0EVkHzSUbms.

6. Lawyer, William and Matthew Margetts."Left for Dead: How Many Survive Abortion?" 2021. Human Life International. March, 12 2021.www.hli.org/resources/abortion-survival-statistics/.

7. "NOMINATION of SANDRA DAY O'CONNOR HEARINGS before the COMMITTEE on the JUDICIABY UNITED STATES SENATE NINETY-SEVENTH CONGBESS FIRST SESSION on the NOMINATION or JUDGE SANDRA DAY O'CONNOR OP ARIZONA to SERVE as an ASSOCIATE JUSTICE of the SUPREME COURT of the UNITED STATES." September 9-11, 1981. https://www.govinfo.gov/content/pkg/GPO-CHRG-OCONNOR/pdf/GPO-CHRG-OCONNOR.pdf.

8. *Washington Post*. "Eric Holder Testifies before House Judiciary Committee." *YouTube*, May 15, 2013. 2:43:10.

9. "NOMINATION of SANDRA DAY O'CONNOR HEARINGS before the COMMITTEE on the JUDICIABY UNITED STATES SENATE NINETY-SEVENTH CONGBESS FIRST SESSION on the NOMINATION or JUDGE SANDRA DAY O'CONNOR OP ARIZONA to SERVE as an ASSOCIATE JUSTICE of the SUPREME COURT of the UNITED STATES." September 9-11, 1981. https://www.govinfo.gov/content/pkg/GPO-CHRG-OCONNOR/pdf/GPO-CHRG-OCONNOR.pdf.

10. "Calendar No 2 118th Congress 1st Session." January 25, 2023. https://www.congress.gov/118/bills/hr26/BILLS-118hr26pcs.pdf.

11. Mosley, Patrina. "Why We Need the Born-Alive Abortion Survivors Protection Act." FRC, n.d. https://www.frc.org/op-eds/why-we-need-the-born-alive-abortion-survivors-protection-act.

12. Ben Sasse, "Sasse Opening Statement at Born-Alive Hearing," February 11, 2020, https://www.youtube.com/watch?v=kdJ0d3Q_EYo.

13. Hadley, Arkes. *Born-Alive Act Redux!* The Catholic Thing. January 21, 2023. https://www.thecatholicthing.org/2023/01/21/born-alive-act-redux-2/.

14. "NRLC Letters to U.S. House of Representatives in Support of the Born-Alive Infants Protection Act." National Right to Life, July 22, 2020. www.nrlc.org/federal/bornaliveinfants/lettertocongress/.

15. "Pro-Life Law Protects Babies Who Survive Their Abortions." National Catholic Register, August 11, 2002. https://www.ncregister.com/news/pro-life-law-protects-babies-who-survive-their-abortions.

16. "Executive Office of the President Office of Management and Budget." March 12, 2002. https://georgewbush-whitehouse.archives.gov/omb/legislative/sap/107-2/107PDFs/HR2175-House.pdf.

17. "President Signs Born-Alive Infants Protection Act." The White House, August 5, 2002. https://georgewbush-whitehouse.archives.gov/news/releases/2002/08/20020805-6.html.

18. "Calendar No. 2 118th Congress 1st Session." January 25, 2023. https://www.congress.gov/118/bills/hr26/BILLS-118hr26pcs.pdf

19. Hadley, Arkes. *Born-Alive Act Redux!* The Catholic Thing. January 21, 2023. https://www.thecatholicthing.org/2023/01/21/born-alive-act-redux-2/.

20. "18 U.S. Code § 3559 – Sentencing Classification of Offenses." LII/ Legal Information Institute. 2019. https://www.law.cornell.edu/uscode/text/18/3559; "18 U.S. Code § 1112 – Manslaughter." LII/ Legal Information Institute. https://www.law.cornell.edu/uscode/text/18/1112#:~:text=Whoever%20is%20guilty%20of%20voluntary%20manslaughter%2C%20shall%20be,imprisoned%20not%20more%20than%208%20years%2C%20or%20both.

21. Byron, Roger. "Children of a Lesser Law: The Failure of the Born-Alive Infants Protection Act and a Plan for Its Redemption." Regent University Law Review. Accessed August 8, 2023. https://www.regent.edu/acad/schlaw/student_life/studentorgs/lawreview/docs/issues/v19n1/08Byronvol19.1(corrected).pdf.

22. Life Dynamics Inc. "Abortion Clinic Employees -- 'Babies Born Alive Daily.'" May 14, 2013. https://www.youtube.com/watch?v=9fhyJItGPko.

23. Ibid.

24. Ertelt, Steven. "20 Texas Lawmakers Demand Probe of Douglas Karpen, Killed Babies Born Alive." *LifeNews.Com*, June 6, 2013. https://www.lifenews.com/2013/06/05/20-texas-lawmakers-demand-probe-of-douglas-karpen-killed-babies-born-alive/.

25. Williams, Seth. "In RE County Investigating Grand Jury XXIII." Court of Common Pleas First Judicial District of Pennsylvania Criminal Trial Provision, January 17, 2011. Accessed January 23, 2023. https://rtl.org/wp-content/uploads/2018/08/GrandJurySummary.pdf.

26. Ibid.

27. Ibid.

28. Lattanzio, Vince. "Gosnell Sentenced to 3 Life Terms, Jurors Open Up." *NBC10 Philadelphia*, May 15, 2013. https://www.nbcphiladelphia.com/news/national-international/gosnell-sentenced-on-other-crimes/2088707/.

29. Anti-Abortion Uprising, Progressive. "Higher Quality #JusticeForTheFive Press Conference," April 6, 2022. https://www.youtube.com/watch?v=Eg6nOvvBD4s&feature=youtu.be.

30. Epner JEG, Jonas HS, Seckinger DL. Late-term Abortion. *JAMA*. 1998;280(8):724–729. doi:10.1001/jama.280.8.724.

31. Parents. "There's No Such Thing as 'Late-Term Abortion'—Here Are the Facts," December 15, 2022. https://www.parents.com/pregnancy/my-body/pregnancy-health/theres-no-such-thing-as-late-term-abortion-here-are-the-facts/.

32. Action, Live. "Inhuman: Undercover in America's Late-Term Abortion Industry - Washington, D.C.," April 28, 2013. https://www.youtube.com/watch?v=NxOWyumLufA&feature=youtu.be.

33. "Lankford, Jordan, Colleagues Demand Investigation into Deaths of Five Babies Aborted in DC." Press release, April 5, 2022. https://www.lankford.senate.gov/news/press-releases/lankford-jordan-colleagues-demand-investigation-into-deaths-of-five-babies-aborted-in-dc.

34. Thomas J. Monaghan to LeRoy H. Carhart, June 28, 1993, *Re: State v. LeRoy H. Carhart*, M.D., www.abortiondocs.org/wp-content/uploads/2012/04/Carhart_Case_Dismissed_NE.pdf.

35. Operation Rescue, "In Memory of Christian Gilbert, 1985-2005." www.operationrescue.org/noblog/in-memory-of-christin-gilbert-1985-2005/.

36. American Family News. "Could Notorious Carhart Be Forced to Quit Bloody Abortion Business?," August 26, 2022. https://afn.net/pro-life/2022/08/26/could-notorious-carhart-be-forced-to-quit-bloody-abortion-business/.

37. gofundme.com. "CARE Abortion Clinic - Pueblo, Colorado, Organized by LEROY CARHART," n.d. https://www.gofundme.com/f/3zkep-abortion-access?qid=d37518461d6199b9cccb792531cf6471.

38. Martin, Michel. "Abortion Doctor Upholds Legacy of Fallen Colleague," January 2010. Accessed January 22, 2023. www.npr.org/templates/story/story.php?storyId=122851800.

39. Eyal Press. "A Botched Operation." *The New Yorker*, January 27, 2014. https://www.newyorker.com/magazine/2014/02/03/a-botched-operation.

40. "Final Report on the Investigation of Dr. Ulrich Klopfer." Attorney General State of Indiana. December 28, 2020. secure.in.gov/attorneygeneral/files/KLOPFER-Final-Report-12-28.pdf.

41. Indiana Attorney General Todd Rokita. "Information Regarding Dr Ulrich Klopfer." Accessed January 23, 2023. https://www.in.gov/attorneygeneral/about-the-office/appeals/victim-services/information-regarding-dr-ulrich-klopfer/.

42. Berry, Susan. "Abortion Clinic Exposé: Kermit Gosnell Was Just 'Tip of the Iceberg.'" *Breitbart*, December 13, 2016.

43. American Life League, "Gosnell Murders Not the Exception," news release, May 13, 2013. Lifenews.com/2013/06/05/20-texas-lawmakers-demand-probe-of-douglas-karpen-killed-babies-born-alive/.

44. We The People LVN. "WtP Leavenworth – Value Them Both Discussion Forum – July 2022." YouTube video, 54:10. July 25, 2022. www.youtube.com/watch?v=ljV0t1Lwa5g.

45. Action, Live. "Inhuman: Undercover in America's Late-Term Abortion Industry - Washington, D.C.," April 28, 2013. https://www.youtube.com/watch?v=NxOWyumLufA&feature=youtu.be.

46. American Life League, "Gosnell Murders Not the Exception," news release, May 13, 2013. Lifenews.com/2013/06/05/20-texas-lawmakers-demand-probe-of-douglas-karpen-killed-babies-born-alive/.

47. Kliff, Sarah. "The Gosnell Case: Here's What You Need to Know." *The Washington Post*, April 13, 2013. Accessed January 24, 2023. https://www.washingtonpost.com/news/wonk/wp/2013/04/15/the-gosnell-case-heres-what-you-need-to-know/.

48. Americans United for Life. *Unsafe: America's Abortion Industry Endangers Women: A 50-State Investigative Report on the Dirty and Dangerous Abortion Industry*. 2nd ed., 2021.

49. Guttmacher Institute. "Induced Abortion in the United States." Guttmacher Institute. February 14, 2019. https://www.guttmacher.org/fact-sheet/induced-abortion-united-states.

50. Coleman, Priscilla K., Catherine T. Coyle, and Vincent M. Rue. 2010. "Late-Term Elective Abortion and Susceptibility to Posttraumatic Stress Symptoms." *Journal of Pregnancy* 2010: 1–10. https://doi.org/10.1155/2010/130519.

51. Guttmacher Institute. "Abortion Reporting Requirements," January 3, 2023. https://www.guttmacher.org/state-policy/explore/abortion-reporting-requirements.

52. Jennings, Katie. "Abortion by the Numbers." Forbes. May 7, 2022. https://www.forbes.com/sites/katiejennings/2022/05/07/abortion-by-the-numbers/?sh=1fa6db3160a8.

53. "Partial Birth Abortion Fiasco: Saved Not One | American Right to Life," n.d. https://americanrtl.org/news/partial-birth-abortion-fiasco-saved-not-one.

54. Ibid.

55. Justia Law. "Gonzales v. Carhart, 550 U.S. 124 (2007)," n.d. https://supreme.justia.com/cases/federal/us/550/124/.

56. Ibid.

57. New, Michael J. *Analyzing the Impact of U.S. Antiabortion Legislation in the Post-Casey Era: A Reassessment*. State Politics & Policy Quarterly, September, 2014.Vol. 14, No. 3. www.jstor.org/stable/24710980?seq=28.

58. Guttmacher Institute. "Abortion Reporting Requirements," January 3, 2023. https://www.guttmacher.org/state-policy/explore/abortion-reporting-requirements.

59. New, Michael J. *Analyzing the Impact of U.S. Antiabortion Legislation in the Post-Casey Era: A Reassessment*. State Politics & Policy Quarterly, September, 2014.Vol. 14, No. 3. Pg. 229. www.jstor.org/stable/24710980?seq=28.

60. Ibid.

61. Lindberg, Laura. *Changing Patterns of Contraceptive Use and the Decline in Rates of Pregnancy and Birth Among U.S. Adolescents, 2007-2014*. Journal of Adolescent Health, August 1, 2018. https://www.jahonline.org/article/S1054-139X(18)30200-3/fulltext.

62. New, Michael J. *Analyzing the Impact of U.S. Antiabortion Legislation in the Post-Casey Era: A Reassessment.* State Politics & Policy Quarterly, September, 2014.Vol. 14, No. 3, Pg. 258. www.jstor.org/stable/24710980?seq=28.

63. Ibid. Pg. 258.

64. Ibid. Pg. 258.

65. Ibid. Pg. 258.

66. Ibid. Pg. 260.

67. Ibid. Pg. 259.

68. Grossu, Arina. "Peer-reviewed studies find state pro-life laws reduce abortion rates" *Washington Examiner.* August 14, 2014. www.washingtonexaminer.com/peer-reviewed-studies-find-state-pro-life-laws-reduce-abortion-rates.

69. New, Michael J. *Analyzing the Impact of U.S. Antiabortion Legislation in the Post-Casey Era: A Reassessment.* State Politics & Policy Quarterly, September, 2014.Vol. 14, No. 3, Pg. 255. www.jstor.org/stable/24710980?seq=28.

70. Grossu, Arina. "Peer-reviewed studies find state pro-life laws reduce abortion rates" *Washington Examiner.* August 14, 2014. www.washingtonexaminer.com/peer-reviewed-studies-find-state-pro-life-laws-reduce-abortion-rates.

71. abortionNO. "Debate: Pro-Life Incrementalism vs Abolitionist Immediatism." *YouTube* video, 34:46. July 8, 2015. www.youtube.com/watch?v=5oi4vVTae30.

72. Quigley, Mallory. "Pro-life Surge in the States: 530 Pro-life Bills Introduced in 221, 61 New Laws Enacted." Susan B. Anthony Pro-Life America, April 30, 2021. sbaprolife.org/newsroom/press-releases/pro-life-surge-in-the-states-530-pro-life-bills-introduced-2021-61-new-laws-enacted.

73. Keller, Timothy. "Christian freedom of conscience in politics." *Facebook*, September 16, 2020.

74. Foley, Ryan. "Andy Stanley says divisive politicians are 'terrible leaders,' urges embrace of the 'messy middle.'" The Christian Post, March 17, 2022. www.christianpost.com/news/andy-stanley-divisive-politicians-terrible-leaders.html.

75. Smietana, Bob. "Brent Leatherwood, new ERLC president, says he won't tell Christians how to vote." Religion News Service. September 16, 2022. https://religionnews.com/2022/09/16/brent-leatherwood-new-erlc-president-says-he-wont-tell-christians-how-to-vote/.

76. Brito, Uri. "Phil Vischer, Veggie Tales, and the Nuance of Abortion." Kuyperian Commentary. May 21, 2022. https://kuyperian.com/phil-vischer-veggie-tales-and-the-nuance-of-abortion/.

77. Klusendorf, Scott. "Defending Pro-Life Incrementalism." October 4, 2021 in Issues Etc. Podcast, 01:45. https://issuesetc.org/2021/10/04/2771-defending-pro-life-incrementalism-scott-klusendorf-10-4-21/.

78. Sproul, R.C. "The Meaning of God's Will." Ligonier. May 20, 2019. https://www.ligonier.org/learn/articles/meaning-of-gods-will.

79. Tozer, A.W. *The Pursuit of God*. Minneapolis: Bethany House, 2013.

80. Enyart, Bob. "Focus on the Strategy." *YouTube* video, 7:30. December 9, 2014. www.youtube.com/watch?v=r4esSBgE10Y.

Recovering Protestant Ethics

1. Veith, Gene Edward. "The Protestant Work Ethic" Ligonier Ministries, September 1, 2006. https://www.ligonier.org/learn/articles/protestant-work-ethic.

2. Montesquieu. Esprit des Lois, Book XX, chap. 7.

3. Kennedy, James. "What if Jesus Had Never Been Born?" Pg. 9.

4. Brownson, Orestes. "The Slavery Question Once More." *Brownson Quarterly Review*, April, 1857. www.orestesbrownson.org/739.html.

5. Brownson, Orestes. "Slavery and the Incoming Administration." *Brownson Quarterly Review*, 1857. www.orestesbrownson.org/736.html.

6. Offenbacher, Martin. "Konfession und soziale Schichtung." Blackamoor: 1900. Pg. 58.

7. Bryan Caplan, "'Catholic' versus 'Protestant' Ethics." Econlib, April 5, 2018, https://www.econlib.org/archives/2012/04/catholic_versus.html.

8. Mitchell D. Creinin, "Medical Abortion with Methotrexate 75 Mg Intramuscularly and Vaginal Misoprostol," *Contraception* 56, no. 6 (December 1, 1997): 367–71, https://doi.org/10.1016/s0010-7824(97)00173-x.

9. Johnson, Abby. "I had no idea how little people knew about the treatment of ectopic pregnancies in a prolife and ethical way. So let me attempt to flesh this out..." *Facebook*, June 19, 2014. https://www.facebook.com/abbyjohnsonprolife/posts/pfbid02Pef9muTmr7GFZ9BAx4c7mfntoHyvxPJWnt1pRR6BAR37EM3PKTBus2t3JVc6Ua4l.

10. Bianchi, Diana W.: *Fetology: Diagnosis and Management of the Fetal Patient*. New York: McGraw-Hill, 2000, pg. xii.

11. Wallace, C.J. 1995. "Transplantations of Ectopic Pregnancy from Fallopian Tube to Cavity of Uterus." *The Linacre Quarterly* 62 (1): 67-69. https://doi.org/10.1080/20508549.1995.11878293.

12. Clark JF. Embryo transfer in vivo. J Natl Med Assoc. 1982 Aug; 74(8):721-4. PMID: 7131571; PMCID: PMC2552973.

13. "Periviable Birth." The College of Obstetricians and Gynecologists. No. 6. October 2017. https://www.acog.org/clinical/clinical-guidance/obstetric-care-consensus/articles/2017/10/periviable-birth.

14. Fortenberry, Bill. *Ectopic Life: What Your Doctor Doesn't Know About Ectopic Pregnancy*. 2023. Pg. 14.

15. Abolish Abortion Florida. "Could This Lead to Saving Ectopic Babies?" *Rumble*, October 23, 2022. https://rumble.com/v1pht1r-could-this-lead-to-saving-ectopic-babies.html?fbclid=IwAR3GL8y3FFgEG3pZm2aZmH-NgRqpJmPipS2CAWFF3Tt2ysZlH7KoP2mGxII.

16. Ibid.

17. Ibid.

18. Fortenberry, Bill. *Ectopic Life: What Your Doctor Doesn't Know About Ectopic Pregnancy*. 2023. Pg. 21.

19. Gunter, Brian. "HB 813 does not ban the removal of an ectopic pregnancy..." *Facebook*, May 11, 2022. https://m.facebook.com/story.php?story_fbid=pfbid02pWceZgKdpEouDbjsvkHbTKKR68jHDPGtBUryszRPPPwBWDHFM2u2fJJYyua6VrtHl&id=511510702&mibextid=Nif5oz.

20. Foundation to Abolish Abortion. "Overview: Louisiana 2022 HB 813." https://faa.life/louisiana-2022-hb-813.

21. webmaster@oklegislature.gov. (n.d.). *Bill Information*. http://www.oklegislature.gov/BillInfo.aspx?Bill=SB1729&Session=2400

22. Williams, L.A. "Southern Baptists Divided over Right Way to Oppose Abortion." *Christian Action League*, May 20, 2022. https://christianactionleague.org/southern-baptists-divided-over-right-way-to-oppose-abortion/.

23. *Acyutananda*. "Why It's Not Murder." *Human Defense Initiative, November 6, 2021. https://humandefense.com/why-its-not-murder/.

24. Fortenberry, Bill. Pg. 21.

25. Ibid.

26. Wayne State University. "Aborton Debate at Wayne State U. – Nadine Strossen v. Scott Klusendorf." *YouTube*, December 1, 2016. https:// www.youtube.com/watch?v=jzHwHX601no.

27. "Abortion and 'Health of the Mother.'" Focus on the Family. Accessed August 7, 2023. https://www.focusonthefamily.com/family-qa/abortion-and-health-of-the-mother/.

28. Students for Life. "Ectopic pregnancies pose a serious threat to the life of the mother and are unsurvivable ..." *Facebook*, July 14, 2022. https:// www.facebook.com/studentsforlife/posts/pfbid02XECfLQmiKbejGRYZjSWYPjbi5cqjAGpYFanMT8i9mLxqTm73HjfdTtpPucfewh33l.

29. Dannenfelser, Marjorie, Kristan Hawkins. "We're two pro-life women who say 'no' to prosecuting women for abortions." *Fox News*. August 3, 2022. https://www.foxnews.com/opinion/two-pro-life-women-say-no-prosecuting-women-abortions.

30. Rose, Lila. "Treating an ectopic pregnancy is not an abortion." *Facebook*, August 9, 2019. https://www.facebook.com/lilagracerose/posts/pfbid0fHx3MfCbxqBc6MtQcjiojhcKddjMW8w5N82SbtkUq2ws8AbDaGDvx2aZFkFTJvajl.

31. Created Equal. "In an ectopic pregnancy treatment, the goal is to save as many lives as possible..." *Facebook*, January 29, 2023. www.facebook.com/CreatedEqual/posts/pfbid0xWmnsmKBgjokodSAFuXhSCLR14s9juqmrYQLuoBMVhVsTwjqH2CntuyigwtUc7ycl.

32. "What is AAPLOG's Position on Treatment of Ectopic Pregnancy?" American Association of Pro-Life Obstetricians and Gynecologists. March 1, 2023. https://aaplog.org/what-is-aaplogs-position-on-treatment-of-ectopic-pregnancy/#:~:text=For%20these%20reasons%20the%20American%20Association%20of%20Pro-Life,to%20be%20the%20wrongful%20taking%20of%20human%20life.

33. Bockmann, John. "Treatment for Ectopic Pregnancy is Not Abortion." Secular Pro-Life, July 11, 2022. https://secularprolife.org/2022/07/treatment-for-ectopic-pregnancy-is-not-abortion/.

34. Ortiz-Catalan, Max, Enzo Mastinu, Paolo Sassu, Oskar Aszmann, and Rickard Brånemark. "Self-Contained Neuromusculoskeletal Arm Prostheses." *New England Journal of Medicine* 382 (18): 1732–38. April 30, 2020. https://doi.org/10.1056/nejmoa1917537.

35. Barber, Bart. Twitter Post. September 16, 2022, 7:49 AM. https://twitter.com/bartbarber/status/1570756745613692936.

36. *While not addressed within this chapter, IVF is an extension of the abortion industry and cannot be reformed like ectopic treatment; it must be abolished altogether. For further information on the unbiblical nature and unethical practices of IVF, visit www.rescuethose.com to request a booklet on this issue.*

Reforming Judicial Dogma

1. Hart, William David. "SLAVES, FETUSES, AND ANIMALS: Race and Ethical Rhetoric." *The Journal of Religious Ethics* 42, no. 4 (2014): 661–90. http://www.jstor.org/stable/24586118.

2. Cali, C.R. *The Doctrine of Balaam*, Wrath and Grace, 2019, pg. 90.

3. *Planned Parenthood v. Casey*, opencasebook.org/documents/106/, accessed January 30, 2023.

4. Ibid.

5. Timm, C. Jane. "What Supreme Court justices said about Roe and abortion in their confirmations." NBC News, June 24, 2022. www.nbcnews.com/politics/supreme-court/supreme-court-justices-said-roe-abortion-confirmations-rcna35246.

6. *Planned Parenthood v. Casey*, opencasebook.org/documents/106/, accessed January 30, 2023.

7. "Alito Confirmation Hearings: on Abortion." *On the Issues*, www.ontheissues.org/Archive/Alito_Hearings_Abortion.htm.

8. Thomas, Rusty Lee. "Biblical Strategies to Abolish Abortion." Covenant Books, 2022. Pg. 95-96.

9. "Webster v. Reproductive Health Services, 492 U.S. 490 (1989)," Justia Law, n.d., https://supreme.justia.com/cases/federal/us/492/490/.

10. Ertelt, Steven. "Pro-life group backs Donald Trump: 'We applaud his list of pro-life candidates for Supreme Court." *Life News*, June 28, 2016. www.lifenews.com/2016/06/28/pro-life-group-backs-donald-trump-we-applaud-his-list-of-pro-life-candidates-for-supreme-court/.

11. Franz, Wanda. Press release. *West Virginians for Life*, accessed April 4, 2023. archive1.wvforlife.org/blog/2016/07/25/wvl-pac-endorses-donald-trump-for-president/.

12. Watson, Kathryn. "Reactions to Trump's decision to nominate Brett Kavanaugh." CBS News, July 10, 2018. www.cbsnews.com/news/reactions-to-trumps-decision-to-nominate-brett-kavanaugh-live-updates/.

13. "U.S. Senate: About the Senate & the U.S. Constitution | Oath of Office." n.d. https://www.senate.gov/about/origins-foundations/senate-and-constitution/oath-of-office.htm#:~:text=I%20do%20solemnly%20swear%20(or,that%20I%20will%20well%20and.

14. Torres-Spelliscy, Ciara. "The cautionary tale of Abe Fortas." *Brennan Center for Justice*, February 6, 2018. www.brennancenter.org/our-work/analysis-opinion/cautionary-tale-abe-fortas.

15. Woodward, Bob. "Fortas tie to Wolfson is detailed." *Washington Post*, January 23, 1977. www.washingtonpost.com/archive/politics/1977/01/23/fortas-tie-to-wolfson-is-detailed/0b15ab1b-ca34-4a99-be65-51967ea123a6/.

16. Willke, Barbara and John C. Willke. *Why Can't We Love Them Both*. 2nd ed., Hayes, 1997.

17. Southard, Nathaniel ed., and Child, Lydia Maria, 1802-1880 comp. "The American Anti-Slavery Almanac, for 1841," 1841. https://jstor.org/stable/community.28591790.

18. Catenacci, Thomas. "Maxines Waters reacts to Dobbs ruling: 'the hell with the Supreme Court. We will defy them.'" *Fox News*, June 24, 2022. www.foxnews.com/politics/maxine-waters-reacts-dobbs-ruling-hell-supreme-court-we-will-defy-them.

19. "Joint statement from elected prosecutors." *Fair and Just Prosecution*, June 24, 2022. www.fairandjustprosecution.org/wp-content/uploads/2022/06/FJP-Post-Dobbs-Abortion-Joint-Statement.pdf.

20. International Coalition of Abolitionist Societies. "We are unifying people together to ABOLISH abortion." *Facebook*, November 5, 2014. www.facebook.com/AbolitionistCoalition/photos/a.518435131625965/523940027742142.

21. POLITICO. "Mike Johnson Told Us What He Really Thinks About Joe Biden, Hakeem Jeffries and Donald Trump," May 10, 2024. https://www.politico.com/news/magazine/2024/05/10/mike-johnson-interview-strategy-00157133.

22. John of Salisbury, "The statesmen's book of John of Salisbury: being the fourth, fifth and sixth books, and selection from the seventh and eighth books, of the Policraticus." New York: A.A. Knopf, 1927. www.archive.org/details/statesmansbookof0000unse/page/n49/mode/2up.

23. Boot, Joseph. *Ruler of Kings*, Wilberforce Publications, 2022. Pg. 172.

24. Trewhella, Matthew. "The doctrine of the lesser magistrates." Matthew Trewhella, 2013. Pg. 11.

25. "Kentucky and Virginia Resolutions." n.d. Monticello. Accessed November 9, 2023. https://www.monticello.org/research-education/thomas-jefferson-encyclopedia/kentucky-and-virginia-resolutions/#fn-src-12.

26. Wycliffe, John. "De civili dominio." New York: Johnson Reprint Corp. 1966.; ReformationSA.org. "John Wycliffe – the Morning Star of the Reformation," October 29, 2020. https:// www.reformationsa.org/history-articles/john-wycliffe-the-morning-star-of-the-reformation.

27. Arkes, Hadley. "Natural Rights and the Right to Choose." New York: Cambridge University Press, 2002. Pg. 152.

28. Ibid. Pg. 153.

29. Ibid. Pg. 150.

30. "Anarchism (Stanford Encyclopedia of Philosophy)," October 26, 2021. https://plato.stanford.edu/entries/anarchism/.

31. Lea, Jessica. "UPDATE: John MacArthur's Church Wins Legal Battle Against CA, LA County." ChurchLeaders, September 1, 2021. https://churchleaders.com/news/404470-john-macarthur-reveals-covid-19-lawsuit.html.

32. Bendix, Aria, Pete Williams, Daniel Barnes, David Li, Marc Caputo, Jay Blackman, Kelly O'Donnell, and Lindsey Pipia. "Florida Judge Overturns CDC Travel Mask Mandate, Says It's 'Unlawful.'" *NBC News*, April 19, 2022. https://www.nbcnews.com/news/us-news/florida-court-overturns-cdc-travel-mask-mandate-unlawful-rcna24853.

33. McArthur, Stu. "Equal Protection Feedback." Email message to author, March 5, 2023.

34. Clinton, Robert Lowry. "Judicial Supremacy and Our Two Constitutions: Reflections on the Historical Record." *The Heritage Foundation*, n.d. https://www.heritage.org/courts/report/judicial-supremacy-and-our-two-constitutions-reflections-the-historical-record.

35. Weiner, Greg. "July 21: The Council of Revision." The Constitutionalist, July 22, 2021. https://the constitutionalist.org/2021/07/22/july-21-the-council-of-revision/.

36. Hamilton, Alexander, James Madison, and John Jay. *The Federalist Papers*. Cutchogue: Buccaneer Books, Inc., 1992, pgs. 392-399.

37. Clinton, Robert Lowry. "Judicial Supremacy and Our Two Constitutions: Reflections on the Historical Record." *The Heritage Foundation*, n.d. https://www.heritage.org/courts/report/judicial-supremacy-and-our-two-constitutions-reflections-the-historical-record.

38. Ibid.

39. Cultural Research Center. "Release #6: What does it mean when people say they are Christian?" *Arizona Christian University*, August 31, 2021.

Unthinkable

1. Pavone, Frank. "This is our mission!" *Facebook*, April 3, 2022. www.facebook.com/fatherfrankpavone/posts/pfbid0EWyY2mwypcdVL4aGJ7dJAqkn3ycMSwC5LLvLY5owNPkFjwuZGMr2xDQ6ZMfqemHcl.

2. Flanders, Nancy. *Live Action*, January 1, 2021, https://www.liveaction.org/news/pro-lifers-unite-2021-abortion-unthinkable.

3. Graham, Elizabeth. The Ethics & Religious Liberty Commission, June 14, 2022 https://erlc.com/resource-library/articles/why-we-aim-to-make-abortion-illegal-unthinkable-and-unnecessary/

4. Anderson, Ryan T. & Desanctis, Alexandra. *National Review*, July 11, 2022, www.nationalreview.com/magazine/2022/07/11/making-abortion-illegal-and-unthinkable/.

5. Finney, Peter. *Clarion Herald*, March 11, 2014, www.clarionherald.org/news/early-feminists-would-view-abortion-as-unthinkable.

6. Montgomery, David. "Why the head of the antiabortion March for Life will keep marching." *Washington Post*, May 14, 2022. www.washingtonpost.com/magazine/2022/05/14/jeanne-mancini/.

7. Raymer, Brittany. "Abby Johnson shares how it's up to us to stop abortions, not the president." *Daily Citizen*, January 26, 2021. dailycitizen.focusonthefamily.com/abby-johnson-shares-how-its-up-to-us-to-stop-abortions-not-the-president/.

8. Acyutananda. "Should we make abortion unthinkable, or should we make children convenient?" *Secular Pro-Life*, September 15, 2019. secularprolife.org/2019/09/should-we-make-abortion-unthinkable-or/.

9. Ibid.

10. Simon, Stephanie. "Offering Abortion, Rebirth." *Los Angeles Times*, March 2, 2019. https://www.latimes.com/archives/la-xpm-2005-nov-29-na-abortion29-story.html.

11. "How Should Women Be Punished If Abortion Becomes Illegal?" Right to Life CA, *YouTube*, 23:37. December 18, 2013. www.youtube.com. Accessed May 21, 2023. https://www.youtube.com/watch?v=uuONbERruPc.

12. Schwarz, Stephen. "The moral question of abortion." Chicago: Loyola University Press, 1990.

13. "S31E06 Firing Line W/ William F. Buckley 'the Rhetoric of Abortion' Naomi Wolf, Helen Alvare." n.d. Www.youtube.com. Accessed April 11, 2023. http://www.youtube.com/watch?v=uj1y6NGwqYk.

14. Speed, Jon. "King Josiah's smashmouth abolitionism." Free the States, March 20, 2020. www.freethestates.org/2020/03/king-josiahs-smashmouth-abolitionism/.

15. Kevan Myers interview. Text message to author, September 30, 2023.

16. Tuma, Mary. Far-Right Texas Legislator Files Bill to Completely Outlaw Abortion." Austin Chronicle, February 4, 2019. https:// 04/far-right-legislator-files-bill-to-completely-outlaw-abortion/. www.austinchronicle.com/daily/news/2019-02-.

17. Arkes, Hadley. "Natural Rights and the Right to Choose." New York: Cambridge University Press, 2002. Pg. 144-145.

18. Acyutananda. "Should we make abortion unthinkable, or should we make children convenient?" *Secular Pro-Life*, September 15, 2019. secularprolife.org/2019/09/should-we-make-abortion-unthinkable-or/.

19. Brown-Kaiser, Liz, Brennan Leach, Kate Santaliz, and Julie Tsirkin. "Republicans Are Trying to Find a New Term for 'Pro-Life' to Stave off More Electoral Losses." *NBC News*. September 8, 2023. https://www.nbcnews.com/politics/congress/republicans-try-find-new-term-life-stave-electoral-losses-rcna103924.

20. Ibid.

21. Ibid.

22. Ulloa, Jazmine. "Nikki Haley Aims to Turn Her Debate Moment into Momentum." *The New York Times*, August 24, 2023.

23. Lee, Samuel. (@samuelhlee), "Any bills to authorize murder charges against women who undergo abortions are dead on arrival. I've killed lots of bills in my 40 years as a pro-life lobbyist and I guarantee they'll be LOTS of pro-life lawmakers in both chambers who'll kill these. #MOLeg." Twitter, December 8, 2023. https:// twitter.com/samuelhlee/status/1733259099498774717?s=12&t=kgthL5L3y0srPW5GP8ormA.

24. Lovasco, Tony. (@tonylovasco), "Charging women with murder for having an abortion may be an intellectually consistent position. It's also an incredibly bad idea. Compassion saves more lives than threats of vengeance, which only push more folks to the pro-choice camp. I won't support these bills." Twitter, December 8, 2023. https:// twitter.com/tonylovasco/status/1733365012851273859.

25. Donovan, Alexi, and Martino, B.J. Key Findings From A Nationwide Survey Of Voters. (The Tarrance Group, 2023). https:// sbaprolife.org/wp-content/uploads/2023/06/SBA-Pro-Life-America-Survey-Findings.pdf.

26. Medical School. "Dr. Julie Amaon's Mission to Expand Access to Reproductive Healthcare," January 4, 2023. https://med.umn.edu/familymedicine/news/dr-julie-amaons-mission-expand-access-reproductive-healthcare.

27. Zeisloft, Ben. "Texas City Let 'Abortion Store' Tell Women How to Order Lethal Pills, Documents Show." The Sentinel, June 28, 2023. https://republicsentinel.com/articles/texas-city-let-abortion-store-tell-women-how-to-order-lethal-pills-documents-show?fbclid=IwAR3fWn-IIsbtxEhe-Iicr81X9SZ2MOqbMGDfWXe1ob68cDFQ9mEOfqbT4ZU.

28. Aiken, Abigail R. A., Jennifer E. Starling, James G. Scott, and Rebecca Gomperts. 2022. "Requests for Self-Managed Medication Abortion Provided Using Online Telemedicine in 30 US States before and after the Dobbs v Jackson Women's Health Organization Decision." JAMA 328 (17): 1768. November 1, 2022. https://doi.org/10.1001/jama.2022.18865.

29. Statista Research Department. 2018. "United States - Pro-Choice and Pro-Life Supporters in 2018 | Statistic." Statista, 2018. https://www.statista.com/statistics/225975/share-of-americans-who-are-pro-life-or-pro-choice/.

30. "History of National Right to Life." National Right to Life. National Right to Life, February 18, 2011. https://www.nrlc.org/about/history/.

31. Garrison, William Lloyd. "No Compromise with the Evil of Slavery." Internet Archive, 1854, pg. 21, www.archive.org/details/nocompromisewit00garrgoog/page/n30/mode/2up.

32. Kissling, Frances. "Abortion Rights Are under Attack, and Pro-choice Advocates Are Caught in a Time Warp." Washington Post. The Washington Post Company, February 18, 2011. https://doi.org/01/04/2023.

33. Heyrick, Elizabeth Coltman. Immediate, Not Gradual Abolition. Philadelphia: Philadelphia A.S. Society, 1837, pg. 10-11.

34. Wilberforce, William. Letter on the Abolition of the Slave Trade, p. 294-295.

35. "Debates in the Anti-Slavery Convention." The Voice of Freedom, September 7, 1839. https://chroniclingamerica.loc.gov/lccn/sn84022687/1839-09-07/ed-1/seq-1/#date1=1770&index=11&rows=20&searchType=advanced&language=&sequence=0&words=Abolition+abolition&proxdistance=5&date2=1963&ortext=Abolition+&proxtext=&phrasetext=&andtext=&dateFilterType=yearRange&page=1.

36. The Voice of Freedom, November 9, 1839.

37. Abolitionists Rising, "Everything we say about the pro-life movement is true." YouTube, February 14, 2024. https://www.youtube.com/watch?v=npQPfr2hwUk&t=202s.

38. Yilek, Caitlin. "DeSantis Says He Does Not Support Criminalizing Women Who Get Abortions." *CBS News*, September 14, 2023. https://www.cbsnews.com/news/ron-desantis-abortion-florida-law-women-penalities/.

39. Phifer, Donica. "Trump Gives Support to 3 Abortion Exceptions: Medical, Rape and Incest." *Newsweek*, May 19, 2019. https://www.newsweek.com/donald-trump-says-he-strongly-pro-life-supports-rape-incest-and-medical-1429695.

40. Smerconish. "GOP Candidate Ramaswamy shares views on abortion, civics, Ukraine." *CNN Politics*, 2024. https://www.cnn.com/videos/politics/2023/05/13/smr-vivek-ramaswamy-interview.cnn.

41. "Debates in the Anti-Slavery Convention." *The Voice of Freedom*, September 7, 1839. https://chroniclingamerica.loc.gov/lccn/sn84022687/1839-09-07/ed-1/seq-1/#date1=1770&index=11&rows=20&searchType=advanced&language=&sequence=0&words=Abolition+abolition&proxdistance=5&date2=1963&ortext=Abolition+&proxtext=&phrasetext=&andtext=&dateFilterType=yearRange&page=1.

42. Morrow, Molly. "The Anti-Abortion Movement Is at a Crossroads," *The Nation*, February 3, 2024, https://www.thenation.com/article/activism/march-for-life-2024-election-anti-abortion-crossroads/tnamp/.

43. Ibid.

44. abortionNO, "Debate: Pro-Life Incrementalism vs Abolitionist Immediatism." YouTube, July 8, 2015. https://www.youtube.com/watch?v=5oi4vVTae30&t=2089s.

45. North, Gary. *Tools of Dominion: The Case Laws of Exodus*. Texas: The Institute for Christian Economics, 1990, pg. 386.

46. Heyrick, Elizabeth Coltman. *Immediate, Not Gradual Abolition*. Philadelphia: Philadelphia A.S. Society, 1837.

47. North, Gary. *Tools of Dominion: The Case Laws of Exodus*. Texas: The Institute for Christian Economics, 1990, pg. 383.

48. Cruso, Timothy. *The Christian laver. Or, a discourse opening the nature of participation with, and demonstrating the necessity of purification by Christ [electronic resource].* London: J.R. for J. Salusbury at the Rising Sun, 1690.

49. Trewhella, Matthew. "He is judging the form of Christianity prevalent in our nation. He will reform and purify His bride. And when you have a form of Christianity that is incapable of reforming itself, He uses judgement to reform and purify. Judgement begins in the house of the Lord." *Facebook*, May 14, 2023. www.facebook.com/matt.trewhella.7/posts/pfbid0qjqVHBUiZs2nKG5w2nRYqeXvF3s2Ht fE5axBXF8ThpJ1yv2n4upHS5BezoJwJtuNl.

50. Saint Augustine. "On Christian Doctrine." 397 A.D.

51. Thomas Watson. "The Doctrine of Repentance." 1668. Pgs. 117-118.

Ecclesia Reformata, Semper Reformanda

1. Marbach, Lizzie. "Commentary: The real story behind why I was fired from Ohio Right to Life." *Blaze Media*, August 21, 2023. Https:// www.theblaze.com/column/opinion/commentary-the-real-story-behind-why-i-was-fired-from-ohio-right-to-life.

2. Prior, Karen Swallow. "Loving Our Pro-Choice Neighbors in Word and Deed." *Christianity Today*, December 1, 2015. https://www.christianitytoday.com/ct/2015/december-web-only/loving-our-pro-choice-neighbors-in-word-and-deed.html.

3. Williams, Mary Elizabeth. "So What If Abortion Ends Life?" *Salon*, January 23, 2013. https://www.salon.com/2013/01/23/so_what_if_abortion_ends_life/.

4. Claire, Miriam. *The Abortion Dilemma: Personal Views on a Public Issue.* New York: Insight Books, 1995, pg. 60.

5. "How to Win This Week | Republicans Must Talk About Abortion | Ep. 53." Kristan Hawkins. October 26, 2022. Video, https://www.youtube.com/watch?v=4G6NDdscZ64.; MONTANARO, DOMENICO. 2019. "NPR Choice Page." Npr.org. June 7, 2019. https://www.npr.org/2019/06/07/730183531/poll-majority-want-to-keep-abortion-legal-but-they-also-want-restrictions.

6. Owens, Mary. "SBA List Is Now Susan B. Anthony Pro-Life America - SBA Pro-Life America." SBA Pro-Life America, June 1, 2022. https://sbaprolife.org/home/sba-list-is-now-susan-b-anthony-pro-life-america?fbclid=IwAR 2uXvszXGrWbjU2o0HR-6IIUMk8qZOeIgdpb0QVhAfyhDbW-TV69Dxc0MU.

7. Brown, Seth. "Mike Pence featured speaker at 'Life Wins!' event in Raleigh." Biblical Recorder, September 4, 2020. https://www.brnow.org/news/mike-pence-featured-speaker-a t-life-wins-event-in-raleigh/; SBA Pro-Life America, "Life is winning." Facebook, August 8, 2020, https://www.facebook.com/SBAProLife/posts/pfbid0JYsvmaM9u4GwcDvGkNdkXdriGq nV29gmeyei85sDKXW3Q4ZrvHNH8BZGTsTY4Zp3l.

8. abortionNO, "Debate: Pro-Life Incrementalism vs Abolitionist Immediatism." YouTube, July 8, 2015. https://www.youtube.com/watch?v=5oi4vVTae30&t=2089s.

9. Cooper, Don. "Former Pro-Life Leader Reviews the Cunningham/Hunter Debate on Immediatism." Abolish Human Abortion. Abolitionist Society of Oklahoma, May 20, 2015. https://doi.org/http://blog.abolishhumanabortion.com/2015/05/former-pro-life-leader-reviews.html.

10. Douthat, Ross. "The Case Against Abortion." The New York Times, November 30, 2021. https://www.nytimes.com/2021/11/30/opinion/abortion-dobbs-supreme-court.html.

11. Marbach, Lizzie. "Commentary: The real story behind why I was fired from Ohio Right to Life." *Blaze Media*, August 21, 2023. Https:// www.theblaze.com/column/opinion/commentary-the-real-story-behind-why-i-was-fired-from-ohio-right-to-life.

12. *Green Mountain Freeman*, Montpelier, VT December 21, 1854. https://www.loc.gov/item/sn84023209/1854-12-21/ed-1/.

13. North, Gary. *Tools of Dominion: The Case Laws of Exodus*. Texas: The Institute for Christian Economics, 1990, pg. 383-386.

14. Higham, Vernon. *The Turn of the Tide*. Wheaton: International Awakening, 1994, pg. xi.

15. Pew Research Center. "1. Americans' Views on Whether, and in What Circumstances, Abortion Should Be Legal." Pew Research Center's Religion & Public Life Project. May 6, 2022. https://www.pewresearch.org/religion/2022/05/06/americans-views-on-whether-and-in-what-circumstances-abortion-should-be-legal/.

16. Highman, Vernon. *The Turn of the Tide*. Wheaton: International Awakening, 1994.

17. Ibid.

18. Sandlin, Andrew, [P. Andrew Sandlin]. "Christians Who Do Not Pray with a Lot of Faith and Confidence Never Fail to Get What They Do Not Expect." *Facebook*, December 5, 2022. Accessed January 21, 2023. https://www.facebook.com/p.andrew.sandlin/posts/pfbid02X3CuufVsMo7G6XcBwVXPXXJko3rZnd2zchtpjG6Hgz7tswkfXCnDmkJGKmDmaFR9l.

19. Barnes, Albert. "The church and slavery." *Parry & McMillan*, 1857, pg. 20, www.archive.org/details/churchslavery00barn/page/20/mode/2up, accessed May 25, 2023.

20. Metaxas, Eric. *Amazing Grace*. New York: NY, HarperCollins, 2007, pg. 207.

Resources

1. Speed, Jon. "Let's Talk IVF..." *Facebook*, June 17, 2023. https://www.facebook.com/share/v/eCw49FtFbBufHtQq/

www.ingramcontent.com/pod-product-compliance
Lightning Source LLC
Chambersburg PA
CBHW060451090426
42735CB00011B/1963